Diagnosing the Philippine Economy
Toward Inclusive Growth

Diagnosing the Philippine Economy
Toward Inclusive Growth

Edited by

Dante Canlas,

Muhammad Ehsan Khan,

and

Juzhong Zhuang

Published for the
Asian Development Bank by

A Co-publication of the Asian Development Bank and Anthem Press

Anthem Press
www.anthempress.com

Asian Development Bank
www.adb.org

This edition first published in 2011 by

ANTHEM PRESS
75-76 Blackfriars Road,
London SE1 8HA, UK
or PO Box 9779, London SW19 7ZG, UK
and 244 Madison Ave. #116, New York, NY
10016, USA

and
Asian Development Bank
6 ADB Avenue, Mandaluyong City, 1550
Metro Manila, Philippines

British Library Cataloguing in Publication Data
A catalogue record for this book is available from the British Library.

Library of Congress Cataloging in Publication Data
A catalog record for this book has been requested.

ISBN-13: 978 0 85728 994 0 (Pbk)
ISBN-10: 0 85728 994 2 (Pbk)

Foreword

The last two decades or so have seen considerable advances in thinking on development policies. The thinking in the late 1980s and early 1990s was very much guided by the Washington Consensus. Subsequent experiences of many countries, including those in Latin America and Africa, however, showed that the policy prescriptions based on the Washington Consensus did not always deliver the expected development outcomes. The disappointment with the Washington Consensus led to a continued search for new approaches to development strategy. A new consensus has in the meantime emerged that the economic and political environment differs a great deal among countries, and there is no "one-size-fits-all" solution to development problems; thus, identifying the binding constraints to development and sequencing policy priorities contingent on country-specific circumstances are critical for igniting and sustaining growth and accelerating the pace of poverty reduction.

The Asian Development Bank (ADB) is committed to achieving its vision of an Asia and Pacific region free of poverty. This vision is restated in its recently adopted long-term strategic framework 2008–2020 (Strategy 2020), under which ADB will support its developing member countries to reduce poverty and improve their peoples' living conditions and quality of life. Strategy 2020 directs ADB to do so by focusing its development assistance, finance, policy advice, and knowledge solutions on three distinct but complementary development agendas: inclusive growth, environmentally sustainable growth, and regional integration. Under Strategy 2020, ADB is also committed to continuing efforts to enhance the effectiveness and results of its development aid. One such effort, in collaboration with government agencies, is to continue to strengthen country diagnosis in formulating ADB's country partnership strategies. This strengthening aims to ensure that ADB's assistance programs target each developing member country's most needed areas, that is, addresses its binding development constraints.

The study—*Philippines: Critical Development Constraints*—is the first in a series of studies under an ADB regional technical assistance project, "Strengthening Country Diagnosis and Analysis of Binding Development Constraints in Selected Developing Member Countries." The purposes of the study are to identify critical impediments to long-term economic growth and equitable development in the Philippines and to recommend policy options that stand a good chance of overcoming the impediments. To this end, ADB commissioned a team of experts on the Philippine economy to undertake diagnoses in a number of areas, including macroeconomic management, human capital, infrastructure investment, governance, industrial policy, and combating poverty. This book presents key findings of the team's diagnoses.

It is hoped that this book will be of value to a wide spectrum of readers—policy makers, academics, development partners, nongovernment organizations, civil society, students of development and economics, and the general public, especially those who care about and are interested in the Philippines and its prosperity.

Ursula Schaefer-Preuss
Vice-President, Knowledge Management and Sustainable Development
Asian Development Bank

Preface

The Philippines has long considered sustained growth of income and employment, along with poverty reduction and improved distribution of income and wealth, as major development goals. In pursuit of these goals, the country embarked on an industrialization drive after gaining political independence more than a half century ago. The drive continues today. The primary strategy involves transforming an economy that still has a large agriculture sector into an industrialized one. Through this strategy, policy makers aim to move individuals, households, and enterprises from low- to high-productivity sectors and activities to trigger and propagate the desired economic and social transformation.

A look at the Philippines' development performance over the past six decades, however, indicates that the country has not done as impressively as many of its East and Southeast Asian neighbors, such as Malaysia, Thailand, and the four newly industrialized economies—Hong Kong, China; the Republic of Korea; Singapore; and Taipei,China. Philippine economic growth has not only been slower, it has also been interrupted frequently by episodes of macroeconomic instability, financial and fiscal crises, and recessions. In the 1950s and 1960s, the Philippines had one of the highest per capita gross domestic products (GDPs) in the region—higher than the People's Republic of China, Indonesia, and Thailand. But, the country has now fallen behind. As a result, household incomes have not risen significantly, poverty incidence has declined only slowly, and inequality remains high. In 2006, about one in every four families and one in every three Filipinos lived below the official poverty lines. Meanwhile, the Gini ratio exceeded 45%—among the highest in the region.

Since the start of the new millennium, however, the Philippine economy has been experiencing its longest running recovery. In 2007, real GDP posted a 7.2% growth rate, the highest in the last 30 years, despite unfavorable economic and political shocks. This has provided grounds for a good deal of optimism that the Philippines may be on the threshold of moving on a faster track toward achieving its major development goals. But, there are also concerns over whether the current pace of growth can be sustained and even improved, as the country's domestic investment has remained weak and its share of GDP has continued to fall, especially in view of the deteriorated external environment due to the ongoing global financial and economic turmoil.

Given the economy's newfound strength, the Government of the Philippines is eager to demonstrate its capacity to eliminate poverty and to reduce income inequality. In this connection, the government has started updating its Medium-Term Philippine Development Plan, aiming to move onto the track of inclusive growth. The Asian Development Bank (ADB) is committed to assisting the government to achieve its development goals. In coordination with the National Economic and Development Authority (NEDA), ADB initiated the study, Philippines: Critical Development Constraints, aimed at identifying key barriers to inclusive growth—barriers that call for urgent corrective action.

The study aims, first, to identify critical impediments to long-run economic growth and equitable development. Next, it recommends policy adjustments that have a good chance of overcoming the evident critical development constraints. To achieve these objectives, the background studies that were prepared by a team of experts follow a growth diagnostic approach proposed by Ricardo Hausmann, Dani Rodrik, and Andrew Velasco of Harvard University. The approach looks promising. It recognizes that developing countries such as the Philippines generally have limited capacities to implement simultaneously a wide array of policy reforms. The policy reform process may thus usefully start with the constraints whose easing delivers the greatest expected returns, material or otherwise, to society.

The areas that the study focused on, broadly stated, are macroeconomic management; financial intermediation; infrastructure; human capital, especially education and health; industrial policy; governance and institutions; and social policy and programs. In investigating which constraints seem most critical, the authors marshaled a variety of economic and financial data and evidence from investment surveys and regression analyses. This book aims to make accessible to policy makers and observers of Philippine economic development both the synthesis report, in Part 1, and the background studies, in Part 2.

The study was led by Muhammad Ehsan Khan. Juzhong Zhuang, Assistant Chief Economist, Economics and Research Department, ADB, provided oversight and overall direction. Dante B. Canlas, Muhammad Ehsan Khan, and Juzhong Zhuang, with the assistance of Maria Rowena M. Cham, coordinated the background studies that are presented in Chapters 4–10 of this book and synthesized them in Part 1.

Contributors to the background studies include Arsenio M. Balisacan, Professor of Economics, University of the Philippines Diliman; Emmanuel S. de Dios, Professor of Economics at the University of the Philippines; Jane Carangal-San Jose, Senior Information Resources and Services Officer at ADB; Joseph Anthony Y. Lim, Professor of Economics at Ateneo University; Gilbert M. Llanto, Senior Research Fellow at the Philippine Institute for Development Studies; Hyun H. Son, Economist at ADB; and Clarence Pascual, Economics Consultant.

The completion of the study would not have been possible without input and assistance from numerous people. In addition to writing Chapter 6, Gilbert M. Llanto assisted with refining and condensing Chapters 4 and 5. Assistance with Chapters 4 and 5 was also provided by Amador Foronda, who collected and processed the myriad data required; Clarence Pascual, who provided initial editing and sequencing of the papers and some regression analyses; and Marife Lou Bacate and Damaris Yarcia, who collected data in the early stage of the study. Lawrence Nelson Guevara provided research for Chapter 6. Sharon Faye Piza of the Asia Pacific Policy Center and Lily Tallafer of the Southeast Asian Regional Center for Graduate Study and Research in Agriculture (SEARCA) assisted with Chapter 9. Geoffrey Ducanes provided research assistance for Chapter 10. Juliet F. Vanta assisted with formatting and proofreading, and Jill Gale de Villa edited the book.

The government provided essential support to the study, for which we are grateful. In particular, we thank NEDA's Deputy Director General, Margarita R. Songco, for serving as the government focal point for the study and providing guidance. We are also grateful for the support and feedback from Undersecretary Gil S. Beltran, Department of Finance; Director General Rodolfo V. Vicerra, Congressional Planning and Budget Department, House of Representatives; Assistant Director General Ruben S. Reinoso, NEDA; Director Gisela C. Lopez, Department of Budget and Management; and Alberto A. Lim, Makati Business Club.

The book also benefited from the comments and feedback received from participants of the two consultation workshops organized as part of the study who represented key government agencies, academic and research institutions, development partners, and the private sector. Tom Crouch, deputy director general, Southeast Asia Department, ADB, and Joven Balbosa, formerly ADB's Philippine country team leader, helped coordinate consultations with the government and other stakeholders.

Our deep appreciation goes to Ifzal Ali, former chief economist, ADB, for his guidance, strong support, and encouragement at various stages of the study.

The views and opinions expressed in this book are those of the authors and do not necessarily reflect those of the people consulted. Neither do they represent the views and policies of ADB or its Board of Governors or the governments they represent.

Dante B. Canlas
Muhammad Ehsan Khan
Juzhong Zhuang

December 2008

Contributors

Arsenio M. Balisacan is Professor of Economics at the University of the Philippines Diliman. He is also the director of Southeast Asian Regional Center for Graduate Study and Research in Agriculture (SEARCA). He has been the President of the Human Development Network and Chairman of the Board of Advisors of the Asian Institute of Management–Mirant Center for Bridging Societal Divides. He is a former Under-Secretary of the Department of Agriculture and President of the Philippine Economic Society.

Dante B. Canlas is the Enrique Virata Professor of Economics at the University of the Philippines and Editor of *The Philippine Review of Economics*. He is also the Chief Executive Officer for the Millennium Challenge Corporation's Philippine Program. He has served as the Secretary of Socioeconomic Planning; Director General of the National Economic and Development Authority (NEDA); Executive Director of the Board of Directors of the Asian Development Bank (ADB); and President of the Philippine Economic Society. His current areas of research are macroeconomics, money, and labor.

Maria Rowena M. Cham is an Economics Officer at ADB and has worked at NEDA and the Power Sector Asset and Liabilities Management (PSALM) Corporation.

Emmanuel S. de Dios is Professor of Economics at the University of the Philippines, where he chairs the Economics Department. His areas of interest include institutions and economic development, economic geography, choice theory, and the history of thought.

Jane Carangal-San Jose is a Senior Information Resources and Services Officer at ADB.

Muhammad Ehsan Khan is a Senior Economist in ADB's Economics and Research Department and has served as a Project Economist in ADB's Southeast Asia Department. He is leading ADB's work in the area of growth diagnostics, including studies on Nepal and the Philippines.

Joseph Anthony Y. Lim is a Professor of Economics at Ateneo de Manila University. He has also taught at the University of the Philippines. His areas of interest include macroeconomics, finance and trade, and investment theories. His current research focuses on the use of product space theory to explain the structural transformation, or lack of it, in Asian economies.

Gilbert M. Llanto is a Senior Research Fellow at the Philippine Institute for Development Studies. He has served as Deputy Director General of NEDA and Vice President of the Philippine Institute for Development Studies. He is a member of the Board of Editors of the *Philippine Journal of Development*. His current research interests are public economics, decentralization, and the political economy of policy reforms.

Hyun H. Son is an Economist at ADB. She has previously worked at the International Poverty Center and the World Bank. Her research work focuses on various aspects of inclusive growth, particularly the links between inequality and growth and measurements of inequality.

Juzhong Zhuang is an Assistant Chief Economist in ADB's Economics and Research Department. He has served as a Principal Economist and Senior Economist in ADB's Office of Regional Economic Integration. His recent areas of research are inclusive growth and growth diagnostics, early warning systems for financial crises, and economics of climate change.

Abbreviations
and Acronyms

ADB	—	Asian Development Bank
APEC	—	Asia–Pacific Economic Cooperation
APIS	—	Annual Poverty Indicator Survey
APPC	—	Asia Pacific Policy Center
ARB	—	agrarian reform beneficiary
ARC	—	agrarian reform community
ARMM	—	Autonomous Region in Muslim Mindanao
ASEAN	—	Association of Southeast Asian Nations
BHS	—	barangay health station
BOP	—	balance of payments
BOT	—	build–operate–transfer
BSP	—	Bangko Sentral ng Philippines (Philippine Central Bank)
CARP	—	Comprehensive Agrarian Reform Program
CIDSS	—	Comprehensive and Integrated Delivery of Social Services
CLOA	—	collective land ownership award
DAR	—	Department of Agrarian Reform
EDSA	—	Epifanio de los Santos Avenue
EPIRA	—	Electric Power Industry Restructuring Act
FDI	—	foreign direct investment
FIES	—	Family Income and Expenditure Survey
GDP	—	gross domestic product
GNP	—	gross national product
GOCC	—	government-owned and -controlled corporation
GRDP	—	gross regional domestic product
HDI	—	Human Development Index
IMF	—	International Monetary Fund
IRA	—	internal revenue allotment
KALAHI	—	Kapit-Bisig Laban sa Kahirapan (Linking Arms against Poverty)
LGU	—	local government unit
LRT	—	Light Rail Transit
MDG	—	Millennium Development Goal

MERALCO	—	Manila Electric Company
MRT	—	Metro Rail Transit
MTPDP	—	Medium-Term Philippine Development Plan
MVUC	—	motor vehicle user charge
NCR	—	National Capital Region
NEDA	—	National Economic and Development Authority
NFA	—	National Food Authority
NIE	—	newly industrializing economy
NPC	—	National Power Corporation
NTC	—	National Telecommunications Commission
ODA	—	official development assistance
OECD	—	Organisation for Economic Co-operation and Development
PEGR	—	poverty equivalent growth rate
PLDT	—	Philippine Long Distance Telephone Company
PPP	—	public–private partnership
PRC	—	People's Republic of China
PSALM	—	Power Sector Assets and Liabilities Management Corporation
R&D	—	research and development
RHU	—	rural health unit
RORO	—	roll-on-roll-off
SARS	—	severe acute respiratory syndrome
SMEs	—	small and medium-sized enterprises
SMS	—	short messaging service
TFP	—	total factor productivity
Transco	—	National Transmission Corporation
US	—	United States
USAID	—	United States Agency for International Development
VOIP	—	voice over internet protocol
WESM	—	wholesale spot electricity market

Contents

1. Introduction

Dante B. Canlas, Muhammad Ehsan Khan, and Juzhong Zhuang

1.1. Objectives

The Philippines' economic growth during the past five decades has not been impressive compared with that of many of its neighbors; in per capita terms, the growth was even less favorable. As a result, the pace of poverty reduction has been slow, and income inequality remains high. In 2006, about one in four Philippine families and 32.9% of the population were deemed poor, and the Gini coefficient of per capita income was slightly over 45%, among the highest in Southeast Asia.[1]

The Philippine Government is committed to sustained growth, the rewards from which are within reach of every Filipino. The commitment is spelled out in the current Medium-Term Philippine Development Plan.

This book presents the work undertaken for the Philippine country diagnostic study under the Asian Development Bank regional technical assistance project, Strengthening Country Diagnosis and Analysis of Binding Development Constraints in Selected Developing Member Countries. A summary of the findings was published in *Philippines: Critical Development Constraints* (ADB 2008). This book presents more in-depth work on the various aspects of the Philippine economy and the constraints that curtail its effort to grow and tackle poverty. The discussions in the book will help improve the understanding of the Philippine economy and the challenges that the policy makers face. It will be of value to people who have been following the developments in the region and the Philippines.

1.2. Methodology

The study adopts a diagnostic approach and broadly follows growth diagnostics developed by Hausmann, Rodrik, and Velasco (2005). The growth diagnostics approach provides a consistent framework for identifying the most critical or "binding" constraints to growth and for discerning the priorities and sequence of policies required to ignite and sustain growth. The growth diagnostics approach differs from the laundry list approach, as implied by

---

[1]   The Gini coefficient is a commonly used measure of income inequality.

the Washington consensus, and recognizes that the economic and political environment differs a great deal among developing countries—there is no "one-size-fits-all" solution to development problems; thus, the ordering of policy priorities contingent on country-specific circumstances is critically important. Further, countries at an early stage of development may not have adequate capacity to implement a wide array of policy reforms at the same time. With the diagnostic approach, reforms can start with easing a few critical areas that most constrain growth. Therefore, the approach offers a practical tool for policy makers and development planners to use in formulating country-specific growth strategies. The application of growth diagnostics is one of the efforts in the search for new approaches to growth strategy after the Washington consensus was questioned in recent years.

The growth diagnostics approach starts with a set of proximate determinants of growth, investigates which of these pose the greatest impediments or are the most critical constraints to higher growth, and figures out specific distortions behind the impediments. The point of departure of the inquiry is a standard endogenous growth model in which growth depends on the social return to accumulation, private appropriability of this social return, and the cost of financing (Box 1.1). Each of these three broad determinants of growth is, in turn, a function of many other factors, which can be presented in a problem tree (Figure 1.1).

The problem tree provides a framework for diagnosing critical constraints to growth. The diagnosis starts by asking what keeps the level of private investment and entrepreneurship low. Is it low social return to investment, inadequate private appropriability of the social return, or high cost of financing? If it is low social return, is that due to insufficient levels of complementary factors of production—in particular, human capital, technical know-how, and/or infrastructure? If the impediment is poor private appropriability, is it due to macro vulnerability, high taxation, poor property rights and contract enforcement, labor–capital conflicts, information and learning externalities, and/or coordination failures? If high cost of finance is the problem, is it due to low domestic savings, poor intermediation in the domestic financial markets, or poor integration with external financial markets?

At each node of the problem tree, the diagnosis looks for signals that will help answer the question. The two types of diagnostic signals are price signals and nonprice signals. Examples of price signals are returns to education, interest rates, and cost of transport. For example, if education is undersupplied, returns to skills/education will be high and unemployment for skilled people will be low. If investment is constrained by savings, interest rates will be high, and growth will respond to changes in available savings (e.g., inflows of foreign resources). If poor transport links are a serious constraint, bottlenecks will occur and private costs of transport will be high.

2

Box 1.1: An Endogenous Growth Model

A standard endogenous growth model yields the result that, at the steady state, consumption and capital grow according to

$$\frac{\dot{c}_t}{c_t} = \frac{\dot{k}_t}{k_t} = s \left[r(1-\tau) - \rho \right]$$

where a dot over a variable denotes the rate of change over time, and where other definitions are as follows:

c = per capita consumption,
k = per capita capital,
σ = elasticity of intertemporal substitution in consumption,
r = rate of (the expected) social return to investment,
$1-\tau$ = private appropriability of social return, and
ρ = cost of financing.

- The rate of (the expected) social return to investment (r) is a function of the availability of complementary factors of production such as infrastructure, technical know-how, and human capital. Lack of complementary factors reduces social return to investment and, with given private appropriability and cost of financing, leads to lower private return to investment and hence to lower private investment.
- The private appropriability of social return (1-τ) is a function of (i) micro risks such as high taxation, poor property rights and contract enforcement, and labor-capital conflicts; (ii) macro risks such as high inflation, currency crises, and financial meltdown; and (iii) market failures due to issues such as learning and information externalities, and coordination failures, with (i) and (ii) being interpreted as government failures. Higher micro and macro risks and larger market failures lower the private appropriability of social return and, with a given social return and cost of financing, lead to lower (expected) private return to investment and hence to lower private investment.
- The cost of financing (ρ) is a function of domestic savings rate, efficiency of domestic financial intermediation, the extent of integration with external financial markets, and perceived country risks. Higher cost of financing, with given (expected) social return to investment and private appropriability, leads to lower private investment.

Source: Hausmann, Rodrik, and Velasco (2005).

Figure 1.1: Growth Diagnostics Framework

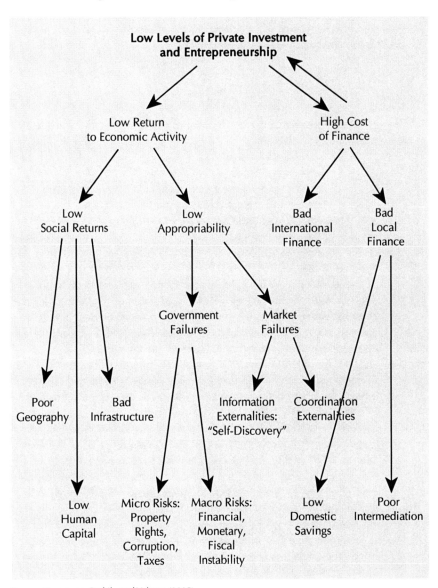

Source: Hausmann, Rodrik, and Velasco (2005).

The use of nonprice signals is based on the idea that when a constraint binds, it results in activities designed to get around it. For example, high taxation could lead to "high informality" (e.g., underreporting of income, resulting in lower tax revenues); poor legal institutions could result in high demand for informal mechanisms of conflict resolution and contract enforcement; and poor financial intermediation could lead to internalization of finance through business groups. Cross-country and cross-period benchmarking and results of business surveys are useful means of gauging whether particular diagnostic evidence signals a binding constraint for the country concerned.

Although the growth diagnostics approach was developed to identify the binding constraints to growth and associated policy priorities, the approach can be expanded and applied to other areas of policy analysis, such as identifying critical constraints to poverty reduction (Figure 1.2). Slow pace of poverty reduction can be caused by the lack of economic opportunities due to poor growth, weak human capacities that prevent individuals from participating in the growth process, the absence of effective and adequate social safety nets, and/or inequitable access to opportunities due to poor governance and weak institutions. Each of these could be due to many other factors. The growth diagnostics approach focuses on identifying the root causes of poverty and critical constraints to poverty reduction.

Figure 1.2: Diagnostic Framework for Poverty

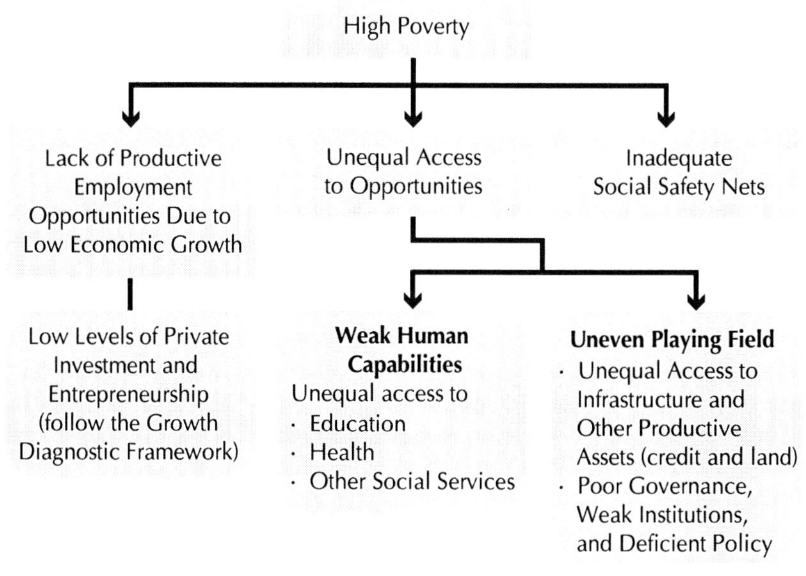

Source: Authors.

1.3. Summary of the Key Findings

The book consists of two parts. Part A, comprising Chapters 2 and 3, presents an overview and a synthesis of the main findings of the Philippine country diagnostic study. Part B, comprising Chapters 4–10, presents the background studies that informed Part A.

In Chapter 2, Dante B. Canlas, Maria Rowena M. Cham, and Juzhong Zhuang describe and try to account for the Philippines' performance in growth and poverty reduction in the past several decades and the evolution of the government's development policy. They argue that, compared to many of its neighbors, the Philippines' economic growth record has not been impressive and, in per capita terms, was even less favorable. Furthermore, growth was never smooth. For example, the economy contracted in 1984–1985, 1990, and 1998. As a result, the pace of poverty reduction has been slow and income inequality remains high. Inappropriate development strategies; macroeconomic instabilities due to inconsistent fiscal, monetary, and exchange rate policies; unfavorable external economic shocks; natural disasters; poor governance; and political upheavals, including martial law rules during 1972–1985, were among the key causes underlying the Philippines' poor development performance.

Canlas, Cham, and Zhuang note that since the People Power Revolution in 1986, successive democratically elected administrations have initiated various policy and structural reforms aimed at accelerating the pace of economic growth and poverty reduction, and these have had some visible impact on the Philippine economy, barring the reversal experienced during the 1997 Asian financial crisis. During 2001–2006, the Philippines posted its highest annual growth in gross domestic product (GDP) of the previous 2.5 decades, reaching 4.6%. In 2007, growth accelerated to 7.2%, the fastest pace in the last three decades. Despite the improved performance, Canlas, Cham, and Zhuang argue that the list of unfinished reform programs remains long, and more difficult reforms are yet to be implemented. In particular, the country's sluggish domestic investment and its declining share in GDP raises the question of whether the recent pace of growth can be sustained. Moreover, the slow reduction in poverty incidence and the very high Gini coefficient of per capita income suggest that the fruits of economic growth have not been widely shared among Filipinos. They argue that, while the public sector plays an important role in investing in infrastructure, the private sector should be the driving force of investment required for sustaining growth and accelerating the pace of poverty reduction in the medium and long term. Therefore, the identification of the critical constraints to investment, economic growth, and poverty reduction become vitally important.

In Chapter 3, Canlas, Muhammad Ehsan Khan, and Zhuang examine the critical constraints to investment, economic growth, and poverty reduction for the Philippines in the next 5–10 years on the basis of the background studies and other data and information available. Following the growth diagnostics framework and using a variety of empirical evidence— macroeconomic and financial indicators, findings from investment and business surveys, regression analysis, insights from in-depth case studies, and benchmarking with other similarly situated countries—they identify the following critical constraints to private investment and growth:

(i)   tight fiscal situation due largely to weak revenue generation;
(ii) inadequate infrastructure, particularly in electricity and transport;
(iii) weak investor confidence due to governance concerns, particularly corruption and political instability; and
(iv) inability to address market failures leading to a small and narrow industrial base.

Using the diagnostic framework for poverty depicted in Figure 1.2, they identify the following critical constraints to poverty reduction:

(i)   lack and slow growth of productive employment opportunities;
(ii) inequitable access to development opportunities, especially education, health, infrastructure, and productive assets such as credit and land; and
(iii) inadequate social protection and social safety nets.

Canlas, Khan, and Zhuang argue that many of these critical constraints are interlinked. For instance, only when the fiscal situation improves sufficiently will the government be in a position to allocate more resources to infrastructure investment. Improved infrastructure alone is not enough to lower the costs of doing business and stimulate private investment, and it needs to be accompanied by significant improvements in investor confidence, which requires the government to adequately address governance concerns by reducing corruption and improving political stability. Removing these three constraints (tight fiscal space, inadequate infrastructure, and weak investor confidence) will result in increased private investments from domestic and foreign sources. But, to ensure that growth can be sustained at a high level, the government will also need to address market failures to encourage investments in expanding and diversifying the manufacturing sector and exports, and in upgrading technology. Sustained and high growth, resulting from elimination of the critical constraints, will create more productive employment opportunities. However, expansion in employment opportunities may not lead to significant poverty reduction unless inequalities in access to development opportunities are removed or reduced by instituting good governance and better policies. At the same time, inadequacies in the social safety nets should be addressed to keep the most vulnerable groups from extreme deprivation.

Canlas, Khan, and Zhuang emphasize that governance concerns not only weaken investor confidence, they underlie most other critical constraints. For instance, corruption undermines tax collection, political instability hinders investment and growth and reduces the tax base, and both contribute to the tightness of the fiscal space. Poor infrastructure is a result of insufficient development spending and of poor governance, the latter causing leakages and misappropriation of public funds. Similarly, poor governance hinders the pace of poverty reduction, as it reduces growth of incomes and productive employment opportunities. It is also a major factor contributing to inequalities in access to education, health, infrastructure, and other productive assets, and contributing to weaknesses of many poverty reduction programs. Therefore, addressing governance concerns will go a long way toward relaxing the critical constraints to growth and poverty reduction and should be made a top development priority in the Philippines.

Canlas, Khan, and Zhuang also look at other possible constraints, such as the level of domestic savings, the efficiency of domestic financial intermediation, the cost of international borrowing, and the stock of human capital. They argue that currently these seem to be less critical than the ones listed above. However, in the longer term, some of the other constraints could become critical as the Philippine economy reaches a higher growth trajectory—examples are the needs for a higher level of domestic savings and for a higher skill and knowledge base to support the development of new and emerging industries.

In Chapter 4, the first of the seven background studies in Part 2, Joseph Anthony Y. Lim traces the long record of past macroeconomic mismanagement that yielded poor aggregate economic performance. For instance, inconsistent fiscal, monetary, and exchange rate policies conspired to produce balance-of-payments crises and collapse of the exchange value of the peso against the United States dollar. The crises triggered the adoption of structural policy reform programs. He argues that, at this point, ensuring that the fiscal policy reforms continue is imperative.

Chapter 5, also by Lim, discusses the changing structure of the Philippine economy. It shows a declining share of agriculture in total output that is being compensated for not by an increase in industry share but in that of services. Trade and investment policies have contributed to the emergence of manufactured exports high in scale and technological content, but this is not reflected in domestic manufacturing output. To sustain growth in the long run, Lim argues that raising the scale and technological content of domestic manufacturing as well is vital.

Chapter 6, by Gilbert M. Llanto, emphasizes limits to growth arising from weak infrastructure support, especially in transport and electricity. This effectively impedes broad-based growth. He notes the large financing requirements of upgrading the country's infrastructure system and concludes that the only way to meet these requirements is through public–private partnerships. The Philippines has a legal framework for this partnership—the BOT or build–operate–transfer law—that Llanto finds laudable; however, the law needs some fine-tuning to facilitate contractual performance. Capacity development aimed at raising the technical, legal, and financial expertise of government agencies responsible for infrastructure development is essential. He finds the new government procurement law a meaningful step in the right direction.

Chapter 7, by Hyun H. Son, examines whether human capital is a constraint to growth. Son starts with the observation that has puzzled many about the Philippines: despite increasing educational attainment, labor productivity remains low, particularly when compared with that of the high middle-income and industrializing economies in the region. Using an aggregate growth decomposition model, she finds that education matters for the growth of output per worker; uneven total factor productivity and low contribution from capital are what depress output per worker. At a micro level, she finds that education improves employability, with the more educated workers crowding out the less educated ones for available jobs. Given the increasing number of educated people, human capital does not appear to be a constraint to growth and private investment, at least under the existing industry structure.

Chapter 8, by Son and Jane Carangal-San Jose, studies the links between growth and equity-related issues, including the extent to which spatial or regional income disparities lie at the root of the poverty problem. Their empirical investigation suggests that spatial disparity could be a binding constraint to inclusive growth and could severely hamper efforts to eliminate poverty. For example, populations in both the Bicol Region and the Autonomous Region in Muslim Mindanao are poor and have low educational achievement.

Chapter 9, by Arsenio M. Balisacan, emphasizes findings that the poverty-reducing effects of the country's growth have been tepid. He notes the strong spatial dimension of poverty and asserts that if the regional income disparities persist, social cohesion could be unhinged, thereby impeding long-run economic growth. He observes that the mixed success of the government's various poverty alleviation programs over time indicates the need for profound redesigning of projects to minimize leakages.

Finally, Chapter 10, by Emmanuel S. de Dios, analyzes the impact of key aspects of governance on investment and growth. Using regression analysis, he finds corruption and political instability to be the most critical constraints to foreign investments and, hence, to sustained and equitable growth. He considers electoral reforms crucial to overcoming barriers to political instability, and argues that adequate checks and balance of power between the executive, legislative, and judiciary branches of government and the adequate professionalization of the bureaucracy and its isolation from political influences are essential to curbing corruption.

References

Asian Development Bank (ADB). 2008. *Philippines: Critical Development Constraints*. Manila.

Hausmann, R., D. Rodrik, and A. Velasco. 2005. *Growth Diagnostics*. Cambridge, MA: John F. Kennedy School of Government, Harvard University.

Part A
Overview and Synthesis

2. Development Performance and Policy

Dante B. Canlas, Maria Rowena M. Cham, and Juzhong Zhuang

The Philippine experience after World War II, relative to that of other countries in East and Southeast Asia, has caught the attention of eminent economists studying growth and development. Lucas (1993), for example, asked why the Philippines was not part of the "economic miracle"—the remarkable East Asian transformation featuring Hong Kong, China; the Republic of Korea; Singapore; and Taipei,China. This section describes and tries to account for performance in growth and poverty reduction in the past several decades and the evolution of the Philippine Government's development policy.

2.1. Synopsis of Philippine Growth

Following the Philippines' political independence in 1946, in the 1950s, the country embarked on an industrialization drive. During 1950–2006, the Philippine gross domestic product (GDP), expressed in 1985 prices, expanded 11.2 times—an average growth of 4.4% each year. But the growth rate was never smooth. For instance, the economy contracted in 1984–1985, 1990, and 1998.

Accounting for growth in population—which rose from about 19 million in 1950 to 87 million in 2006, for an average annual growth of about 2.75%—in 1960 the Philippines had a per capita GDP of about $612 expressed in 2000 United States (US) dollars (Table 2.1). By this measure, it was ahead of Indonesia, with a per capita income of $196, and Thailand, with $329. The Philippines trailed Hong Kong, China; the Republic of Korea; Malaysia; Singapore; and Taipei,China. By 1984, Thailand's per capita GDP of $933 had overtaken the Philippines' $908. In 2006, the Philippines' per capita GDP was $1,175, compared with Thailand's $2,549.[1]

---

[1] Oshima (1987) describes how Thailand overtook Philippine per capita GDP in the 1980s, focusing on country differentials in labor productivity in the aggregate and in the three major sectors of agriculture, industry, and services.

During 2001–2006, the Philippines posted its highest average per capita GDP growth of the past 2.5 decades, at 2.7%; at that rate, per capita GDP would double in about 25 years.

As shown in Table 2.2, during 1981–1990, the average annual change of Philippine per capita GDP was a negative 0.6%; in contrast, Thailand grew 6.3%, overtaking the Philippines. The entire 1980s were a "lost decade" for Philippine growth: the government declared a moratorium on foreign debt servicing in 1983, and, in 1984–1985, the country had its first recession in the postwar era. The economy recovered in 1986, and this was sustained until 1989, when political shocks slowed it down. Because growth in the

Table 2.1: Per Capita Gross Domestic Product (in 2000 $)

Economy	1960	1983	1984	2006
Hong Kong, China	1,960	13,028	14,163	31,779
Indonesia	196	444	467	983
Korea, Republic of	1,110	3,884	4,147	13,865
Malaysia	784	2,059	2,161	4,623
Philippines	612	1,004	908	1,175
Singapore	2,251	10,386	11,042	27,685
Taipei,China[a]	1,468	2,846	3,169	15,482
Thailand	329	897	933	2,549

[a] Data for Taipei,China for 1960 are in constant 1996 United States dollars.
Sources: Data from CEPD (various years), IMF (various years), and World Bank (various years).

Table 2.2: Annual Average Growth Rate of Real Per Capita Gross Domestic Product, 1951–2006 (%)

Period	Hong Kong, China	Indonesia	Korea, Rep. of	Malaysia	Philippines	Singapore	Taipei, China	Thailand
1951–1960	9.2	4.0	5.1	3.6	3.3	5.4	7.6	5.7
1961–1970	7.1	2.0	5.8	3.4	1.8	7.4	9.6	4.8
1971–1980	6.8	5.3	5.4	5.3	3.1	7.1	9.3	4.3
1981–1990	5.4	4.3	7.7	3.2	−0.6	5.0	8.2	6.3
1991–2000	3.0	2.9	5.2	4.6	0.9	4.7	5.5	2.4
2001–2006	4.0	3.3	4.2	2.7	2.7	3.2	3.4	4.0

Sources: Data from CEPD (various years), IMF (various years), and World Bank (various years).

second half of the 1980s could not offset the dismal performance in the first half, the average annual per capita GDP shrank during the decade.

Natural disasters intervened as the economy entered the 1990s. A major earthquake devastated parts of the central and northern Philippines in 1990, and was followed by the eruption of Mount Pinatubo in 1991. The volcano's destruction was severe enough to cause a contraction that year. In 1992, presidential elections were held, but before the incoming administration could start working on its development agenda, it had to overcome a severe electric power crisis. The crisis was defused in 1994, allowing the economy to gain strength until 1997, when the Asian financial crisis broke. The Philippines caught the contagion from that crisis. Another recession materialized in 1998, which was also a presidential election year. The contraction proved short lived. In 1999, the economy recovered. The recovery continued until another political shock hit in late 2000, when the incumbent President stepped down and a new administration took over in January 2001.

A number of external shocks again struck the economy as it entered the new millennium. For example, in 2001, the information technology sector retreated on a global scale, causing the country's top manufactured exports (semiconductors) to decline. Then came the terrorist attacks on the US on 11 September and the war against terrorism, and the risk and uncertainty it engendered in the Philippines, particularly in the Autonomous Region in Muslim Mindanao. In addition, public health shocks (the onset of the severe acute respiratory syndrome [SARS] and avian influenza) intervened. Though the diseases had minimal direct effects on the Philippines, negative externalities were caused by limited information about the geographic extent of these diseases. Nevertheless, the economy showed some resiliency as real per capita GDP managed to grow an average of 2.7% during 2000–2006.

At this growth rate, real per capita GDP will double every 25 years. In all likelihood, the Philippines will not be able to catch up with Thailand if its growth rate stays at a mere 2.7%. Doubling this growth rate would bring real per capita GDP up to $2,350, which is still less than Thailand's in 2006.

Hong Kong, China; the Republic of Korea; Singapore; and Taipei,China—often referred to as newly industrializing economies (NIEs)—have undergone remarkable economic transformation and modernization since the 1960s and now export manufactured products on a global scale. The four NIEs in East and Southeast Asia are regarded as models of successful industrialization and are often referred to as "economic miracles." In contrast, the Philippines did not make a similar transformation.

2.2. Accounting for Sources of Growth

The Philippines' growth record during the last four decades leaves much to be desired compared with that of its East and Southeast Asian neighbors. What have been the key drivers of and reasons behind its slow and erratic growth?

On the supply side, the three major sectors (agriculture, industry, and services) grew steadily during the 1950s, 1960s, and 1970s (Table 2.3). But the economic crises in the mid 1980s, early 1990s, and late 1990s slowed the growth considerably. During the recession in the early 1980s, industry was the hardest hit as the growth rate for the period slipped to 0.6% from a high 7.9% in the previous decade. Industry recovered in the 1990s and stabilized in the 2000s, but services proved to be the main contributor to growth starting in the 1980s. In the 1990s, agriculture contributed 12.9% to GDP growth; industry, 35.3%; and services, 51.9%. During 2001–2006, agriculture's average contribution to GDP growth increased to 15.9%, that of industry decreased to about 22.6%, while that of services increased to almost 61.5%.

Figure 2.1 depicts the output share of the major sectors. Agriculture, including fishery and forestry, was a major source of income and employment from the 1950s to 1980s. In 1986, agriculture's share of real GDP was about 25%. In 2006, this had declined to about 19.5%. The biggest subsector in agriculture is crops, and, during 1986–2006, its share of real GDP fell from 23.0% to 18.6%. Forestry's share declined from 1.7% in 1986 to 0.1% in 2006, reflecting the rapid rate of deforestation that had taken place.

In the course of economic development, the share of agriculture to real GDP is expected to decline. Industry is normally expected to pick up the slack. This did not happen in the Philippines. The share of industry was highest in the 1960s and 1970s as import substitution policies, which were oriented mainly toward the domestic market, extended high rates of effective protection to local industries against imports. In the 1980s, industry's share began to decline. In 1986, industry's share of real GDP was 35.0%; in 2006, the share had dropped to 32.5%. The biggest subsector in industry is manufacturing. In 1986, manufacturing's share of real GDP was 24.7%; this fell to 24.0% in 2006. Food processing is the most important manufacturing subsector.

Philippine industry contributed only 33% of GDP during 2001–2006. This contrasts sharply with many of its neighbors in the Association of Southeast Asian Nations (ASEAN). During the same period, industry contributed about 45–46% of GDP in Indonesia, Malaysia, and Thailand (Table 2.4).

Due to the service sector's high growth rates, its share in GDP increased and exceeded that of industry starting in the mid 1980s. In 1986, services'

Table 2.3: Annual Average Gross Domestic Product Growth and Contributions of Major Production Sectors (%)

Period	GDP Growth Rate	Agriculture		Industry		Services	
		Growth Rate	Contribution to GDP Growth	Growth Rate	Contribution to GDP Growth	Growth Rate	Contribution to GDP Growth
1951–1960	6.4	5.0	25.5	7.5	34.1	7.0	40.4
1961–1970	4.9	4.3	26.0	5.7	37.0	4.8	37.0
1971–1980	5.9	4.1	17.6	7.9	49.6	5.3	32.8
1981–1990	1.8	1.2	16.3	0.6	8.5	3.4	75.3
1991–2000	3.1	1.9	12.9	3.1	35.3	3.7	51.9
2001–2006	4.6	3.7	15.9	3.2	22.6	6.1	61.5

GDP = gross domestic product.
Source: Estimates by the National Economic and Development Authority based on NSCB (*National Income Accounts* various years).

Table 2.4: Average Shares of Major Production Sectors in Gross Domestic Product, 2001–2006 (%)

Economy	Agriculture	Industry	Services
Indonesia	15.1	44.8	40.1
Malaysia	8.5	45.1	46.4
Philippines	19.6	33.3	47.1
Taipei,China	1.7	28.7	69.7
Thailand	9.3	46.0	44.7
Viet Nam	20.7	38.8	40.5

Sources: Estimates by the National Economic and Development Authority based on NSCB (*Philippine Statistical Yearbook* various years) for the Philippines; data from ADB (2007) and World Bank (various years) for all other economies.

Figure 2.1: Sector Shares in Gross Domestic Product (%)

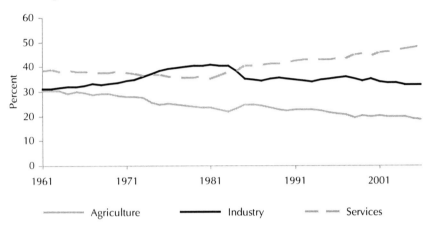

Source: Data from NSCB. *National Income Accounts* (various years).

share was 40.6%; in 2006, this had risen to 48.7%. Trade, both retail and wholesale, was the biggest subsector in services. In 1986, trade's share in real GDP was 14.7%; this increased to 16.9% in 2006, helped in no small amount by the enactment of the Retail Trade Liberalization Law. Other than government services, all subsectors of services (such as transport, telecommunications, finance, and private services) were part of the economic expansion.

On the demand side, the share of private consumption in GDP in the Philippines averaged about 75% during the 1950s and 1960s and declined to just below 70% in 1970s. Since then, it has been on a rising trend and reached 78% during 2000–2006 (Table 2.5). Consequently, private consumption has been the most important driver of GDP growth, averaging 89% of that growth in the 1990s and slightly declining to 81.9% afterward (Table 2.6). Meanwhile, the contributions of investment to GDP growth have stayed below one third of that of private consumption in most periods, and the average contribution fell to –7.2% during 2000–2006. As for government spending, its share in GDP has continued to be below that of comparator countries—and has consistently been less than 10% of GDP. The dominant role of private consumption in driving GDP growth in the Philippines is also in sharp contrast with many of its ASEAN neighbors, where the role of private consumption is much less significant, and the contributions of investment and net exports are more important (Table 2.7).

The Philippines' regions show a high level of disparity in their growth patterns (Table 2.8). The National Capital Region (NCR) is the largest contributor to GDP growth, followed by Region IV (Southern Tagalog) and

Table 2.5: Annual Average Shares of Expenditure Components in Gross Domestic Product, 1951–2006 (%)

Period	Consumption		Government		Investment		Net Exports
	Growth Rate	Share in GDP	Growth Rate	Share in GDP	Growth Rate	Share in GDP	Share in GDP
1951–1960	6.5	74.9	4.5	7.3	5.8	18.4	–5
1961–1970	4.7	74.2	5.5	7.1	6.3	20.7	–3
1971–1980	4.7	67.7	7.0	8.7	9.5	25.2	–4
1981–1990	3.0	70.1	1.5	7.6	3.0	21.3	–2
1991–2000	3.5	77.8	3.5	8.0	4.0	23.0	–9
2001–2006	4.9	78.4	0.4	6.8	–1.3	19.7	–7

GDP = gross domestic product.
Note: Figures do not add up because of statistical discrepancy in the National Income Accounts data of the National Statistical Coordination Board.
Source: Estimates by the National Economic and Development Authority based on NSCB (*National Income Accounts* various years).

Table 2.6: Contribution to Annual Average Gross Domestic Product Growth by Expenditure Component, 1951–2006 (%)

Period	Consumption		Government		Investment		Net Exports
	Growth Rate	Contribution to GDP Growth	Growth Rate	Contribution to GDP Growth	Growth Rate	Contribution to GDP Growth	Contribution to GDP Growth
1951–1960	6.5	75.4	4.5	5.2	5.8	15.5	–2.2
1961–1970	4.7	71.3	5.5	7.9	6.3	24.7	–4.6
1971–1980	4.7	54.1	7.0	9.9	9.5	36.7	–1.7
1981–1990	3.0	118.0	1.5	6.1	3.0	11.9	–23.7
1991–2000	3.5	89.0	3.5	9.0	4.0	26.0	–1.3
2001–2006	4.9	81.9	0.4	0.2	–1.3	–7.2	1.9

GDP = gross domestic product.
Note: Figures do not add up because of statistical discrepancy in the National Income Accounts data of the National Statistical Coordination Board.
Source: Estimates by the National Economic and Development Authority based on NSCB (*National Income Accounts* various years).

Region III (Central Luzon). During 2001–2006, the Philippines' average annual GDP growth rate was 4.6%, of which 75% was contributed by 5 of the 17 regions. The NCR accounted for over 39% of GDP growth; Region IV, 14%; and Region III, 7%.

Table 2.7: Average Shares of Expenditure Components in Gross Domestic Product, 2001–2006 (%)

Economy	Consumption	Government	Investment	Net Exports
Indonesia	61.0	7.4	22.9	8.8
Malaysia	48.1	14.3	27.8	9.7
Philippines	78.4	6.8	19.7	–7.4
Taipei,China	59.1	13.1	18.3	9.5
Thailand	54.7	8.7	23.0	13.6
Viet Nam	65.4	6.6	34.8	–6.8

Note: For the Philippines, figures do not add up because of statistical discrepancy in the National Income Accounts data of the National Statistical Coordination Board.
Sources: Estimates by the National Economic and Development Authority based on NSCB (*National Income Accounts* various years) for the Philippines; CEPD (various years) for Taipei,China; and World Bank (various years) for all other economies.

Table 2.8: Regional Contribution to Gross Domestic Product and Gross Domestic Product Growth (%)

Period	National Capital Region	Region IV (Southern Tagalog)	Region III (Central Luzon)	Region VI (Western Visayas)	Region VII (Central Visayas)	Other Regions
Gross Regional Domestic Product—Regional Shares						
1981–1990	29.6	14.8	9.3	7.4	6.4	32.5
1991–2000	30.3	15.7	9.5	7.2	6.7	30.7
2001–2006	31.2	15.4	8.8	7.2	7.1	30.3
Gross Regional Domestic Product—Contribution to Growth						
1981–1990	34.5	17.1	12.3	4.6	8.2	23.4
1991–2000	31.4	16.3	7.9	7.4	9.0	28.1
2001–2006	39.0	14.4	6.7	7.8	7.2	25.0

Source: Data from NSCB. *National Income Accounts* (various years).

Table 2.9 decomposes real GDP growth into the growth of labor and capital, weighted by their shares in GDP, plus a residual that represents growth of total factor productivity (TFP), capturing factors such as technological progress and efficiency gains due to policy and institutional reforms. The share of capital income (α) is estimated at 0.65 using a regression model. Under constant returns to scale, the share of labor income is $1-\alpha$, which is equal to 0.35. The results show that much of the growth in real

GDP in the 1960s and until the 1990s was attributed to growth in capital and labor and came minimally from growth in TFP. In fact, TFP growth was negative in the 1970s and 1980s. But the tide seems to have turned in 2001–2006, with TFP growth at 2.41%.

TFP growth is a main source of long-run growth. Many studies have found that TFP growth in the Philippines was weak and volatile over time (Cororaton 2002). During some decades, such as the 1980s, average TFP growth was negative. Compared with other countries in Southeast Asia, the Philippines obviously performed weakly in TFP growth (Table 2.10), which could partly explain why Thailand overtook the Philippines' per capita GDP and growth rate in the 1980s.

Table 2.9: Contribution of Factors of Production to Gross Domestic Product Growth (percentage point)

Period	Contribution of Capital Stock Growth [$\alpha(\Delta K/K)$]	Contribution of Labor Growth [$(1-\alpha)(\Delta L/L)$]	Contribution of TFP Growth ($\Delta A/A$)
1961–1970	3.98	1.18	0.06
1971–1980	4.57	1.38	–0.64
1981–1990	2.05	1.37	–1.62
1991–2000	1.77	0.87	0.25
2001–2006	1.12	1.24	2.41

TFP = total factor productivity.
Note: In the column heads, K = capital stock, ΔK = change in capital stock, L = labor force, ΔL = change in labor force, A = total factor productivity, ΔA = change in total factor productivity, α = share of capital stock, and 1-α = share of labor.
Source: Estimations based on NSCB (*Philippine Statistical Yearbook* various years).

Table 2.10: Annual Average Growth of Total Factor Productivity in Selected Asian Countries (%)

Period	Indonesia	Malaysia	Philippines	Thailand	Viet Nam
1980–1984	–0.32	0.74	–2.34	0.37	–
1985–1989	–0.47	0.20	0.49	3.66	2.02
1990–1994	0.82	3.36	–1.68	2.14	4.12
1995–1999	3.67	0.32	1.03	–2.16	3.22
1980–2000	–0.80	1.29	–0.37	1.00	3.27

– = not available.
Source: APO (2004).

2.3. Recent Trends in Poverty and Inequality

Due to the modest growth of the Philippine economy during the last 5.5 decades, real incomes of households have not risen significantly, the poverty incidence has declined only slowly, and inequality remains high. Poverty and inequality amid growth is a constant reminder of the challenges that the Philippines faces in the new millennium.

2.3.1. Poverty

In eradicating poverty, the Philippines has lagged far behind most of its East and Southeast Asian neighbors, particularly the People's Republic of China (PRC), Indonesia, Thailand, and Viet Nam. In 2003, using the official poverty lines, 30% of Filipinos and 24% of Philippine families were classified as poor (Figure 2.2). At the $1-a-day poverty line, the poverty incidence was about 13.2%. In contrast, the PRC and Viet Nam started with higher levels of poverty than the Philippines during the early 1980s, but their absolute poverty rates soon dwindled and became lower than those of the Philippines in the early 2000s. Using the $1-a-day poverty line, the PRC's absolute poverty rate was about 10.8% and that of Viet Nam about

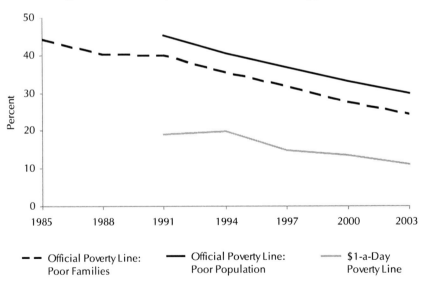

Figure 2.2: Poverty Incidence in the Philippines (%)

Source: Data from ADB (2005).

Figure 2.3: Poverty Incidence Based on $1-a-Day in Selected Countries

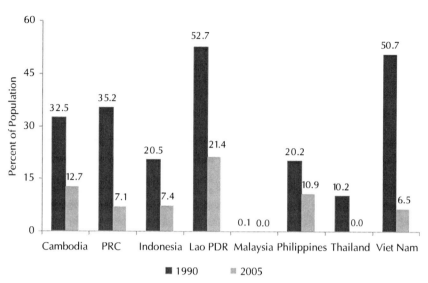

Lao PDR = Lao People's Democratic Republic, PRC = People's Republic of China.
Note: Data for Cambodia are for 1993 and 2004; for PRC, 1993 and 2004; for Indonesia, 1993 and 2002; for Lao PDR, 1992 and 2002; for Malaysia, 1993 and 2004; for Philippines, 1994 and 2003; for Thailand, 1992 and 2002; and for Viet Nam, 1993 and 2004.
Source: ADB (2007).

8.4%. Both Malaysia and Thailand have virtually eliminated absolute poverty (Figure 2.3). The latest data show that the poverty incidence increased to 32.9% for the population and 26.9% for families at the official poverty lines in 2006.

As in most Asian developing countries, poverty in the Philippines is largely a rural phenomenon. Two of every three poor people in the country are in rural areas and depend predominantly on agricultural employment and incomes. Poverty incidence among agricultural households is about four times that of the rest of the population. Although the share of agriculture in the total labor force has gone down from about one half in the late 1980s to only a little more than one third by the mid 2000s, the sector continues to account for nearly two thirds of total poverty. Further, there were large variations in poverty incidence across regions. In 2003, the poverty incidence was the highest in the Autonomous Region in Muslim Mindanao at 63.9%; Bicol, 45.7%; and Western Mindanao, 48.2%; and was lowest in

23

the NCR (4.9%).[2] The highest concentration of the poor was in the Visayas and Mindanao, with 48.3% of the poor living in these regions in 2003.

The large regional variation in poverty incidence has been attributed partly to a relatively large variation in access to infrastructure and social services across regions and island groups. A widely held view, for example, is that development efforts in the Philippines have favored Luzon and discriminated against the Visayas and (especially) Mindanao, leading to substantial regional differences in access to economic opportunities, rates of poverty reduction, and the incidence of armed conflicts. For instance, the *Philippine Human Development Report 2005* shows that measures of deprivation—such as disparities in access to reliable water supply, electricity, and (especially) education—predict well the occurrence of armed encounters (HDN 2005).

Several studies have examined the causes of poverty in the Philippines. Balisacan (2007a) found that multidimensional deprivation in the Philippines—as manifested not only in low incomes but also in inadequate human capabilities such as poor health and educational achievements and in limited access to the means to achieving these capabilities—is closely linked to agriculture. Cluster analysis of provincial data indicates that the share of agriculture in employment increases with the level of provincial deprivation, being lowest (about 6%) in the least deprived provinces and highest (about 65%) in the extremely deprived provinces. Thus, moving rural populations out of the agriculture sector has the potential advantage of overcoming many dimensions of deprivation at the same time.

Balisacan (2007b) also looked at the statistical significance of the channels by which income growth, together with a host of other factors, influence poverty reduction. The study grouped all the factors into initial economic and institutional conditions and time-varying policy variables. Among the initial conditions, the level of human capital stock was found to be statistically significant: an increase of 10% in the mortality rate relative to the mean for all provinces (84.7 in 1988) would reduce the rate of provincial income growth by 0.2% per year. All the time-varying policy variables were found to be significant and have the expected signs. Improvements in literacy and access to infrastructure (electricity and roads) had a positive

---

[2]   These figures were estimated using consistency-confirming poverty lines. As shown in Balisacan (2003), the official estimates are not an accurate guide to ascertaining changes in poverty over time, across the country's regions or provinces, or between rural and urban areas, because the standard of living implied by the poverty lines varies for each region and over time. In contrast, consistency-confirming poverty lines are fixed for various subpopulation groups and periods in terms of the level of living they imply. Moreover, they use expenditure per capita as a proxy measure for individual welfare, while the official methodology uses income per capita as the relevant indicator.

effect on income growth. Most interestingly, increments in implementation of land reform (the Comprehensive Agrarian Reform Program) had a positive and significant effect on the mean income growth rate. A 25% increase in the pace of implementing land reform would raise the income growth rate by 0.6% per year. This is a significant result considering that land reform is often seen as a policy tool mainly for achieving noneconomic objectives. The result suggests that addressing access to productive assets would improve efficiency, thereby raising the economy's subsequent income growth rates.

2.3.2. Inequality

The Philippines also has a relatively high level of inequality compared with most of its regional neighbors. In 2003, the richest 20% of Philippine families received more than half of the national income, while the poorest 20% accounted for only one twentieth. The Gini coefficient of per capita income was 0.44 in the Philippines in 2003, compared with 0.34 in Indonesia, 0.40 in Malaysia, and 0.42 in Thailand (Figure 2.4). During 1994–2003, the Philippines' Gini coefficient rose by 7%, suggesting that income

Figure 2.4: Gini Coefficient for Per Capita Income
and Expenditure for Selected Countries

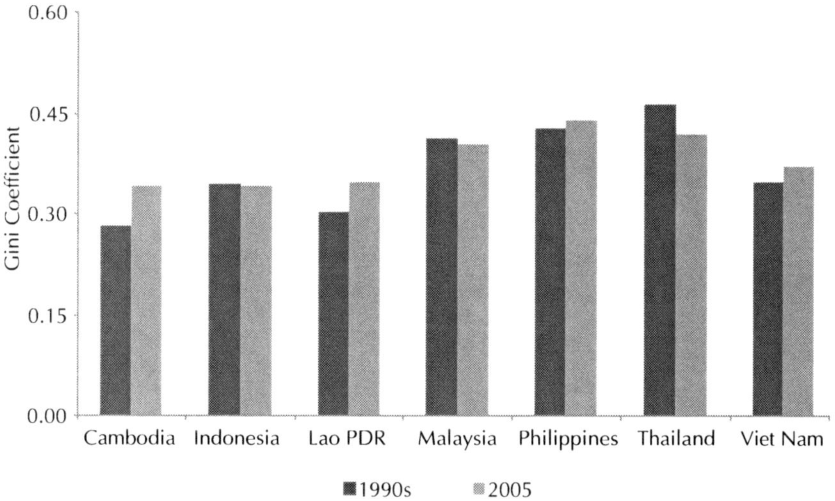

Lao PDR = Lao People's Democratic Republic.
Note: Data for Cambodia are for 1993 and 2005; Indonesia, 1993 and 2002; Lao PDR, 1992 and 2002; Malaysia, 1993 and 2004; Philippines, 1994 and 2003; Thailand, 1992 and 2002; and Viet Nam, 1993 and 2004.
Source: ADB (2007).

distribution had worsened during this period. The income distribution worsened during 1994–1997, then improved during 2000–2003; but in 2003, the Gini coefficient was still higher than the 1994 level. Thus, while average per capita income has increased, the benefits of growth have not been shared equally by all segments of the population.

Decomposing the country's total inequality into two components— between-region inequality and within-region inequality—shows that more than 90% of the inequality in 2003 was due to inequality among individuals within each region, while less than 10% could be explained by differences in mean per capita income or expenditure across regions (Table 2.11). Decomposing the total inequality into within education levels and between levels shows that about 65% of the inequality can be explained by differences in per capita income or expenditure of individuals with the same education attainments. However, about 35% can be explained by differences in the education subgroups (Table 2.12),[3] which indicates that improvements in human capital could help reduce inequalities and promote pro-poor growth.

Table 2.11: Inequality Decomposition by Region

	1994	1997	2000	2003
Per Capita Welfare of Income				
Theil's Index: Total	0.316	0.390	0.386	0.367
Of Which				
Within regions	0.278	0.340	0.339	0.340
(as a share of total)	(88.1%)	(87.1%)	(87.8%)	(92.8%)
Between regions	0.038	0.050	0.047	0.027
(as a share of total)	(11.9%)	(12.9%)	(12.2%)	(7.2%)
Per Capita Welfare of Expenditure				
Theil's Index: Total	0.260	0.305	0.306	0.283
Of Which				
Within regions	0.225	0.257	0.261	0.257
(as a share of total)	(86.6%)	(84.3%)	(85.3%)	(90.8%)
Between regions	0.035	0.048	0.045	0.026
(as a share of total)	(13.4%)	(15.7%)	(14.7%)	(9.2%)

Source: Son (2007).

---

[3] Education levels of household heads were divided into seven groups: (i) no education, (ii) incomplete primary education, (iii) complete primary education, (iv) incomplete secondary education, (v) complete secondary education, (vi) incomplete college education, and (vii) complete college education and higher levels.

Table 2.12: Inequality Decomposition by Education Level

	1994	1997	2000	2003
Per Capita Welfare of Income				
Theil's Index: Total	0.316	0.390	0.386	0.367
Of Which				
Within educational levels	0.222	0.252	0.246	0.241
(as a share of total)	(70.3%)	(64.7%)	(63.7%)	(65.8%)
Between educational levels	0.094	0.138	0.140	0.125
(as a share of total)	(29.7%)	(35.3%)	(36.3%)	(34.2%)
Per Capita Welfare of Expenditure				
Theil's Index: Total	0.260	0.305	0.306	0.283
Of Which				
Within educational levels	0.178	0.193	0.190	0.182
(as a share of total)	(68.6%)	(63.3%)	(62.1%)	(64.3%)
Between educational levels	0.081	0.112	0.116	0.101
(as a share of total)	(31.4%)	(36.7%)	(37.9%)	(35.7%)

Source: Son (2007).

2.4. Evolution of the Philippines' Development Policy

In the last 5.5 decades, the Philippines experienced not only dramatic economic ups and downs, but also political upheavals. The country was under martial law rule for 13 years starting in 1972. In 1986, the People Power Revolution restored democracy. Since then, successive democratically elected administrations have initiated various policy and structural reforms aimed at accelerating the pace of economic growth and poverty reduction.

2.4.1. Development Policy before 1986

In the 1950s, the country's development policy was centered around an industrialization strategy based on import substitution. The strategy was able to raise the level of capital per worker, allowing GDP to grow by about 6.4% annually during the decade. Import substitution, however, soon lost steam and, during 1960–1970, per capita GDP growth slowed to an annual average of 4.9%. The Philippines adhered to import substitution well into the 1970s and the first half of the 1980s, long after the four Asian NIEs had shifted to export-led industrialization.

Import substitution rested on protectionist trade barriers, including high tariffs and quantitative restrictions against imports, and on foreign exchange controls. From the elaborate system of trade protection and foreign exchange controls emerged favored domestic industries, mostly heavy and upstream, that absorbed a good deal of official foreign reserves and contributed to persistent balance-of-payments difficulties. In addition, smuggling of imported goods, abetted by corrupt officials, became pervasive. The restrictive foreign trade regime benefited mostly the owners and employees of industries the government chose to promote based on policies that were later consolidated under the Investment Incentives Act of 1967. The investment and industrial promotion policies, consisting mainly of tax and customs duties exemptions, did little to bring sustainable growth and poverty reduction.

Associated with the import substitution strategy was a fixed or managed exchange rate regime, which periodically collapsed from the weight of countercyclical fiscal and monetary policies. Each of the peso collapses was generally accompanied by a balance-of-payments crisis, forcing the government to seek liquidity support from the International Monetary Fund. The countercyclical policies resulted in large and persistent deficits in the current account and in the national government budget. To finance the twin deficits, the government borrowed abroad, thereby enlarging its foreign debt. The fiscal deficits were automatically accommodated by the central bank. Because the central bank was not independent from the government, its monetary management was inconsistent, inflation increased, and official foreign reserves were eroded. In the early 1980s, the Philippines was forced to declare a moratorium on foreign debt servicing, after the oil price shocks brought in high interest rates worldwide.

The dismal economic performance could also be traced to poor governance during the 1970s. A good deal of the foreign debt, it turned out later, consisted of loans that financed projects of political cronies of the then President. Most of the projects failed, and because the loans were coursed through government financial institutions they were eventually assumed by the government.

2.4.2. Development Policy from 1986

In 1986, the Philippine economy emerged from martial law rule with serious imbalances. The consolidated public sector deficit reached about 6%, and external debt was close to 100% of gross national product. Foreign reserves fell to a level equivalent to less than 1 month of imports. Inflation hit 50% in 1984 before falling to 23% in 1985. Real GDP recorded 2 consecutive years of negative growth, at −7% (in 1984 and 1985). The central bank was saddled with massive liabilities, and the finance sector was plagued by huge nonperforming loans of the two government financial institutions—the Development Bank of the Philippines and the Philippine National Bank. Social indicators were just as disappointing: unemployment was high and poverty was pervasive.

Key policies and reform agendas of the administrations since 1986 were mostly documented in the medium-term Philippine development plans (MTPDPs).[4] A review of the MTPDPs reveals that policies and reforms pursued since the restoration of democracy broadly fall into the following areas: monetary and fiscal reforms for restoring and maintaining macroeconomic stability; trade, industrial, and financial reforms for improving economic efficiency and competitiveness; governance reform and decentralization for improving the effectiveness of the national and local governments; and social policies and programs for fighting poverty, improving income distribution, and achieving the Millennium Development Goals. These policies and reforms are embodied in a number of well-publicized initiatives or programs implemented since 1986, including trade liberalization, tariff reduction, and accession to the World Trade Organization (WTO); fiscal consolidation and tax reform; creation of an independent central bank with inflation targeting as a key policy tool; privatization of several government-owned and -controlled corporations, such as the Philippine National Bank and Petron (a petroleum refining and distribution company); power sector restructuring and reform; comprehensive agrarian reform; banking sector reform and capital market development; devolution of public services delivery to local government units; and declaration of poverty reduction as the overarching development goal and commitment to social programs for alleviating poverty and achieving Millennium Development Goals.

The current MTPDP covers 2004–2010. The plan fleshes out the policies to support the Arroyo administration's 10-point agenda: (i) creation of 10 million jobs through support for entrepreneurship and agribusiness; (ii) strengthening of education through infrastructure support; (iii) balancing of the national budget through fiscal reforms; (iv) decentralization of progress and development by developing transportation networks and digital infrastructure; (v) greater and better provision of power and water supply; (vi) decongestion of Metro Manila by expanding new centers of government, business, and community outside Metro Manila; (vii) development of Clark and Subic as the logistics center in Asia; (viii) automation of the electoral process; (ix) peace agreements with rebel groups; and (x) closure of divisive issues caused by the "people power movements " of EDSA 1, 2, and 3.

---

4   The MTPDP is the most important planning document of the government. It spells out the strategic framework to guide the government's policies, normally for the coming 6 years.

Policies and reforms initiated and implemented so far have had some visible impact on the Philippine economy, barring the reversal experienced during the 1997 Asian financial crisis. During 2001–2006, the Philippines posted its highest annual GDP growth of the past 2.5 decades, reaching 4.6%. In 2007, growth accelerated to 7.2%, the fastest pace in the last three decades. At the same time, inflation was under control and was now at the lowest level in the last 20 years. The external payments position has also become more sustainable than in recent decades.

However, the Philippines' policy and structural reform is by no means complete. The list of unfinished reform programs remains long and, arguably, more difficult reforms are yet to be implemented. In particular, the country's domestic investment remains sluggish, and its share in GDP has continued to decline. This raises the question of whether the recent pace of growth can be sustained. Moreover, the reduction in poverty incidence has been slow, and the Gini coefficient of per capita income remains very high, suggesting that the fruits of economic growth have not been widely shared among Filipinos. The next chapters will examine the critical constraints to sustainable growth and poverty reduction in the Philippines now and in the coming 5–10 years.

References

Asian Development Bank (ADB). 2005. *Poverty in the Philippines: Income, Assets, and Access.* www.abd.org/documents/books/Poverty-in-the -Philippines/default.asp

_____. 2007. *Key Indicators: Inequality in Asia.* Manila.

Asian Productivity Organization (APO). 2004. *Total Factor Productivity Growth: Survey Report.* Tokyo.

Balisacan, A. 2003. Poverty Comparison in the Philippines: Is What We Know about the Poor Robust? In C. M. Edmonds, ed. *Reducing Poverty in Asia: Emerging Issues in Growth, Targeting, and Measurement.* Cheltenham: Edward Elgar.

_____. 2007a. Local Growth and Poverty Reduction. In A. Balisacan and H. Hill, eds. *The Dynamics of Regional Development: The Philippines in East Asia.* Cheltenham: Edward Elgar.

_____. 2007b. *An Analysis of Chronic Poverty in the Philippines.* Quezon City: University of the Philippines Diliman.

Cororaton, C. 2002. Total Factor Productivity in the Philippines. In Asian Productivity Organization. *Total Factor Productivity Growth: Survey Report.* Tokyo.

Council for Economic Planning and Development (CEPD). various years. *Statistical Data Book.* Taipei,China.

Human Development Network Inc. (HDN). 2005. *Philippine Human Development Report 2005*. Manila.

International Monetary Fund (IMF). various years. *World Economic Outlook*. www.imf.org/external/pubs/ft/weo/2006/02/index.htm

Lucas, R. E. 1993. Making a Miracle. *Econometrica*. 61(2): 251–272.

National Statistical Coordination Board (NSCB). various years. *National Income Accounts*. Makati City.

_____. various years. *Philippine Statistical Yearbook*. Makati City.

Oshima, H. 1987. *Economic Growth in Monsoon Asia: A Comparative Study*. Tokyo: Tokyo University Press.

Son, H. H. 2007. Human Capital and Economic Growth. Background report to the *Philippines: Critical Development Constraints*. www.adb.org/Projects/Country-Diagnostic-Studies/default/ast.

World Bank. various years. *World Development Indicators*. Washington, DC.

3. Critical Constraints to Growth and Poverty Reduction

Dante B. Canlas, Muhammad Ehsan Khan, and Juzhong Zhuang

The Philippines, under a succession of administrations since 1986, has been committed to sustained growth of income and employment, stable prices, poverty eradication, and improved distribution of income and wealth in an open economy setting. In pursuit of these development goals, the national and local governments have ushered in wide-ranging economic and social policy reform programs. Under the reform programs, real gross domestic product (GDP) doubled between 1986 and 2006—a growth rate of about 3.5% each year. However, this pace of growth leaves much to be desired when compared with that of many of the Philippines' East and Southeast Asian neighbors. In recent years, growth has picked up and in 2007 real GDP grew at 7.2%. But there is no room for complacency. Private investment remains weak, raising the question of whether the current pace of growth is sustainable. In 2006, about 26.9% of families and 32.9% of the population still lived in poverty, a reminder of the difficulties that many individuals are still going through. And inequality in the distribution of household incomes remains high by regional standards.

Moving forward, the challenge for the Philippines is to sustain the current pace of growth or even accelerate it, while making every Filipino a winner in the growth process. To meet this challenge, a key step is to identify the most critical factors that constrain growth and poverty reduction. The diagnostic approach this study adopted to identify the critical constraints is informed by basic insights from recent literature that seeks to account for international differences in the levels and growth rates of per capita income. Section 3.1 presents a diagnosis of factors that may be constraining economic growth, section 3.2 provides an analysis of constraints to poverty reduction, and section 3.3 synthesizes the chapter.

3.1. Critical Constraints to Growth

Since the 1990s, the Philippines' overall investment rate has almost constantly lagged behind its neighbors' rates. Investment fell in many Southeast Asian countries following the 1997 Asian financial crisis. However, while investment has recovered in most of the countries, in the Philippines, the share of gross domestic investment in GDP has continued to fall and is presently at the lowest level since the crisis years of the early 1980s (Figure 3.1).

Figure 3.1: Comparison of Investment Rates
(% of gross domestic product)

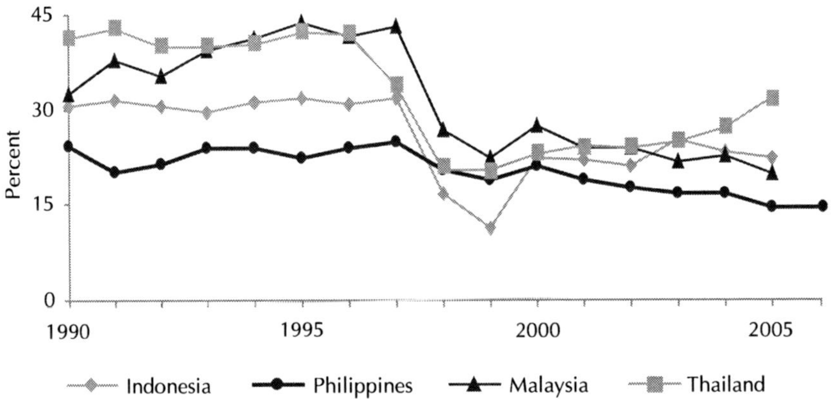

Investment = gross capital formation.
Sources: Data from NSCB (various years) and World Bank (2007).

Although investment has remained weak, GDP growth has picked up in recent years, in particular since 2005. The increase is driven by strong private consumption, which was in turn partly supported by rising remittance inflows. One possible explanation for the fall in the investment rate amid recovery of GDP growth is the growing share of the service sector in total output in the Philippines (ADB 2007c). A substantial part of the economic activities in services may require less investment to produce a unit of output than is true for industry. This implies that a larger share of services in GDP translates to a lower share of investment in GDP. However, data on credit use show that the biggest service subsectors—trade and transport, communications, and storage—are also the largest borrowers, after manufacturing. Such subsectors (especially transport, communications, and storage) are no less investment-intensive than industry. Therefore, the

34

large share of the service sector in total output is not likely to be a major contributing factor to the low investment rate.

Another possible explanation for the recent divergence in the GDP growth and investment rates could be that the Philippine economy has had excess capacity, which enabled it to register higher growth even with declining investment levels. This possibility is supported by the survey data on capacity utilization of the manufacturing sector. The 2003 Annual Survey of Philippine Business and Industry reported low capacity utilization levels across all size groups of manufacturing establishments (NSO 2004). Almost 50% of the large establishments reported operating at less than 70% of their installed capacity. Small establishments fared significantly better, but still with almost 20% of them reporting a capacity utilization level of less than 70% (Figure 3.2). The same survey in 2005 did not provide similar information, but the Monthly Integrated Survey of Selected Industries found that the average capacity utilization for the manufacturing sector rose from about 74% in 2003 to close to 81% in the second half of 2007 (NSO 2007), suggesting that the declining investment was at least partly compensated for by the increased capacity utilization.

Figure 3.2: Capacity Utilization of Small and Large Manufacturing Establishments, 2003

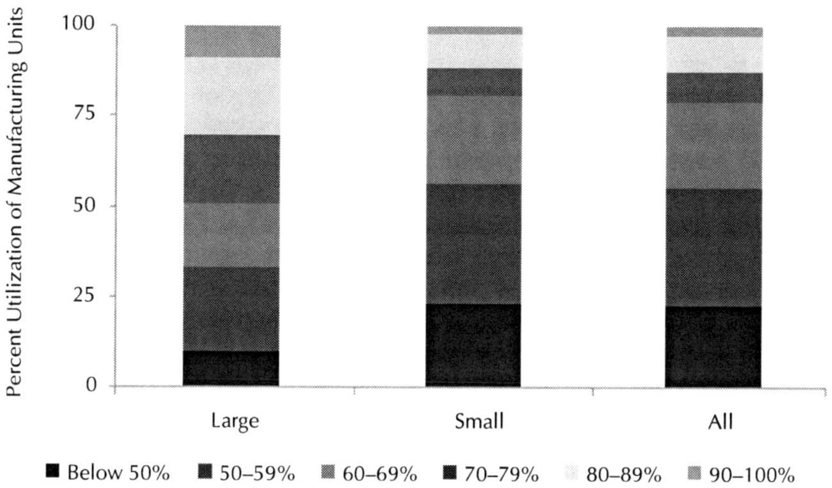

Source: Data from NSO (2004).

Therefore, the recent pace of growth may not be sustainable unless the declining trend in investment is reversed. While the public sector plays an important role of investing in infrastructure, the private sector should be the driving force of investment required for sustaining growth in the medium and long term. What are the constraints underlying the low level of private investment in the Philippines? Is it due to low social return to investment, low private appropriability, high cost of financing, or some combination of the three? This study will now look at some empirical evidence.

3.1.1. Cost of Finance

Low domestic savings could push the real interest rate up, inefficient financial intermediation could make access to finance difficult, and both could lead to a high cost of funds in domestic financial markets. For a small open economy such as the Philippines, access to the international capital market provides an alternative source of financing and, hence, the cost of international borrowing is also an important determinant of cost of financing for investors. In addition, in the Philippines, remittances from overseas workers provide another important source of finance.

Domestic savings. The Philippines' gross domestic savings rate has always been modest. In 1998, the savings rate fell below 13% of GDP, the lowest in more than 50 years. Although the savings rate has been improving since and reached about 20% of GDP in 2006, it was still the lowest among Association of Southeast Asian Nations (ASEAN) countries (Figure 3.3). One may argue that the savings rate should be a function of the level of income. When income is low, a country needs to spend more on basic consumption goods, and its savings rate will therefore be lower than that of a country with a higher income level. However, a comparison with savings rates of selected East and Southeast Asian countries when their levels of per capita GDP in purchasing power parity (PPP) terms were similar to that of the Philippines shows that the Philippine domestic savings rate was low (Table 3.1). In fact, the Philippines' domestic savings rate was similar to rates of Latin American countries that in the past faced periodic recessions and crises, which brought down the savings rate. Notably, by 2006, the Philippines' domestic savings rate had been overtaken by the rates of Argentina and Chile and was only slightly higher than those of Brazil and Mexico.

The Philippines' low domestic savings rate was likely one of the impediments to the country attaining the high and sustainable growth rates achieved by many of its neighbors in the last several decades. In the long term, the Philippines' growth prospects will benefit from a higher level of domestic savings. A comparison of the gross domestic savings and gross domestic investment rates shows that, prior to 2002, the savings levels lagged behind the investment levels; but the tide has since turned, with the ratio of domestic savings to GDP exceeding that of domestic investments to GDP by 1.4 percentage points in 2002, 2.9 percentage points in 2003,

Figure 3.3: Comparison of Gross Domestic Savings, 1980–2006
(% of gross domestic product)

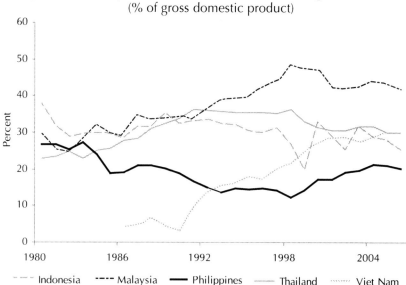

- ~~~~ Indonesia   ---- Malaysia   ▬ Philippines   ─── Thailand   ········ Viet Nam

Note: Gross domestic savings for the Philippines is calculated as the difference between gross domestic product and final consumption.
Sources: Data from NSCB (various years) for the Philippines and World Bank (various years) for other countries.

Table 3.1: Comparison of Gross Domestic Savings with Neighboring Countries at Comparable Per Capita GDP in PPP Terms

Country	Comparable Period	Per Capita GDP (in 2000 $)	Gross Domestic Savings (% of GDP)
China, People's Republic of	2002–2003	4,805	40.4–43.4
Korea, Republic of	1978–1981	4,847	23.9–29.3
Malaysia	1984–1987	4,584	29.4–34.7
Philippines	2005–2006	4,652	20.2–21.0
Thailand	1990–1991	4,758	33.8–36.3

GDP = gross domestic product, PPP = purchasing power parity.
Sources: Data from NSCB (various years) for the Philippines and World Bank (various years) for all other countries.

4.5 percentage points in 2004, 6.4 percentage points in 2005, and 5.9 percentage points in 2006 (Figure 3.4).

At the same time, the Philippines' current account was in surplus for almost 5 consecutive years starting in 2003, the longest time span in the last 40 years. During 2003–2006, although the trade account was in deficit, the deficit was more than offset by the growing overseas workers'

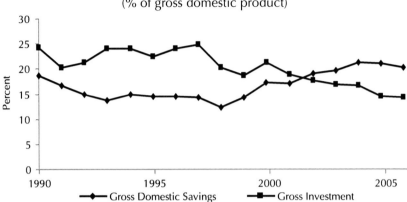

Figure 3.4: Gross Domestic Savings and Investments
(% of gross domestic product)

Note: Gross investment refers to gross domestic capital formation, which is calculated as the difference between gross domestic product and final consumption.
Source: Data from NSCB (various years).

remittances, leading to positive net resource transfers and enabling the country to reduce its external indebtedness (Figure 3.5). According to the central bank (Bangko Sentral ng Pilipinas [BSP]), the overseas remittances grew by more than 19% annually during 2002–2006, reaching more than $12 billon in 2006 and equivalent to about 11% of GDP in the same year (BSP 2007). These developments suggest that the modest domestic savings rate does not constitute a critical constraint to investment and growth at present. However, if the declining trend in investment were to reverse, the modest domestic savings rate could start to curtail investment and growth.

Domestic financial intermediation. As in most of its regional neighbors, the Philippines' financial system is dominated by banks. In 2006, bank credit accounted for 44% of total corporate domestic financing, equity accounted for 55%, and corporate bonds accounted for 1% (Figure 3.6). Judging from the banking sector's lending–deposit interest rate spreads, the efficiency of domestic financial intermediation in the Philippines is comparable to that in some of its neighbors, such as Thailand (Figure 3.7). Therefore, poor domestic financial intermediation is unlikely to have constituted a critical constraint to growth. However, compared with some developed countries, such as France, Italy, and the United Kingdom, the efficiency of Philippine financial intermediation has significant room for improvement. The declining returns on assets and on equity of the banking sector after the 1997 Asian financial crisis are also a reason for concern, which does not bode well for overall financial intermediation. According to Torreja (2003), returns on assets of the banking sector declined from 2.07% in 1995 to 0.45% in 2002, and returns on equity from 14.78% to 2.76% in the same period.

Figure 3.5: Comparison of External Indebtedness
(% of gross domestic product)

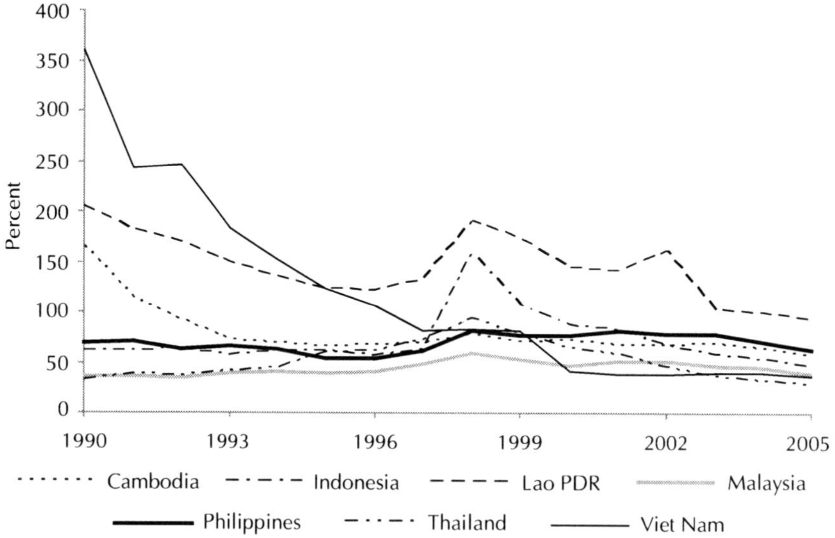

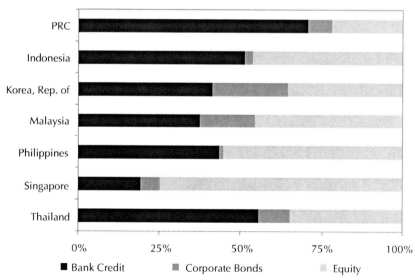

Lao PDR = Lao People's Democratic Republic.
Source: World Bank (various years).

Figure 3.6: Sources of Corporate Domestic Financing, End 2006 (%)

PRC = People's Republic of China.
Note: Calculated on the basis of outstanding values of bank loans, corporate bonds, and equity marketization.
Source: Data from ADB (2008).

Figure 3.7: Comparison of Spreads between Lending and Deposit Rates

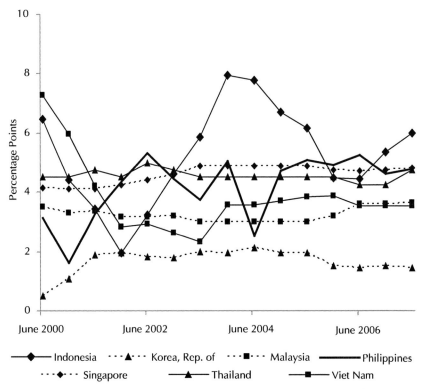

Note: Spread is the difference between the weighted average lending rate and the weighted deposit rate.
Source: Data from IMF (2007).

Growth of real domestic credit. After the 1997 Asian financial crisis, most affected countries experienced stagnation in real domestic credit, and the Philippines is no exception (Figure 3.8). And like most of the countries (including Indonesia, Malaysia, and Thailand), the ratio of domestic credit to GDP has continued to decline over the last 10 years. The decline, however, is more likely to reflect weak borrowing appetite of the corporate sector than the lack of liquidity in the banking sector. The most telling evidence for this is commercial banks' soaring excess reserves (Figure 3.9). Until 1994, the banking system's available reserves were more or less close to the required level, dipping into negative territory in times of crises and uncertainty (1983–1985 and 1990–1992). Low excess reserves owing to high reserve requirements explain the credit crunch in 1983–1992. In contrast, the current credit slump has been accompanied by soaring excess reserves. The banks may be getting a smaller percentage of the total savings but, even with that, they are not lending to the private sector. Instead, they are holding more government bonds.

The bulk of banks' excess reserves is accounted for by investments in treasury bills (2% of such investments qualify as reserves according to BSP rules). The share of loans to bank assets has fallen with the rise in bank holdings of government securities. This is consistent with the findings from the Investment Climate Survey that only 10% of business establishments surveyed indicated that access to financing was a major or severe constraint (ADB–World Bank 2005). This raises an important issue for regulators: the function of banks is to lend not to the government but to the private sector.

Borrowing costs. The Philippines has historically had very high lending rates, which have no doubt constrained economic growth. Figure 3.10 shows a negative correlation between the nominal average commercial lending rates and per capita GDP growth rates over time: high lending rates were associated with low per capita GDP growth rates. Since 2003, however, the nominal lending rate has declined significantly and is now close to the lowest level in 40 years, while the GDP growth rate is at the highest level. In real terms, the lending rate is currently also low by historical standards and is comparable to

Figure 3.8: Comparison of Ratios of Domestic Credit to Gross Domestic Product

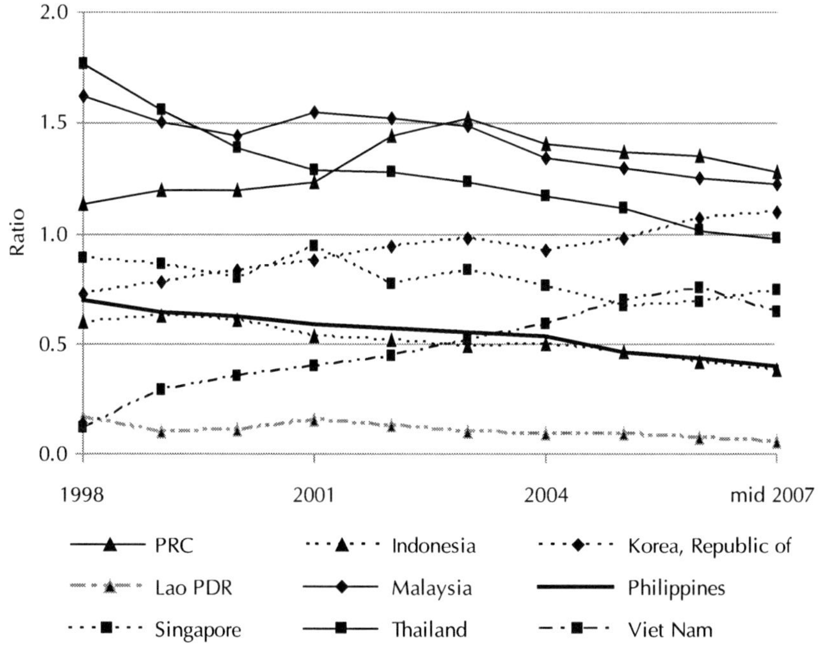

Lao PDR = Lao People's Democratic Republic, PRC = People's Republic of China.
Sources: Data from Bank of Thailand (2007) for Thailand and IMF (2007) for all other countries.

Figure 3.9: Available and Required Reserves Assets of the Banking Sector (% of deposits)

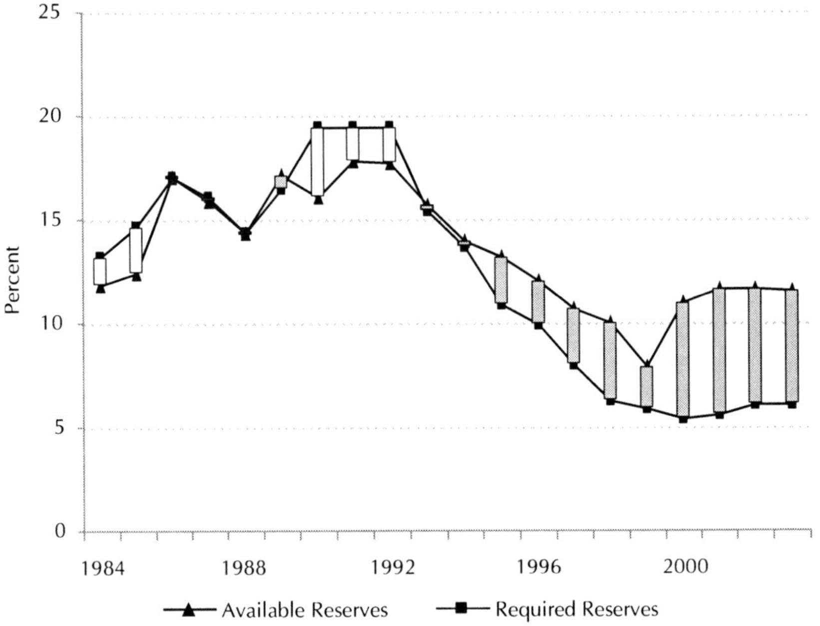

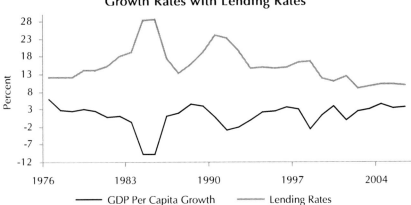

Note: Grey bar indicates that available reserves are more than required reserves and white bar indicates the reverse.
Source: Data from BSP (2007).

Figure 3.10: Comparison of Per Capita Gross Domestic Product Growth Rates with Lending Rates

GDP = gross domestic product.
Note: The lending rate is the average nominal commercial lending rate.
Source: Data from IMF (2007).

the rates in some of the Philippines' neighbors (Figure 3.11). Thus, the cost of borrowing from domestic banks is unlikely to have constituted a critical constraint to private investment and growth.

A key reason for the decline in the lending rates appears to be the corporate sector's weak demand for credit, which in turn reflects weak corporate investment. Weak corporate investment as a cause of weak credit growth is further evidenced by the fact that significant reductions in the lending rate after the 1997 Asian financial crisis did not spur investment spending. The decline in inflation to the low single-digit level has also helped bring down interest rates. But while lending rates have eased, they have not dropped as much as they should, certainly not as much as the decline in the treasury bill rates. What has kept lending rates from falling further is BSP's high overnight borrowing rate (Figure 3.12). Since the second half of 2001, the gap between the central bank's rate and the 91-day treasury bill

Figure 3.11: Comparison of Real Domestic Interest Rates

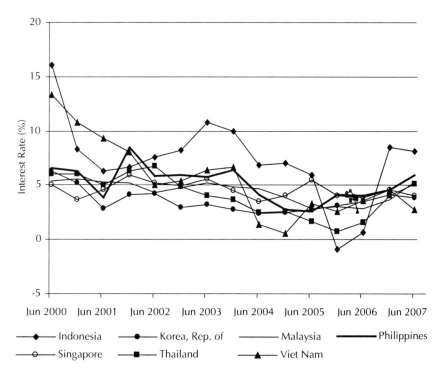

Note: The real domestic interest rate is the domestic interest rate of net inflation.
Source: Data from IMF (2007).

Figure 3.12: Trends in Lending Rates (%)

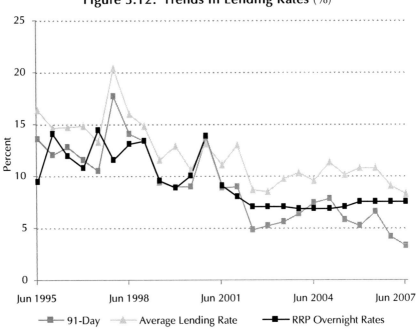

RRP = reverse repurchase.
Note: The 91-day is the rate for a 91-day treasury bill. The average lending rate is the weighted average interest rate charged by commercial banks on loans granted during a given period. The RRP overnight rate is the interest rate at which the Bangko Sentral ng Pilipinas borrows from banks with government securities as collateral.
Source: Data from BSP (2007).

rate has been growing. Thus, what currently matters is not just the treasury bill rate, but BSP's overnight borrowing rate, which has prevented further reductions in the rate at which banks lend to the private sector.

Access to international finance. Investors in the Philippines enjoy access to foreign financing through financial markets that are at various stages of development and that continue to evolve using a variety of instruments from recent financial reforms. Financial markets consist of money markets (offshore and local), capital markets (debt and equity), foreign exchange markets (spot and forward), and derivatives (options, swaps, futures, and structured products). The latter are the most recent and least developed of these markets.

A measure of the ease of access to international financial markets may be the sovereign spreads. The comparison of sovereign spreads in Figure 3.13 shows that the Philippines had one of the highest levels of spreads among its regional neighbors, but that the spreads have been

Figure 3.13: Comparison of Sovereign Spreads

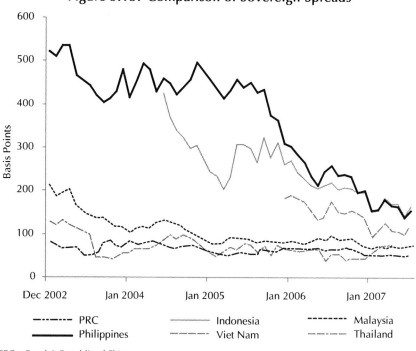

PRC = People's Republic of China.
Note: Sovereign spread is the difference between the yield of a United States treasury bond and the treasury bond of the pertinent country.
Source: Data from JP Morgan (2007).

declining recently and are now at par with those for Indonesia. This suggests that the access to international financial markets may have been poor in the past but has improved significantly recently and may not be a critical constraint.

Financing of small and medium-sized enterprises. Although access to and cost of finance do not currently constitute a critical constraint to private investment and economic growth overall in the Philippines, many small and medium-sized enterprises (SMEs) find access to financial services difficult. According to the 2005 Annual Survey of Philippine Business and Industry, SMEs account for about 97% of the enterprises in the country and about 49% of the employment in enterprises (NSO 2006); however, SMEs account for less than 17% of the revenues and only about 12% of the assets. SMEs represent a potential new growth area but are unable to realize their potential partly because they lack access to credit. The investment climate survey indicated that 25% of respondent firms claimed limited access to credit and that over 80% of SMEs had no access to overdraft or credit line facilities, which greatly hampered their ability to do business and grow (ADB–World Bank 2005). In addition, over 70% of small and 47% of medium-sized firms reported that they had to produce collateral to borrow from banks. Feedback from the smaller firms suggested that, in addition to poor access to financial services, they also faced higher costs of financing—interest rates offered to the smaller firms were 10–12% when funds were being made available to large firms at about 7%.

3.1.2. Social Returns to Investments

The returns to society of investments are diminished or enhanced depending on investments made in complementary factors of production, such as human capital and infrastructure. Investments in such complementary factors often have significant externalities. However, because such investments could be underprovided if left entirely to the market, they require public sector intervention. Human capital may augment labor (i.e., raise the efficiency of individual workers). Human capital also contributes to knowledge, giving rise to innovations that raise the productivity of all factors of production and are an important source of long-run growth. Infrastructure or social overhead capital supports private production through connectivity of places and integration of markets, linking suppliers to producers and facilitating distribution of commodities, all helping to lower the costs of doing business and increase returns to private investment.

Human Capital
Unemployment by education level. The high level of unemployment among educated workers suggests that the lack of human capital is currently not a critical constraint to growth. Table 3.2 shows that in 2006, the unemployment rate was close to zero for workers with no schooling, 1.0% for workers with elementary schooling, 3.3% for workers with high school education, and 2.9% for workers with college education. The overall unemployment rate declined from 10.2% in 2002 to 7.3% in 2006, and the pace of decline was faster for workers with elementary schooling than for the workers with high school and college education. *Asian Development Outlook 2007* reports that the education levels among the workforce are rising and a large number of the college graduates are taking low productivity jobs: for example, the median years of schooling among taxi drivers in the Philippines is 10 while it is 9 in Indonesia and 6 in Thailand (ADB 2007a).

Returns to education. Declining returns to education across the education levels also suggest that the lack of human capital is currently not a critical constraint to growth. If skilled human capital were indeed a constraint

Table 3.2: Unemployment Rates by Education Level

Education Levels	Unemployment Rate		Contribution to Total Unemployment	
	2002	2006	2002	2006
No Grade Completed	0.2	0.0	1.5	0.5
Elementary	2.1	1.0	20.8	14.0
Not completed	1.0	0.4	9.6	6.0
Completed	1.1	0.6	11.2	8.1
High School	4.3	3.3	42.7	45.5
Not completed	1.4	0.9	14.2	12.1
Completed	2.9	2.4	28.5	33.4
College	3.6	2.9	35.0	40.0
Not completed	1.8	1.5	17.4	21.0
Completed	1.8	1.4	17.6	19.0
Total	10.2	7.3	100.0	100.0

Source: Data from NSO (n.d.).

to growth, the demand for skilled workers would be high and, as a result, the returns to skilled workers would be high. Empirical estimates of rates of return to education suggest otherwise: rates of return across the education levels are declining although the differences in the average rate of return to tertiary education (16.6%) and to primary and secondary education (2.2% and 5.2%, respectively) are large. However, a recent cross-country comparison suggests that the difference in levels of returns may not be as large across the education levels and is not excessive when compared to those in regional neighbors such as Indonesia and Thailand (ADB 2007a).

Other evidence also suggests that, overall, the lack of human capital is not a critical constraint to growth in the Philippines.

- The Commission on Higher Education reported that more than 447,000 students graduated from universities and colleges nationwide in April 2006, but many of the graduates would add to the 2.8 million unemployed and 6.9 million underemployed Filipinos as of January 2006 (Dela Cruz 2007).
- The latest Labor Force Survey showed that while more than 400,000 students graduate from tertiary educational institutions each year, the number of employed professionals in the Philippines increased by only 31,000 to 1.414 million as of January 2006 from 1.383 million a year earlier, and the number of technicians and associate professionals increased by just 26,000 to 869,000 from

843,000 a year earlier. In comparison, the number of sales workers surged by 135,000, and the number of laborers and unskilled
workers went up by 382,000 (Dela Cruz 2007).

- Findings of the Investment Climate Survey (although limited to a few
  industries) also back the conclusions in the preceding paragraphs
  (ADB–World Bank 2005). The survey reported that only about
  12% of the responding firms considered that availability of human
  capital was a constraint to doing business in the Philippines.

Skilled requirements of emerging industries. While the lack of human
capital is not a critical constraint to growth in the Philippines overall, it may
be an issue in emerging industries. Study findings based on the 2004 labor
force statistics suggest that the earnings of professional workers in emerging
industries such as financial intermediation, information technology, call centers, and real estate, were 3–4 times those of unskilled workers in the same
industries (DOLE various years). Conversely, for more established industries, such as manufacturing, construction, and private education and health
services, professional workers' earnings were only 2.0–2.5 times those of
unskilled workers. These patterns suggest that human capital may be a constraint in some emerging industries. This argument is supported by the views
of the European Chamber of Commerce, which recently flagged the scarcity
of skilled workers in industries such as information technology and business
process outsourcing as a major constraint (Sto. Domingo and Rubio 2007).

Scarcity of skilled workers is also one reason for returns to education
being much higher for the tertiary level than for the primary and secondary
levels (Table 3.3). The emerging industries in information and communications technology and business process outsourcing generally employ college
graduates at rates much higher than those in the traditional service trades.
With rising skill intensity in the service sector, it is reasonable to expect a
higher rate of return for education in services than in agriculture and industry. Table 3.3 shows that in services the rate of return to education is 9.36%,
compared with 0.89% in agriculture and 7.23% in industry, in 2003.

Out-migration. Out-migration of highly skilled workers may not be a
critical constraint to growth. Statistics reported by the Philippine Overseas
Employment Administration suggest that the majority of migrant workers
are employed in low-technology occupations (POEA 2007). According to the
2006 data, over 80% of the 308,000 newly hired workers were employed in
low-paying and/or -skill occupation groups (Table 3.4). Less than 4% of new
hires were employed in engineering and related occupations. However, the
statistics do not provide insights into how many of the workers may have
higher skill levels but were forced to accept employment in occupations
requiring less skill because they were unable to find employment that better

Table 3.3: Rates of Return by Education Level and Sector (%)

	1997	2000	2003
Education Level			
Primary	2.50	2.42	2.22
Secondary	6.75	5.57	5.16
Tertiary	19.80	17.62	16.57
Sector			
Agriculture	0.84	0.96	0.89
Industry	7.57	7.01	7.23
Services	11.42	9.90	9.36

Sources: Data from NSO Family Income and Expenditure Surveys and Labor Force Surveys (various years).

Table 3.4: Selected New Deployment of Overseas Workers by Occupational Group, 2006

Occupational Group	Newly Hired Workers	Percent of Total
Household Workers	91,451	29.7
Factory Workers	43,234	14.0
Construction Workers	43,040	14.0
Medical Workers	17,731	5.8
Hotel and Restaurant Workers	15,693	5.1
Caregivers and Caretakers	14,412	4.7
Building Caretakers	12,294	4.0
Engineers	11,169	3.6
Dressmakers and Tailors	7,831	2.5
Performing Artists	7,431	2.4
All New Deployment	**308,142**	**100.0**

Source: Data from POEA (2007).

matched their skill level. The investor feedback gathered by the Global Competitiveness Report also suggests that less than 4% of the investors considered that brain drain may be a problem in the Philippines (IMD 2007).

Infrastructure

Infrastructure in general. Inadequacies in infrastructure are a critical constraint to investment and growth. The Philippines' investment in infrastructure as a percentage of GDP has been low and erratic (Figure 3.14). Government expenditure on infrastructure investment, after peaking at 4% of GDP in 1994, has slipped back to about 2% of GDP. Trends in private investment in infrastructure have been even more erratic. Following the crisis in the

Figure 3.14: Public and Private Sector Investments in Infrastructure
(% of gross domestic product)

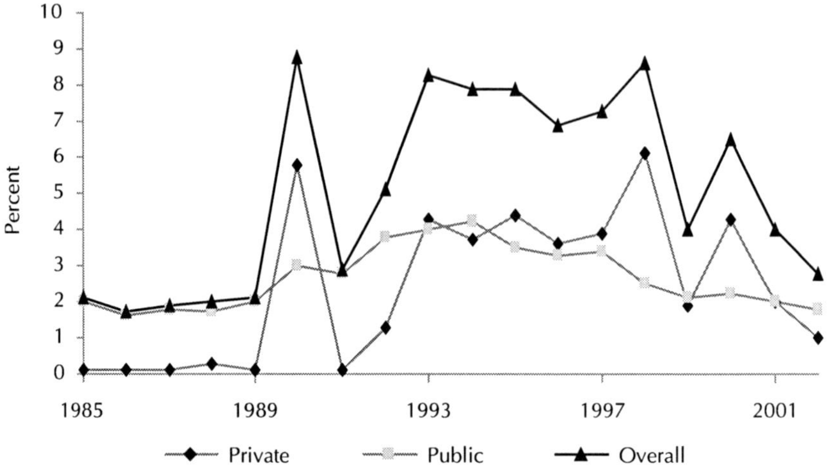

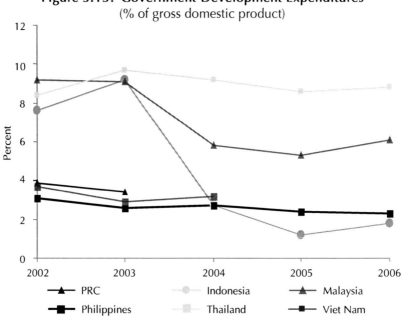

Source: World Bank (2005).

Figure 3.15: Government Development Expenditures
(% of gross domestic product)

PRC = People's Republic of China.
Sources: Data from NBSC (2007) for the PRC and ADB (2007c) for all other countries.

mid 1980s, private investment in infrastructure remained below 0.5% of GDP until the early 1990s, when private sector investment in power led to a sharp jump. Private sector investment has hovered near 2–4% of GDP since then, but dipped below 1% in 2002.

The Philippines has invested less in infrastructure than have most of its regional neighbors (Figure 3.15). In 2005, for example, the national government capital expenditure as a share of GDP was 8.6% for Viet Nam, 5.3% for Malaysia, and 3.0% for the Republic of Korea, but was only 2.4% for the Philippines. Major development partners have been urging the

Figure 3.16: Comparison of Road Network Coverage, 2003–2004

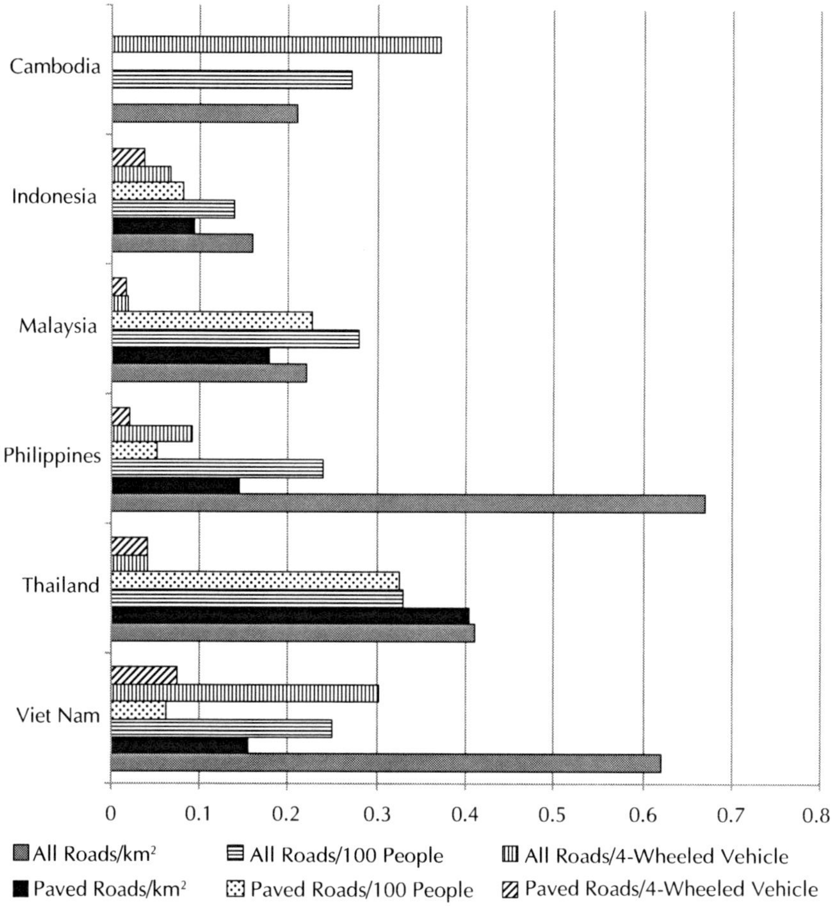

km² = square kilometer.
Note: Total length is for 2003–2004 for all countries. Paved length for Indonesia is for 2002; Viet Nam, for 1998; and for all other countries, for 2003. Paved length data for Cambodia are not available.
Source: Data from World Bank (2005 and various years).

51

government to raise infrastructure investment levels to at least 5.0% of GDP. Current levels of investment are insufficient for keeping up with the growing needs of the economy and the population; the investments also fall short of the levels required for maintaining the existing infrastructure.

Due to the dearth of investment in infrastructure, the availability of key infrastructure in the Philippines compares unfavorably with that in many of its regional neighbors. While the country's road length per unit area is one of the highest in the region, the per capita and per vehicle road lengths are among the lowest in Southeast Asia (Figure 3.16). Further, only 22% of the road network in the Philippines is paved, compared with 99% in Thailand, 81% in Malaysia, and 58% in Indonesia. For paved roads, the Philippines' road length is among the lowest in Southeast Asia, whether in terms of per unit area, per capita, or per vehicle. Similarly, per capita power consumption levels in the Philippines are about one third those in Thailand and one fifth those in Malaysia (Figure 3.17). In telecommunications, the Philippines is also behind Malaysia and Thailand in terms of per capita availability of phone lines, but the difference is not as large as in the case of power consumption (Figure 3.18).

The low levels of investment in and poor condition of Philippine infrastructure have increased the cost of doing business in the country (see succeeding sections) and had significant adverse impact on the perceived competitiveness and attractiveness of the Philippines as an investment destination.

Figure 3.17: Comparison of Per Capita Electricity Consumption, 2002–2004 (kWh)

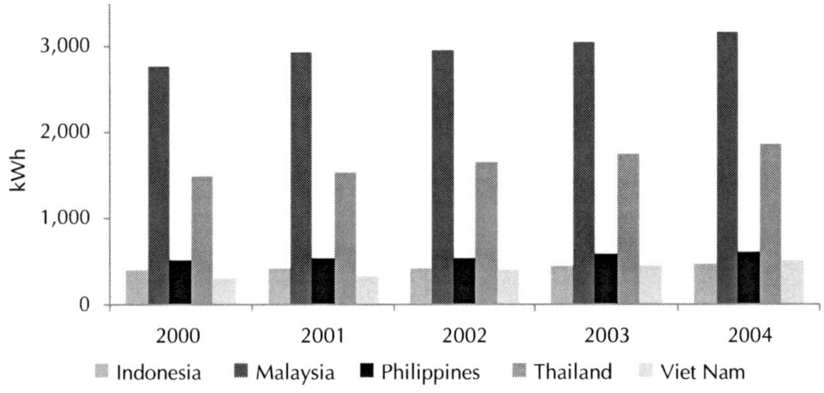

kWh = kilowatt-hour.
Source: Data from World Bank (various years).

Figure 3.18: Comparison of Fixed Line and Mobile Telephone Subscriptions, 2000–2005 (per 1,000 people)

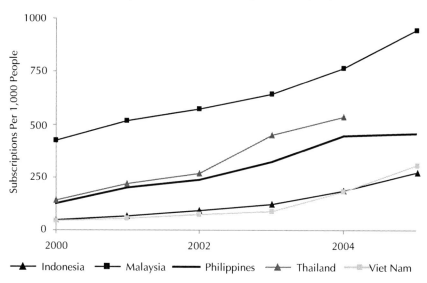

Source: Data from World Bank (various years).

- A recent cross country study (World Bank–TSE 2007) ranked the Philippines 86th among 150 countries in adequacy of infrastructure and behind most of its regional neighbors except the Lao People's Democratic Republic (Figure 3.19).
- The World Economic Forum in 2003–2004 ranked the Philippines 66th of 102 countries in its Growth Competitiveness Index, partly because of the poor state of Philippine infrastructure (WEF 2004).
- In terms of overall infrastructure quality, the Philippines ranked 88th (of 125 countries) in the 2006 Global Competitiveness Index of the World Economic Forum, a slight improvement from its 89th rank in 2004 (WEF 2004).
- In terms of adequacy of infrastructure, the Philippines slid to 51st in 2007 of 61 countries from 49th in 2006 according to the 2007 World Competitiveness Yearbook (IMD 2007). Among its regional neighbors, the Philippines trails Thailand (46th, 2007) but is ahead of Indonesia (54th, 2007).
- Figure 3.20 shows that, since the 1997 Asian financial crisis, the Philippines ranked the lowest in foreign direct investment inflows among the major regional neighbors (ADB 2007c).

Figure 3.19: Infrastructure Quality Ranking, 2006–2007

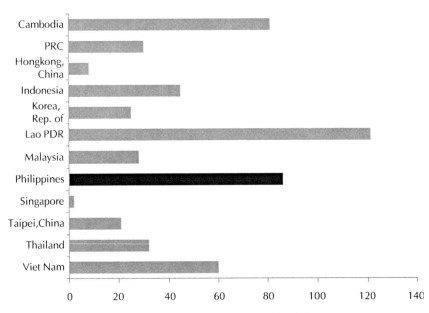

Lao PDR = Lao People's Democratic Republic, PRC = People's Republic of China.
Note: Rankings of 150 countries; a higher ranking indicates poorer infrastructure quality.
Source: Data from World Bank–TSE (2007).

Figure 3.20: Annual Average Foreign Direct Investment, 2002–2006
($ million)

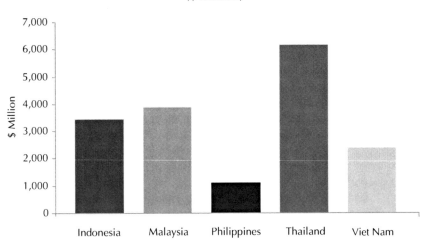

Source: Data from ADB (2007a).

Increased cost of doing business and the inability to attract more foreign investment have constrained growth at both national and subnational levels. Empirical testing as part of this study finds a robust relationship between economic growth and infrastructure in the Philippines and that the causality from infrastructure to economic growth is highly significant. The findings also confirm earlier studies (including Llanto 2004) showing that poor infrastructure and lack of investment in infrastructure have constrained growth. The study's empirical testing also indicates that infrastructure has a positive and significant effect on growth in regional incomes, and the regions with better infrastructure have had higher growth rates. This is consistent with findings that show that adequacy of infrastructure services and different levels of infrastructure development have led to differences in regional growth in the Philippines (Lamberte, Alburo, and Patalinghug 2003; Basilio and Gundaya 1997).

Electricity supply and transport network. Within infrastructure, expensive and unreliable electric supply and inefficient transport network are the two most critical constraints to growth. Of the firms in the Investment Climate Survey, 62% rated public infrastructure and services in the Philippines as "somewhat inefficient to very inefficient." This is particularly due to poor shipping services in the country, which led to a 4.7% loss in production (ADB–World Bank 2005). Of the firms, 52% viewed Philippine public works as unsatisfactory. Recent studies by the Asian Development Bank, World Bank, and other agencies indicate that expensive and unreliable electricity supply and inefficient transport networks are the two most critical constraints in the infrastructure sector to growth in the Philippines. The government had initiated a number of key reforms in power and transport, some of which are yet to be completed (Box 3.1).

For the transport network:

(i)   A recent World Bank study noted that more than half of the country's road network was in poor or bad condition, leading to vehicle operating and intercity freight costs that are more than 50% higher than in regional neighbors such as Indonesia and Thailand. The same study estimated that the high level of congestion on the main roads alone is costing the nation as much as P185 billion a year in 2006 prices (World Bank 2005).

(ii) The port of Manila ranked 31st among the top 50 ports worldwide in the 2005 World Port Rankings in terms of container traffic, with a total of 2,665 twenty-foot equivalent units (WCPL 2005). The Philippines was way behind other ASEAN ports in the top 50 list, which includes Singapore (1st); Hong Kong, China (2nd); Busan, Republic of Korea (5th); Port Klang, Malaysia (14th); Tanjung

Pelepas, Indonesia (19th); Laem Chabang, Thailand (20th); and Tanjung Priok, Indonesia (24th).

(iii) The Philippines has the highest cost in the ASEAN for exporting a container, partly because of inefficiencies in port handling. The World Bank's recent Doing Business indicators noted that the cost of exporting a 20-foot container from the Philippines is 16–51% higher than from the People's Republic of China, Singapore, or Thailand (World Bank–IFC 2007).

(iv) About 18% of firms participating in the 2005 Investment Climate Survey reported that the inadequate transport network was a major constraint to investment (ADB–World Bank 2005).

(v) Firms experience delays 5.6% of the time when picking up goods for delivery to or delivering supplies from the domestic market. Firms in the National Capital Region (NCR) experience longer delays than those in nearby CALABARZON (comprising Cavite, Laguna, Batangas, Rizal, and Quezon provinces) and Cebu and Davao areas due to greater traffic congestion and inadequate transport network linking the NCR to other regional domestic markets. The proportion of paved roads to total roads indicates that undependable roads limit transport of goods and access to inputs and markets in a timely manner.

For electricity:

(i) A study of 10 Southeast Asian cities noted that the power tariffs for businesses in Manila were 20–80% higher than tariffs in the other 9 cities (Leung, Thanh, and Viseth 2003).

(ii) The reliability of electricity supply has been poor and the Investment Climate Survey shows that SMEs had been losing up to 8% of their production due to frequent power disruptions. As many as 33% of surveyed firms reported that lack of dependable and affordable electricity supply was a major constraint for them (ADB–World Bank 2005). Losses due to power failure amounted, on average, to 8% of production. Power outages hurt SMEs most, costing them about 8–11% of production, compared with 6% for large firms.

The findings are based on feedback from the businesses operating in the Philippines and may not fully reflect the views of investors that may have stayed away from investing in the country. A survey by the Japan External Trade Organization in 2006 may be more useful in gauging views of such investors and similarly found that about 32% of the Japanese firms' international operations considered the underdeveloped infrastructure as a critical bottleneck (JETRO 2006).

Box 3.1: Unfinished Reform Agenda for the Power and Transport Sectors

Electric power. The passage of the Electric Power Industry Restructuring Act (EPIRA) was instrumental in introducing important reforms in the power sector in the following areas:

- separating the competitive from the monopolistic components of the industry, such as generation versus transmission and distribution versus supply of electricity;
- unbundling the cost components of power rates to ensure transparency and to distinguish the efficient utilities from the inefficient ones; and
- promoting efficiency and providing reliable and competitively priced electricity, while giving customers a full range of choices.

Reform measures achieved under the EPIRA include (i) creating the National Transmission Corporation (TransCo), (ii) creating the Power Sector Assets and Liabilities Management Corporation to dispose of government-owned generation assets, (iii) establishing a wholesale spot electricity market, (iv) unbundling power rates, and (iv) reviewing the independent power purchase contracts of the National Power Corporation.

The EPIRA provides for the establishment of a wholesale electricity spot market, which is a mechanism for determining the price of electricity not covered by bilateral contracts between sellers and purchasers of electricity. Because it is a spot market, electricity is traded in real time. As a wholesale market, it is open to distributors directly connected to customers, large users, and supply aggregators.

To enhance growth of gross domestic product, the government has to address the following constraints: (i) financial viability of the National Power Corporation and Power Sector Assets and Liabilities Management Corporation, (ii) the need for new investments in the power sector in view of the forecast of power shortage in the near future, (iii) improved management of the wholesale electricity spot market for credible competition, (iv) privatization of the rest of the generation assets, and (v) an efficient and credible regulatory framework and institution.

Transport. The Philippines' transport system relies heavily on the road network, which handles about 90% of the country's passenger movement and about 50% of freight. The road network provides the most common means of transporting passengers and economic goods within the islands as well as between them, using the recently inaugurated roll-on-roll-off shipping facilities. A light rail transport system is concentrated in Metro Manila, and a partly functioning heavy rail system operates to some destinations outside Metro Manila. A string of ports and airports connects the country's major economic centers.

continued on next page

57

> **Box 3.1: Unfinished Reform Agenda for the Power and Transport Sectors** *continued*
>
> Several issues must be addressed. While the Philippine road network is extensive, much of it is in poor condition. Only 70% of the national road network is paved. The national road network is a mere 12% of the total public road network. *Barangay* (village) roads are mostly unpaved and in poor condition, and comprise more than half of the road network. Most of the road network has been devolved to local government units. The road network has deteriorated due to the central and local governments' neglect of basic road maintenance and underinvestment in new roads.
>
> This is ironic because the problem does not fully rest with insufficient funds for road maintenance. Republic Act 8794 created the Road Fund, earmarked for maintaining national and local roads and controlling air pollution from motor vehicles. The Road Fund has accumulated a substantial amount of money since May 2001, when the collection of a motor vehicle user charge from vehicle owners commenced—about P22.6 billion was collected from May 2001 to April 2005. The efficiency with which these funds are used could be improved.
>
> The Philippine light rail system is administered by the Light Rail Transit Authority. Metro Manila has three light rail transit lines. The main issues are (i) the failure to link a 5-kilometer portion from North Avenue, Quezon City, to the major transport hub at Monumento, Caloocan City; (ii) insufficient capacity and number of coaches, especially during peak hours, causing stress to the many passengers; (iii) interruption of operations due to mechanical and or electrical failure, especially during adverse weather conditions—the light rail system does not have a dedicated power source; and (iv) the huge subsidy burden on the government arising from failure to adjust the fare to cover costs.
>
> Source: Author.

3.1.3. Appropriability of Returns to Investments

Private parties will invest only when they expect to capture adequate returns from their investments. Anything that weakens the capture discourages investment and, ultimately, slows growth. Risks to such appropriability can emanate from either government or market failures. Government failures increase either macro or micro risks. The macro risks may include fiscal and financial crises; the micro risks may be bad governance such as corruption, weak rule of law, overly burdensome taxation, and labor–capital conflicts. Market failures affecting appropriability normally reflect information and learning externalities and coordination failures.

Macroeconomic Risks

Macroeconomic instabilities. The Philippines has had periodic macroeconomic instabilities (Figure 3.21) often resulting from persistent fiscal and current account deficits, overborrowing and overlending activities in the banking sector, and excessive exposure to short-term external debt. These often depressed investor confidence and led to capital flight, sharp currency depreciation, and economic recessions. Sharp monetary contraction and high interest rates to stave off currency depreciation and inflationary

Figure 3.21: Gross Domestic Product Growth and External and Internal Shocks

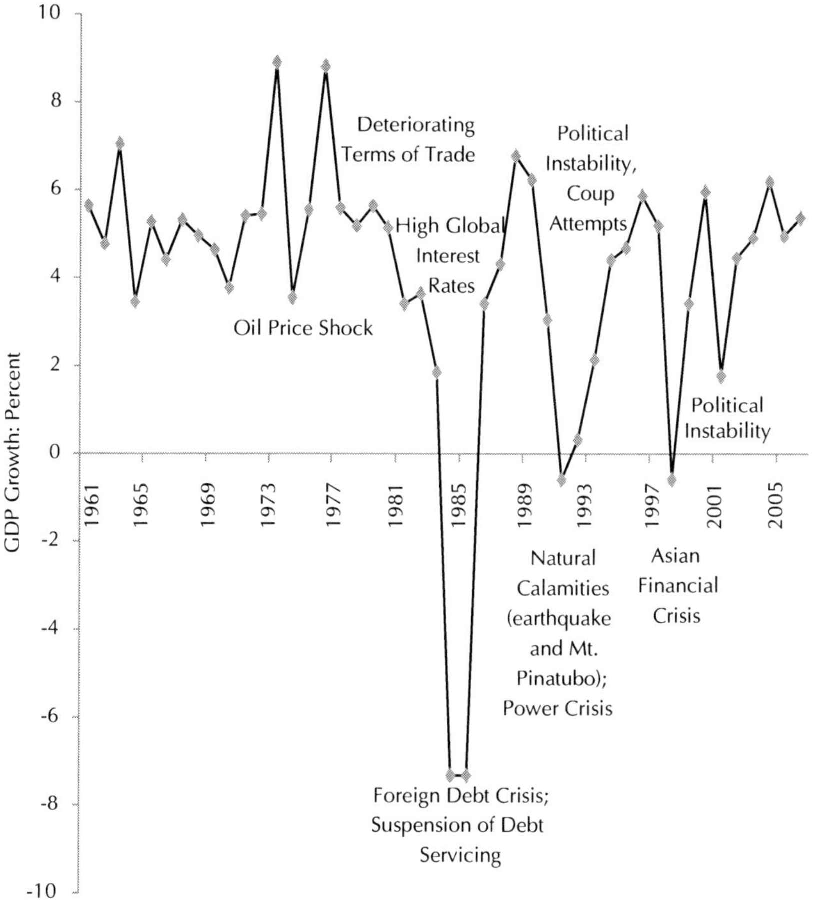

GDP = gross domestic product.
Sources: Data from NSCB (various years) and Vos and Yap (1996).

pressures during these crisis periods aggravated the economic downturn. The 1984–1985 economic collapse cost the Philippines a decade of potential economic growth and development. Major recession or low growth episodes occurred in 1960, 1970, 1982–1985, 1991–1993, 1998, and 2001, and were associated with the macroeconomic instabilities in the last five decades. Indeed, these periodic and frequent downturns largely explain why the Philippines has lagged behind many of its regional neighbors.

Despite some improvement in recent years, macroeconomic instability has remained a key investor concern. The Philippines' macroeconomic situation has recently improved, with GDP growth picking up, inflation going down, and external positions improving (Figure 3.22), but investors remain wary of macroeconomic instabilities and resulting uncertainties in the economic policies. About 40% of firms responding to the Investment Climate Survey considered macroeconomic instability, and 29% of them considered the economic policy uncertainty as major or severe constraints (ADB–World Bank 2005). Among respondents, medium-sized establishments appeared to be most affected, with almost 52% ranking macroeconomic instability and about 43% ranking economic policy uncertainty as the major or most severe constraint.

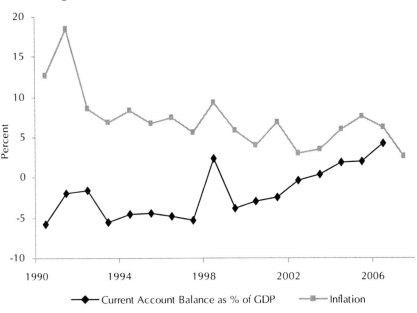

Figure 3.22: Inflation and Current Account Balance

GDP = gross domestic product.
Sources: Data from ADB (various years) and World Bank (various years).

Fiscal deficits and tax collection. The Philippines recorded fiscal deficits for most of the last 2.5 decades (Figure 3.23). The country went through additional serious fiscal and public debt distress during 2002–2005, resulting in sovereign credit downgrades and difficulties in accessing foreign capital. The most important cause of the deficits in recent years has been weak revenue generation, in particular, tax collection. Since 2001, Philippine Government revenue as a share of GDP has been the lowest in East and Southeast Asia (Figure 3.24).

A very disturbing trend was the decline in the tax effort in the post-Asian financial crisis years of 1999–2005 (Figure 3.25). Part of the reason for the decline was lower profitability or greater losses of many businesses that were still feeling the impact of the Asian financial crisis. The excise tax system, which was based on specific tax rates without inflation indexation, and some provisions of the Comprehensive Tax Reform Law of 1997, which allowed significant exemptions to big corporations and high-income individuals, also contributed to the decline in the tax effort. Moreover, there were serious weaknesses in tax administration. The decline in the tax effort was arrested in 2003 and, except for 2004, tax collection improved. But it remained below pre-Asian financial crisis levels. During 2003–2006, the government made significant progress in lowering the fiscal deficits, but at very high costs. The deficits were reduced mainly through deep cuts in social and economic services (including infrastructure) as interest

Figure 3.23: Philippine National Government Deficits
(% of gross domestic product)

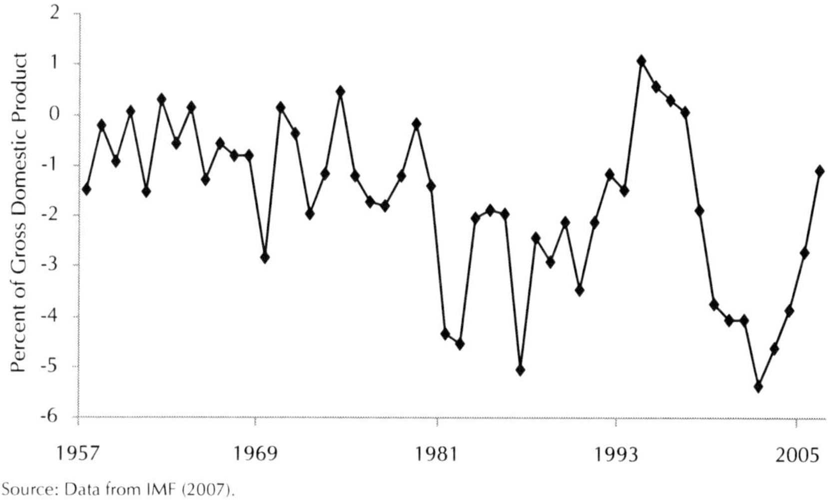

Source: Data from IMF (2007).

61

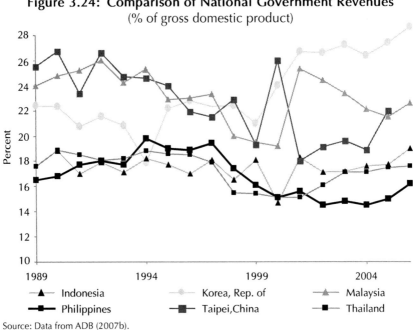

Figure 3.24: Comparison of National Government Revenues
(% of gross domestic product)

Source: Data from ADB (2007b).

Figure 3.25: Comparison of Tax Revenues
(% of gross domestic product)

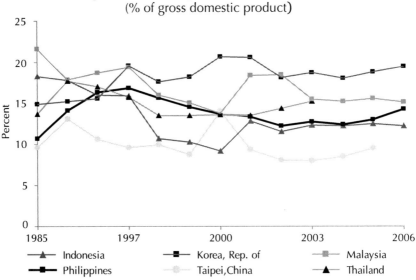

Source: ADB (various years).

Figure 3.26: Government Expenditures by Type of Service
(% of gross domestic product)

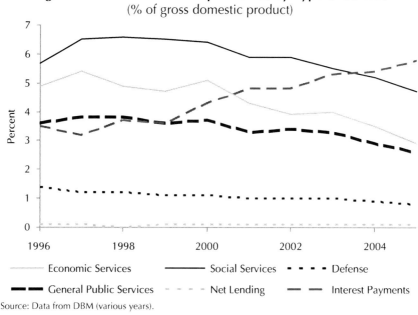

Source: Data from DBM (various years).

payments went up, accounting for around 30% of the total budget in 2006 (Figure 3.26).

As budget deficits persist, the urge to tax intensifies. The passage of the reformed value-added tax law and improved financial condition of the state-owned National Power Corporation (losses from which aggravated public deficits during 2002–2005) also helped reduce fiscal deficits in 2006. But tax collection appears to have faltered again in 2007 as fiscal targets in the first 9 months were missed and the government again spent less than planned to achieve its fiscal targets. Furthermore, to make up for the missed tax revenue targets, the government is accelerating sale of shares of its stocks in private corporations. Amid these concerns, the government has announced that it is still committed to a balanced budget by 2008, 2 years ahead of the original target date.

With the public debt at 64.0% of GDP in 2006, interest payment reached 5.5% of GDP and 31.1% of the budget in the same year. The Philippines, given its large public debt, is vulnerable to increases in interest rates, which may rise with high inflation (the rising oil price is the most immediate threat to inflation) or the need to stave off currency speculation during a sudden crisis. The risk of defaulting on foreign debt, which always dents appropriability of investment returns, may not be high at this time; but the

Philippines is always vulnerable to currency risks. Such risks may reverse the stable situation very quickly—as happened during the Asian financial crisis. The tight fiscal situation is also constraining the public sector's ability to finance key infrastructure and services.

Monetary management and financial reform. The monetary and financial market reforms implemented since the Asian financial crisis rendered the risk of new crises low. BSP's inflation targeting succeeded in moving the inflation rate to very low levels. In 2007, the inflation rate averaged only 2.8%, way below BSP's target of 4–5%. At the same time, efforts to broaden and deepen financial and capital markets will help to enhance investment and saving levels and rates. Recent mergers and acquisitions have allowed major commercial banks to raise their capitalization prodigiously.

Microeconomic Risks

Governance, political stability, and control of corruption. Several studies have indicated that poor governance is a major concern for the Philippines, seriously affects appropriability for private investors, and is a critical constraint to investment and growth. Governance outcomes collected by Kaufmann, Kraay, and Mastruzzi (2006) indicate that, for most years the study covered, the Philippines scored respectably in the aspect of "voice and accountability" compared with other countries with similar per capita income levels. This largely reflects the formal guarantees of civil liberties, a free media, democratic processes, and checks and balances prescribed in the country's constitution and affirmed in public discourse. The Philippines also scored relatively well in terms of regulatory quality and about average in "government effectiveness," though more ambiguously for the "rule of law." In political stability and control of corruption, however, the Philippines fell consistently below the average (Table 3.5).

Using the same data from Kaufmann, Kraay, and Mastruzzi, Figures 3.27 and 3.28 show the Philippines' percentile ranking on individual governance aspects—control of corruption and political stability. The shifting pattern across countries becomes apparent, particularly in the last few years. For corruption, Thailand has remained several notches above the Philippines, but the Philippines' loss of momentum is apparent and has allowed Viet Nam and (fairly soon) Indonesia to catch up with it. In terms of stability, Viet Nam rates the highest, consistently doing better than the 50th percentile. Again, the Philippines has slipped, particularly relative to 1998.

Findings of the study based on regression analysis were that corruption, political instability, and weak rule of law have had significant negative effects on investment. The findings also suggest that the 1980s turned into a "lost decade" of growth for the Philippines because of its failure to attract

Figure 3.27: Control of Corruption in Selected Countries, Percentile Rankings

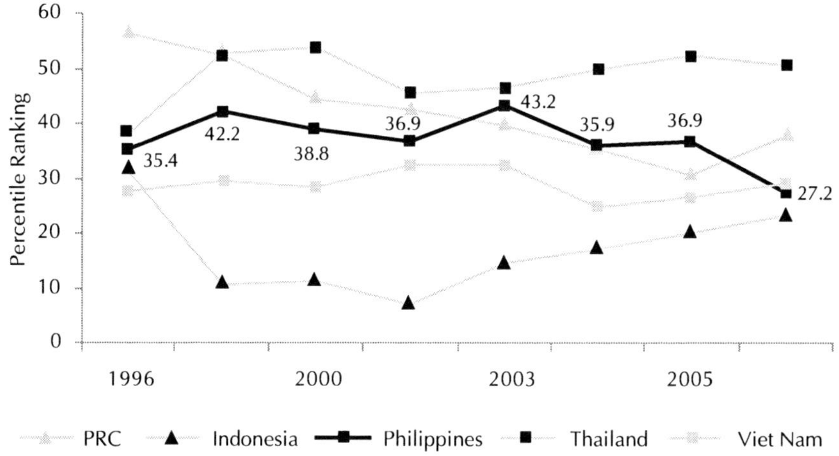

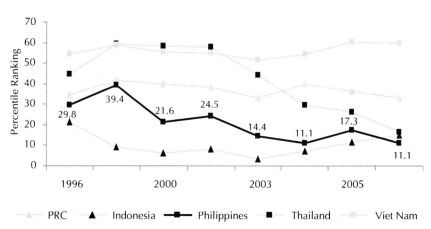

PRC = People's Republic of China.
Note: Higher scores indicate better control of corruption.
Source: Kaufmann, Kraay, and Mastruzzi (2007) as generated from http://info.worldbank.org/governance/wgi2007

Figure 3.28: Political Stability in Selected Countries, Percentile Rankings

PRC = People's Republic of China.
Note: Higher scores indicate more stability.
Source: Kaufmann, Kraay, and Mastruzzi (2007) as generated from http://info.worldbank.org/governance/wgi2007

Table 3.5: Governance Indicators for the Philippines, Selected Years

Governance Indicator	1996	1998	2002	2003	2004	2005	2006
Voice and Accountability		+	+	+	+	+	+
Political Stability	–	–	–	–	–	–	–
Government Effectiveness	+					+	+
Regulatory Quality	+	+	+	+		+	+
Rule of Law	+	+	–	–	–	–	–
Control of Corruption	–	–	–	–	–	–	–

Note: + or – denotes a governance score for the Philippines that is significantly better (+) or worse (–) at the 5% level or less, compared to countries with similar gross domestic product per capita for the period. No entry means no significant difference.
Source: ADB staff computations using data from Kaufmann, Kraay, and Mastruzzi (2007).

Figure 3.29: Government Stability Index for Selected Countries
(1 = least stable to 12 = most stable; 1984–2006)

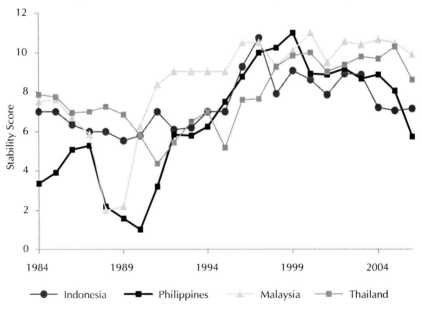

Source: Data from PRSG (2007).

the massive wave of relocating direct foreign investments that followed the Plaza Accord. Instead, for most of the decade the country was mired in deep political turmoil, which placed it at a significant disadvantage relative to some of its neighbors as a foreign investment destination (Figures 3.29

Figure 3.30: Foreign Direct Investment Flows for Selected Countries, 1980–1996 (in million current $)

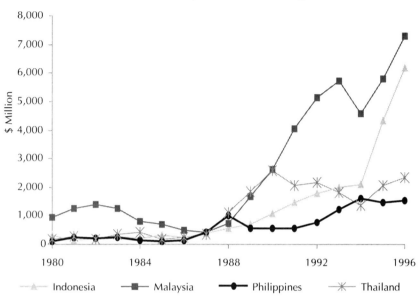

Source: Data from UNCTAD (2007).

and 3.30). Nor has the problem disappeared—instability was manifested in a number of political events (in 2000, 2005–2006, and 2007) that sorely tested normal constitutional processes. More generally, the perception of worsening corruption figures significantly in an explanation of the investment rate, and may partly explain the downturn in investment in recent years. This effect is mediated largely through lending rates, which reflect a premium for worsening corruption, political instability, and internal conflict. It thus becomes evident that poor governance weakens the appropriability of returns from investments and, in the long run, contributes to low-level real per capita GDP.

Governance issues are linked to other major constraints on growth. The thin fiscal buffer is due in no small degree to persistent corruption and patronage problems in revenue collection. Despite the government's efforts to improve tax administration, the leakage remains huge. Governance issues (both in terms of bureaucratic ineffectiveness and leakages due to corruption) have perennially plagued the government's fiscal position, leading to low levels of spending on infrastructure and social services. A cause for concern is that beyond ad hoc changes in top agency personnel and short-lived integrity campaigns, definitive and systemic solutions to these problems appear to have eluded all past administrations.

Tax administration. High tax rate and poor tax administration are critical constraints. Of firms responding to the Investment Climate Survey, 32% considered the high tax rate as a major or severe constraint to doing business in the Philippines (ADB–World Bank 2005). This is also apparent from a comparison of the corporate income tax rates in Table 3.6, which shows that the corporate income tax rate in the Philippines is the highest among comparable ASEAN neighbors. If the tax system is not transparent or the tax laws are difficult to interpret, taxation easily turns into a source for rent seeking. Survey respondents also raised inefficiencies and lack of transparencies in the tax administration as a constraint to doing business, with about 26% of the firms considering these as major or severe constraints. The *Global Competitiveness Report 2003–2004* ranked the Philippines 97th among 102 countries on the frequency of irregular payments in tax collection—the highest among the neighboring countries (WEF 2004).

Table 3.6: Corporate Income Tax and Value-Added Tax Rates in Selected Economies (%)

Economy	Corporate Income Tax	Value-Added Tax
China, People's Republic of	30	5–17
Hong Kong, China	17.5	none
Indonesia	10–30	10
Malaysia	28	none
Philippines	35	12
Thailand	30	7
Viet Nam	28	0–10

Sources: For the Philippines, www.bir.gov.ph; for Indonesia, www.usasean.org/Indonesia/business_guide/taxation.asp; for Hong Kong, China www.gov.hk; for People's Republic of China, www.abailaw.com/english/tax; for all other economies, www.aseansec.org/6524.htm, all accessed in November 2007.

Business procedures. Cumbersome business procedures and overregulation are constraints. Cumbersome processes and rules tend to induce firms to engage in corrupt practices to avoid bureaucratic red tape. Surveys of investors indicate that the red tape associated with starting and operating a business is considered a constraint. According to the *Global Competitiveness Report 2003–2004*, among neighboring countries, only Indonesia had more cumbersome processes for setting up a new business than the Philippines: in the Philippines, it took about 59 days to register a business compared with 8 days for Singapore; 11 for Hong Kong, China; 31 for Malaysia; and 42 for Thailand (WEF 2004).

The same report also noted that the regulatory burden was more severe in the Philippines than in its neighbors and other developing countries in

Asia. The Philippines ranked 98th out of 102 countries where most comparable neighbors ranged from 20th to 40th.

Contract enforcement and property rights. Evidence on whether contract
enforcement and property rights are constraining growth has shown a changing trend. The *Global Competitiveness Report 2003–2004* findings showed
that, in terms of contract enforcement, the Philippines fared better than its
neighbors in 2004 (WEF 2004). The number of days required to enforce a
contract in the Philippines averaged 164, which was lower than Thailand
(575); Malaysia (270); Indonesia (225); the People's Republic of China
(180); and Hong Kong, China (180). This appears to be consistent with the
findings of the World Business Environment Survey 2000, which compared
the confidence level of firms in the legal system upholding contract and property rights (IFC 2000). Survey findings suggested that the Philippines compared well with its regional neighbors—the confidence level of 80% for the
Philippines was lower than the 90% for Malaysia but similar to the 82% for
Thailand and much higher than the 42% for Indonesia.

However, more updated data suggest that some of the investor confidence in the contracts and the property rights being upheld may have
eroded. A survey by the Makati Business Club in 2007 as input to the World
Economic Forum's Global Competitive Index revealed that the respondents
considered contract enforcement as one of the top two constraints faced by
the businesses (WEF 2007). This may partly be a result of gradual worsening of the business environment, but at least in part must have also been
a result of a number of high profile cases, such as that involving Ninoy
Aquino International Airport (NAIA) Terminal III.

Labor market regulation. Labor costs and labor market rigidities may or
may not be a constraint. Labor costs in the Philippines are higher than in
most regional neighbors. As evident from Figure 3.31, the minimum wage
in the Philippine was about 4–5 times higher than that in Indonesia and
Viet Nam, while labor productivity was not higher by similar proportion.
Thailand had lower minimum wage rates and higher labor productivity
levels, and Malaysia had a higher minimum wage rate but much higher
productivity levels.

In addition to high labor costs, market rigidities such as the difficulties
in hiring and firing labor may deter investors. A comparison with regional
neighbors on labor-related regulations (Table 3.7) suggests that it is difficult to hire and fire employees in the Philippines, and the cost of firing
an employee can be as high as 91 weeks of salary. Thus, investors, both
existing and new, may view the Philippine labor market as very rigid and a
constraint to investment.

Figure 3.31: Comparison of Minimum Wage Rates and Labor Productivity in Selected Countries, 2003

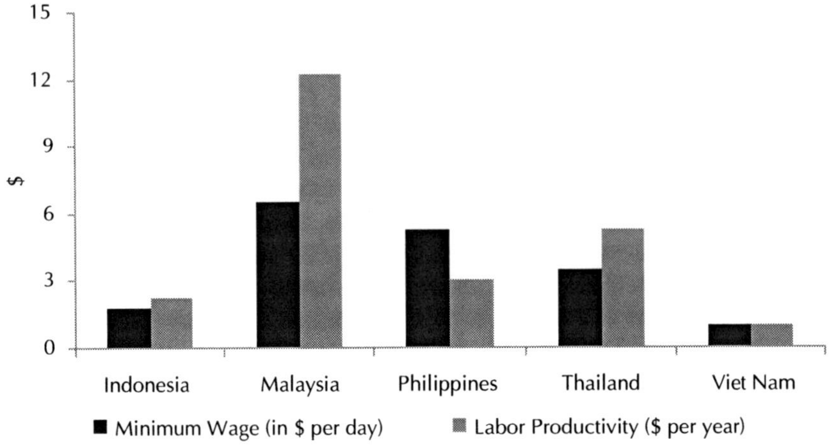

■ Minimum Wage (in $ per day)   ▦ Labor Productivity ($ per year)

Source: Data from ADB–World Bank (2005).

Table 3.7: Comparison of Labor-Related Regulations with Regional Countries, 2006

Country	Difficulty of Hiring Index (0–100)	Difficulty of Firing Index (0–100)	Rigidity of Employment Index (0–100)	Nonwage Labor Cost (% of salary)	Firing Cost (weeks of salary)
Indonesia	61	50	50	10	108
Malaysia	0	10	10	13	88
Philippines	56	20	39	9	91
Thailand	33	20	18	5	54
Viet Nam	0	40	37	17	87

Note: High scores on individual indexes represent more rigidities and low scores represent more flexibility.
Source: Data from World Bank–IFC (2007).

However, results of the 2005 Investment Climate Survey suggest that the responding firms did not consider the mandated minimum wage rate to be a major or severe constraint, as less than 30% of the firms answered the question relating to the minimum wage rate (ADB–World Bank 2005). While 75% of respondents to the question considered the minimum wage rate to be a major concern, this is only 20% of all firms responding to the survey. Patterns in the feedback suggested that the food and food processing and garment industries may be more affected than other industries by the rigidities relating to the mandated minimum wage rates. Firms' apparent lack of concern for the high minimum wage rates may be because they are not effectively implemented. Feedback from the 2005 survey suggested that the firms get around the labor regulations by hiring temporary workers during peak production periods—as many as 30% of the workforce may comprise temporary hires.

Market Failures

Narrow industrial base. A relatively small and narrow industrial base may be a critical constraint to growth. Compared with most Southeast Asian countries, the Philippines' manufacturing sector is small. In 2005, the share of manufacturing in GDP was 23.3% in the Philippines but was 27.5% in Indonesia, 30.6% in Malaysia, and 34.8% in Thailand (Figure 3.32). The level of manufacturing exports has also been low by regional standards. During 2000–2005, manufacturing exports (in constant 2000 dollars) grew at about 1.4% per year in the Philippines compared with 6.4% in Indonesia, 7.6% in Malaysia, and 11.8% in Thailand (Figure 3.33). No doubt, constraints identified previously, in particular inadequate infrastructure, macroeconomic instability, concerns over poor governance, and political instability, have contributed to the poor performance of the Philippine manufacturing sector by lowering social returns to investment and/or private appropriability. Recent literature, however, points to another set of factors that could also lead to low private appropriability—market failures.

The market failures emphasized in this context are information and learning externalities, and coordination failures, and these have been proposed to explain the lack of export growth and diversification in some developing countries (Hausmann and Rodrik 2006). An example of information externality is a situation wherein the benefits of successfully introducing products and production processes that are well established elsewhere but new to a country may spill over to third parties without giving due remuneration to the original proponent, which bears the cost of the introduction. Presence of such information externality could lead to underinvestment in new products and production processes, yielding a low level of diversification and innovation. Similarly, an example of learning externality is when the benefits from investing in developing the capacity of a workforce may spill over to third parties when the trained workers switch employers, acting as a disincentive to training a workforce. Reference to coordination failures recognizes that a firm's productivity depends not only on its own efforts and the general economic conditions, but also on how the upstream and downstream firms link and perform, and its access to infrastructure, regulations, and other public goods. Similar to information and learning externalities, coordination failures can deter investment. The presence of these market failures calls for nonmarket corrective actions.

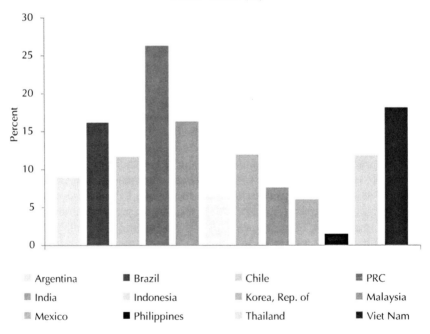

Figure 3.32: Comparison of the Shares of Manufacturing in Gross Domestic Product, 2005 (%)

40
35
30
25
20
15
10
5
0
Percent
Indonesia
Malaysia
Philippines
Thailand
Viet Nam

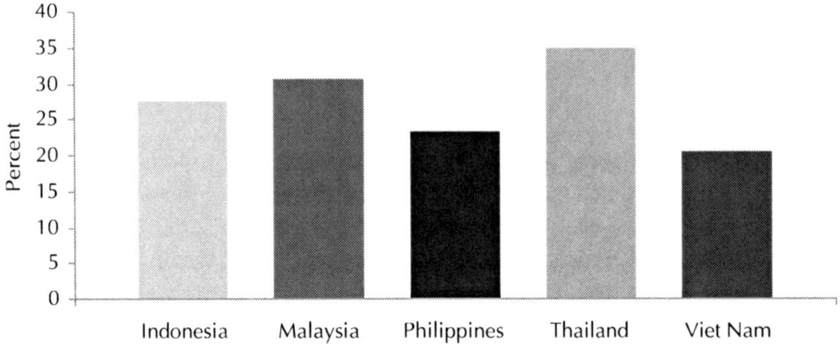

Source: Data from World Bank (various years).

Figure 3.33: Comparison of Growth Rates of Manufacturing Exports, 2000–2005 (%)

30
25
20
15
10
5
0
Percent
Argentina
Brazil
Chile
PRC
India
Indonesia
Korea, Rep. of
Malaysia
Mexico
Philippines
Thailand
Viet Nam

PRC = People's Republic of China.
Source: Data from World Bank (various years).

Though direct evidence for such market failures is difficult to find in the Philippines, the following broad symptoms suggest that they exist.

- **Manufacturing exports.** Manufactured exports are slow to diversify and innovate and have low value added. More than 60% of the country's merchandise exports come from two main categories: electrical machinery and apparatus, and nonelectrical appliances and machinery. Both categories primarily involve assemblies of semiconductors and electronic equipment, with low value added. In 2005, the ratio of imports to exports of electrical and nonelectrical machinery was 90.3% for the Philippines, compared with 66.9% for the Republic of Korea and 83.1% for Malaysia. The lack of diversification in the Philippines is also evident from the fact that since 1997 only two export product groups crossed the $10 million threshold and only four that were above $10 million crossed the $100 million threshold.

- **Domestic manufacturing.** Domestic manufacturing has low technological and scale quality, and upgrading is slow. Classifying all the manufactured goods into four groups according to the productivity level associated with each shows that the Philippine manufacturing sector focused most on goods in the group with low productivity—food, beverage, tobacco, textile, footwear, clothing, and wearing apparel (13.3% of GDP in 2005). The share of goods in the group with high productivity—paper and pulp, printing and publishing, rubber manufactures, electrical machinery, nonelectrical machinery, transport equipment, chemicals, and miscellaneous manufactures—is small (5.7%). The corresponding figures for Malaysia are 3.0% and 20.3% and for Taipei,China are 2.1% and 12.3%, respectively (Figure 3.34). These findings are consistent with the findings that growth of total factor productivity in the Philippines has been lower than in its regional neighbors (Chapter 1). Further, the composition of domestic manufacturing in the Philippines is very different from that of manufactured exports. This is unlike in the Republic of Korea and Malaysia, where exports and domestic manufacturing are both concentrated in high-technology and -scale products, indicating that their export sectors are strongly integrated with their domestic manufacturing.

- **Research and development.** The Philippines ranked very low in spending on research and development (R&D). A survey of R&D expenditure in the most recent year (depending on data availability) by countries worldwide showed that the Philippines only spent 0.11% of GDP on R&D, one of the lowest in the world, and ranked 89th out of 103 countries (IMD 2007). In comparison, neighboring

Figure 3.34: Comparison of Manufacturing Subsectors by Technology Level of Production Process (% of gross domestic product)

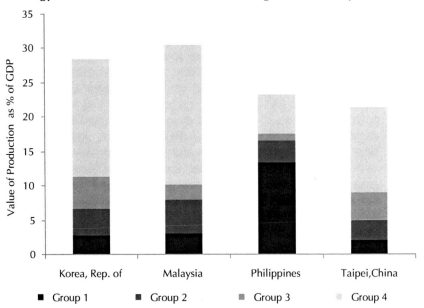

GDP = gross domestic product.
Note: Groupings are based on the commodity-specific index, PRODY, which is a weighted average of the per capita GDPs of countries exporting a given product (Hausmann, Hwang, and Rodrik 2006).
Group 1 commodities have PRODY scores below 6,000 and include food, beverage, tobacco, textile, clothing, and footwear. Group 2 commodities have PRODY scores of 6,000–9,000 and include wood, furniture and fixtures, and nonmetal minerals. Group 3 commodities have PRODY scores of 9,000–10,500 and include metals, metal manufactures, and leather-made products. Group 4 commodities are with PRODY scores of greater than 10,500 and include paper and pulp, paper and publishing, rubber manufactures, electrical and nonelectrical machineries, transport equipment, and chemicals.
Source: Lim (2007).

Malaysia spends 0.69% of its GDP on R&D, and Thailand spends 0.26%. The low R&D spending can partly explain the slowness of technological upgrade in the Philippines.

- **Links between universities and R&D.** Links between the university system and industries' R&D and skill requirements are weak. The 2005 Investment Climate Survey states: "Given the Philippines' relatively well-developed university system, it is surprising that only one of 716 firms reported universities (and other public institutions) as the most important source of new technology. Moreover, only three firms rated universities as the second, and two firms as the third, most important source of new technology" (ADB–World Bank 2005, p. 35).

Most firms in the survey claimed that technology improvements in the Philippines are mainly derived from technology embodied in new equipment and machinery or from trained and skilled personnel, not from any government, academic, or even the firms' R&D support. It appears that no universities are clearly linked to providing R&D or skilled engineers to high value-added electronic or semiconductor products produced within the country or highly skilled business process outsourcing such as software development, medical diagnostics, and computerized designs for fashion and cinema.

- **High education in science and technology.** Incentives to pursue higher education in science and technology are low. As shown in Table 3.8, Commission on Higher Education statistics on Philippine public and private universities suggest that few students are seeking higher education and even fewer do so in the technology-related disciplines (CHED 2007). Of about 295,000 students who earned bachelors degrees in 2002–2003, only just over 15,000 graduated with master's degrees and less than 1,800 obtained a doctorate. In the technology-related disciplines, only about 300 graduated with a master's degree in engineering and technology and about 160 in mathematics and computer science. Only 6 students graduated with doctorates in engineering and technology and 13 in computer science. These statistics do not show whether the lack of interest in pursuing higher education in technology-related disciplines is constraining investment in technology upgrades or if the lack of technology-related jobs is keeping the students from pursuing higher education in these sectors.

The challenge for the Philippines is upgrading the technology for and scale of its domestic manufacturing. As it does so, growth will be enhanced to the extent that new value continues to be added to manufactured

Table 3.8: Number of Graduates in Technology-Related Disciplines, 2002–2003

Discipline	Baccalaureate		Master's		Doctoral	
	Number	% of All Disciplines	Number	% of All Disciplines	Number	% of All Disciplines
Engineering and Technology	42,187	12.6	305	2.0	6	0.3
Information Technology	24,163	7.2	126	0.8	1	<0.1
All	334,307		15,215		1,748	

Source: Data from CHED (2007).

products for export and for the domestic market. Old products with stagnant value added will be replaced by new products that embody new knowledge. Furthermore, low focus on R&D reduces the country's chances of rapid growth, because the Philippines is slow in moving toward high value addition and products with increasing returns to scale.

The evidence suggests some forms of information externalities and coordination failures that call for corrective action. Hausmann and Rodrik (2006) and Murphy, Schleifer, and Vishny (1989) asserted the need for the state to be proactive in solving coordination failures and setting up complementary inputs and legal and physical infrastructure of potentially dynamic sectors, especially those with positive externalities. The state must also actively give economic incentives to "first movers" willing to undertake risky innovation and entry into new activities and ventures that have high positive externalities and information spillovers. These so-called Schumpeterian activities encourage entry into technology and knowledge-intensive areas that exhibit increasing returns to scale that lead to higher growth.

3.2. Critical Constraints to Poverty Reduction

Low growth has been a major factor in the stagnant level of poverty in the Philippines. Several studies have shown that the response of poverty incidence to economic growth in the Philippines is greatly muted compared to that in many of its Asian neighbors. For example, the growth elasticity of poverty reduction was 3.5 for Thailand and 3.0 for Indonesia, while it was only 1.3 for the Philippines (Balisacan 2003, Balisacan and Fuwa 2004). Part of the reason is the high level of inequality, which has continued to worsen. Thus, there is a great need for making growth more inclusive in the Philippines. This section looks at access to economic opportunities, human development, basic social services and productive assets, and social safety nets as potential critical constraints to broadening the inclusiveness of growth in the Philippines.

3.2.1. Access to Economic Opportunities

Employment opportunities. The lack and slow growth of productive employment opportunities are a critical constraint to poverty reduction and equitable development. The Philippines has consistently underperformed most of its regional neighbors in providing productive employment opportunities to its growing labor force. Since the early 1990s, the unemployment rate in the

Philippines has remained persistently high and has fluctuated between 8% and 12%, compared with 1.5–4.4% in Thailand and 2.5–5.0% in Malaysia (Figure 3.35). Even among the employed population, the level of under-employment was high at 22.7% in 2006, compared with 4.0% in 2000 in Thailand. Moreover, productivity of jobs in the Philippines is much lower than that in many of its neighbors. Figure 3.36 shows that the Philippines' total labor productivity had a very low rank in East and Southeast Asia and had stagnated for the last 30 years, while total labor productivity in countries such as Malaysia and Thailand improved steadily during the same period.

Figure 3.35: Unemployment Levels in Selected Countries (%)

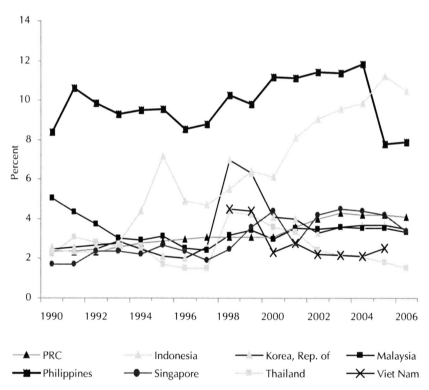

PRC = People's Republic of China.
Notes: Philippine data have a break in 2005 due to the change in the definition of unemployment.
PRC data refers to unemployment rate of urban areas only.
Indonesia data have adjustments beginning in 1997.
Source: Data from ADB (n.d.).

Figure 3.36: Total Labor Productivity
(constant 2000 $, logarithmic scale)

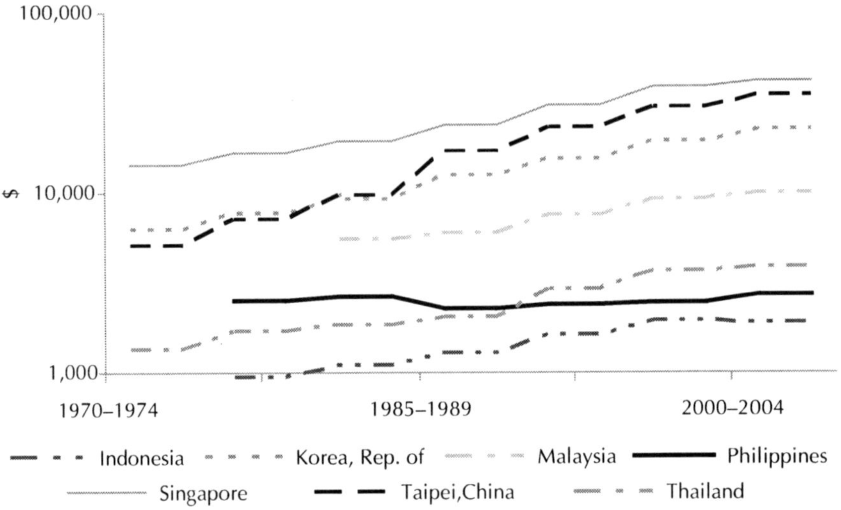

Note: Labor productivity is per labor gross domestic product in constant 2000 $.
Source: Data from ADB (2007c).

Unequal access to employment opportunities. Access to productive employment opportunities is unequal between the rich and poor. Even among the available employment opportunities, the poor are getting far less productive jobs than the rich. A recent study (ADB 2007d) showed that the average hourly wage earnings for workers from the bottom 20% of income distribution were 86% lower than those for workers from the top 20% (Figure 3.37). Son (2007b) found that in 2003, on average, the workers from poor households worked 15% less hours per week than those from an average household. This suggests that the higher employment rate in workers from poor households may be misleading and may hide their unequal access to employment opportunities. The same study also found that poor households rely more on domestic remittances and much less on remittances from abroad than do average households. Thus, the poor may not have equal opportunities to work overseas. This discussion provides indirect evidence (but not conclusive proof) that poor households have unfavorable access to employment.

3.2.2. Human Development

Balisacan (2007b) found that inadequate human capabilities are often a key underlying cause of poverty and inequality in the Philippines.

Figure 3.37: Inequality in Average Weekly Real Wages of Urban Full-Time Employees (2002 $)

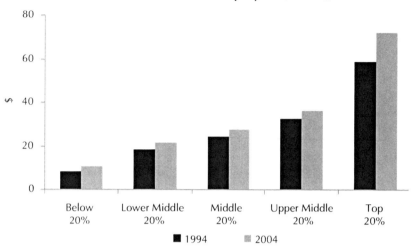

Source: Data from ADB (2007d).

Improved human capacities can improve the poor's opportunity to benefit from growth, and lack of or weak human capacities hamper their chance to fully benefit from growth. Two key determinants of human capacities are education and health attainments.

Primary and secondary education. Access to primary education is near universal levels in the Philippines, but access to secondary education is lower and not equitable. Although the Philippines' enrollment rate is over 96% at the primary level, there is substantial room for improvement in the enrollment rate for secondary education, which currently averages about 73%. School attendance varies significantly between regions, especially at the secondary level, and is below the national average in poorer regions—such as Bicol, parts of Mindanao (especially the Autonomous Region in Muslim Mindanao), and the Visayas.

Using the opportunity curve proposed by Ali and Son (2007) and Annual Poverty Indicator Survey data (NSO various years), one can find that while access to primary education does not exhibit significant inequalities among income groups, significant inequality exists in the access to secondary education. The average access to secondary education (enrollment rate) for the bottom 10 percentile of the population was less than 55%, but it was about 75% for the top 10 percentile (Figure 3.38). Further, access to secondary education increased between 1998 and 2004, but the increase was greater for households with higher income than for those with lower

79

Figure 3.38: Opportunity Curve of Access to Primary and Secondary Education, 1998 and 2004

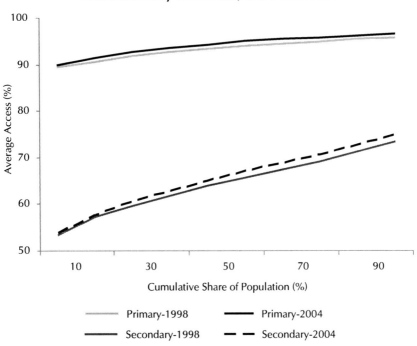

Note: The opportunity curve as proposed by Ali and Son (2007) plots the distribution of access to opportunities for a particular service or asset. A downward sloping curve suggests that opportunities available to the poor are greater than those available to the non-poor. An upward sloping curve indicates that opportunities are distributed inequitably.
Source: Son (2007a).

income, supporting earlier claims that education has become less afford-able to the poor.

Access to health services. Access to health services is low and not equitable. Using the same methodology shows that the access to overall health services is inequitable and that the services are largely used by those at the top end of the income distribution (Figure 3.39). In 2004, the average access to health services (measured by the proportion of the sick who sought treatment in health facilities)[1] was a little over 30% for the bottom 20% of the population, while it was close to 45% for the top two percentiles. Further, access to health services declined during 1998–2004, and the decline was far greater at the

---

[1] Including government hospitals, private hospitals, private clinics, rural health units, village health stations, or other health facilities.

Figure 3.39: Opportunity Curve of Access to Health Facilities, 1998 and 2004

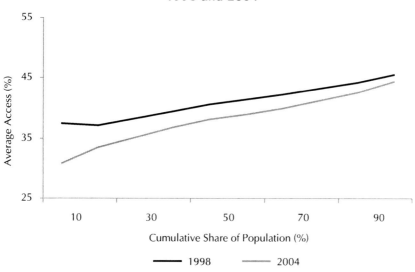

Note: The opportunity curve proposed by Ali and Son (2007) plots the distribution of access to opportunities for a particular service or asset. A downward-sloping curve suggests that opportunities available to the poor are greater than those available to the non-poor. An upward sloping curve indicates that opportunities are distributed inequitably.
Source: Son (2007a).

bottom than at the top end of the income distribution. Thus, the provision of health services became less equitable between 1998 and 2004.

Another finding was that private health facilities, which were considered by clients as providing better quality of services, were more heavily used by patients from the higher income groups (about 15%) than from the lower ones (about 5%). People at the lower end of the income distribution used public health facilities such as rural health units and village health stations more than those at the upper end. Such facilities are generally perceived to provide low-quality health services: diagnosis is poor, resulting in repeat visits; medicines and supplies are inferior and rarely available; staff members are often absent, especially in rural areas, and are perceived to lack medical and people skills; and waiting time is long, schedules are inconvenient, and facilities are rundown (World Bank 2001).

Results from the National Statistics Office's 2004 Annual Poverty Indicators Survey also showed that use of health facilities varies across regions (NSO 2004). People living in Mindanao tended to under use health services. Health status indicators vary widely across regions and provinces within the country. For instance, the NCR had an infant mortality rate of about 20, which is very close to the norm of developed countries, whereas some parts of Mindanao had mortality rates of about 100, similar to that of the least-developed countries. The wide gap in health status calls for an effective system of health service delivery that will reach the disadvantaged areas and regions. Disparity in health care between regions and income groups persists in the Philippines due to the fragmented administration of health services and the high costs of operating public hospitals. Administrative fragmentation occurs at different levels because of a lack of referral networking among health care providers. In the past, the national government controlled all public health facilities from the central office to the regional districts. However, health care has been decentralized, and the regional health units are run by the municipalities, while the provincial and district hospitals are controlled by the provinces. This has proven disadvantageous because the less capable health centers have difficulty accessing the services of hospitals that have well-trained doctors and better facilities. In some cases, health units are linked because of informal personal contacts rather than institutionalized arrangements. Such personal networking would not be necessary if interrelationships among the health units could be formally established.

3.2.3. Access to Basic Social Services and Productive Assets

Balisacan (2007b) also found that limited access to basic social services and productive assets is often a key cause underlying poverty and inequality in the Philippines. This section discusses the access to basic social infrastructure and services.

Figure 3.40: Access to Key Infrastructure Services, 2004

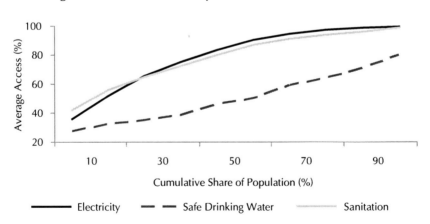

Source: Son (2007).

Access to basic infrastructure and services. The 2004 Annual Poverty Indicators Survey shows that, on average, about 50% of the population did not have access to safe drinking water, and roughly 20% was without access to electricity (NSO various years). But there were great variations across income groups. During 1998–2004, the access for the lowest 10 percentile of the population to electricity was about 35%, to safe drinking water was 25%, and to safe sanitation was a little over 40%, but the corresponding portions were 100%, 80%, and 100% for the top two 10 percentiles (Figure 3.40). Access

Figure 3.41: Access to Electricity and Potable Water, 2004

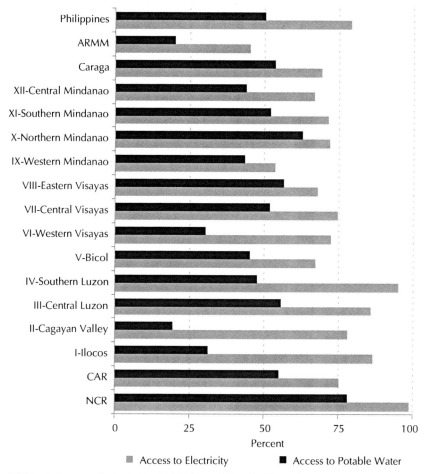

Percent

▨ Access to Electricity   ■ Access to Potable Water

ARMM = Autonomous Region in Muslim Mindanao; CAR = Cordillera Administrative Region; NCR = National Capital Region.
Source: Son (2007).

across regions was also highly unequal (Figure 3.41), with the NCR far better served than the Autonomous Region in Muslim Mindanao.

Figure 3.42 compares the per capita and per unit area of road infrastructure across the regions, and shows large disparities between rich and poor regions. Predictably, the NCR is far better served than the other regions, and poorer provinces have the shortest road network both in terms of length per population and land area.

Access to finance by the poor. For the poor, access to finance is key not only for smoothing consumption during adverse shocks but also for taking advantage of the opportunities arising from greater openness, new production

Figure 3.42: Regional Availability of Roads, 2004

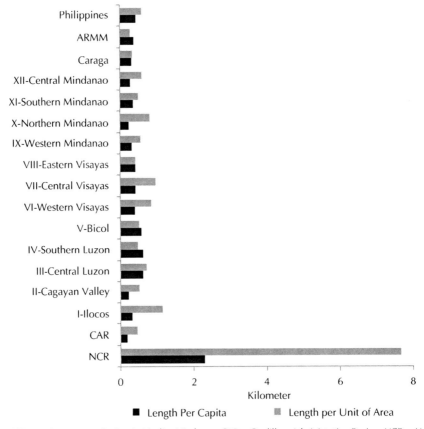

ARMM = Autonomous Region in Muslim Mindanao; CAR = Cordillera Administrative Region; NCR = National Capital Region.
Source: Data from NSCB (2004) and DPWH (2007).

technologies, and market diversification. The formal financial intermediary system tends to bypass the poor, especially in rural areas where agriculture is their main economic activity. Poor infrastructure combined with spatial dispersion and seasonality of agricultural production makes lending to small-scale farmers and fishers costly and risky. While microfinance has spread considerably in the past 10 years to help fill the unmet need for financial services, a majority of poor families in the poorer regions still do not have access to microfinance services (Figure 3.43). Moreover, providers of microfinance cater largely to nonfarm enterprises, and poor agricultural households generally do not have access to microfinance services. The key challenge is to develop mechanisms enabling microfinance to reach agriculture and grow

Figure 3.43: Regional Distribution of Active Microfinance Loans, 2007

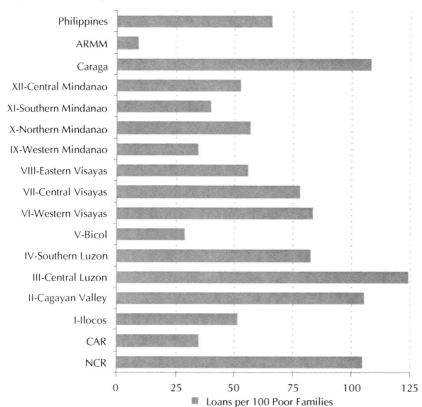

ARMM = Autonomous Region in Muslim Mindanao; CAR = Cordillera Administrative Region; NCR = National Capital Region.
Source: Magnitude of poor families is based on 2000 Family Income and Expenditure Survey data (NSO various years). Active client data is based on preliminary data on 2007 from the People's Credit and Finance Corporation, provided by the Department of Finance.

at a substantially accelerated pace in order to achieve national outreach and necessary sustainability.

Access to land. Evidence from a number of studies, including Balisacan and Pernia (2002), Quisumbing et al. (2004), and Balisacan (2007a), suggests that access to land is one of the key determinants of welfare in the rural areas of the Philippines. However, access to land is highly inequitable and is gradually worsening. The Gini coefficient of land distribution increased from about 0.53 in 1960 to about 0.57 in 2002 (Table 3.9), which compares unfavorably with a decline in the coefficient for East Asia and the Pacific, from 0.47 to 0.41, over the same period. Other indicators of access to land also paint a dismal picture with both the average farm size and land–labor ratio fast declining as the land is passed on from one generation to the next. Between 1960 and 2002, the average farm size shrank by about 44% and the land–labor ratio by over 48%. The studies on the land distribution also suggest that the lack of access to land not only limits the ability of the poor to engage in agriculture, but also curtails their ability to invest in human capital and productivity enhancements and to access financial services.

Table 3.9: Average Farm Size and Landholding Distribution

Year	Average Farm Size (ha)	Land-Labor Ratio	Percent of Farms Above 10 ha	Percent of Farms Above 25 ha	Percent of Area Above 10 ha	Percent of Area Above 25 ha	Gini Coefficient
1960	3.6	1.34	5.5	0.5	38.3	15.4	0.53
1971	3.5	1.16	4.8	0.6	33.8	17.1	0.54
1980	2.8	1.08	3.5	–	26.0	–	0.54
1991	2.2	0.88	2.3	0.3	23.5	10.6	0.57
2002	2.0	0.69	1.8	0.2	19.4	8.1	0.57

– = not available; ha = hectare.
Source: Balisacan (2007a).

Increasing inequalities in access to land tends to offset the progress that has been made on land reform through the Comprehensive Agrarian Reform Program, and the fact that the land distribution could have been much more inequitable in its absence. At the end of 2006, about 84% of the target of 8.06 million hectares had been distributed (Balisacan 2007a), largely comprising nonprivate agricultural, publicly alienable and disposable, and public forest lands. In contrast, only 18% of lands identified for compulsory acquisition had been acquired and distributed. Most beneficiaries of the program have not received land titles, support services, and key infrastructure that were to accompany the land reforms as part of the program. A key challenge for the country remains implementation of the unfinished land reform agenda, which will help check rising inequalities in land distribution.

3.2.4. Social Safety Nets

Social protection programs. Compared with other Asian countries, the Philippines is often seen to have a wide scope of programs for social protection (Sta. Ana 2002, Ortiz 2001). However, the 1997 Asian financial crisis exposed the weaknesses of the country's social protection system, as evident in low coverage (in terms of beneficiaries and level of benefits), absence of and/or weaknesses in targeting methodologies and techniques, and operational constraints due to the lack of coordination among the programs' implementers (Torregosa 2005). These issues cut across the social protection programs in the areas of social assistance, health, education, housing, livelihood creation, and disaster relief.

- The social protection system has low coverage, partly due to the lack of funding. Over the years, persistent budget deficits have led the government to reduce spending on social services substantially (Cook, Kabeer, and Suwannarat 2003; Torregosa 2005). During 2001–2005, the share of central government spending on the social sector was 22% in the Philippines, compared with 45% in Thailand, 37% in Malaysia, and 11% in Indonesia (Figure 3.44). Further, due to limited financing from the government budget, continued reliance on foreign grants and funding threatens sustainability of social safety net programs.
- The problem of insufficient funding is exacerbated by poor targeting, leading to significant leakages and wastage of resources on the non-poor and the near-poor. Poor targeting is partly a result of the lack of reliable poverty measures, especially at the local level, and partly due to poor governance. National surveys, often conducted at long intervals, generate poverty statistics only at the province level, making it difficult to identify and validate the poorest families being targeted (Reyes 2002, Torregosa 2005). Worse, many programs lack built-in monitoring and evaluation components, which make impact assessment difficult.
- Social protection programs in the Philippines are not well coordinated and are often implemented piecemeal due to their individual mandates. This causes waste because of overlaps and redundancies in sectoral or geographical beneficiaries. A consolidation of the programs would help to harmonize implementation.

Figure 3.44: Annual Average Social Expenditures as a Percent of Total Government Expenditures for Selected Countries, 2001–2005

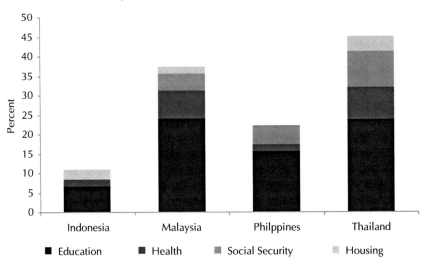

Note: The housing value for the Philippines is 0.2%.
Source: Data from ADB (2007d).

Disaster relief. Disasters, both natural and manmade, have been a major source of poverty and vulnerability in the Philippines. An average of 20 typhoons, accompanied by strong winds, intense rainfall, and flooding, buffet the country every year, and in recent years, hydrologic events have become more intense and more frequent (presumably due to global climate change). The most vulnerable areas of the country are the Eastern Visayas and Southern, Central, and Northern Luzon, the first two being among the country's poorest regions. Agriculture, the sector on which two thirds of the poor depend for income and sustenance, is most vulnerable to vagaries of climate and weather and to the incidence of pests and diseases. In 2004–2006, disasters, particularly typhoons and associated hydrologic events, adversely affected an annual average of about 8 million people, mostly in rural areas. This was an increase of over 50% from 1994–1996 (Table 3.10). Only about one half of the affected people received assistance from government and private relief institutions. Of those assisted, the value of the assistance was a miniscule amount, not even representing 1% of the average income during "normal" times of the poorest 30% of the population. This is a serious concern considering that disasters often inflict severe damage and loss to property and destroy the only means of livelihood for the poor. Failing to receive assistance, they risk falling to perpetual poverty traps.

Table 3.10: Disasters and Assistance to Affected Persons

Type of Disaster	Number of Persons Affected (annual average)		Number of Persons Assisted (annual average)		Assistance Per Affected Person (pesos)		As Percent of Income of Poor Person	
	1994–1996	2004–2006	1994–1996	2004–2006	1994–1996	2004–2006	1994–1996	2004–2006
Typhoon	4,092,023	5,928,979	2,221,036	2,992,873	7	16	0.14	0.18
Flooding	829,560	1,864,245	326,826	1,039,266	6	20	0.12	0.22
Strong Wind/Waves	2,877	14,381	1,936	10,304	21	83	0.41	0.92
Sea Tragedy	515	906	271	411	2,083	170	39.56	1.88
Tremors/Landslides	6,761	7,778	289	7,109	11	977	0.21	10.78
Volcanic Activity	35,872	15,811	28,210	15,811	117	630	2.23	6.95
Others	71,386	1,332	14,748	1,182	0	260	0.00	2.87
Total	5,038,994	7,833,432	2,593,316	4,066,955	8	19	0.15	0.21

Note: The average income of poor person is average of the poorest 30% of the population.
Sources: Data from Department of Social Welfare and Development (DSWD) and Family Income and Expenditure Surveys (NSO various years).

Major antipoverty programs. Some of the major poverty reduction programs have not lived up to expectations. Since 1986, various Philippine presidents have stressed direct antipoverty programs as the core objective of the administration. Antipoverty action is embodied in the government's Medium-Term Philippine Development Plan that is drawn up every 6 years. The agenda has evolved from one of alleviating poverty to a more holistic approach to eradicating it. Each president has had flagship poverty reduction projects. Despite the plethora of measures, various evaluations suggest that the government's antipoverty efforts may not have lived up to expectations. A budgeting issue revolves around whether to allocate a separate budget line for poverty-related projects or to give agencies the responsibility to request for budgetary funds. In addition, shortcomings have been identified in programming and institutional issues (ADB 2005, Balisacan and Edillon 2005).

- **Programming-related issues.** The antipoverty programs have been weak because they are often short-lived, poorly targeted, lacking in accountability, not well coordinated, and wanting in key components. Framing the poverty plans has been cumbersome and lengthy, and problematic because every administration tends to introduce new poverty programs while discontinuing ones that are associated with the previous government, even if they have been making good progress. This shortens the lifespan of the programs, making it difficult to realize the full impact of poverty initiatives.
- **Institutional issues.** Institutions that carry out antipoverty programs have been weakened by high staff turnover, politicization, and redundancy. Every change in administration since 1988 resulted in appointing new agency heads and recruiting new staff down to the director level. Rapid staff turnover negates continuity and slows the pace of antipoverty efforts. Poverty programs are often pursued to meet short-term political goals. The operations of the National Anti- Poverty Commission since 1988 have been highly politicized (ADB 2005). Political influence is rife throughout the process—from appointing agency heads, to choosing "basic sector" representatives and target beneficiaries, and to distributing the budget and goods for poverty alleviation.

3.3. Summary and Conclusions

Many factors are at work in the growth and development process, but, in the long run, a country's prosperity and the welfare of its people are determined by the accumulation of physical and human capital, their efficient utilization, and equitable access to the opportunities that the growth and development process generates. What factors have been hindering these in the Philippines? Using a variety of evidence—macroeconomic, financial, and social indicators; findings from investment and business surveys; regression analysis; insights from in-depth case studies; and benchmarking with other similarly situated countries—the study determined that the following are critical constraints to growth and poverty reduction in the Philippines during the next 5–10 years:

(i) Critical constraints to growth are
   • tight fiscal situation;
   • inadequate infrastructure, particularly in electricity and transport;
   • weak investor confidence due to governance concerns, in particular, corruption and political instability; and
   • inability to address market failures leading to a small and narrow industrial base.
(ii) Critical constraints to poverty reduction are
   • lack and slow growth of productive employment opportunities;
   • inequitable access to development opportunities, especially education, health, infrastructure, and productive assets; and
   • inadequate social protection and social safety nets.

Many of these critical constraints are interlinked. Only when the fiscal situation improves sufficiently will the government be in a position to allocate more resources to infrastructure investment. However, improved infrastructure alone is not enough to lower the cost of doing business and to stimulate private investment. Better infrastructure needs to be accompanied by significant improvements in investor confidence, which can be achieved if the government adequately addresses governance concerns by implementing initiatives aimed at reducing corruption and improving political stability. Removing these three constraints—tight fiscal space, inadequate infrastructure, and weak investor confidence—will result in increased private investments from domestic and foreign sources. But, to ensure that growth can be sustained at a level similar to that achieved by many East and Southeast Asian economies in recent decades, the government will also need to address the market failures (such as information and coordination externalities) in order to encourage investments in diversifying and expanding the manufacturing sector and exports, and in upgrading the level of technology.

Sustained and high growth, resulting from removing critical constraints, will create more productive employment opportunities. This is essential because insufficient employment is the most critical constraint to poverty reduction in the Philippines. However, the expansion in employment opportunities may not lead to significant poverty reduction unless inequalities in access to development opportunities are reduced and removed by instituting good governance and better policies. Removal of constraints due to unequal access will greatly help accelerate the pace of poverty reduction, but they may not suffice to reduce poverty sufficiently unless the inadequacies in the social safety nets are addressed so as to keep the most vulnerable groups, such as the elderly and destitute, from extreme deprivation. Similarly, people who graduate from poverty may still be vulnerable to natural disasters or economic shocks unless the inadequacies in social protection are remedied.

Governance concerns not only weaken investor confidence, they underlie most other critical constraints just listed. For instance, corruption undermines tax collection, political instability hinders investment and growth and reduces the tax base, and both contribute to the "tightness of the fiscal space." Poor conditions of infrastructure are a result of insufficient development spending and of poor governance, which causes leakages and improper appropriation of public funds. Similarly, poor governance hinders the pace of poverty reduction, as it reduces growth of incomes and productive employment opportunities. It is also a major contributing factor to inequalities in access to education, health, infrastructure, and other productive assets, as well as to weaknesses of many poverty reduction programs. Therefore, addressing governance concerns will go a long way toward relaxing the critical constraints to growth and poverty reduction and should be made a top development priority in the Philippines.

This study found other possible constraints (such as the level of domestic savings, the efficiency of domestic financial intermediation, the cost of international borrowing, and the stock of human capital) to be less critical than the ones just listed. However, in the longer term, as the Philippine economy reaches a higher growth trajectory, some constraints that are currently less critical could become more so. They include the needs for a higher level of domestic savings and for a higher skill and knowledge base to support the development of new and emerging industries.

References

Ali, I., and H. H. Son. 2007. *Defining and Measuring Inclusive Growth: Application to the Philippines*. ERD Working Paper No. 98. Manila: Asian Development Bank.

Asian Development Bank (ADB). 2005. *Poverty in the Philippines: Income, Assets, and Access.* www.adb.org/documents/books/Poverty-in-the -Philippines/default.asp

_____. 2007a. *Achieving Broad-based Growth by Sustained Reforms and Higher Investment—Report on the Proceedings of 2007 Philippine Development Forum.* www.adb.org/Documents/Board/2007/IN53 -07.pdf

_____. 2007b. Change Amid Growth. In *Asian Development Outlook.* Manila.

_____. 2007c. *Growth Amid Change in Developing Asia.* www.adb.org/ documents/books/growth-amid-change/Growth-Amid-Change.pdf

_____. 2007d. *Key Indicators 2007: Inequality in Asia.* Manila.

_____. 2008. *Asian Bonds Online.* http://asianbondsonline.adb.org/ regional/regional.php

_____. n.d. Statistical Database System. www.adb.org/Statistics/sdbs.asp

_____. various years. *Key Indicators.* Manila.

Asian Development Bank and World Bank (ADB–World Bank). 2005. *Improving the Investment Climate in the Philippines.* Manila: ADB.

Balisacan, A. 2003. Poverty Comparison in the Philippines: Is What We Know about the Poor Robust? In C.M. Edmonds, ed. *Reducing Poverty in Asia: Emerging Issues in Growth, Targeting, and Measurement.* Cheltenham: Edward Elgar.

_____. 2007a. Agrarian Reform and Poverty Reduction in the Philippines. Paper presented at the Policy Dialogue on Agrarian Reform Issues in Rural Development and Poverty Alleviation. Manila. 30 May. www.dar .gov.ph

_____. 2007b. Local Growth and Poverty Reduction. In A.M. Balisacan and H. Hill, eds. *The Dynamics of Regional Development: The Philippines in East Asia.* Cheltenham: Edward Elgar.

Balisacan, A., and R. Edillon. 2005. Poverty Targeting in the Philippines. In J. Weiss, ed., *Poverty Targeting in Asia: Experiences from India, Indonesia, the Philippines, People's Republic of China and Thailand.* Tokyo: ADB Institute.

Balisacan, A., and N. Fuwa. 2004. Going Beyond Cross-Country Averages: Growth, Inequality and Poverty Reduction in the Philippines. *World Development.* 32(11): 1891–907.

Balisacan, A. and E. Pernia. 2002. *What Else Besides Growth Matters to Poverty Reduction in the Philippines?* ERD Policy Brief No. 5. Manila: ADB.

Bangko Sentral ng Pilipinas (BSP). 2007. *Key Statistical Indicators.* www.bsp.gov.ph/statistics/statistics_key.asp

Bank of Thailand. 2007. *Bank of Thailand Public Finance Statistics.* www.bot.or.th/English/Statistics/EconomicAndFinancial/PublicFinance/Pages/Index.aspx

Basilio, L., and D. Gundaya. 1997. The Impact of Collective Public Infrastructure on Regional Income Disparities. Quezon City: University of the Philippines, School of Economics. Unpublished thesis.

Commission on Higher Education (CHED). 2007. *2002–2003 Annual Report.* www.ched.gov.ph/statistics/index.htm.

Cook, S., N. Kabeer and G. Suwannarat. 2003. *Social Protection in Asia.* New Delhi: The Ford Foundation and Har-Anand Publications PVT Ltd.

Dela Cruz, R. 2007. College Grads Find Landing Jobs Difficult. *Manila Standard Today.* 11 April. www.manilastandardtoday.com/?page=business05_april11_2006

Department of Budget Management (DBM). various years. *Budget of Expenditures and Sources of Financing.* Manila. Available: www.dbm.gov.ph/dbm_publications/

Department of Labor and Employment (DOLE). various years. *Labor Force Statistical Yearbook.* Manila.

Department of Public Works and Highways (DPWH). 2007. *Infrastructure Statistics.* www.dpwh.gov.ph/infrastructure/infra_stat/index

Hausmann, R., J. Hwang, and D. Rodrik. 2006. *What You Export Matters.* NBER Working Paper No. 11905. Cambridge, MA: National Bureau of Economic Research.

Hausmann, R., and D. Rodrik. 2006. Doomed to Choose: Industrial Policy as Predicament. Paper prepared for the Blue Sky Seminar of the Center for International Development at Harvard University. Cambridge, MA. 9 September.

International Finance Corporation (IFC). 2000. *World Business Environment Survey 2000.* Washington, DC.

International Institute for Management Development (IMD). 2007. *World Competitiveness Yearbook.* www.imd.ch/research/publications/wcy/index.cfm

International Monetary Fund (IMF). 2007. *International Financial Statistics.* www.imfstatistics.org/imf/about.asp

Japan External Trade Organization (JETRO). 2006. *FY2005 Survey of Japanese Firms' International Operations.* www.jetro.go.jp/en/stats/survey/pdf/2006_04_biz.pdf

JP Morgan. 2007. *Emerging Markets Bond Index Global Sovereign Spreads.* http://mm.jpmorgan.com/servlet/PortalFW?pageName=bi_emi_embig

Kaufmann, D., A. Kraay, and M. Mastruzzi. 2006. *Governance Matters V: Aggregate and Individual Governance Indicators for 1996–2005*. World Bank Policy Research Department Working Paper. www.worldbank .org/wbi/governance/govdata

_____. 2007. *Goverance Matters VI: Governance Indicators for 1996–2006*. Policy Research Department Working Paper No. 4280. http://info .worldbank.org/governance/wgi2007//

Lamberte, M., F. Alburo, and E. Patalinghug. 2003. *Philippines Private Sector Assessment Study*. Manila: ADB. Consultants' report.

Leung, S., V. T. Thanh, and K. R. Viseth. 2003. *Integration and Transition— Vietnam, Cambodia and Lao PDR*. International and Development Economics Working Paper 05-1. Canberra: Asia Pacific School of Economics and Government, Australian National University.

Lim, J. 2007. Identifying Critical Constraints in Macroeconomic Management. Available: www.adb.org/Projects/Country-Diagnostic -Studies/default.asp

Llanto, G., 2004. *Infrastructure Development: Experience and Policy Options for the Future*. Makati: Philippine Institute for Development Studies.

Murphy, K., A. Schleifer, and R. Vishny. 1989. Industrialization and the Big Push. *Journal of Political Economy*. 97(5): 1003–26.

National Bureau of Statistics of China (NBSC). 2007. *China Statistical Yearbook 2007*. Beijing.

National Statistical Coordination Board (NSCB). 2004. *Philippine Countryside in Figures 2004*. Makati.

_____. various years. *Philippine Statistical Yearbook*. Makati.

National Statistics Office (NSO). 2004. *2003 Annual Survey of Philippine Business and Industry*. Manila.

_____. 2006. *2005 Annual Survey of Philippine Business and Industry*. Manila.

_____. 2007. *Monthly Integrated Survey of Selected Industries*. www .census.gov.ph/data/sectordata/datamfg.html

_____. 2004 and various years. *Annual Poverty Indicators Survey*. Manila.

_____. various years. *Family Income and Expenditure Survey*. Manila.

_____. various years. *Philippine Labor Force Survey*. Manila.

_____. n.d. *Index of Labor Force Statistics*. www.census.gov.ph/data/ sectordata/datalfs.html

Ortiz, I., ed. 2001. *Social Protection in Asia and the Pacific*. www.adb.org/ documents/books/social_protection/social_protection.pdf

Philippine Overseas Employment Administration (POEA). 2007. *OFW Global Presence: A Compendium of Overseas Employment Statistics 2006*. www.poea.gov.ph/stats /2006Stats.pdf

Political Risk Services Group (PRSG). 2007. *International Country Risk Guide*. www.prsgroup.com /ICRG.aspx

Quisumbing, A., J. Estudillo, and K. Otsuka. 2004. *Land and Schooling: Transferring Wealth Across Generations*. Baltimore, MD: Johns Hopkins University Press.

Reyes, C. M. 2002. *The Poverty Fight: Have We Made An Impact?* Philippine Institute of Development Studies 25th Anniversary Symposium Series on Perspective Papers. Makati: Philippine Institute of Development Studies.

Son, H. H. 2007a. Human Capital and Economic Growth. Background report to *Philippines: Critical Development Constraints*. www.adb.org/Projects/Country Diagnostic-Studies/default.asp

_____. 2007b. The Role of Labor Markets in Explaining Growth and Inequality: The Philippines Case. Paper presented at the 45th Annual Meeting of the Philippine Economic Society. Manila.

Sta. Ana III, F. 2002. Social Protection in the Philippines. Briefing paper presented at the United Nations Development Programme interregional workshop, Social Protection in an Insecure Era: A South–South Exchange on Alternative Policy Responses to Globalization. Santiago de Chile. 14–16 May.

Sto. Domingo, B., and R.A. Rubio. 2007. Businesses Move to Address Human Capital Challenge. In *Business World*, 18 October. www.itmatters.com.ph/news.php?id=101807b

Torregosa, C. L. 2005. *Looking into Social Protection Programs in the Philippines: Towards Building and Implementing an Operational Definition and a Convergent Framework*. Manila: United Nations Development Programme (UNDP).

Torreja, M. 2003. Philippine Financial System. In *Money and Banking in the Philippines: Perspectives from Bangko Sentral ng Pilipinas*. Manila: Bangko Sentral ng Pilipinas.

United Nations Conference on Trade and Development (UNCTAD). 2007. *UNCTAD Statistics*. www.unctad.org/Templates/Page.asp?intItemID=1584&lang=1

Vos, R., and J. Yap. 1996. *The Philippine Economy: Stray Cat of East Asia?* The Hague: Institute of Social Studies.

World Bank. 2001. *World Development Report*. Washington, DC.

_____. 2005. *Philippines: Meeting Infrastructure Challenges*. www.worldbank.org/transport/transportresults/regions/eap/infra-chall-philippines.pdf

_____. 2007. *Investment Climate Survey*. Washington, DC. Available: http://iresearch/worldbank.org/InvestmentClimate/

_____. various years. *World Development Indicators*. Washington, DC.

World Bank and International Finance Corporation (World Bank–IFC). 2007. *Doing Business 2007: How to Reform*. www.doingbusiness.org

World Bank and Turku School of Economics (World Bank–TSE). 2007. *Connecting to Complete: Trade Logistics in the Global Economy.* Washington, DC.

World Container Port League (WCPL). 2005. *Containerisation International Yearbook, 2005.* www.prlog.org/10008201-containerisation-international-yearbook-2007.pdf

World Economic Forum (WEF). 2004, 2007, and various years. *Global Competitiveness Report.* www.gcr.weforum.org

Part B
Background Studies

4. Macroeconomic Management

Joseph Anthony Y. Lim

4.1. Introduction

The Philippines has performed poorly against the major economies of East Asia and Latin America (Table 4.1). It had the lowest average annual growth rate in the last half century, next only to Argentina. Even during growth periods (1960–1980, 1993–1997, and 2003–2005), the Philippines did not grow as fast as the more successful countries. Its best years equal only those of Brazil and Mexico in the dismal decade of the 1980s. And the Philippines suffered major recessions due to balance-of-payments (BOP) and financial crises, yielding negative average annual growth in the periods 1980–1991 and 1997–1999.

This puts the Philippines in a league with the major Latin American economies—Argentina, Brazil, and Mexico—which suffered recessions or stagnation, with almost zero growth of gross domestic product (GDP) per capita in the 1980s and 1990s. In recent years, however, Argentina has done very well (next only to the People's Republic of China), and the Philippines has not been doing too badly either. The Philippines has been growing at a better pace than have Brazil and Mexico, and at par with the Republic of Korea. In 2007, the Philippines' growth rate was 7.3%.

What explains the rather poor performance during most years?

This chapter starts with a restatement of the importance of macroeconomic stability for growth and investments and discusses how inefficient macroeconomic management is a major reason for the poor performance of the Philippines vis-à-vis other East Asian and Latin American countries. The Philippines' poor growth record is linked with inefficient macroeconomic management, which has two main components: fiscal policy and monetary policy. A brief discussion of postwar Philippine economic history provides an excellent backdrop to the main thesis of this chapter—that macroeconomic instability is a critical constraint to growth. The second part of the chapter brings to the fore the constraints on growth imposed by fiscal deficits and poor monetary policy.

Table 4.1: Annual Growth Rate of Per Capita Gross Domestic Product of Selected Countries for Various Growth Periods Based on Per Capita Gross Domestic Product at Constant 2000 US Dollars

Average Growth Rate[a]	1960–2005	1960–1980	1980–1991	1991–1993	1993–1997	1997–1999	1999–2002	2002–2005
Argentina	0.96	1.83	-1.76	7.41	2.78	-0.96	-6.42	7.97
Brazil	2.23	4.57	-0.50	0.60	2.47	-1.04	1.06	1.17
Chile	2.55	1.54	2.42	7.62	5.88	-0.11	2.12	4.34
China, People's Republic of[b]	6.00	2.89	7.71	12.75	9.63	6.68	7.84	9.42
India	2.71	1.19	3.14	3.14	4.86	4.75	2.65	7.11
Indonesia	3.55	3.58	4.68	5.53	5.55	-7.68	3.00	3.71
Korea, Rep. of	5.66	5.47	7.54	5.05	6.20	0.27	5.66	3.44
Malaysia	3.93	4.38	3.57	6.52	6.30	-3.20	2.18	4.07
Mexico	1.98	3.53	-0.06	0.92	0.74	2.94	1.20	1.78
Philippines	1.38	2.43	-0.92	-1.06	2.78	-0.64	2.06	3.49
Thailand	4.55	4.56	6.17	6.73	4.38	-4.29	3.10	4.97
Viet Nam[b]	4.86	–	2.46	6.23	7.07	3.86	5.62	6.64

– = not available.
Notes:
[a] Annual growth rate is estimated by $F(T) = F(0) (1+r)^T$ where $F(T)$ is the final value, $F(0)$ is the initial value, r is the annual growth rate, and T is the number of years. This leads to $r = [F(T)/F(0)]^{1/T} - 1$.
[b] Data for the People's Republic of China start in 1975 and data for Viet Nam start only in 1984.
Source: World Bank (2007).

Macroeconomic stability is important for growth and investments because it provides a good business environment, comprising

(i)   continuous periods of growth and high business confidence free from financial, BOP, and debt crises;

(ii)   lack of high current account deficits (that is, large gaps between investments and savings) and high fiscal deficits;

(iii) manageable external debt burden, as a heavy burden constrains the financing of public expenditures and foreign exchange for imports needed for development;

(iv)   price stability, which enables businesses to predict input and output prices reasonably to encourage production and investments; and

(v)   lack of strong contractionary policies such as high interest rates; damaging speculative attacks on the currency; and fiscal cutbacks in public spending, especially public infrastructure.

Unless all the ingredients for a good environment are present, firms will be discouraged from expanding production and making long-term investments in the economy.

4.2. Philippine Postwar Experience

The history of the Philippines since World War II is marked by frequent economic and political crises that led to periodic economic downturns and stagnation.

4.2.1. Immediate Postwar Period

The first half of the 1950s saw the best growth performance in Philippine history, as import-substituting industries flourished. Next to Japan, the Philippines was widely seen as the front-runner to achieve successful development in East Asia. The process of industrialization was launched with the share of manufacturing rising quickly to 25% of GDP by the end of the 1950s from only 7% in 1946. This marked the start of the sustained decline in the share of the agriculture sector.

The anticipated economic take-off, however, failed to materialize. Industrialization did not develop backward links, hampered by a small domestic market characterized by high income inequality, a lack of cohesive industrial strategy, and corrupt practices in the issuance of import licenses with alternating administrations using state power to expand their rent-seeking activities. A key weakness of the import-substituting strategy was the inability to outgrow initial dependence on imported raw materials, intermediate inputs, and capital equipment. With policy makers preferring an overvalued peso, trade and current account deficits became the rule. International reserves, in terms of import cover, shrank throughout the 1950s, culminating in the intense BOP crisis during 1957–1961. Pressures to devalue the peso became difficult to stave off.

4.2.2. 1962–1970: Trade and Foreign Exchange Liberalization, International Monetary Fund Entry, and Balance-of-Payments Crisis

A regime defending the import substitution strategy was replaced in 1962 by the Macapagal administration, which won the elections on a platform of trade and foreign exchange liberalization. The peso was devalued and International Monetary Fund (IMF) help sought, marking the beginning of IMF's deep involvement in economic policy making and management.

The Philippines under the ensuing Marcos administration entered another BOP crisis in 1969–1970 as foreign debt began to bunch up and as trade deficits continued. In 1970, the Philippines entered another IMF–sponsored structural adjustment program that called for drastic devaluation and pushed for an outward-oriented economic strategy.

4.2.3. 1971–1981: Authoritarian Rule and Martial Law

The declaration of martial law in 1972 was followed by a decade of high growth. Massive borrowings from multilateral institutions and foreign banks rolling in petrodollars financed a spending spree in public infrastructure that lasted till the late 1970s. The period was also marked by inconsistent implementation of an outward-looking strategy combining export promotion with the protection of economic sectors dominated by close Marcos allies.

The debt-driven growth of this era survived the first oil price shock in 1973–1974, but not the Latin American crisis of 1982, which took its toll as access to long- and medium-term debt was virtually cut off, and short-term debt instruments were obtained at exceedingly high interest rates. The peso devaluation in July 1983—followed by the assassination of Marcos' political rival, which touched off a domestic political crisis—set the stage for the worst BOP crisis in the country's history. A moratorium on external debt payments amid sharp depreciation of the currency was declared in the third quarter of 1983, 2 years after the start of the world recession and about a year after foreign debt crises erupted in Brazil and Mexico.

Policy makers followed the monetarist policy prescribed by IMF. Liquidity and credit were contracted in 1984–1986 to stem capital outflows and control inflation that resulted from the sharp currency devaluations. The credit contraction deepened the recession. Financial conditions deteriorated rapidly, as happened in countries hard-hit by the Asian financial crisis a decade later. Firm closures and work stoppages hit key industries. The Central Bank and state-owned banks were left holding nonperforming assets of the private sector. A long time elapsed before these assets were disposed of; the financial sector, especially hard-hit government financial institutions, was rehabilitated; and a new central bank free of crippling debt burden was established—reforms accomplished during the Aquino and Ramos administrations.

As investment share fell, the share of consumption rose. The other side of rising consumption is falling gross domestic savings. Poverty and income distribution data show that poverty rates and income distribution worsened during this period.

On the supply side, industry and manufacturing suffered the most. The economic collapse precipitated the premature decline in the share of industry, unlike in the more successful countries where industry, after reaching maturity, retreats to give way to services. The recession was accompanied by high inflation, which reached 50% in 1984 and more than 20% in 1985. As the economy hit rock bottom in 1986, inflation fell to zero and (briefly) negative levels, and external balance was restored as imports contracted.

This period saw gross national product per capita shrinking by almost 20% from 1983 to 1985, setting the economy back a full decade as the country lost its chance to become part of the East Asian success story. The resulting depression was perhaps worse than the Indonesian experience in 1998.

In sum, from 1946 until the early 1980s, gross national product per capita increased steadily, except for 3 years—1958, 1960, and 1970—all of which saw BOP crises. Since the 1980s, the Philippine economy has been highly volatile, experiencing four recessions and stagnation within two decades—in 1983–1985, 1991–1993, 1998, and 2001. Except in 2001, these periods were marked by BOP difficulties. The 1984–1985 period, which involved both an external debt crisis and financial crisis, marked the deepest crisis in the country's modern history.

4.2.4. 1986–1993: Recovery, Recession, and Power Shortages

The resolution of the political crisis in 1985–1986, through the assumption to power of the Aquino government, offered a golden opportunity for reformers in government to institute structural adjustments with the backing of multilateral development banks. Import restrictions were lifted, large-scale privatization of state-owned enterprises was pursued, and tax reforms were implemented (Lim and Montes 2002).

The economy slowly recovered as the decade came to a close, but not without IMF assistance and government pump-priming efforts. The resulting fiscal and external deficits proved unsustainable in 1989 and 1990, especially as the public and external sectors continued to suffer from debt overhang after the government had to assume a substantial amount of private debt.

The government, under IMF supervision, responded to the external and fiscal deficits and double-digit inflation rates with tight monetary policy, reduced fiscal spending, and higher indirect taxes. Interest rates jumped to over 20% in 1990–1991, and fiscal spending was slashed (partly to allow the servicing of accumulated debts). On the political front, a series of military challenges against the Aquino administration sapped business confidence, which had been showing signs of revival. With the first Gulf War, the external environment turned negative: oil prices rose in the global market, and the peso came under pressure. The stage was set for the 1991 recession. Economic recovery was delayed by widespread power shortages, a result of sustained cutbacks in public investments in the previous decade.

4.2.5. 1993–1998: Liberalization, Surge, and Contagion

A new administration under Fidel Ramos, who took office in 1992, pursued liberalization in earnest. It reduced tariff rates (most import restrictions had been eliminated by the early 1990s) and locked the country into international agreements to open the economy to international trade and investment flows—the Association of Southeast Asian Nations (ASEAN) Free Trade Area, Asia-Pacific Economic Cooperation (APEC), and World Trade Organization (WTO). Throughout the 1990s, the Philippines unilaterally reduced tariff rates on many items way below the rates it had set for itself in the agreements. Not surprisingly, export and import shares grew at an unprecedented pace during the opening up (globalization) period, starting in the late 1980s up to the 1997 Asian financial crisis, with the share of exports and imports increasing by more than 50% during the period.

A key reform in the period was capital account liberalization initiated in 1991 and completed in the last quarter of 1993. The move opened the country to volatile private capital flows, reviving moribund asset and financial markets. Positive developments in the domestic front—the fast-track construction of power plants (which later would lead to higher electricity costs); the success of the Brady Plan in reducing foreign debt payments; the creation of Bangko Sentral ng Pilipinas (BSP), the new debt-free central bank; and the economic recovery in the first 4 years of the Ramos administration—seemed to justify the exuberance and optimism in financial markets. During this period, economic growth was spurred by rapid credit expansion, lower interest rates, and improving fiscal position. The switch to positive fiscal balances, falling inflation rates, and continuing foreign capital inflows fuelled even more optimism for the Ramos growth strategy. The peso appreciated as capital inflows intensified until the second quarter of 1997.

However, not all indicators were bright. The external sector continued to register sizeable current account deficits, and the investment–savings gap widened during this period. As is well known, the foreign inflows came largely in the form of short-term debt and portfolio investments ("hot money"). Unhedged dollar borrowings (used to finance real estate, construction, speculative, and manufacturing activities) and "hot money" fueled a bubble in asset and equity markets, paving the way for the country's participation in the Asian financial crisis. The financial crisis, in addition to the El Niño weather phenomenon that had detrimental effects on agriculture, halted growth and the economy contracted in 1998.

BSP initially reacted to the financial turmoil by defending the currency by using international reserves, raising its repurchase rates and liquidity

reserve ratios in a bid to stem the currency depreciation. These moves has-
tened the loss of confidence and the deterioration in the quality of loan
portfolios. In addition to monetary tightening, the IMF program required
the economy to attain a fiscal surplus at the height of the crisis, which
obviously could not be achieved, further eroding confidence. These policy
responses, much like in other affected countries, weakened the financial
and real sectors and ushered in a recession in 1998.

4.2.6. 1999 On: Post-Asian Financial Crisis

Political volatility during the Estrada administration ensured that economic recovery from 1999 to 2001 would be lackluster, with GDP growth
rates averaging less than 4% in these years. 2001 was a low-growth year
as the Estrada administration was rocked by a scandal involving accu-
sations of illegal gambling that reached the President himself, who was
forced out of office by another "people-power" revolt finally backed by
the military forces. Estrada was replaced by the vice president, Gloria
Macapagal-Arroyo. The Arroyo administration in turn, has been rocked by
coup rumors and political scandals. The low-growth year was also accompanied by a global recession, led by the weak performance of the United
States (US) economy.

The low confidence in the Philippine economy is shown by the developments in BOP and exchange rate movements. There were net capital
outflows and currency depreciation in 2001–2005, as the Arroyo administration was rocked with coup threats and corruption scandals, the most
serious one being the rigging of the presidential election in 2004, which
Arroyo won. The lack of confidence was aggravated by a fiscal crisis
wherein continuing declines of the tax effort and losses from the government-owned National Power Corporation led to high fiscal deficits and
a high public debt burden. The imposition of an expanded value-added
tax (the "R-VAT") and the improved performance of the National Power
Corporation subdued the emerging fiscal crisis. Once it was clear that
coups and attempts to impeach the President were unsuccessful, portfolio
flows started to pour in, lifting the country's stock and sovereign bond
markets in 2006 to 2007. But the external shock of the subprime crisis in
the US, starting in July 2007, reversed this in a matter of weeks. Portfolio
inflows and outflows then alternated with the outflows spurred by the US
subprime crisis and political instabilities besetting the Arroyo administration. Despite the problems, GDP annual growth rates quickened in 2002
and 2006 to 4–6%. In 2007, the GDP growth increased further to 7% in
real terms.

4.3. Macroeconomic Instability as a Constraint to Growth

4.3.1. Vulnerability to Crisis

A substantial investment–savings gap and foreign exchange constraints hampered Philippine economic growth from the postwar period until 2003. Foreign exchange constraints, as indicated by large current account deficits and large gaps between investments and savings, exposed the Philippines to high risks of BOP crises that led to economic collapse, recession, or financial debacle. Such problems are more likely to occur if large current account deficits are accompanied by high short-term debts, a high ratio of domestic credit to international reserves, a low stock of international reserves, high debt burden, and high lending rates. Figures 4.1 and 4.2 show that large gaps between gross capital formation and savings and large current account deficits preceded the slowdowns or recessions in 1960, 1970, 1983–1985, 1991, and 1998. The economic collapse in 1984–1985 was deep enough to retard Philippine growth for a decade. The Philippines seems to share this crisis vulnerability with Latin American countries, especially in the 1980s. On the other hand, while Indonesia, the Republic of Korea, Malaysia, and Thailand also had significant current account deficits, fiscal deficits, and exposure to short-term debt in the 1970s and early 1980s, they did not suffer economic collapse because their strong export sector and relative political stability attracted substantial foreign direct investments.

Figure 4.1: Gross National Savings and Gross Capital Formation, in Percent of Gross Domestic Product versus Gross National Product Growth Rate

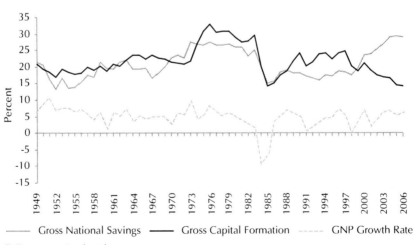

GNP = gross national product.
Source: NSCB (various years).

Figure 4.2: Current Account Balance, in Percent of Gross Domestic Product versus Gross Domestic Product Growth Rate

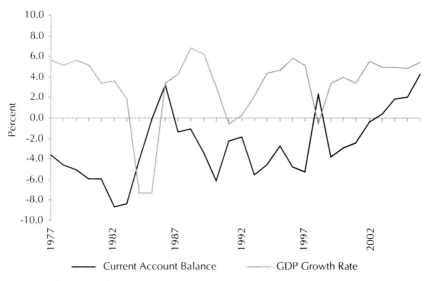

GDP = gross domestic product.
Source: IMF (2007).

Appendix A shows a logit regression analysis with a binary dependent variable with a value of 1 during crisis years (1983–1985, 1991, and 1998). The most significant explanatory variables in the logit regressions of Appendix A are (i) the lagged ratio of domestic credit to international reserves; (ii) the lagged ratio of short-term debt to international reserves; (iii) the lending rate; (iv) lagged international reserves expressed in number of months of imports; and (v) lagged current account deficit as percent of GDP. Unfortunately, these variables are quite collinear so that if any two variables are used in a logit regression, their z-values become insignificant even if their likelihood-ratio chi-square statistic is significant at more than 1%.

The emerging picture is that the Philippine economy becomes vulnerable to crisis when it has to rely on huge domestic and foreign borrowing to sustain its development momentum without a concerted effort to raise significant tax revenues to help close the investment–savings gap. This leads to a high risk of debt default when currency attacks occur, and the monetary authorities are forced to raise interest rates to fight these attacks and reduce the inflationary pressures. Crises are also likely to happen when (i) short-term debts, which are used to finance current account deficits, are large with respect to international reserves; and (ii) currency speculation and losses of confidence trigger monetary contraction and high interest rates, exacerbating the problem.

4.3.2. The Fiscal Deficit and Public Debt

Huge fiscal deficits, which have long hounded the Philippine economy, have constrained growth and poverty reduction. Figure 3.23 in Chapter 3 shows the national government deficit as percent of GDP. High fiscal deficits can be traced to three factors: low tax effort, huge public debt service burden, and financial losses of major government corporations.

Low tax effort has significantly contributed to three periods with extremely high fiscal deficits: the early 1980s, the mid 1980s, and 2002–2004. Appendix B shows the result of a regression analysis demonstrating the inferior quality of tax effort from 1998 on. Episodes of fiscal deficits have preceded at least two major recessions in Philippine postwar economic history. These major recessions are remarkable in depth and severity of impact, especially on domestic manufacturing firms and poor households.

The recession years were generally characterized by cuts in infrastructure and other vital economic and social spending. The cutbacks in public expenditure effectively tamed the fiscal deficit, but at a very high cost. Lower deficits have been achieved mainly through deep cuts in social and economic services (Figure 3.26) and public construction during 1998–2006, thereby bringing down gross fixed capital formation in the same period (Figure 4.3).

Figure 4.3: Gross Fixed Capital Formation and Public Construction,
(% of gross domestic product)

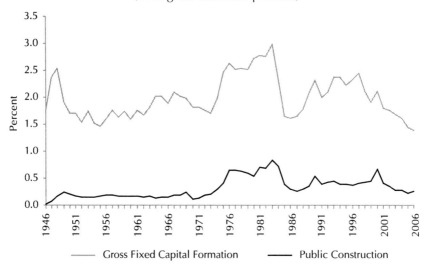

Source: NSCB (various years).

The result of an empirical estimation by this study shows that indeed one of the main causes of the low investment rate during this period was low public construction brought about by spending cuts (Appendix C). Thus, the fiscal bind restricted spending for public infrastructure and other vital economic and social spending, which significantly reduced the investment rate, thus constraining growth.

There were serious attempts to bring down the fiscal deficit: value-added taxation was introduced in the late 1980s and privatization of government assets in the post-Marcos years somewhat eased the pressure of the deficit. The government posted rare fiscal surpluses in 1994–1997, but the additional revenues really came from a nonrecurrent source—the sale of government assets. Relatively high growth rates in 1994–1997 helped raise the tax effort as it peaked at 17% in 1997, but tax revenue collections continued to fall short of the economy's rapidly growing expenditure requirements. The most disturbing phenomenon is the decline in tax effort in the post-Asian financial crisis years of 1999–2005 during a period of economic recovery and growth. The reasons for the decline are (i) the reduction in tariff collection due to import liberalization; (ii) the significant tax exemptions given to big corporations and high-income individuals under the Comprehensive Tax Reform Law of 1997; and (iii) a deteriorating tax administration, saddled by corruption. Figures 4.4a and b show that Philippine tax effort pales in comparison with key East Asian economies and is inferior to some Latin American countries (see also Figure 3.24 of Chapter 3).

Because of its inability to raise sufficient tax revenues, the government resorted to heavy domestic and foreign borrowing to finance growth. However, the temporary relief provided by the liquidity coming from debt vanished as public debt mounted and debt service obligations (interest and principal payments) absorbed as much as 80% of government revenues, leaving only a slim margin for growth spending (Table 4.2). As of 2006, national government debt stood at 64% of GDP while interest payment was as high as 5.5% of GDP and 31.1% of the national government budget in 2006. The Philippines' fiscal debt burden is now much worse than those of its East Asian neighbors and some Latin American counterparts. In particular, Indonesia, which suffered major debt and financial turmoil during the Asian financial crisis, now has a lower debt service ratio than does the Philippines.

The irony is that debt service obligations, which were incurred to finance development expenditures, now absorb a great portion of budgetary allocations, in effect reducing the government's ability to finance development. To be able to service the debt, the government also had to curtail expenditure on public construction and social and economic services (Figure 4.3).

Figure 4.4: Government Revenue as a Percent of Gross Domestic Product

a: Selected Asian Countries

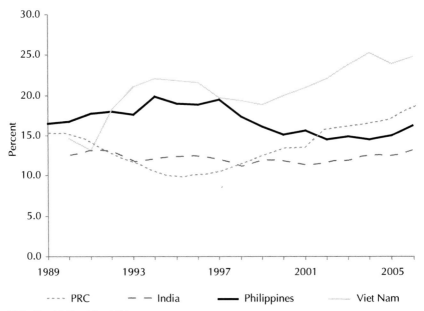

PRC = People's Republic of China.
Source: IMF (2007).

b: Selected Latin American Countries and the Philippines

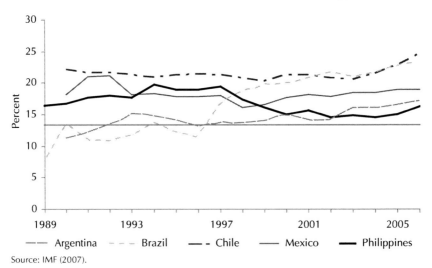

Source: IMF (2007).

Table 4.2: Public Debt Service and Public Debt Burden

	1998	1999	2000	2001	2002	2003	2004	2005	2006
As % of Government Revenues									
National Government Debt Service Payments	35.6	42.9	44.3	48.4	61.9	73.5	85.1	83.2	87.2
Interest	21.6	22.2	27.4	30.8	32.1	35.4	36.9	36.7	31.7
Principal	14.0	20.7	16.9	17.6	29.8	38.1	48.2	46.5	55.6
As % of GDP									
Total National Government Debt	56.1	59.6	64.6	65.7	71.0	77.7	78.2	71.5	63.8
Domestic	31.9	32.9	31.8	34.4	37.1	39.5	41.1	39.8	35.7
Foreign	24.2	26.8	32.7	31.3	33.9	38.3	37.2	31.7	28.1
As % of GDP									
Total Public Sector Debt	94.6	101.4	109.3	106.0	110.2	117.5	108.7	92.6	73.9
Domestic	35.2	32.8	32.5	32.7	34.4	35.5	35.1	32.1	28.7
Foreign	59.5	68.6	76.8	73.3	75.9	82.1	73.7	60.5	45.2
As % of GDP									
Total Expenditure Less Interest Payment	16.4	15.9	16.1	14.8	15.2	14.2	13.0	12.2	12.2
Interest payment	3.7	3.6	4.2	4.8	4.7	5.2	5.4	5.5	5.1
Total expenditure	20.2	19.5	20.3	19.6	19.9	19.5	18.3	17.7	17.3
Interest Payment as % of Budget	18.6	18.3	20.6	24.5	23.5	27.0	29.2	31.1	29.7

GDP = gross domestic product.
Note: GDP was estimated as 7/6 times the GDP of the first semester of 2007.
Sources: BSP (2007), Bureau of the Treasury (2007), and DBM (2007).

In summary, the huge debt service burden; financial losses of government corporations such as the National Food Authority and National Power Corporation; and, above all, low tax effort were responsible for the high fiscal deficits. In turn, the deficits have had a deleterious effect on growth through two main channels: a low investment rate and deep cuts in economic and social services.

4.3.3. Inflation, High Interest Rates, and Monetary Contraction

Episodes of high inflation (10% and above) in the Philippines can be attributed to two factors: currency devaluations and oil price shocks (Figure 4.5).

Figure 4.5: Consumer Price Index Inflation and Growth of Exchange Rate

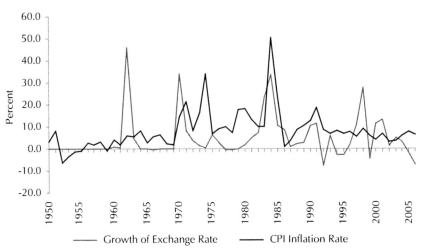

CPI = consumer price index.
Source: BSP (2007).

In the 1970s, double-digit inflation can be traced to the 1970 devaluation and the first oil price shock in 1973–1974. In the 1980s, high inflation rates were caused initially by the second oil price shock and worldwide inflation in 1979–1981, followed by the significant devaluations in 1983 and 1984. These devaluations, accompanied by deep economic and political instability, brought about record inflation rates in the late 1980s.

In the 1990s, the moderate devaluation in 1990–1991 plus the oil price shock due to the first Gulf War caused a rise in inflation. The significant devaluation during the Asian financial crisis in 1998 brought a slight uptick in inflation, but nowhere near the high inflation that had occurred in previous devaluations. Inflation rose again in 2004–2005 because of high world oil prices but subsided to as low as 3% in 2007 before rising again in 2008.

The high inflation from the 1970s to the 1990s had profound and adverse consequences on Philippine growth performance. In general, the Philippines had higher inflation than the other Asian countries over the years (Figure 4.6). This could partly explain the weak investor confidence in the Philippines in the 1970s through the 1990s. While Philippine inflation has not been much worse than Indonesia's, except in the mid 1980s to the early 1990s, the latter outperformed the Philippines during this period, except during the Asian financial crisis. This is mainly because Philippine inflation was primarily brought about by BOP crises and currency devaluations followed by monetary contraction to counter the ill effects of rising

Figure 4.6: Consumer Price Index Inflation Rates—Republic of Korea; Malaysia; Philippines; Taipei,China; and Thailand

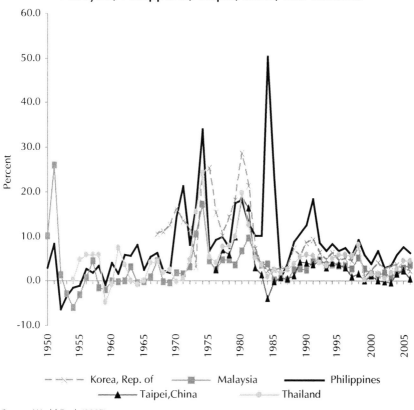

Source: World Bank (2007).

prices, while in the case of Indonesia, inflation before the Asian financial crisis was not triggered by BOP crises, and their authorities did not undertake contractionary monetary policies.

Monetary contraction brought about high interest rates, which dampened investments and risk taking. In the early 1980s, quarterly monetary targeting became the norm in fighting inflation. Monetary targets were tightened every time the BOP deteriorated and inflation increased. These targets were achieved through (i) a high required reserve ratio, (ii) high policy rates of the central bank, and (iii) open market sale of central bank bills and government securities in order to reduce the monetary base. The central bank's open market operations were particularly effective in reducing money supply by siphoning off excess liquidity in the economy.

A review of the experience of other countries with monetary growth reveals two things. First, the high growth countries—the People's Republic

Figure 4.7: Gross Domestic Product and Money Plus Quasi Money, in Real Terms: Philippines

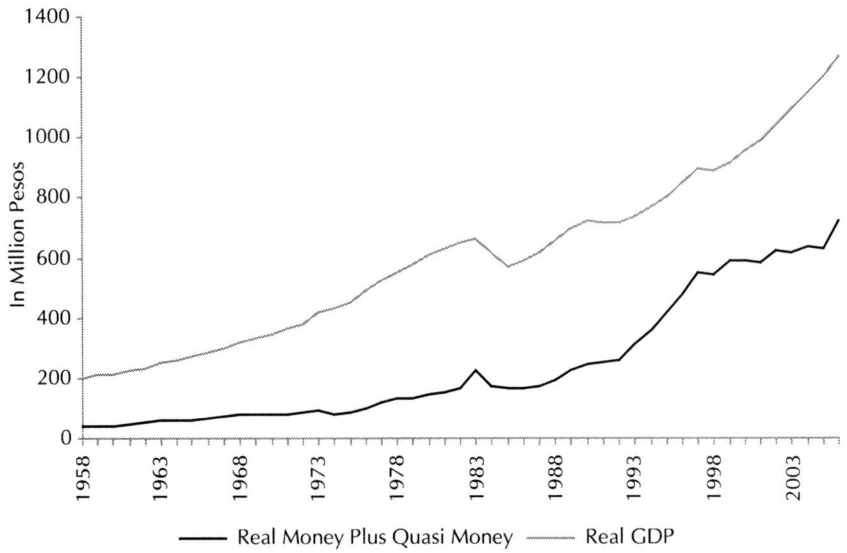

GDP = gross domestic product.
Source: BSP (2007).

of China; India; Indonesia; the Republic of Korea; Malaysia; Taipei,China; and Thailand—showed sustained growth in real money supply until the Asian financial crisis, in contrast to the monetary and credit contraction and concomitant low growth in the Philippines.[1] Second, the Latin American countries, like the Philippines, had many instances of monetary contraction during their crises. Declines in money supply in Argentina, Brazil, Chile, and Mexico were accompanied by recessions, stagnation, or low growth— in the mid 1970s, early to mid 1980s, late 1980s, 1994, and 2001–2002 for Argentina; 1980–1983 and the volatile monetary movements in the hyperinflation 1989–1992 period in Brazil; mid 1970s and early 1980s for Chile; and early 1980s, 1988, and 1994–1995 for Mexico.

In summary, it is highly probable that the restrictive monetary response to inflation partly paved the way for the country's economic recession in the

---

[1]   The Asian financial crisis prompted Indonesia, Malaysia, and Thailand to contract real money supply temporarily only in 1998. The Republic of Korea did not engage in monetary contraction until 2004 in the wake of the Asian financial crisis. This, along with the debt workout arrangement that the Government of the Republic of Korea promptly undertook, partly explains the Korean economy's quick recovery compared to the other economies.

late 1980s. There is a strong positive relationship between real GDP and real money supply (Figure 4.7). Real monetary contraction in 1984–1985, 1991, and 1998 was accompanied by real output contraction. A similar relationship is exhibited by lending rates and growth rate of per capita GDP (Figure 3.10, Chapter 3). Regression analysis showed high lending rates significantly constraining investment growth (Appendix C) and both the lending rate and investment rate significantly contributing to GDP growth (Appendix D). Thus, credit and monetary contraction during the crisis years deepened the economic recession and slowdown.

4.4. Policy Implications

This chapter shows that inefficient macroeconomic management adversely impacts growth through inappropriate fiscal and monetary policies. The chapter focuses particularly on the growth implications of fiscal deficit and contractionary monetary policy, which brings about a regime of high interest rates. The vulnerability to periodic BOP crisis arises because of perennial fiscal deficits, which are partly responsible for the huge investment–savings gap (current account deficits). The inadequacy of tax revenues forces the government to rely on domestic and foreign borrowing to finance development. Excessive reliance on foreign borrowing, especially short-term debt, exposes the country to the volatility of foreign currency markets and speculative attacks against the currency. Contractionary monetary policy is used as a defensive strategy against high inflation that is triggered by currency depreciations and BOP crisis. The regime of high interest rates that is the progeny of contractionary monetary policy creates conditions for an economic slowdown or worse, a recession.

4.4.1. Fiscal Policy

In the current period, the main macroeconomic constraint is the fiscal deficit basically brought about by the low tax effort. Sustained revenue generation is required to finance the spending needed on public investments, infrastructure, and social and economic services that will spur the economy to a higher and better quality growth path. In combination with efficient expenditure and debt management, an increase in tax effort is also needed to avoid public debt crises and defaults due to external (e.g., currency depreciation) or domestic (e.g., a downturn of manufacturing) shocks. Measures to increase tax effort include improving tax administration and tax collection and broadening the tax base. Furthermore, proper public debt management is needed to reduce the debt burden. This includes relying more on low-interest domestic debt, retiring foreign debt faster as the peso strengthens, taking advantage of grants and beneficial concessional loans, and more judicious use of official development assistance.

The Philippine Government has publicly vowed to expand its revenue generation capability. This is good policy, and the government should exert vigorous efforts to achieve it.

4.4.2. Monetary Policy

Monetary policy should be countercyclical. During good times, when trade and current account deficits increase because of high growth, expansion of money supply should be moderate as a general policy. During recessions and currency attacks, monetary policy should not be overly contractionary, in order to avoid high interest rates and excessive credit contraction that deepen crisis and increase debt defaults as firms' and banks' balance sheets deteriorate.

High inflation, especially during BOP crises, has been met by monetary contraction, which aggravated recession or reduced the growth rate. Because much of the inflationary pressure on the Philippine economy comes from supply-side shocks, an immediate monetary demand-reduction response to fight inflation may be inappropriate. The government should find better measures to address supply-side shocks (such as oil price shocks, adverse weather, and natural calamities) that trigger price increases. Oil and food price shocks are emerging as a major potential inflationary pressure. BSP has been wise not to contract money supply and increase interest rates by correctly distinguishing supply-side from demand-side inflation.

The current policy of the BSP to be more lax with monetary policy, and the series of reductions in the overnight lending and borrowing rate is moving in the right direction in tackling both the lower inflation situation and the strong appreciation of the peso.

Appendix 4.A: Crisis Logit Regressions

Dummy	Coef.	z	P>|z|	z	P>|z|	z	P>|z|	z	P>|z|	z	P>|z|	z	P>|z|	z	P>|z|
lcabpct	-1.111	-2.00	0.05												
lstdbt	0.003			2.54	0.01										
ldc_res	0.005					2.66	0.01								
lres_mos	-2.290							-2.09	0.04						
dbtxgs	0.013									2.08	0.04				
dbtgnp	0.085											2.08	0.04		
lendrate	0.425													2.45	0.01
Number of obervations		29		29		29		29		30		30		30	
LR $\chi^2(1)$		12.10		8.36		12.63		13.71		5.25		5.38		12.85	
Prob > χ^2		0.00		0.00		0.00		0.00		0.02		0.02		0.00	
Pseudo R^2		0.45		0.31		0.47		0.51		0.19		0.20		0.48	
Log likelihood		-7.28		-9.15		-7.02		-6.48		-10.89		-10.83		-7.09	

cabpct = lagged current account balance, as % of gross domestic product; dbtgnp = external debt, as % of gross national product; dbtxgs = external debt, as % of exports of goods and services; dc_res = lagged domestic credit, as % of international reserves (less gold); lendrate = lending rate; res_mos = lagged international reserves (less gold), in months of merchandise imports; stdbt = lagged short-term debt, as % of international reserves (less gold).
Source: Author.

Appendix 4.B: Regression of Tax Revenue to Nominal Gross Domestic Product and Dummy, Indicating Years with Difficulties in Tax Collection

```
--------------------------------------------------------------------
lntaxrev | Coef. Std. Err. t P>|t| [95% Conf. Interval]
-------------+------------------------------------------------------
lnnomgdp | 1.102783 .0394928 27.92 0.000 1.021886 1.183681
dumtax | –.1059586 .0298771 -3.55 0.001 –.1671592 –.0447581
_cons | –3.429059 .5621183 -6.10 0.000 –4.580506 –2.277612
-------------+------------------------------------------------------
rho | .7449577
--------------------------------------------------------------------
Durbin-Watson statistic (original) 0.868314
Durbin-Watson statistic (transformed) 2.118829

Source | SS df MS Number of obs = 31
-------------+----------------------------- F( 2, 28) = 390.03
Model | 2.87221044 2 1.43610522 Prob > F = 0.0000
Residual | .103096128 28 .003682005 R-squared = 0.9653
-------------+----------------------------- Adj R-squared = 0.9629
Total | 2.97530657 30 .099176886 Root MSE = .06068
```

where lntaxrev = log of tax revenue in current prices
lnnomgdp = log of nominal gross domestic product in current prices
dumtax = dummy for years with difficulties in tax collection

Appendix 4.C: Regression of the Investment Rate to Public Construction and Lending Rate

```
-------------------------------------------------------------------------
D.lninvr85 | Coef. Std. Err. t P>|t| [95% Conf. Interval]
-------------+-----------------------------------------------------------
D.lninvr85(–1) .2599368 .159525 1.63 0.115 –.0679716 .5878451
 |
D.lnlendrate –.2358056 .1103429 –2.14 0.042 –.4626186 –.0089926
 |
D.lnpbcr85 | .3796791 .0677979 5.60 0.000 .2403186 .5190397
 |
_cons | .0096519 .0158808 0.61 0.549 –.0229916 .0422953
-------------------------------------------------------------------------
Durbin-Watson d-statistic( 4, 30) = 1.397964
```

```
 Source | SS df MS Number of obs = 30
------------+------------------------------- F( 3, 26) = 15.47
 Model | .325411477 3 .108470492 Prob > F = 0.0000
 Residual | .182253986 26 .007009769 R-squared = 0.6410
------------+------------------------------- Adj R-squared = 0.5996
 Total | .507665463 29 .017505706 Root MSE = .08372
```

where D.lninvr85 = difference in the log of gross investment, real 1985 prices
D.lnlendrate = difference in the log of lending rate
D.lnpbcr85 = difference in the log of public construction, real 1985 prices

Appendix 4.D: Regression of the First Difference of the Logarithm of Real Gross Domestic Product at 1985 Prices

D.lngdpr85	Coeff	Std. Err.	T	P>l t l	[95% Conf. Interval]	
D.lngdpr85 (-1)	0.3590	0.1049	3.42	0.0020	0.1419	0.5760
D.lnagrir85	0.4731	0.1139	4.16	0.0000	0.2376	0.7087
D.lnlendrate	−0.0378	0.0128	−2.07	0.0500	−0.0756	−0.0000
D.lninvr85	0.1604	0.0255	6.30	0.0000	0.1077	0.2132
D.CABpctgdp	0.0020	0.0011	1.81	0.0830	−0.0003	0.0043
Constant	0.0058	0.0044	1.31	0.2020	−0.0034	0.0150

Durbin-Watson d-Statistic (6, 29) =			1.8184	Number of obs =	29
				F (5, 23) =	36.65

Source	SS	df	MS	Pro > F =	0.00000
Model	0.03075	5.0000	0.00615	R-Squared =	0.88850
Residual	0.00386	23.0000	0.00017	Adj R-squared =	0.56430
Total	0.03461	28.0000	0.00124	Root MSE =	0.01295

where D.lngdpr85 = first difference in the log of gross domestic product, real 1985 Prices
D.lnagri85 = first difference in the log of agriculture/fishery/forestry real 1985 prices
D.lnlendrate = first difference in the log of lending rate
D.lninvr85 = first difference in the log of gross investments, real 1985 prices
D.CABpctgdp = first difference in current account balance as % of gross domestic product

122

References

Bangko Sentral ng Pilipinas (BSP). 2007. *Key Statistical Indicators.* www
.bsp.gov.ph/statistics/statistics_key.asp

Bureau of the Treasury. 2007. *Bureau of the Treasury Statistical Portal.* www
.treasury.gov.ph/statdata/statdata.html

Department of Budget and Management (DBM). 2007. *Budget Expenditures
and Sources of Financing.* Manila. www/dbm/gov/dbm_publications/
all_pub_2006.htm

International Monetary Fund (IMF). 2007. *International Financial Statistics.*
www.imfstatistics.org/imf/about.asp

Lim, J., and M. Montes. 2002. Structural Adjustment after Structural
Adjustment, but Why Still No Development in the Philippines? Paper
presented at the Asian Economic Panel Meeting. Seoul. 25–26 October.

National Statistical Coordination Bureau (NSCB). various years. *Philippine
Statistical Yearbook.* Makati City.

World Bank. 2007 and various years. *World Development Indicators.*
Washington, DC.

5. Trade, Investments, and Domestic Production

Joseph Anthony Y. Lim

5.1. Introduction

The economic collapse in 1983–1985 and periodic slowdowns and recessions thereafter led to the sharp decline in Philippine industry's share of gross domestic product (GDP) as well as that of investment from the early 1980s. The premature halt in the growth of the industrial and capital formation sector reduced the country's capacity to improve its technology and to scale up production, which would have brought the economy to much higher growth and development. As industry's share declined, services took over as the lead growth sector. This is unlike the experience of more developed countries such as Taipei,China, where the service sector and consumption share of GDP rose only after the highly industrialized stage and where industrial and manufacturing activities have reached maturity. Figure 5.1 shows the Philippines' drop and stagnation in the share of industry compared with that of its more successful East Asian neighbors.

Except for Taipei,China[1] and the Philippines, all East Asian high-growth performers had increased their investment–GDP ratio until the 1997 Asian financial crisis (Figure 5.2). In fact, other Asian countries' investment–GDP ratios continued to exceed that of the Philippines by 2006 notwithstanding the decline in their investment–GDP ratios during the 1997 Asian financial crisis and thereafter. Investments in all countries in the figure, except Malaysia and the Philippines, had a mild recovery during 2000–2006.

---

[1]   In contrast to the Philippines, Taipei,China is a more mature economy that now exhibits a lower investment–GDP ratio and a higher consumption–GDP ratio as the population takes advantage of the higher standard of living brought about by a rapidly growing economy.

Figure 5.1: Industry Share (% gross domestic product)

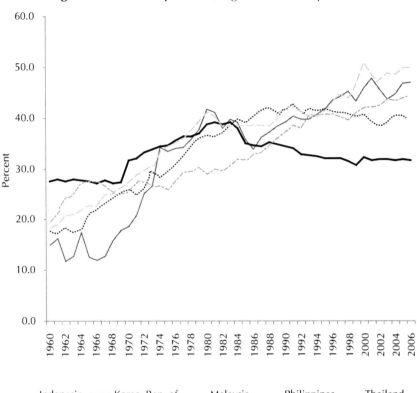

Source: IMF (2007).

While Philippine export and import shares in GDP rose sharply since the 1990s, the same was true for all countries due to globalization and the institution of World Trade Organization (WTO) and regional and bilateral trade agreements in the 1990s and 2000s. Table 5.1 shows the growth rates of exports of goods based on 2000 United States (US) dollars for selected countries.

For the period 1960–2005, Philippine exports grew the least among comparator countries. The Philippines was somewhat at par with Argentina and Indonesia, whose low export growth was only above 5% annually during the period. Except for Mexico, all the other countries whose exports grew much faster than the Philippines also had much higher GDP per capita growth than the Philippines (Table 5.1).

Figure 5.2: Gross Capital Formation of Selected Asian Countries
(% of gross domestic product)

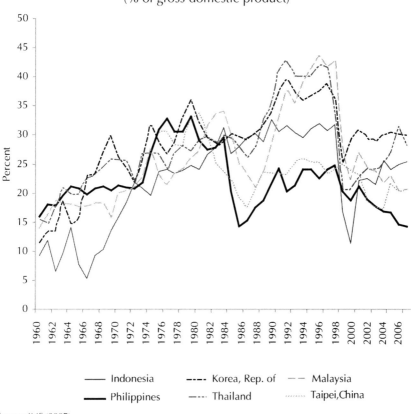

Source: IMF (2007).

The lackluster performance in exports and investments and the inability to transition to high productivity sectors adversely impact Philippine growth prospects. Clearly, growth will continue to be subdued unless policy makers are able to address the factors constraining trade and investments. In this regard, Hausmann, Rodrik, and Velasco (2005) identify government and market failures as some of the key variables that might lead to low appropriability of economic returns, which inhibits investments and expansion in tradable goods, in turn constraining growth.

Table 5.1: Export Growth Rate (based on export values at constant 2000 $ prices)

Country	1960–2005	1960–1980	1980–1985	1985–1993	1993–1997	1997–1999	1999–2002	2002–2005
Philippines	5.57	6.35	–3.89	8.12	16.06	–9.54	5.55	7.72
Early East Asian Developers								
Indonesia	5.15	6.56	–5.73	9.78	8.25	–12.92	7.94	9.29
Korea, Republic of	17.75	24.46	10.08	11.67	18.52	13.63	9.49	14.48
Malaysia	8.65	6.80	7.10	13.75	13.70	6.64	3.90	10.12
Thailand	10.41	9.87	8.09	17.56	7.52	8.64	8.02	6.98
Late Asian Developers[a]								
China, People's Republic of	12.60	14.99	6.57	7.65	12.91	11.09	22.81	26.47
India	8.84	8.55	1.02	9.56	11.44	15.92	6.09	16.50
Viet Nam	20.45	–	–	18.85	31.23	13.49	13.06	21.24
Latin American Countries								
Argentina	5.64	5.18	4.78	3.26	14.28	4.51	2.85	9.16
Brazil	7.86	7.91	10.45	5.73	4.38	6.44	9.90	12.79
Chile	7.19	6.86	1.85	10.31	11.40	6.27	4.61	8.11
Mexico	8.92	8.63	9.51	6.09	19.03	12.26	4.38	7.00

– = not available.
[a] Data for the People's Republic of China start at 1978, for India at 1970, and for Viet Nam at 1989.
Source: World Bank (various years).

5.2. Government Failures Constraining Growth, Trade, and Investments

Investments and expansion in trade will obviously be stimulated only in an environment with (i) macroeconomic and political stability, (ii) clear property rights and contract enforcement, (iii) low transaction costs and easy establishment of businesses, (iv) no corrupt practices that hamper business start-up and operations, (v) clear economic policies and policy directions, (vi) safety for people and strict adherence to the rule of law and order, (vii) good infrastructure, and (viii) reasonable taxation of sales and income. Conversely, investments will be low and trade stagnant where government has failed to motivate an environment conducive to it.

5.2.1. Government Failures as Revealed by Surveys

Do government failures significantly hinder trade and investments? The results of surveys reporting major constraints on business operations and investments seem to confirm major government failures as significant hurdles to the expansion of trade and investments in the country.

In 2007, the Makati Business Club conducted a survey for the Global Competitiveness Report of the World Economic Forum. The Makati Business Club surveyed 72 of its 700 members between 19 October and 9 November 2007. The top two constraints that respondents identified were licensing obstacles and contract enforcement. The survey (also undertaken by the Makati Business Club for the Philippines in 2007–2008, with 37 of its members responding) identified several major constraints (Figure 5.3). Topping the list were corruption, inadequate infrastructure, policy instability, and inefficient government bureaucracy. Appendix 5.A gives some results of the Global Competitiveness Index for the Philippines for 2007–2008. The Philippines ranked very low with respect to institutions (95th among 131 countries), infrastructure (94th), labor market efficiency (100th), macroeconomic stability (77th), financial market sophistication (77th), and quality of business environment (73rd); and ranked 71st overall. The Philippines had a lower overall ranking than all the Association of Southeast Asian Nations (ASEAN) countries except Cambodia.[2] It also ranked below Colombia, El Salvador, Mexico, Sri Lanka, and Turkey.

---

[2] Brunei Darussalam, Lao People's Democratic Republic, and Myanmar were not included in the survey.

Figure 5.3: Share of Firms Rating Constraints as Major or Severe

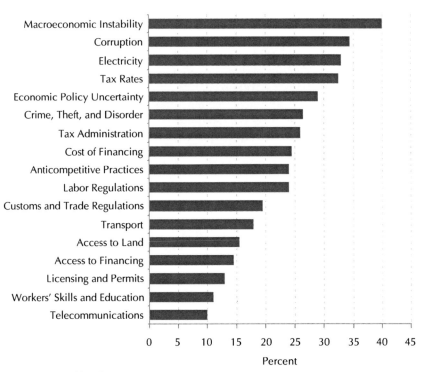

Source: ADB–World Bank (2005).

The 2003 Asian Development Bank (ADB) Investment Climate Survey of 716 firms in the Philippines showed that the biggest constraint—as cited by 40% of the firms—was macroeconomic instability (Figure 5.3). In order of importance, the other factors cited by about one third of the respondents were corruption, high electricity costs, and high tax rates. Other problems with high ratings were economic policy uncertainty (29%); crime, theft, and disorder (26%), and tax administration (26%). Macroeconomic instability scored the highest in the survey, because 2003 was the height of the fiscal crisis in the Philippines (ADB–World Bank 2005). This problem has been declining starting in 2006, which is the main reason that the Philippines was able to improve its ranking in the Global Competitiveness Index 2007.

The 2003 Investment Climate Survey further found long delays in obtaining government licenses or permits (Figure 5.4), corroborating the findings of the Makati Business Club survey. The worst hit in terms of getting licenses to operate were medium-sized firms, which had to wait an average of almost 40 days for a business permit or operating license.

Figure 5.4: Number of Days to Obtain Government License or Permit by Firm Size

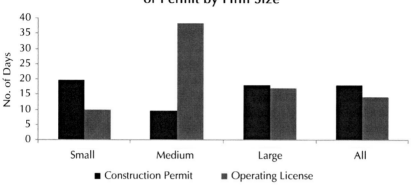

Source: ADB–World Bank (2005)

Various surveys of members by the American Chamber of Commerce in the Philippines in 2006 (Table 5.2) revealed the following major concerns: (i) corruption—cited by 77% of respondents; (ii) defective or unclear laws and regulations—cited by 52%; (iii) bad infrastructure—cited by 50%; and (iv) tax structure—cited by 45%.

The resulting picture is that significant government failures constrain growth and investments. The failures are bureaucratic red tape, corruption, defective or unclear laws and regulations, bad infrastructure (especially high electricity costs), unclear economic policies and policy direction, and long delays in setting up businesses.

Table 5.2: Local Business Environment Factors

Strengths (a score of 60% or more is significant)				Major Concerns (a score of 30% or more is significant)			
Factors	2004	2005	2006	Factors	2004	2005	2006
Availability of Low-Cost Labor	–	–	71%	Laws and Regulations	48%	63%	52%
Availability of Trained Personnel	73%	63%	67%	Corruption	91%	88%	77%
Office Lease Cost	–	–	59%	Local Protectionism	49%	46%	39%
Housing Cost	–	–	63%	Tax Structure	49%	56%	45%
				Infrastructure	69%	68%	50%
				Availability of Raw Materials	20%	42%	35%

– = no data.
Source: American Chamber of Commerce (2006).

5.2.2. Currency Overvaluation

Currency overvaluation is considered both a government and market failure because it depends on the government's exchange rate regime and monetary policy as well as failures in the international financial markets, as in the irrational exuberance of "hot money" pouring into emerging markets or sudden panics and flight from currency during speculative attacks.[3] Overvaluation has a strongly detrimental effect on industrialization and incentives for trade and investments.

The exchange rate is a crucial variable that critically affects industrial policy. However, this variable did not emerge as a major problem in the surveys, because different businesses have different interests in the exchange rate. For obvious reasons, only exporters complained strongly about the overvaluation during critical periods. Families of overseas Filipino workers also noted difficulties resulting from the strong appreciation of the peso since 2006. Empirical estimation for this chapter shows that exports are very affected by world trade and a dummy denoting the strong trade liberalization years before the 1997 Asian financial crisis. The world trade variable is also positively related to the exchange rate at the 5% level (Appendix 5.B).

An overvalued currency reduces the economic incentives for both the suppliers and demanders of Philippine exports. As exports are retarded over time, the economy loses the opportunity not only to earn foreign exchange but also for "learning by doing," by competing internationally and adopting best techniques and processes learned in the international sector.

Empirical estimation also shows that imports are mainly determined by GDP and the exchange rate (Appendix 5.B). Currency depreciation tames import growth as foreign goods become expensive. This is important for firms producing for the domestic market, since it reduces import competition.

An overvalued currency encourages imports and reduces incentives to produce domestically. It leads to strong import competition, which creates a disincentive for firms to enter potentially high productivity sectors. Empirical estimation shows that currency overvaluation retards the shift of domestic industries to high-productivity sectors.

The next section provides evidence that market failure has stymied the growth and technological advancement of Philippine export and domestic manufacturing.

---

3   "Hot money" refers to inflows that may be readily reversed, e.g., investments in the stock markets that can enter and leave a market easily.

5.2.3. The Lack of Technological and Scale Upgrading in Philippine Export and Domestic Manufacturing due to Market Failures

Due to market failure, Philippine export and domestic manufacturing have not climbed the technological, scale, and productivity ladder. This is because market failure problems have not encouraged entrepreneurial and innovative activities in the Philippines, as exports tend to concentrate on a few high-technology but low value-added products while domestic manufacturing has gravitated around traditional labor-intensive and/or low-skilled activities, e.g., food, beverage, textile, footwear, clothing, and wearing apparel.

Concentration on a few high-technology, low value-added products in exports. To examine the export performance of the Philippines over time, the study constructed a measure of the quality of a country's exports called EXPY, as in Hausmann, Hwang, and Rodrik (2006). This measure captures the income level associated with a country's export basket. The measure proceeds from the idea that commodities exported by richer countries are associated with higher productivity levels or "quality" than those exported by poorer countries. This gives commodity-specific scores, which are then used to construct country-specific indexes of the quality of a country's exports.

The commodity-specific index, called PRODY, is a weighted average of the per capita GDPs of countries exporting a given product. PRODY represents the income level associated with that product. Let countries be indexed by j and goods by k. Total exports of country j equals

$$X_j = \sum_k x_{jk}$$

Let the per capita GDP of country j be denoted by Y_j. Then the productivity level associated with a product k, $PRODY_k$ equals

$$PRODY_k = \sum_j \frac{\left(x_{jk}/X_j\right)}{\sum_j \left(x_{jk}/X_j\right)} Y_j$$

The index represents a weighted average of per capita GDPs where the weights correspond to the revealed comparative advantage of a country in good k.

The productivity level associated with a country i's export basket, $EXPY_j$ is the weighted average of the PRODYs for that country, where the weights are the value shares of the products in the country's total exports.

$$EXPY_i = \sum_i \left(\frac{x_{it}}{X_i} \right) PRODY_k$$

Export data come from the UN Comtrade Database at the 2-digit level (SITC Revision 1) with 60 commodities for 1970 to 2006.

Appendix 5.C shows the composition of Philippine merchandise exports based on the 60 commodities ranked from highest to the lowest PRODY score. The Philippines had changed its export composition over the years from low-technology and -scale products (wood, lumber, and cork; oil products, mainly coconut oil; sugar; and metal ores or mineral products). In the mid 1970s to 1990s, the Philippines started to produce manufactured exports such as semiconductors (under electrical machinery, apparatus, and appliances); clothing; and furniture. In the 1990s, electrical machinery, apparatus, and appliances started to dominate exports, exceeding 50% of total merchandise exports. In the second half of the 1990s, machinery other than electrical became the second largest export, comprising 20% of total merchandise exports by 2000. Since 1997, machinery—electrical and nonelectrical—has comprised 60% to more than 70% of the Philippines' total merchandise exports. This share has diminished slightly since 2001.

Figure 5.5 shows the Philippines performing well on the EXPY score compared to its higher growth neighbors. The Philippines' EXPY score was low in 1970 and has risen fast through the years. By 2004–2006, the Philippines was second only to the Republic of Korea in EXPY score. However, in recent years, EXPY scores of Indonesia, Malaysia, and the Philippines tapered off.

No doubt, the Philippines' high score was due to the high concentration of two merchandise exports—electrical machinery and apparatus, and other than electrical machinery. Together these two exports comprised more than 60% of total merchandise exports. These export categories have high PRODY scores, which may be an advantage as well as a disadvantage. The advantage is that the Philippines is now exporting at the high end of export product lines, which implies a strong potential for a huge expansion of technological electronic know-how. The disadvantage has two aspects. The first is that the overconcentration in two product categories in the 2-digit coding scheme shows a lack of diversification, which will be perilous for the economy if there is a slump in global electronics and machinery sectors. The second disadvantage is that because the two sectors are highly import-intensive, the value added may not be very high.

Figure 5.5: Export Productivity Score of Selected East Asian Countries

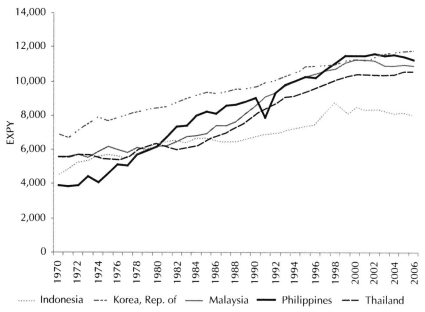

EXPY = a measure of the quality of a country's exports.
Source: Author's calculation based on the UN Comtrade Database.

Table 5.3 shows the ratio of imports to exports of electrical and nonelectrical machinery of three countries (the Republic of Korea, Malaysia, and the Philippines) that rely heavily on this sector for their exports. Clearly, the Philippines, with the highest import–export ratio, is the most dependent on this sector. This implies low value added from the two export products. The challenge for the Philippine export sector is to go into backward links in the two general export categories so the country can climb the technological, scale, and productivity ladder.

Low Technological and Scale Upgrading in Domestic Manufacturing.
In terms of technological and scale upgrading, the Philippine domestic manufacturing sector does not do well in the range and type of products it produces. Using the PRODY scores of the commodities in Table 5.3, the economic sectors in the manufacturing sectors can be classified as

(i) group 1—PRODY scores below 6,000: food, beverage, tobacco, textile, footwear, clothing, and wearing apparel;

(ii) group 2—PRODY scores of 6,000–9,000: wood and cork products, furniture and fixtures, nonmetal minerals, petroleum, and coal;

Table 5.3: Import and Export of Electrical and Nonelectrical Machinery (%)

Economy	2000	2001	2002	2003	2004	2005
Ratio of Imports to Exports						
Korea, Republic of	77.2	72.1	69.7	64.1	65.6	66.9
Malaysia	82.4	83.5	83.2	85.3	82.5	83.1
Philippines	81.4	95.5	94.9	91.7	93.7	90.3
Share of Electrical and Nonelectrical Machinery in Total Merchandise Exports						
Korea, Republic of	38.9	42.3	43.6	43.5	40.9	38.8
Malaysia	57.1	57.5	54.4	52.1	51.8	50.1
Philippines	71.3	73.2	71.2	71.4	69.0	66.1

Source: Calculated from UN Comtrade Database, SITC Revision-1, 2-digit codes.

(iii) group 3—PRODY scores from 9,000–10,500: metals, metal manufactures, and leather-made products (travel, handbags, etc.); and

(iv) group 4—PRODY scores over 10,500: paper and pulp, printing
and publishing, rubber manufactures, electrical machinery, nonelectrical machinery, transport equipment, chemicals, and miscellaneous manufactures.

More detailed manufacturing data are used here for the Republic of
Korea; Malaysia; the Philippines; and Taipei,China. Based on the above
classification, the shares in GDP of the different groups of manufacturing
subsectors are shown in Table 5.4.

Table 5.5 shows that Philippine manufacturing is more concentrated
on group 1 while the other countries' manufacturing sector is concentrated
in group 4, the higher technology and scale subsectors. The fall in the share
of group 1 in the other three countries over time is very distinct.[4]

The composition of Philippine exports is very different from that of its
domestic manufacturing. In contrast, in the three comparator countries,
exports and domestic manufacturing are both consistently concentrated in
high-technology and -scale products. Table 5.6 gives more detailed informa-

---

[4] Taipei,China's shares in GDP of all subgroups are falling because the economy's total
share of industry in GDP is falling fast, as service share is increasing in the transition to
a developed and mature economy.

Table 5.4: Manufacturing Subsectors' Share of GDP (%)

Economy/ Group	1981	1985	1987	1990	1993	1995	1998	2000	2003	2004	2005
Korea, Republic of											
Group 1	8.2	7.4	7.8	5.5	4.9	4.1	4.1	4.1	3.1	3.0	2.8
Group 2	3.7	4.2	4.4	4.0	4.5	4.0	4.2	3.8	3.7	3.9	3.9
Group 3	2.9	3.5	4.2	3.9	3.7	3.9	3.7	3.8	3.4	4.2	4.6
Group 4	10.2	12.2	13.9	13.8	13.6	15.6	15.3	17.8	16.2	17.4	17.2
Malaysia											
Group 1	–	–	5.1	4.7	4.4	4.2	4.6	3.2	3.6	3.3	3.0
Group 2	–	–	3.8	3.9	4.3	4.6	4.1	5.4	5.0	4.9	5.0
Group 3	–	–	1.2	1.7	1.9	1.5	1.9	1.8	1.9	2.5	2.2
Group 4	–	–	9.7	13.9	15.2	16.0	18.2	22.2	20.6	20.8	20.3
Philippines											
Group 1	14.3	15.2	15.3	14.7	13.7	13.1	12.6	12.5	13.4	13.4	13.3
Group 2	4.7	4.4	3.9	4.1	3.9	3.5	2.9	3.1	2.9	2.7	3.3
Group 3	1.1	1.3	1.3	1.4	1.2	1.2	0.9	0.7	1.1	1.1	1.0
Group 4	5.4	4.3	4.4	4.7	4.9	5.2	5.4	5.9	5.9	5.9	5.7
Taipei,China											
Group 1	9.5	9.8	9.1	6.6	5.2	4.0	3.3	3.0	2.6	2.3	2.1
Group 2	4.9	4.4	5.2	3.7	4.2	3.8	3.3	2.6	2.7	3.1	2.9
Group 3	4.3	5.3	5.2	4.6	4.1	3.6	3.5	3.3	3.0	3.8	4.0
Group 4	14.9	16.2	17.8	16.3	14.5	14.0	14.7	14.9	14.1	12.7	12.3

– = no data.
Source: Calculated from national accounts data of the selected countries. ADB (n.d.).

tion on the shares in GDP of Philippine economic sectors. The Philippines is not doing well in the high-technology and high-scale manufacturing sectors. However, as the service sector takes the lead in the growth of output, the share of potentially high-technology and high-scale service sectors such as communication, financial intermediation, and business services, especially business process outsourcing, improves perceptibly. The shares of educational and health and medical services, which are important for human capital formation, are also improving. The share of public utilities (electricity, gas, and water) in total output is also improving.

Table 5.5: Share in Gross Domestic Product of Production Sectors, Philippines (%)

Sector and Subsector	1967	1970	1975	1980	1985	1990	1995	2000	2004	2005	2006	1st Half 2007
Agriculture, Fisheries, Forestry	**27.4**	**29.5**	**30.3**	**25.1**	**24.6**	**21.9**	**21.6**	**15.8**	**15.1**	**14.3**	**14.2**	**13.1**
a. Agriculture	22.8	25.6	27.9	22.5	23.0	21.1	21.4	15.7	15.0	14.3	14.1	13.0
b. Forestry	4.5	3.9	2.5	2.6	1.6	0.8	0.2	0.1	0.1	0.1	0.1	0.1
Industry	**31.5**	**31.9**	**35.0**	**38.8**	**35.1**	**34.5**	**32.1**	**32.3**	**31.7**	**31.9**	**31.6**	**31.6**
a. Mining and Quarrying	1.1	2.1	1.3	2.2	2.1	1.5	0.9	0.6	1.1	1.2	1.3	1.8
b. Manufacturing	24.2	24.9	25.7	25.7	25.2	24.8	23.0	22.2	23.0	23.3	22.9	21.2
Group 1	**12.7**	**13.1**	**13.8**	**13.6**	**15.2**	**14.7**	**13.1**	**12.5**	**13.4**	**13.3**	**12.9**	**12.3**
Food Manufactures	8.9	9.6	9.2	9.0	11.3	10.4	9.2	9.5	11.0	11.0	10.8	10.6
Beverage Industries	0.7	0.8	0.8	0.9	1.1	1.1	1.1	1.0	0.8	0.7	0.7	0.6
Tobacco Manufactures	0.8	0.7	1.1	0.8	0.9	0.7	0.6	0.5	0.2	0.2	0.1	0.1
Textile Manufactures	1.0	1.1	1.5	1.4	0.9	0.9	0.6	0.3	0.3	0.4	0.3	0.3
Footwear Wearing Apparel	1.4	1.0	1.2	1.4	1.0	1.6	1.6	1.2	1.1	1.0	0.9	0.8
Group 2	**4.3**	**4.0**	**4.6**	**5.2**	**4.4**	**4.1**	**3.5**	**3.1**	**2.7**	**3.2**	**3.4**	**3.1**
Furniture and Fixtures	1.1	0.9	0.7	0.6	0.3	0.4	0.4	0.4	0.3	0.4	0.3	0.3
Wood and Cork Products	1.4	1.0	0.8	1.1	0.5	0.5	0.3	0.2	0.1	0.1	0.1	0.1
Nonmetallic Mineral Products	0.9	0.8	0.7	0.9	0.5	0.7	0.9	0.6	0.6	0.5	0.5	0.5
Products of Petroleum and Coal	1.0	1.3	2.3	2.6	3.2	2.4	1.9	2.0	1.7	2.3	2.4	2.2
Group 3	**1.6**	**1.7**	**1.3**	**1.2**	**1.3**	**1.4**	**1.2**	**0.7**	**1.1**	**1.0**	**1.1**	**1.0**
Leather and Leather Products	0.0	0.0	0.0	0.0	0.0	0.0	0.0	0.0	0.0	0.0	0.0	0.0
Basic Metal Industries	0.3	0.5	0.5	0.5	0.8	0.8	0.7	0.4	0.7	0.6	0.7	0.6
Metal Industries	1.3	1.2	0.8	0.7	0.5	0.6	0.5	0.4	0.4	0.4	0.4	0.4

continued on next page

Table 5.5 (continued)

Sector and Subsector	1967	1970	1975	1980	1985	1990	1995	2000	2004	2005	2006	1st Half 2007
Group 4	5.5	6.0	6.0	5.7	4.3	4.7	5.2	5.9	5.9	5.7	5.5	4.7
Rubber Products	0.6	0.6	0.7	0.4	0.3	0.3	0.2	0.1	0.1	0.1	0.1	0.1
Chemicals and Chemical Products	1.3	1.8	2.2	2.4	1.8	1.9	1.9	1.6	1.5	1.6	1.5	1.2
Paper and Paper Products	0.2	0.3	0.3	0.5	0.3	0.3	0.2	0.2	0.1	0.1	0.1	0.1
Publishing and Printing	0.4	0.4	0.4	0.3	0.3	0.3	0.3	0.2	0.2	0.2	0.2	0.2
Machinery except Electrical	0.5	0.5	0.3	0.3	0.2	0.2	0.3	0.3	0.3	0.2	0.2	0.1
Electrical Machinery	1.0	1.1	0.7	0.8	0.8	0.9	1.5	2.6	2.8	2.6	2.6	2.1
Transport Equipment	1.4	1.2	1.1	0.8	0.2	0.3	0.4	0.2	0.2	0.2	0.2	0.2
Miscellaneous Manufactures	0.2	0.2	0.3	0.3	0.3	0.5	0.5	0.7	0.7	0.6	0.7	0.6
c. Construction	5.3	4.1	6.7	9.3	5.1	6.0	5.6	6.5	4.4	3.9	3.9	4.7
d. Electricity, Gas, Water	0.8	0.8	1.4	1.6	2.8	2.1	2.6	2.9	3.2	3.6	3.6	3.9
Services	41.1	38.6	34.7	36.1	40.4	43.6	46.3	52.0	53.2	53.7	54.2	55.3
a. Transport, Communications, Storage	3.6	3.4	3.8	4.6	5.5	4.9	4.7	5.9	7.5	7.6	7.4	7.7
Land Transport	–	–	1.5	2.1	3.0	2.4	2.3	2.5	2.7	2.6	2.7	2.7
Water Transport	–	–	0.8	0.8	0.5	0.5	0.4	0.5	0.5	0.5	0.4	0.5
Air Transport	–	–	0.3	0.3	0.2	0.4	0.3	0.3	0.3	0.3	0.3	0.4
Storage	–	–	0.6	0.8	0.7	0.6	0.4	0.4	0.4	0.5	0.5	0.5
Communication	0.5	0.6	0.6	0.6	1.0	1.1	1.2	2.3	3.6	3.7	3.5	3.7

continued on next page

Table 5.5 (continued)

Sector and Subsector	1967	1970	1975	1980	1985	1990	1995	2000	2004	2005	2006	1st Half 2007
b. Trade	9.9	9.7	10.3	12.2	14.5	14.4	13.7	14.1	14.0	14.3	14.5	14.3
Wholesale	–	–	–	5.6	2.7	4.2	3.5	3.1	3.2	3.3	3.2	3.1
Retail	–	–	–	6.6	11.8	10.1	10.2	11.0	10.8	11.0	11.3	11.2
c. Finance	2.5	3.0	3.3	3.9	3.0	3.9	4.1	4.4	4.4	4.8	5.2	5.7
Banks	1.3	1.6	1.5	2.0	1.9	2.8	2.9	3.1	3.1	3.5	3.7	4.1
Non-Banks	0.3	0.5	0.7	0.8	0.4	0.4	0.4	0.4	0.4	0.4	0.6	0.6
Insurance	0.9	1.0	1.0	1.0	0.8	0.7	0.8	0.9	0.9	0.9	0.9	1.0
d. Ownership of Dwellings and Real Estate	9.4	8.3	6.3	5.2	5.6	5.7	6.8	6.6	6.0	5.9	5.8	5.9
e. Private Services	8.5	7.4	5.6	5.3	6.8	7.5	8.9	11.4	13.4	13.6	13.8	14.5
Education	1.2	1.1	0.9	0.8	0.8	1.0	1.5	2.3	2.7	2.6	2.6	2.6
Medical	0.5	0.4	0.5	0.6	0.9	0.9	1.1	1.4	1.6	1.6	1.6	1.6
Business	1.5	1.5	1.1	1.0	1.0	1.0	1.2	1.6	3.0	3.4	3.6	4.2
Recreational	0.5	0.5	0.5	0.4	0.8	0.9	0.8	1.1	1.1	1.1	1.1	1.1
Personal	3.1	2.0	1.2	1.0	1.8	2.1	2.3	2.9	2.9	2.9	2.9	3.0
Hotels and Restaurants	1.2	1.5	1.0	1.0	1.2	1.4	1.7	1.9	1.8	1.8	1.7	1.8
Other Services	0.5	0.5	0.4	0.4	0.3	0.2	0.2	0.3	0.2	0.2	0.2	0.2
f. Government Services	7.2	6.7	5.4	4.9	4.9	7.2	8.1	9.5	7.9	7.5	7.5	7.3

– = not available.
Source: Based on data from NSCB (various years).

5.3. The Inability to Upgrade the Technology and Scale of Manufacturing

Why is Philippine domestic manufacturing concentrated in low-productivity, -technology, and -scale products? The results of panel data regression (Appendix 5.D) conclusively confirm the hypothesis that market failures were behind the inability to upgrade the technology and scale of domestic manufacturing. The most significant explanatory variable is the real effective exchange rate, followed by the share of gross fixed capital formation in GDP and by research and development (R&D). These are significant at the 0.001% level. Per capita GDP is significant at the 5% level. That per capita GDP—a measure of an economy's level of development—has the weakest significance in the regression may indicate that high-technology and -scale output for the economy is not a static phenomenon but can be achieved through correct policies such as not overvaluing the currency and stimulating investments in R&D and science and technology.

The methodology behind panel data analysis consists of using as a dependent variable the per capita manufacturing value added of group 4 (the high-technology and -scale index products identified earlier) for the Republic of Korea, Malaysia, the Philippines, and Taipei,China during the period 1987–2005. This variable is expressed in constant 2000 US dollars, and the following independent variables were found to be significant.

- **GDP per capita in constant US dollar 2000 prices.** As the income per capita of the country increases, the country's demand for and capacity to produce more high-technology and -scale products increase.
- **Share of gross capital formation in GDP.** Because technology is embedded in capital stock, the higher the share a country's investment has in GDP, the higher the probability that the country will move into high-technology and -scale products.
- **Research and development.** High-technology and -scale production require R&D and the scientific community's link to industry. World Development Indicators contain patchy data on R&D expenditures as a percent of GDP. The paper computed the averages of these data for each country, which were used as the level of R&D spending for all the years in the sample period.[5]
- **The real effective exchange rate.** It is hypothesized that overvalued currencies will encourage imports of high-technology and

---

[5] The R&D expenditure as a percent of GDP for Taipei,China was derived separately from an internet search that yielded a 3% R&D expenditure.

-scale products and lessen the incentives to produce them at home. Specifically, the entrepreneur will be discouraged from innovating and taking risks because of stiff import competition made cheap by the overvaluation of currency.

5.3.1. The Lack of Research and Development Promotion

The importance of R&D expenditure, a significant explanatory variable of per capita manufacturing value added (as shown in Appendix 5.D), is emphasized in Table 5.6. The table shows clearly that the Philippines invests very little in R&D—at 0.11% of GDP, which is one of the lowest in the world. In terms of investments in R&D, the Philippines ranks 89th among 103 countries. The Global Competitiveness Index shows distinctly that the Philippines has a very low score in infrastructure, technological readiness, and innovation (Appendix 5.A). ADB–WB (2005), in analyzing the Investment Climate and Productivity Survey, observed "Given the Philippines' relatively well-developed university system, it is surprising that only one of 716 firms reported universities and other public institutions as the most important source of new technology. Moreover, only three firms rated universities as the second, and two firms rated them as the third most important source of new technology." Most firms in the survey noted that technology improvements in the Philippines were mainly derived from technology embodied in new equipment and machinery or from trained and skilled personnel, not from government, academic, or even the firm's own R&D support.

5.3.2. Coordination Failures, Information/Self-Discovery Externalities, and Training Externalities

Only 58% of within-country variations are explained by the panel data regression (Appendix 5.D). This suggests that other variables (that had not been included in the panel data regression because they are hard to identify or measure) may have an impact. The omitted variables may also indicate the inability of domestic manufacturing firms to tackle market failures. One such variable is "information spillovers in self-discovery," an externality according to Hausmann and Rodrik (2006). Because of uncertainty over the success or failure of an innovation, new products and technologies, if left to the markets, may not be introduced because of the "first mover" problem—the first mover shoulders all the risks and all the losses in case of failure, but successes provide competitors with free information concerning the profitability and economic opportunities of the new product or technique. Other producers will then enter the field and reduce the economic rents and profits of the first mover. Thus, innovation is stymied because the private returns from engaging in innovation are lower than the social benefits. This partly explains the low appropriability of returns to innovation. The antidote to this market failure is to provide a subsidy or economic incentive to increase the private returns in line with the social benefits.

Coordination failures occur when complementary inputs (e.g., inter-related industries; specific skills requirements for the specific sector; specific intermediate inputs; infrastructure; logistics and transport systems; and legal and regulatory frameworks for contracts, property rights, and labor norms) that are needed before an industry can take off are nonexistent. Many of these requirements may be sector-specific and would have a higher possibility of not existing for new activities that involve innovation. Furthermore, many of the requirements (e.g., physical infrastructure, legal and regulatory frameworks, and labor norms) cannot be provided by the markets but only by the state.

There are also training externalities. As Becker (1975) pointed out, profit-maximizing firms will provide less than the socially optimal amount of training because they may not get the full benefit of their training expenditure—their trained employees may be hired away by other firms. This market failure prods the state to provide the general and specific skills formation required especially for industries that have positive externalities.

Table 5.6: Research and Development Expenditure by Country, as % of Gross Domestic Product (most

Rank	Country	R&D Exp.	Year	Rank	Country	R&D Exp.	Year
1	Israel	4.46%	2004	27	New Zealand	1.16%	2003
2	Sweden	3.74%	2004	28	Ukraine	1.16%	2002
3	Finland	3.46%	2005	29	Croatia	1.14%	2003
4	Japan	3.15%	2003	30	Italy	1.14%	2003
5	Iceland	3.01%	2004	31	Spain	1.11%	2003
6	United States	2.68%	2004	32	Brazil	0.98%	2003
7	Korea, Republic of	2.64%	2003	33	Estonia	0.91%	2004
8	Denmark	2.63%	2003	34	Hungary	0.88%	2004
9	Switzerland	2.57%	2000	35	India	0.85%	2000
10	Germany	2.49%	2004	36	Moldova	0.81%	1997
11	Austria	2.33%	2005	37	Uganda	0.81%	2001
12	Singapore	2.25%	2004	38	Portugal	0.78%	2003
13	France	2.16%	2004	39	Lithuania	0.76%	2004
14	Canada	1.93%	2004	40	South Africa	0.76%	2001
15	Belgium	1.90%	2003	41	Malaysia	0.69%	2002
16	United Kingdom	1.89%	2003	42	Iran	0.67%	2004
17	The Netherlands	1.85%	2003	43	Turkey	0.66%	2002
18	Luxembourg	1.81%	2003	44	Nepal	0.66%	2002
19	Norway	1.75%	2003	45	Cuba	0.65%	2003
20	Australia	1.70%	2002	46	Tunisia	0.63%	2002
21	Slovenia	1.61%	2004	47	Bangladesh	0.62%	2002
22	China, People's Republic of	1.44%	2004	48	Morocco	0.62%	2002
23	Czech Republic	1.28%	2004	49	Belarus	0.62%	2002
24	Ireland	1.21%	2004	50	Chile	0.61%	2003
25	Russian Federation	1.17%	2004	51	Hong Kong, China	0.60%	2002
26	Serbia	1.17%	2002	52	Mozambique	0.59%	2002

continued on next page

Table 5.6 (continued)

Rank	Country	R&D Exp.	Year	Rank	Country	R&D Exp.	Year
53	Greece	0.58%	2004	79	Kyrgyz Republic	0.20%	2002
54	Poland	0.58%	2004	80	Kuwait	0.20%	2002
55	Slovakia	0.53%	2004	81	Egypt	0.19%	2000
56	Bulgaria	0.51%	2004	82	Viet Nam	0.19%	2002
57	Latvia	0.42%	2004	83	Colombia	0.17%	2001
58	Argentina	0.41%	2003	84	Burkina Faso	0.17%	1997
59	Mexico	0.40%	2002	85	Saint Vincent	0.15%	2002
60	Romania	0.40%	2004	86	Sri Lanka	0.14%	2000
61	Costa Rica	0.39%	2000	87	Madagascar	0.12%	2000
62	Saint Lucia	0.38%	1999	88	Trinidad and Tobago	0.12%	2003
63	Cyprus	0.37%	2004	89	Philippines	0.11%	2002
64	Mauritius	0.35%	2003	90	Seychelles	0.11%	2002
65	Sudan	0.34%	2003	91	Peru	0.10%	2003
66	Panama	0.34%	2003	92	Paraguay	0.10%	2002
67	Azerbaijan	0.30%	2002	93	Bermuda	0.08%	1997
68	Malta	0.29%	2004	94	El Salvador	0.08%	1998
69	Georgia	0.29%	2002	95	Myanmar	0.07%	2001
70	Bolivia	0.28%	2002	96	Jamaica	0.07%	2002
71	Mongolia	0.28%	2002	97	Ecuador	0.07%	2003
72	Venezuela	0.28%	2003	98	Honduras	0.05%	2003
73	Uruguay	0.26%	2002	99	Nicaragua	0.05%	2002
74	Macedonia	0.26%	2002	100	Indonesia	0.05%	2001
75	Thailand	0.26%	2003	101	Brunei	0.03%	2003
76	Armenia	0.25%	2002	102	Zambia	0.01%	1997
77	Kazakhstan	0.22%	2001	103	Lesotho	0.01%	2002
78	Pakistan	0.22%	2002		Weighted Average	0.90%	2002

EXP = expenditure, R&D = research and development.
Source: World Bank (various years).

5.4. Policy Implications

The foregoing discussion clearly shows that both government and market failures constitute severe constraints to growth, investment, and upscaling of production. This section discusses some policy implications and recommendations to tackle the constraints.

5.4.1. Addressing Government Failures

This chapter pointed out critical government failures that policy makers have to address to stimulate investment and expand trade opportunities. Stakeholder surveys pinpointed the specific areas, which are given in the introductory paragraph to section 5.2.

5.4.2. Avoiding Overvaluation of the Exchange Rate

The strong appreciation of the currency in 2006 and 2007 partly contributed to reduced growth in exports in 2007. The value of imports in 2007 was expected to increase, not only because of the strong peso, but also due to the large world oil price hikes starting in September 2007. It is important to tame the appreciation of the peso. This is a very challenging task given the high inflows of overseas workers' remittances and high portfolio flows into the country. To avoid the currently strong appreciation of the peso, the following is recommended.

Discourage high inflows of short-term capital. Because periodically large portfolio inflows contribute to the sharp appreciation of the peso, the Bangko Sentral ng Pilipinas (BSP)[6] should study ways to discourage excessive short-term capital flows into the country during periods of high confidence in the economy and excessive outflows during periods of low confidence or external shocks. The Thai experiment of trying to tax short-term inflows was short-lived because it led to a plunge in the stock market, which frightened the authorities. The problem is that it is easy to liberalize the capital account but very difficult to reverse it. Given the significant capital account liberalization in the 1990s, policy makers should slow further liberalization. For example, BSP can simply maintain the current policy on the maximum amount of foreign currency allowed into the country in any one transaction. Over and beyond this ceiling, BSP permission is required for foreign currency entry.

---

[6]   BSP is the Philippines' central bank.

Consider taxing short-term capital inflows. Another policy to consider is taxing short-term capital inflow. This may cause an initial massive plunge in the stock market, but the plunge may be short-lived (as happened in Malaysia in 1998). This chapter recommends that, before any drastic policy decision is made, a rigorous study should be completed of possible market-based capital controls, e.g., taxation of short-term capital inflows, the imposition of required reserves for short-term capital flows, and their corresponding impact on the financial and external sectors. This is to ensure that productive long-term capital flows (e.g., beneficial foreign direct investment) will not be unduly harmed as investors facing the prospect of capital controls, albeit market-based, start to lose confidence in the economy. Because capital controls may cause financial instability, especially in the stock market, taxing short-term capital flows ("hot money") could be proposed as regional or international policy backed by many developing economies and tolerated by the powerful multilateral agencies and developed economies. A regional policy supported by stakeholders (developing and developed economies, multilateral agencies, and bilateral fund providers) will signify approval for countries planning to impose some form of taxation on short-term inflows in order to avoid volatility in the exchange markets.

Allow more capital outflows. BSP is now liberalizing the capital account by allowing more capital outflows and relaxing the maximum amount of foreign exchange allowed to flow out of the country in order to tame the net inflows from workers' remittances and portfolio inflows. In 2007, BSP substantially increased the maximum amount that local companies may invest overseas using foreign exchange from the banking system. It has also been considering relaxing the restrictions on banks' overseas investments of mutual funds, pension funds, and unit investment trust funds. But this policy may not be effective in view of recent large capital outflows from residents. However, these outflows pale in comparison to the overseas workers' remittances and portfolio inflows during periods of optimism. Thus, some form of market-based capital control on "hot money" should be considered, but cautiously, as suggested above.

Relax the maximum allowable foreign exchange purchase. In April 2007, BSP also relaxed the maximum amount of foreign exchange that individuals and banks may purchase. It is recommended that BSP explore asymmetric maximum limits, relaxing the limits of foreign exchange purchases but tightening the limits of sales (or limiting the maximum for a single transaction when converting foreign currency to the peso). This would hamper speculation on the peso, which is now rampant because multinational banks and multilateral institutions are predicting significant strengthening of the peso over the short and medium term.

5.4.3. Improving and Linking Research and Development with Industries, and Linking Universities with Industries to Address Training Externalities

The negligible attention to R&D reduces the country's chances of successfully joining the march toward high growth. A strong focus on R&D will enable the country to lock in high value addition and products with increasing returns to scale, as explained by endogenous growth theories. The government should increase the focus on and resources for practical R&D to support industries in enhancing their technologies and improving the range and quality of their products. By the same token, linking industries with universities is crucial in view of the training externality. University links to the human capital needs of particular industries and sectors could solve the training externality problem.

The National Innovation Summit in 2007 that sought to achieve an effective national innovative system is a step in the right direction. The system includes support and direction from academe in designing new curricula to enhance the quality of education in order to meet emerging and new global standards. The system also includes measures to counter the "invisible brain drain," wherein the work of local inventors is licensed and patented in other countries. The plan also includes strong domestic protection of indigenous intellectual property rights.

Public–private partnership in strengthening R&D and science and technology for industrial upscaling is commendable. However, this requires the government to commit more resources to R&D activities, which means increasing budgetary allocation for R&D from 0.11% of GDP to perhaps four times that figure. In addition, public and academic activities in R&D need to be consistent with the actual needs of industries. This requires a strong commitment from the National Economic and Development Authority, Department of Trade and Industry, science and technology agencies, private industries, and academic sectors to work together for the achievement of this goal. Unfortunately, the national innovative system plan lacks the important participation of the National Economic and Development Authority and Department of Trade and Industry, and the strong backing of the legislative branch and the Office of the President.

5.4.4. Upgrading the Technology and Scale of the Domestic Economy

Perhaps the most controversial and difficult task is formulating and enacting the needed policies. Panel data regression shows that, to achieve this, the country must (i) avoid overvaluing the currency, (ii) increase the investment rate, and (iii) increase spending on R&D. The more controversial question is, after achieving the above, should the country leave achieving the technological and scale upgrading to the market or be proactive? The endogenous growth literature (Hausmann and Rodrik 2006; Murphy, Shleifer, and Vishny 1989) indicate the need for the state to be proactive in solving coordination failures and setting up complementary inputs and legal and physical infrastructure of potentially dynamic sectors, especially those with positive externality spillover. The state must also actively give economic incentives for "first movers" to undertake risky innovation and engage in new activities with high positive externalities and information spillovers. Economic incentives will encourage entry into technology and knowledge-intensive areas that exhibit increasing returns to scale. Most of the group 4 economic sectors (see section 5.2) that will lead to much higher economic growth belong to these technology- and knowledge-intensive areas.

In the Philippine context, the challenge facing policy makers in electronics and semiconductor industries is how to increase the value-added contribution and to be less import-intensive. Table 5.3 indicates possibilities to improve the production and export of scientific instruments, whose exports have been increasing slowly in recent years. The rapid increase in business process outsourcing should also be able to have stronger backward integration, especially to the telecommunications and information and communications technology sectors.

A noteworthy development is the rapid rise of business process outsourcing in the country. Outsourcing has important links with telecommunications and with information and communications technology, creating opportunities to expand other value-added services (e.g., call centers, computerized fashion design, motion pictures, and software development).

Many sectors included in the government's Investment Priority Plan enjoy generous fiscal incentives, which exacerbates the country's narrow fiscal space. In consultation with the private sector, the list could be trimmed to a few industries with the greatest potential for upscaling, employment generation, and higher value added. In addition, economic incentives, e.g., tax rebates to successful innovators, could be given upon proof that the innovation leads to technology and scale upgrading. Tax incentives should be given based on transparent performance indicators.

Hausmann and Rodrik (2006) may be correct that proactive state incentives will promote technological and scale upgrade of the economy. They also point out that a wise, efficient, honest, transparent, and relatively autonomous state is required to properly handle market and coordination failures. Government interventions cannot be arbitrary and biased. Hausmann and Rodrik (2006) provide guidelines. Interventions are only justified when enough information is available to provide a reasonable probability of success of the targeted industry. The processes and criteria for deciding whether to grant economic incentives to a sector or beneficiaries should be open and transparent, and include time limits.

This chapter tried to show how market and government failures have constrained the growth of investments and the expansion of the tradable sector. Addressing market failures works best when government failures are minimized. Clearly, efficient government is indispensable whether for expanding fiscal space, orchestrating the appropriate monetary and exchange rate policies, or stimulating technology and scale upgrade of export and domestic manufacturing industries.

Appendix 5.A: Global Competitiveness Indexes for the Philippines, 2007–2008

Rank (among 131 countries/economies)		Score (maximum = 7)
Global Competitiveness Index 2007–2008	71	3.99
Global Competitiveness Index 2006–2007 (of 122)	75	3.98
Subindex A: Basic Requirements (2007–2008)	93	3.99
1st Pillar: Institutions	95	3.42
2nd Pillar: Infrastructure	94	2.70
3rd Pillar: Macroeconomic stability	77	4.70
4th Pillar: Health and primary education	86	5.16
Subindex B: Efficiency Enhancers (2007–2008)	60	4.03
5th Pillar : Higher education and training	62	4.02
6th Pillar: Goods market efficiency	64	4.19
7th Pillar: Labor market efficiency	100	4.05
8th Pillar: Financial market sophistication	77	4.06
9th Pillar: Technological readiness	69	3.07
10th Pillar: market size	24	4.77
Subindex C: Innovation and Sophistication Factors (2007–2008)	65	3.61
11th Pillar: Business sophistication	55	4.20
12th Pillar: Innovation	79	3.03
Rank (among 131 countries and economies)		
Business Competitiveness Index 2007–2008	66	
Sophistication of Company Operations and Strategy	46	
Quality of National Business Environment	73	

Source: WEF (2007).

Appendix 5.B: Regressions of Exports and Imports

Regression of Log of Real Exports at 1985 Prices

lnexpr85	Coeff	Std. Err.	t	P>l t l	[95% Conf. Interval]	
lnexpwifs	0.4227	0.0779	5.42	0.000	0.2663	0.5791
lnexchrt	0.1862	0.0929	2.01	0.050	–0.0001	0.3726
Dummy	0.1687	0.0719	2.35	0.023	0.0245	0.3128
Constant	5.4919	0.9719	5.65	0.000	3.5415	7.4422

Rho = 0.87217

Durbin-Watson Statistic (original) = 0.42635

D-W Statistic (transformed) = 1.78814

			Number of obs	=	56
			F (3, 26)	=	32.64

Source	SS	df	MS	Pro > F	=	0.000
Model	0.89258	3	0.29753	R-Squared	=	0.6531
Residual	0.47403	52	0.00912	Adj R-squared	=	0.6331
Total	1.36660	55	0.02485	Root MSE	=	0.0955

where
lnexpr85 = log of exports of goods and services, 1985 prices
lnexpwifs = world exports in US$, derived from *International Financial Statistics* (IMF 2007).
lnexchrt = log of exchange rate
Dummy   = dummy for trade liberalization period 1988 to 1997

Regression of First Difference of Log of Imports in 1985 Prices

D.lnimpr85	Coeff	Std. Err.	t	P>l t l	[95% Conf. Interval]	
D.lnexchrt	-0.2315	0.1338	-1.73	0.089	-0.4998	0.0368
D.lngdpr85	1.1795	0.1660	7.11	0.000	0.8468	1.5123
D.lnpimp_pgdp	-0.6436	0.1760	-3.66	0.001	-0.9965	-0.2908
Constant	0.0117	0.0188	0.63	0.534	-0.0259	0.0494

Durbin-Watson d-Statistic (4, 58) = 1.64950

				Number of obs	=	58
				F (3, 26)	=	20.90
Source	SS	df	MS	Pro > F	=	0.0000
Model	0.93811	3	0.31270	R-Squared	=	0.5373
Residual	0.80794	54	0.01496	Adj R-squared	=	0.5116
Total	1.74605	57	0.03063	Root MSE	=	0.1223

where
D.lnimpr85   = first difference of log of imports of goods and services, 1985 prices
D.lnexchrt   = first difference of peso exchange rate (average of period)
D.lngdpr85   = first difference in the log of gross domestic product (GDP),
                 real 1985 prices
D.lnpimp_pgdp = first difference of log of price of imports ratio to GDP price deflator

The domestic price of imports vis-à-vis the GDP price deflator is heavily affected by the exchange rate since the domestic price of imports is given by the following equation:

Pimp = (exchange rate * border price of imports in $) * (1 + tariff rate)

Appendix 5.C: Composition of Philippine Merchandise Exports

Merchandise Exports	PRODY Score	Percent of Total Merchandise Exports								
		1970	1975	1980	1985	1990	1995	2000	2005	2006
Medicinal and Pharmaceutical Products	19,059	0.13	0.10	0.11	0.15	0.09	0.11	0.05	0.07	0.07
Scientific and Control Instruments, Photo Goods, Clocks	18,091	0.00	0.05	0.48	0.13	0.21	0.35	1.30	2.41	2.32
Machinery, Other than Electric	14,751	0.06	0.32	0.26	0.30	1.14	2.94	20.24	20.10	18.50
Plastic Materials	14,604	0.00	0.18	0.21	0.37	0.40	0.27	0.20	0.29	0.28
Chemical Materials and Products, nes	14,487	0.04	0.29	0.24	0.35	0.30	0.22	0.14	0.14	0.12
Paper, Paperboard, and Manufactures Thereof	13,997	0.03	0.03	0.01	0.02	0.18	0.32	0.24	0.27	0.29
Coin, Other than Gold, not Legal Tender	13,466	0.07	0.00	0.00	0.03	0.00	0.00	0.00	0.00	0.00
Pulp and Paper	13,423	0.06	0.09	0.15	0.29	0.26	0.19	0.10	0.13	0.11
Electrical Machinery, Apparatus, and Appliances	12,226	0.05	6.11	17.24	36.31	41.94	56.58	54.06	48.95	47.61
Dyeing, Tanning, and Coloring Materials	12,121	0.03	0.05	0.02	0.01	0.02	0.05	0.03	0.04	0.04
Transport Equipment	11,984	0.01	0.13	0.66	0.49	0.71	1.40	1.93	5.09	4.02
Rubber Manufactures, nes	11,969	0.01	0.03	0.01	0.03	0.15	0.12	0.21	0.27	0.38
Miscellaneous Manufactured Articles, nes	11,930	0.41	2.33	2.52	2.90	3.96	3.22	1.56	1.42	1.45

continued on next page

Appendix 5.C (continued)

Merchandise Exports	PRODY Score	Percent of Total Merchandise Exports								
		1970	1975	1980	1985	1990	1995	2000	2005	2006
Dairy Products and Eggs	10,774	0.02	0.03	0.04	0.01	0.01	0.00	0.03	0.19	0.19
Chemical Elements and Compounds	10,611	0.26	0.28	0.90	1.52	1.29	0.33	0.23	0.31	0.62
Manufactures of Metal, nes	10,356	0.02	0.07	0.32	0.17	0.23	0.36	0.40	0.35	0.42
Gas, Natural and Manufactured	10,348	0.03	0.00	0.03	0.31	0.60	0.63	0.18	0.08	0.10
Sanitary, Plumbing, Heating, and Lighting Fixtures	10,301	0.07	0.08	0.06	0.04	0.06	0.10	0.13	0.11	0.40
Iron and Steel	9,383	1.09	0.08	0.84	0.87	0.94	0.35	0.09	0.30	0.57
Electric Energy	9,213	0.00	0.00	0.00	0.00	0.00	0.00	0.00	0.00	0.00
Travel Goods, Handbags, and Similar Articles	9,134	0.08	0.46	0.16	0.21	0.53	0.64	0.73	0.18	0.22
Meat and Meat Preparations	9,072	0.00	0.00	0.03	0.01	0.01	0.00	0.00	0.02	0.01
Nonferrous Metals	8,888	0.13	1.66	2.49	5.25	3.55	2.58	0.86	1.18	2.95
Miscellaneous Food Preparations	8,744	0.07	0.07	0.07	0.16	0.20	0.15	0.13	0.16	0.14
Perfume Materials, Toilet and Cleansing Preparations	8,261	0.02	0.06	0.05	0.12	0.18	0.22	0.10	0.20	0.22
Coal, Coke, and Briquettes	8,260	0.00	0.00	0.00	0.00	0.00	0.00	0.00	0.00	0.00
Furniture	8,142	0.13	0.23	1.33	1.81	2.31	1.60	1.01	0.74	0.59
Explosives and Pyrotechnic Products	7,850	0.00	0.04	0.03	0.06	0.08	0.03	0.02	0.02	0.02

continued on next page

Appendix 5.C (continued)

Merchandise Exports	PRODY Score	Percent of Total Merchandise Exports									
		1970	1975	1980	1985	1990	1995	2000	2005	2006
Textile Yarn, Fabrics, Made-Up Articles	7,065	0.51	1.01	1.29	0.83	1.12	1.19	0.77	0.65	0.50
Wood and Cork Manufactures, Excluding Furniture	6,957	4.07	2.70	3.22	2.42	2.36	0.89	0.59	0.39	1.42
Feedstuff for Animals, Excluding Unmilled Cereals	6,898	1.71	1.54	1.47	0.82	0.69	0.47	0.08	0.08	0.08
Fish and Fish Preparations	6,757	0.19	0.74	2.39	3.21	4.83	2.91	1.06	0.84	0.82
Nonmetallic Mineral Manufactures, nes	6,735	0.31	1.47	1.04	0.51	0.69	0.63	0.53	0.99	1.22
Crude Chemicals from Coal, Petroleum, and Gas	6,363	0.00	0.00	0.00	0.16	0.00	0.00	0.00	0.00	0.00
Hides, Skins and Fur Skins, Undressed	6,332	0.02	0.01	0.01	0.00	0.00	0.00	0.00	0.01	0.01
Petroleum and Petroleum Products	6,074	1.60	1.69	0.84	0.43	1.60	0.89	1.15	1.80	2.22
Footwear	5,635	0.10	0.14	1.16	0.84	0.95	0.89	0.20	0.06	0.05
Crude Animal and Vegetable Materials, nes	5,623	0.25	0.28	0.27	0.53	0.76	0.54	0.24	0.20	0.17
Cereals and Cereal Preparations	5,116	0.05	0.04	1.37	0.12	0.12	0.15	0.10	0.19	0.19
Fertilizers, Manufactured	4,762	0.03	0.00	0.01	0.72	0.88	0.70	0.12	0.22	0.18
Leather, Leather Manufactures, nes, and Dressed Fur Skins	4,614	0.00	0.02	0.01	0.03	0.08	0.03	0.02	0.01	0.01

continued on next page

Appendix 5.C (continued)

Merchandise Exports	PRODY Score	Percent of Total Merchandise Exports								
		1970	1975	1980	1985	1990	1995	2000	2005	2006
Wood, Lumber, and Cork	4,503	23.83	8.84	4.89	3.16	0.41	0.16	0.11	0.04	0.05
Animals, nes, including Zoo Animals, Dogs, and Cats	4,281	0.00	0.00	0.01	0.02	0.01	0.01	0.00	0.00	0.00
Live Animals	4,243	0.00	0.01	0.00	0.01	0.00	0.00	0.00	0.01	0.00
Firearms of War and Ammunition Therefor	4,232	0.00	0.00	0.00	0.00	0.01	0.00	0.00	0.00	0.01
Tobacco and Tobacco Manufactures	4,172	1.33	1.56	0.52	0.61	0.60	0.16	0.10	0.35	0.29
Beverages	4,154	0.12	0.06	0.03	0.05	0.11	0.08	0.03	0.11	0.09
Fruit and Vegetables	4,091	5.04	6.94	6.34	7.65	5.16	3.37	1.72	2.13	2.04
Crude Rubber, including Synthetic and Reclaimed	4,015	0.02	0.03	0.15	0.21	0.14	0.16	0.04	0.09	0.10
Animal and Vegetable Oils and Fats, Processed	3,943	0.01	0.04	0.04	0.43	0.15	0.10	0.03	0.08	0.07
Clothing	3,916	0.04	1.49	4.82	5.71	8.32	6.36	6.81	5.66	5.68
Metalliferous Ores and Metal Scrap	3,297	20.76	11.54	17.91	5.26	4.42	1.64	0.72	1.03	1.47
Crude Fertilizers and Crude Minerals, nes	3,013	0.10	0.04	0.08	0.10	0.13	0.09	0.05	0.05	0.04
Sugar, Sugar Preparations, and Honey	2,690	18.67	27.78	11.38	4.09	1.74	0.51	0.22	0.27	0.29
Fixed Vegetable Oils and Fats	2,652	9.21	10.40	9.80	7.53	4.42	4.79	1.23	1.60	1.23
Oil Seeds, Oil Nuts, and Oil Kernels	2,365	7.56	7.85	0.96	0.15	0.28	0.08	0.00	0.00	0.00

continued on next page

Appendix 5.C (continued)

Merchandise Exports	PRODY Score	Percent of Total Merchandise Exports									
		1970	1975	1980	1985	1990	1995	2000	2005	2006
Textile Fibers Not Manufactured and Waste	1,858	1.60	0.72	0.56	0.68	0.27	0.21	0.07	0.08	0.08
Coffee, Tea, Cocoa, Spices, and Manufactures	1,297	0.04	0.21	1.13	1.76	0.36	0.18	0.03	0.03	0.02
EXPY Score: Philippines		**3,884**	**4,598**	**6,168**	**8,202**	**9,034**	**10,239**	**11,470**	**11,457**	**11,271**

EXPY = a measure of the quality of a country's exports, nes = not elsewhere specified, PRODY = an export commodity-specific index measuring the sophistication of the export commodity.
Source: Calculated from UN Comtrade Database, SITC Revision-1, 2-digit codes.

Appendix 5.D: Panel Data Analysis of Output Per Capita of High-Technology and High-Scale Products (Group 4)

Random-effects GLS regression			Number of observations		=	76
Group variable (i) : cntry			Number of groups		=	4

R-sq:	within	=	0.5825	Observations per group: min	=	19
	between	=	0.9896	avg	=	19
	overall	=	0.9457	max	=	19

Random effects u_i ~ Gaussian	Wald chi^2(4)	=	1237.43
Correlation (u_i, X) = 0 (assumed)	Probability > chi^2	=	0.0000

Lnmfgr4	Coeff	Std. Err.	z	P>| z |	[95% Conf. Interval]	
Incapusd	0.1867	0.0930	2.01	0.045	0.0043	0.3690
Ingfcf	1.0438	0.1613	6.47	0.000	0.7277	1.3600
Inreer	-2.6133	0.2508	-10.42	0.000	-3.1049	-2.1218
Inrnd	0.3938	0.0920	4.28	0.000	0.2134	0.5742
Constant	17.3218	1.1535	15.02	0.000	15.0610	19.5826

Sigma_u	=	0	
Sigma_e	=	0.18278	
Rho	=	0	*(fraction of variance due to U-I)*

Where:
lnmfgr4	=	logarithm of per capita value-added output of manufacturing subgroup 4 in 2000 US$
lnpcapusd	=	logarithm of gross domestic product (GDP) per capita in 2000 $
lngfcf	=	logarithm of share of gross fixed capital formation to GDP
lnreer	=	logarithm of real effective exchange rate (2000 = 100) using JP Morgan data reported in *International Financial Statistics* (IMF 2007)
lnrnd	=	logarithm of average of research and development expenditures as percent of GDP for available years from the World Bank (various years) *World Development Indicators* (one value for each country)

References

American Chamber of Commerce. 2006. *Business Outlook Survey: Philippines*. Makati.

Asian Development Bank (ADB). various years. *Key Indicators*. Manila. www.adb.org/Documents/Books/Key_Indicators/

_____. n.d. *Statistical Database System*. https://sdbs.adb.org/sdbs/index .jsp (accessed October 2007)

Asian Development Bank and World Bank (ADB–World Bank). 2003. *Investment Climate and Productivity Survey*. Manila: ADB.

_____. 2005. *Improving the Investment Climate in the Philippines*. Manila.

Becker, G. 1975. *Human Capital*. 2nd edition. Chicago: University of Chicago.

Hausmann, R., J. Hwang, and D. Rodrik. 2006. What You Export Matters. NBER Working Paper No. 11905. Cambridge, MA: National Bureau of Economic Research.

Hausmann, R., and D. Rodrik. 2006. Doomed to Choose: Industrial Policy as Predicament. Paper prepared for the Blue Sky Seminar of the Center for International Development at Harvard University. Cambridge, MA. 9 September.

Hausmann, R., D. Rodrik, and A. Velasco. 2005. *Growth Diagnostics*. http:// ksghome.harvard.edu/~drodrik/barcelonafinalmarch2005.pdf

International Monetary Fund (IMF). 2007. *International Financial Statistics*. www.imfstatistics.org/imf/about/asp

Kaldor, N. 1966. *Causes of the Slow Rate of Economic Growth of the UK. An Inaugural Lecture*. Cambridge: Cambridge University Press.

Makati Business Club (MBC). 2007. *Executive Outlook Survey*. Makati.

Murphy, K. M., A. Shleifer, and R. W. Vishny. 1989. Industrialization and the Big Push. *Journal of Political Economy*. 97(5): 1003–26.

National Statistics (Taipei,China). http://eng.stat.gov.tw/mp.asp?mp=5

National Statistical Coordination Board (NSCB). various years. *National Accounts of the Philippines*. www.nscb.gov.ph/sna/default.asp

United Nations Commodity Trade Statistics Database (UN Comtrade Database). http://comtrade.un.org/db/dqBasicQuery.aspx

World Bank. various years. *World Development Indicators*. www.worldbank .org/data/

World Economic Forum (WEF). 2007. *Global Competitiveness Report: 2007–2008*. www.gcr.weforum.org/

6. Infrastructure

Gilbert M. Llanto

6.1. Introduction

The importance of infrastructure for developing countries cannot be overstated—it is a major driver for growth and poverty reduction. For example, the lack of adequate transport, water, and energy facilities can adversely affect the development of existing industries and may preclude new entrants. An efficient transport and communication infrastructure provides overall mobility for goods and people alike, contributes to reducing input and transaction costs, and enhances the efficiency of markets. Local infrastructure, which may have significant spillover effects, spurs local economic activities while the network characteristics of infrastructure enhance the connectivity of regions and promote domestic integration. The key role of infrastructure in economic growth cannot be overstated. A recent joint study substantiates the decisive role that infrastructure has played in growth and poverty reduction in East Asia and the Pacific (ADB, JBIC, and World Bank 2005).

This chapter takes off from sources-of-growth studies in which application of the growth diagnostic framework points to the possibility that inadequate infrastructure is constraining economic growth. This chapter analyzes specific factors responsible for the lack of infrastructure and then provides policy recommendations to help overcome those constraints. It attempts to provide an empirical basis for the often-claimed key role of infrastructure in fostering economic growth. Thus, the chapter investigates whether poor infrastructure acts as a binding constraint to economic growth. The basis for the popular claim that infrastructure matters to economic growth seems to be anecdotal and founded more on conviction than on empirical analysis. Given the current enthusiasm for evidence-based policy making, empirical analysis assumes practical relevance.

Infrastructure in the Philippines has not kept pace with the requirements of a growing economy, the increase in population, and rising urbanization. The Philippines has not provided infrastructure that is sufficient in quantity and quality to meet global economic challenges as well as poverty reduction goals under such international commitments as the Millennium Development Goals (MDGs). Both the Asian Development Bank (ADB) and the World Bank have noted the negative impact of low-quality infrastructure on the Philippines' global competitiveness. In 2003–2004, the World

Economic Forum's Global Competitiveness Index ranked the Philippines 66th out of 102 countries, partly because of the poor state of Philippine infrastructure (WEF 2004). In terms of overall infrastructure quality (Figure 6.1),[1] the Philippines ranked 88th (out of 125 countries) in the 2006 Global Competitiveness Index, slightly improving from 89th in 2004 (WEF 2006). In terms of adequacy of infrastructure,[2] the Philippines slid to 51st in 2007 (out of 61 countries) from 49th in 2006 according to the 2007 World Competitiveness Yearbook (IMD 2007). Among the countries of the Association of Southeast Asian Nations (ASEAN), however, the Philippines is not far behind Thailand (48th, 2007) and is slightly ahead of Indonesia (54th, 2007). The state of a country's infrastructure is a key determinant of its competitiveness ranking.

Rapid urbanization has swelled the ranks of the urban poor and has created a tremendous demand for housing and social services, secured land tenure, and serviced land, which to a great extent has remained unsatisfied.[3] Access to social services, such as water supply and sanitation and solid waste management, is declining both in terms of coverage and quality. The deteriorating coverage and lack of quality of infrastructure and service delivery are widely considered to be impediments to growth and poverty reduction.

Since the 1997 Asian financial crisis, infrastructure investment has dropped from a peak of 8.5% of gross domestic product (GDP) in 1998 to only 2.8% in 2002. The funding community has advised the government to increase infrastructure investments to at least 5% of GDP, the average infrastructure investment norm of its neighboring countries in the last decade. The government has recognized the constraining effect

---

[1] Overall infrastructure quality is measured in terms of (i) railroad infrastructure development, (ii) quality of port infrastructure, (iii) quality of air transport infrastructure, and (iv) quality of electricity supply and telephone lines.

[2] Adequacy of infrastructure is measured in terms of the extent to which basic, technological, scientific, and human infrastructure resources meet the needs of business.

[3] The Housing and Urban Development Coordinating Council estimates that the Philippine population will increase from 80 million in 2002 to 98.2 million by 2015. The country has one of the highest urbanization rates in the world, with an average urbanization growth rate of 5.1% during 1960–1995. More than half of the population is in urban areas, and this proportion is expected to reach 60% by 2010 if current trends continue. While official data indicate that only about 20% of the 7.5 million urban households fall below the poverty income line (P13,915 per capita per year as of 2001), the poverty income line alone does not capture the dire situation of informal settlers (Llanto 2007a).

Figure 6.1: Infrastructure Rankings, 2006–2007

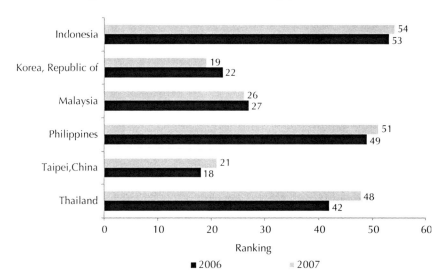

Source: IMD (2007).

of poor infrastructure on economic growth and development and has prioritized the removal of this serious bottleneck. The Medium-Term Philippine Development Plan for 2004–2010 provided broad strategies and identified key infrastructure to be completed or provided by the end of the plan period (NEDA 2004). It stressed the importance of connectivity in an archipelagic economy through good transport and communications networks. The connectivity provided by good infrastructure facilities is expected to open new economic opportunities, reduce transport and transaction costs of doing business, and increase access to social services. The interconnection will also strengthen the socioeconomic, cultural, and political links between and among regions. Eventually, connectivity will decentralize progress and bring development to the countryside.

After this introduction, the succeeding section briefly reviews the theory of and evidence on the impact of infrastructure on economic growth, which helps to shape understanding of the relevant questions pertaining to the link between infrastructure and growth. Section 6.3 reports the results of the empirical tests and draws out their policy implications. Section 6.4 concludes and suggests some policy recommendations.

6.2. Links between Infrastructure and Economic Growth

A diagnostic approach to economic growth identifies a narrow range of factors believed to constrain growth and provides a means of ordering policy priorities given scarce political capital for reform. Economists who give policy advice to developing countries often encounter problems prioritizing the policy reforms that matter most for growth. A wide ranging policy reform program may have less likelihood of success than a more focused and nuanced policy reform strategy. A growth diagnostics framework (Figure 1.1, Chapter 1) applied to the Philippine economy identified weak infrastructure as a constraint to growth and poverty reduction.

A review of recent literature shows the strong link between infrastructure and economic growth. Empirical studies testing the public capital hypothesis indicated that infrastructure has a positive and significant impact on growth and productivity. A pioneering study by Aschauer (1989) argued that the general decline in productivity growth in the United States might be due to a reduction in public capital investments. The early studies triggered a flurry of empirical tests on the link between infrastructure and economic growth that used various econometric models and estimation techniques, (e.g., fixed and random state effects, and different approaches to data measurement) and introduced variables believed to have an impact on growth, other than infrastructure variables. Summarizing the results of the estimates, Gramlich (1994) and Sturm, Kuper, and de Haan (1996) found output elasticities with respect to public capital of about 0.3. Other economists noted that the estimated output elasticities were implausibly high.[4] The estimates of Wang (2002) for seven East Asian countries for 1979–1998 indicated an average elasticity of 0.2% of private production to a 1% increase in public capital.

A different view was that, while there is a definite link between infrastructure investment and economic growth, the causality in either direction had not been established. Thus, physical infrastructure can be regarded as a form of "complementary capital" that requires productive capital (whether physical or human) for investment (and innovation) in order to realize the economic growth potential. Infrastructure can only develop, not create, economic potential—but only where conditions are appropriate (O'Fallon 2003). However, notwithstanding the lively debate among researchers on the link between infrastructure and growth, the preponderance of empirical evidence shows that inadequate or unreliable infrastructure may constrain investments of productive capital and lead to a restriction or reduction of output. Much evidence supports the view that infrastructure has signifi-

---

[4]   Sturm, Jacobs, and Groote (1999) mentioned the criticisms of Aaron (1990), Hulten and
       Schwab (1991), and Munnell (1992).

cant impacts on productivity and growth (Rodriguez 2006). Researchers investigating what type of public capital would have a significant impact on growth found that public transport, telecommunications, and electricity generation were positively correlated with growth. The majority of studies trying to establish a link between (public) investments or capital and economic growth indicate that (i) public capital is complementary and promotes private capital formation; (ii) core infrastructure, such as roads and railways, tend to have the most impact on productivity; and (iii) the direction of causation is from public capital to productivity and not the other way around (Infrastructure Canada 2007). An interesting observation is that infrastructure investments may also be defended on equity grounds, because interregional infrastructure increases the accessibility of peripheral regions and raises their level of competitiveness. This could help stop the process of regional divergence (Rosik 2006). On balance, empirical evidence shows infrastructure provision as having a significant impact on living standards and productivity.

6.3. Empirical Findings and Policy Implications

The brief overview of recent literature on the link between infrastructure and growth motivates a discussion of several questions.[5] This section reports the empirical findings and essays a few policy implications.

6.3.1. Four Enquiries

Is infrastructure a significant determinant of economic growth? This query relates to the public capital hypothesis, which says that higher infrastructure investment will lead to higher growth in the economy. Granger causality tests were used to establish whether public infrastructure capital has a link to or impact on economic growth and productivity. A Cobb-Douglas production function model with real GDP as a left-hand side variable and various types of infrastructure as right-hand side variables was then estimated. Statistical tests were used to determine the impact of aggregate public infrastructure investments on the level and growth of real GDP.[6]

---

[5] Severe data constraints currently limit the extent of empirical testing that may be practicable.

[6] The tests used varying specifications and data measurement. The tests were done at growth at the aggregative level (real GDP), gross regional domestic product, and different measures of infrastructure investments.

Pair-wise Granger causality tests rejected the null hypothesis that infrastructure does not Granger-cause growth. Causality is bidirectional, but the direction running from infrastructure to economic growth showed the higher level of significance. The empirical results of a production function model using time series data support a positive relationship between public infrastructure capital and economic growth. Empirical tests using measures of infrastructure capital (such as national and local government infrastructure expenditure, and national and local government budgetary outlay for infrastructure) show a significant relationship between these infrastructure variables and economic growth. Of particular interest is the significant impact of the capital utilization variable. Both public infrastructure capital and capacity utilization are important determinants of economic growth or output. The regression results show that, while there is a positive and significant link between output and infrastructure (electricity and telecommunications), the way that the stock of capital (which includes infrastructure) was used has a more significant impact on output. It is conceivable that high capacity utilization is correlated with high growth in output.

The results of the empirical tests confirm earlier findings that poor infrastructure and the lack of infrastructure investment have constrained growth (Llanto 2004). Reviewing the past 25 years of infrastructure development in the country, Llanto indicated that the Philippines was failing to make substantial investments in transport, ports and shipping, and communications, thereby weakening its ability to compete on a global basis. The World Bank (2005) drew attention to the problem, noting that "infrastructure deployment has not kept up with high population growth and rapid urbanization, with serious consequences for the country's competitiveness and in particular for its growth and poverty reduction targets..." In sum, empirical results using both a production function approach and Granger causality tests showed the robust relationship between economic growth and infrastructure.[7]

What is the impact of infrastructure on regional growth? Regions with high infrastructure investments tend to have higher economic growth than regions with low infrastructure investments, as shown by Basilio and Gundaya (1997), Manasan and Chatterjee (2003), Manasan and Mercado (1999), and Reyes (2002). Reyes (2002) confirmed that the regions with the lowest gross regional domestic product (GRDP) are also those suffering from the most severe lack of basic infrastructure. As measured by contribution to GRDP, in 2000 the country's richest region, the

---

[7]   These results are consistent with the findings of other studies reported in the brief review of literature.

National Capital Region (NCR), had access to potable water, electricity, sanitary toilet facilities, and road infrastructure that was above the national average. The second-richest region, CALABARZON (Region IV-A), also had above-average access to basic infrastructure, as did the third-richest region, Central Luzon. The country's poorest regions in terms of contribution to GRDP—the Autonomous Region in Muslim Mindanao (ARMM), Cagayan Valley, Caraga (composed of Agusan, Dinagat Islands, and Surigao provinces), and Western Mindanao—also had the least access to basic infrastructure.

Empirical tests by Llanto (2007a) showed that infrastructure has a positive and significant effect on regional growth (incomes). Regional incomes also tend to increase with higher rates of participation in secondary education. Using data on road quality for total road network and local road networks, the empirical tests indicate that the quality of roads has a positive and significant effect on regional growth. The tests show that regional incomes tend to increase with an increase in the quality of road infrastructure, holding the education variable constant. The results of testing for the effects of road density are insignificant, implying perhaps that regional growth depends not only on the availability of roads but also on the quality of the road network.[8]

Llanto's findings are consistent with those of other researchers. The lack of access to adequate infrastructure services and the different levels of infrastructure development have led to differences in regional growth in the Philippines (Lamberte, Alburo, and Patalinghug 2003; Basilio and Gundaya 1997). Empirical work by Manasan and Chatterjee (2003) using total net shift analysis for 14 regions in 1987–2000 indicates a strong correlation between total net shift values and access to infrastructure services. This implies that the richer regions have access to better infrastructure services.

Llanto (2007a) observed that investing in road improvements and the construction of high-quality roads at the regional (local) level, particularly in provinces, municipalities, and the country's smallest administrative divisions—*barangays*—benefits the region more than investments in the national road network alone. This is an important finding in view of the concern about a "missing middle" in the country's road network, referring to the inadequate state of road infrastructure at the provincial level.

---

[8]   Ertekin, Berechman, and Ozbay (2003) examined the impact of accessibility changes on the level of economic development in 18 counties in New Jersey and New York during 1990–2000. They reported that "our model clearly shows that the economic growth is a function of accessibility, among other things, which is related to the transportation system performance measured in terms of travel times." More specifically, they observed that "accessibility is found to have considerable impact on employment growth and total earnings growth value" (p. 21).

The national government takes care of constructing national roads, while cities and municipalities are in charge of local roads. Provinces, however, receive small block grants from the national government and thus have low capacity to construct and maintain provincial roads, hence the issue of a "missing middle" in road infrastructure. This suggests a need to review infrastructure policy at the national and local levels as well as the associated budgetary requirements, especially for network infrastructure such as road networks.

More specifically, returns from infrastructure (road network, energy, ports, etc.) are higher the poorer the region is. The network character of infrastructure and the existence of spillover effects indicate the great importance of infrastructure for regional growth. Hill (2007) stresses that economic development and improved infrastructure and communications systems usually result in more integrated national economies. For example, transport costs fall—relatively if not absolutely—as roads and harbors are constructed. This is important for facilitating labor mobility and for lowering transaction costs, as information on commercial and employment opportunities across regions becomes more accessible to both business and labor. The literature has pointed out that network infrastructure could have important spillover effects, which could be positive or negative, depending on the specific characteristics of regions or areas where the infrastructure is located and the adjoining areas that have access to it. The importance of good infrastructure, such as transport infrastructure in regional development, cannot be overemphasized. An independent organization performed an initial economic impact assessment of the Development Bank of the Philippines' Industrial Restructuring Program, which indicated that the operation of roll-on-roll-off (RORO) transport in the Philippine archipelago had increased transport efficiency, promoted tourism and regional trade, and enhanced agricultural productivity and regional development (CRC 2006).[9]

The importance the government placed on creating efficient transport highways (e.g., linking the road network with the so-called nautical highway using RORO transport systems to interconnect the islands) shows an understanding of the beneficial impacts of network infrastructure. It binds local economies more closely together and works for better domestic integration. The link of the primary road network with secondary roads and with municipal ports is critical for an archipelagic country such as the Philippines to reduce high transport and logistics costs, which have contributed to low productivity and lack of competitiveness of domestic

---

[9] RORO is the interisland movement of land vehicles via seagoing vessels onto which the former are driven.

producers. Missing links in the road and ports infrastructure network create serious bottlenecks to moving people and cargo over island boundaries. An efficient network of road and port infrastructure contributes to overall economic efficiency and has distributive effects as well.

The spillover effects of infrastructure are not self-evident, notwithstanding the intuition that positive externalities may arise from having an efficient infrastructure system (e.g., road infrastructure) that traverses adjoining areas. One would expect a road highway to have positive impacts in the region or area where the highway goes as well as in many neighboring regions or areas. Network infrastructure may help peripheral regions to be better integrated with more developed regions.

The new economic geography models hypothesize that the development of interregional transport infrastructure causes both generative and distributive effects. Negative spillover occurs when rich regions become the main beneficiaries of network infrastructure, and the poor ones are the main losers (Rosik 2006). This happens because both capital and labor locate in regions better endowed with infrastructure and other amenities for economic and business activity. Factor mobility is enhanced by good network transport infrastructure, which may result in poorer areas or regions experiencing decreases in output.[10] This would have been an important aspect of the empirical tests, but because of severe data limitations, the study did not attempt it. Future research should look into this, data permitting.

What type of infrastructure constrains growth? Because the Philippines has a limited financial resource envelope, it will be particularly important to find out which type of infrastructure (e.g., road, energy, water supply, telecommunications) will be binding constraints to economic growth. In a joint survey, ADB–World Bank (2005) identified electricity and transport (among other factors such as macroeconomic instability, corruption, regulatory policy, crime, theft, and disorder) as crucial elements in a good investment climate.

The Philippines has missed substantial private investments because of mediocre infrastructure, which contributes to the high cost of doing business in the country. Based on the World Bank–International Finance Corporation's doing business reports, the Philippines ranked 133rd (of 178 economies) for the year 2007 from 130th (of 175 economies) for 2006,

---

10 In empirical estimates for the United States, Holtz-Eakin and Schwartz (1995) found no evidence of quantitatively significant productivity spillovers, while those of Boarnet (1996) indicate that, in the presence of negative spillovers, the elasticities of output with respect to public capital tend to be smaller.

and 121st (of 155 economies) in 2005 in terms of ease of doing business.[11] The cost of doing business increases with inadequate infrastructure. The effects of inadequate infrastructure were articulated in ADB's 2005 report, which noted the following:

- Of the surveyed firms, 62% rated public infrastructure and services in the Philippines as "somewhat inefficient to very inefficient," particularly due to poor shipping services that lead to a 4.7% loss in production.
- Firms experience delays 5.6% of the time, on the average, when picking up goods for delivery to the domestic market or delivering supplies from the domestic market. Firms in the NCR experience longer delays than those in the CALABARZON, Cebu, and Davao areas, due to greater traffic congestion and inadequate transport network linking the NCR to other regional domestic markets. The proportion of paved roads to total roads indicates less dependable roads that limit transport of goods and access to inputs and markets in a timely manner.
- Of surveyed firms, 54% viewed Philippine public works as unsatisfactory.
- An average of 13 days elapses in order to obtain telephone lines and 10 days to acquire connection to electricity.
- Electricity was considered the most critical concern among business establishments (33%), compared with transport (18%) and telecommunications (10%). Losses owing to power failure amounted, on average, to 8% of production. Power outages hurt small and medium-sized firms most, costing them an equivalent of about 8% and 11% of production, respectively, compared with 6% for large firms.
- Bottlenecks in water supply translate to an average cost of 7% of production, especially in the food and food processing industry.

The empirical tests also considered three types of infrastructure: roads, electricity, and telecommunications. Of these, electricity (for commercial establishments) and telecommunications had a positive and significant im-

---

[11] The ease of doing business index is meant to measure regulations directly affecting businesses and is measured based on the simple average ranking of each of the following subindexes: "starting a business," "dealing with licenses," "employing workers," "registering property," "getting credit," "protecting investors," "paying taxes," "trading across borders," "enforcing contracts," and "closing a business." The index, however, does not account for a country's proximity to large markets, the quality of its infrastructure services (other than services related to trading across borders), the security of property from theft and looting, macroeconomic conditions, or the strength of underlying institutions.

pact on output. This confirmed the results of the 2005 ADB survey, that firms considered electricity to be the most critical concern. While the firms considered telecommunications still problematic, they felt that electricity and transport were the greater issues. The coefficient of the road variable (measured either as road-kilometers or road density), although significant, had the wrong sign (i.e., negative).

Pair-wise Granger causality tests between economic growth and various types of infrastructure showed Granger causality running from infrastructure to real GDP. Similar tests on the People's Republic of China (PRC) and the Republic of Korea showed the same results. Shiu and Lam (2003) found that real GDP and electricity consumption for the PRC were cointegrated, and unidirectional Granger causality ran from electricity consumption to real GDP but not vice versa. On the other hand, for the Republic of Korea, the causality between real GDP and electricity consumption was found to be bidirectional (Yoo 2004).

The results also seem to indicate that different types of infrastructure have different impacts on economic growth. Electricity and telecommunications appear to have a more significant impact on growth than do other types of infrastructure, such as roads. As economic growth becomes more dependent on the output of the service sector, lower-cost electricity and telecommunications infrastructure would be expected to be very critical to economic performance. Cross-border transactions in the service industries done through the internet are increasingly becoming a key source of growth for the Philippines. The country's recent reforms in power and telecommunications are starting to pay off. The greater accessibility of energy and telecommunications services and more competition in these subsectors have contributed to an overall decline in costs, especially in telecommunications; have increased job creation; and have led to a higher level of economic growth—although the price of electricity may still be higher than in neighboring economies.

The tests did not include other types of infrastructure, such as ports, for lack of data. It would be ideal to have data measuring the network characteristic of roads, as, together with ports they constitute the main physical infrastructure linking the islands in an archipelagic setting. Presumably for an archipelagic country such as the Philippines, which depends on maritime transport for the mobility of people and movement of cargo among the islands, inadequate ports and shipping infrastructure may be a principal constraint to economic growth. Limao and Venables (1999) noted that inefficient port infrastructure explains about 40% of predicted maritime transport costs for coastal countries. Clark, Dollar, and Micco (2001) noted that cargo handling accounted for 46% of sea transport costs in the Philippines.

An inadequate road network, which is necessary to link people and markets like ports, could be a major constraint. Different types of infrastructure may not have the same kind of impact on economic growth. For instance, the impact of one type of infrastructure may be localized (i.e., affecting economic activity where it is located, e.g., a local water system). Another type of infrastructure (e.g., network transport infrastructure) may have positive impact in the area where it is located and externalities or spillover effects to other areas. More research on this is needed, but the quality and availability of data would be paramount considerations.

Is infrastructure critical for income convergence between regions? Is there reason to believe that, notwithstanding current income or growth disparities across the regions, there will be convergence over time?[12] Manasan and Mercado (1999) found marked disparities across regions in 1975–1997. Lamberte, Manasan, and Llanto (1993) indicated that the NCR's per capita GRDP was more than twice that of the next richest region, Southern Tagalog, in 1975. However, regional growth disparities declined more rapidly during 1975–1986, although Manasan and Mercado (1999) noted a positive relationship between regional dispersion and the growth rate of GDP. Thus, high levels of economic growth may be accompanied by regional stagnation, slow regional convergence, or even divergence (Cuenca 2004).

Whether there is regional convergence is an interesting question, but it is equally interesting, and perhaps more important, to find out why convergence will or will not happen. It is also interesting to find out whether infrastructure could be a key variable in income convergence or divergence across regions. Cuenca's empirical tests concluded that there is no evidence of absolute convergence among the regions during 1982–2000 and 1985–2000. She found strong and consistent evidence of conditional convergence. Secondary enrollment rate and capital stock have a positive impact on regional growth. Poorer regions grow faster than richer regions in their transition phases, but toward differing steady states of growth.

Thus, if disparities in the level of infrastructure development result in uneven economic growth and income inequality across regions, the regional allocation of infrastructure investments needs improving. The improvement should be aimed at providing opportunity for lagging regions to catch up.

The empirical tests showed that coefficients of the infrastructure variables (road density, energy) have the correct positive sign, but they are

---

[12] Convergence is the reduction of income disparities across regions or countries. It is the tendency of poorer economies to grow faster than richer economies, which results in a reduction of income differential between them (Cuenca 2004).

insignificant. Infant mortality rate, a proxy for the population's health status, has the wrong sign and is not a significant conditioning variable. Only the secondary enrollment rate, a proxy for human capital, is a significant conditioning variable. The finding on enrollment rate validates Cuenca's earlier finding that regions that invest more in education have higher growth. The rate of conditional convergence shown by the coefficient of per capita GRDP ranges from 26% to 28%. Cuenca found a rate of conditional convergence ranging from 24% to 30%. These results indicate the importance of investments in human capital as well as specific types of infrastructure. For the latter, electricity (energy) has consistently come out as a determinant of aggregate output (in the regressions using annual time series) and of regional output (in regressions using panel data for a convergence hypothesis).

Results. Overall, the empirical tests showed the following:

- Infrastructure is a significant determinant of economic growth, and lack of it results in poor growth outcomes. It is a binding constraint to economic growth.
- Regions with better infrastructure tend to have higher economic growth.
- Electricity and telecommunications services are critical factors in economic growth, especially in an economy where the service sector is a strong growth driver.
- Infrastructure and human capital are key conditioning variables in regional convergence. The quality of human capital (soft infrastructure) interacting with hard infrastructure (electricity, telecommunications, and integrated road and port networks) are significant drivers for domestic integration and regional growth.
- The results indicate the importance of investment in human capital (education) and infrastructure in promoting regional growth. Infrastructure development is critical at the subnational level, implying that underinvestment in local infrastructure will have serious consequences for local growth and poverty reduction efforts.

6.3.2. Policy Implications

Poor infrastructure is a binding constraint on economic growth because of its critical importance to private enterprise, the locomotive of growth that is responsible for output and job creation. While infrastructure is not a direct input into the production function, "inadequate supply of infrastructure or unreliability in infrastructure services may inhibit the investment of productive capital, restrict or reduce output" (O'Fallon 2003). For private enterprise to produce output and create jobs, it has to make investments and locate itself where the cost of doing business is relatively low. In Asia, the globalization of private capital (initially Japanese capital and, in the future, Chinese capital) and the drive for competitiveness among firms has led to the unbundling of production processes and cross-border division of labor among a few countries that present the most conducive investment climate. The countries that have absorbed huge investment capital from Japan (primarily Malaysia, Singapore, and Thailand) have one thing in common: very good infrastructure that can be combined with relatively good human capital to produce goods and services. The Philippines may not be a preferred country for investments because of several deterrents, among which poor infrastructure is a major item. The Japan External Trade Organization's survey of Japanese firms' international operations (JETRO 2006) noted that 32.2% of Japanese businesses in the Philippines considered "underdeveloped infrastructure" as a critical bottleneck, as did Japanese respondents in India (57.2%) and Viet Nam (47.9%).[13]

Poor or weak infrastructure has a serious constraining effect on economic growth and poverty reduction. Relative to neighboring countries, the Philippines has performed very poorly in providing this indirect input to growth and productivity and has paid dearly for it in terms of a lower standard of living for the population and generally poor development outcomes, for example, high incidence of poverty relative to other ASEAN countries. That the country has registered modest economic growth in the past few years is not a reason to be complacent about the state of infrastructure. Investments in both human capital and infrastructure will have to be high priority in the development agenda of the government. Future growth will depend on the quality of human and infrastructure capital, especially in lagging regions. Improving the access of the regions to funding for infrastructure should take high priority on the agenda for infrastructure development. Local governments have also underinvested in infrastructure. Manasan (2004) and World Bank (2005) reported that while total infrastructure investments by all local government units (LGUs) combined grew by 6.4% annually during 1990–2001, the ratio of spending by LGUs on infrastructure to their total capital outlays contracted from 59.6% in 1985–1991 to 34.6% in 1992–2002.

---

[13] The Japan External Trade Organization is a Government of Japan-related organization that works to promote mutual trade and investment between Japan and the rest of the world. Originally established in 1958 to promote Japanese exports abroad, the organization is currently promoting foreign direct investment into Japan and helping small to medium-sized Japanese firms maximize their global export potential. The survey covered 729 Japanese companies, of which 177 are doing business in the Philippines. Other major concerns are political and social instability (52.5%) and lack of accumulation of related industries (20.9%).

Because of the importance of transport and other infrastructure in domestic integration and regional convergence, the national government and LGUs should work for better integration and consistency of national, regional, and local infrastructure plans. Policy and planning coordination between the national government and the LGUs in infrastructure development has been poor and ineffective. There is no regional budget allocation system that substantiates regional plans and priorities and supplies an acceptable methodology for ranking interregional priorities (Llanto 2007a). In a review of regional development councils in the Visayas, Llanto and Lasam (2004) found that the councils lacked the political clout to transform regional plans into budgetary allocations. This may be attributed to poor national–regional–local links in planning, programming, and budgeting.

The current inadequate state of infrastructure was the product of years of underinvestment and poor maintenance. The narrow fiscal space has constrained the government's ability to invest in and maintain infrastructure. Relatively low tax effort, inefficiency in project implementation, and reported corruption were principal reasons for the lack of funds for infrastructure. To augment scarce resources, the Philippines has largely relied on official development assistance (ODA) for infrastructure development. However, ODA has been declining, from $13 billion in 2000 to $9 billion in 2006. The most recent *ODA Portfolio Review* reported that infrastructure accounted for $5.5 billion in 2006 (71 loan projects), or 58% of the total ODA loans (NEDA 2007). Of the total, (i) transport received $4.0 billion (42.2%); (ii) energy, power, and electrification, $639 million (6.7%); (iii) water resources, $615 million (6.5%); and (iv) social infrastructure, $199 million (2%). Implementation bottlenecks (Box 6.1) have hampered the efficient use of those funds, resulting in project delays and nonimplementation of projects already approved by both the funding agencies and the government. The government has tried to address the implementation bottlenecks, as reported in the *ODA Portfolio Review*, but has to exert greater effort and political will to remove them completely because they remained unchanged during the 7 years of ODA portfolio reviews (2000–2006).

The Medium Term Philippine development Plan rightly identified the private sector and LGUs as partners in addressing the infrastructure lack. Through build–operate–transfer (BOT) arrangements and other modes of private sector participation, (e.g., concession agreements and management contracts), the government could take advantage of private sector financing and technical and management expertise. Although this strategy was used to solve the energy crisis of the 1990s, the BOT approach faltered after the Asian financial crisis. The government should address a number of issues constraining private sector participation, because the country cannot afford to lose private sector expertise and resources in the quest for

Box 6.1: Bottlenecks in Implementation of Projects Funded by Official Development Assistance

Cost overruns. These are caused by (i) additional civil works (changes in scope, variation orders, and/or supplemental agreements); (ii) increased right-of-way, land acquisition, and/or resettlement costs; (iii) increased unit cost of labor, materials, and equipment; (iv) bids above the budget approved or estimated for the contract; (v) currency exchange rate movement; (vi) increased consultancy services; (vii) increased administrative cost; and (viii) claims for price escalations.

Budget and financing issues. The Philippine Congress' reenactment of the budget for 2006 limited the financing cover for ongoing projects to the 2005 levels. This also meant that no new appropriation was allocated for newly approved projects.

Procurement. Delays in procurement were brought about by (i) lengthy review process, (ii) restraining orders filed by losing bidders, (iii) suspended bidding proceedings due to bidders contesting them and/or delayed approval by the financing institution, and (iv) failed bidding and rebidding of contracts.

Right-of-way and land acquisition. Right-of-way and land acquisition bottlenecks remain a major issue due to (i) delayed judicial action on the titling of acquired properties; (ii) unresolved issues on land ownership; (iii) relocation sites being no longer available; (iv) new squatters occupying cleared areas; and (v) change in local government leadership, priorities, and commitments.

Local government issues. The capacity of local government units (LGUs) to provide the counterpart funding required for projects continues to be a problem. Other LGU issues include the limited technical capability of some LGUs, particularly those in the lower income bracket, and changes in LGU leadership, priorities, and commitments.

Contractor performance. Poor performance of contractors was noted in terms of weak management, late mobilization and/or insufficient equipment and materials on site, insufficient technical skills of personnel, technical problems (i.e., frequent breakdown of equipment and changes in design concept), and uncertainty of the financial capability of the contractor.

Sustainability. Post-completion performance monitoring, operation, and maintenance were weak in some completed projects, which raised concerns on the sustainability of the projects.

Source: NEDA (2007).

improving its infrastructure. Some of the issues identified are (i) uncertainty over government policy on contracts and contract review, (ii) regulatory and political risks, (iii) inability of government line agencies to identify and prepare good projects for tender, (iv) corruption in project identification and procurement, and (v) constraints in the provision of guarantees due to government budgetary problems.

LGUs could help provide much-needed local infrastructure, for example, critical road links to the national arterial highway and port terminals for the government's RORO strategy for efficient mobility of goods and people across the archipelago. However, many LGUs depend on the cash-strapped national government for internal revenue allotments (IRAs) to fund local development and service delivery. The share of IRAs in total LGU income net of borrowings rose from 38% in 1985–1991 to 65% in 1992–2003 for all LGUs combined. IRAs, thus, effectively substitute for own-source revenue generation, which could have been used as an effective tool for financing local development. Only the larger cities and towns were able to raise substantial resources locally to finance local infrastructure development.

In addition, local infrastructure projects tend to be "governor- or mayor-centric," meaning that local infrastructure projects are typically pursued for the furtherance of the parochial political objectives of the local chief executive. Worse, is the reported syndrome of apportioning the local infrastructure budget among local legislators for implementation purposes. This approach, an imitation of the provision of pork barrel funds to national legislators, fragments already scarce local resources and results in uncoordinated and unrelated infrastructure projects. The lack of integration of such infrastructure projects with regional and national development plans has resulted in wasting of local resources and the poor state of subnational infrastructure (Llanto 2007a). Thus, the expectation that LGUs would fill the gap in infrastructure development should be tempered because (i) LGUs often face fiscal constraints, and (ii) local infrastructure development projects may not be integrated with overall regional or national development plans. The latter is a critical issue that the national government and the LGUs should address.

Policy makers have to think "out of the box," so to speak, by developing appropriate incentives for greater LGU participation in infrastructure provision. It may be time to review the national government's control over the more productive tax bases in view of growing local development needs, including local infrastructure. The tax revenue provided for under the Local Government Code has favored cities and municipalities over provinces. Policy makers and the national government could develop appropriate incentives for provinces particularly and LGUs in general to invest in infrastructure through mechanisms such as (i) using ODA funding for critical infrastructure needs of provinces or poor LGUs in general while using BOT schemes and private participation in infrastructure to provide urban infrastructure; (ii) improving the targeting and prioritization strategies of the national government to favor lagging regions or provinces; (iii) providing capability-building funds for project development to poor LGUs; (iv) linking access to ODA funding to the attainment of MDGs or providing performance incentives for LGUs attaining a national objective such as MDGs and other appropriate incentives.

Based on criteria to be developed by the national government in consultation with LGUs (e.g., scale economies, positive externalities, and technical capability) the national government could spearhead efforts to improve the allocation of the infrastructure budget and the spatial location of infrastructure projects. Thus, at one level, the province may be found to be the best implementer of road projects, for example, improving province-wide road networks; in other cases it may be the city, municipality, or even the barangay that should be involved in a particular infrastructure project. Improving the coordination of national and local infrastructure investment plans, adherence to an integrated national–local infrastructure plan, and more innovative use of ODA and private financing (e.g., reviewing the BOT Law and public–private partnership [PPP]) could be important for remedying serious infrastructure gaps.

The readiness of government-owned and -controlled corporations (GOCCs) to take on infrastructure projects should be assessed in view of their fiscal problems. Lenders typically demand sovereign guarantees for loans to GOCCs. The government should closely examine the risk posed by the increasing contingent liabilities arising from the guarantees. The government's total estimated contingent liabilities were P1,672 million as of 2003. The Department of Finance estimated that 54% of the total were liabilities of the infrastructure sector, of which 18.5% was for BOT projects, 35.0% for buy-out costs of independent power producers, 43.0% for guarantees on projects and activities of GOCCs and government financial institutions, and 3% for guarantee institutions (Llanto 2007b).

GOCCs may be able to play a significant role in view of the government's fiscal constraints faced. However, only a few GOCCs may have the resources to engage in infrastructure development. In fact, many GOCCs depend on government subsidies for their continuing operation and, thus, contribute to the consolidated public sector deficit. For GOCCs that have the resources to engage in infrastructure development and can borrow from the capital markets, the government should ensure good corporate governance, transparency, and above-board procurement procedures, in addition to being aware of the potential contingent liabilities arising from sovereign guarantees that may be demanded by foreign lenders.

The decision to invest in infrastructure is an endogenous variable that is influenced by both technocratic and political forces. Government sometimes takes the myopic decision of making across-the-board cuts in capital expenditure, including infrastructure, without due regard for the implications to productivity loss. Such cuts are usually made during times of fiscal stress when adjustment policies may dictate cuts in government spending. The most expedient item to cut back is capital expenditure, because governments usually succumb to political pressure to avoid laying off personnel. The risk posed by indiscriminate cuts in capital expenditure is the deleterious impact on the economy's productivity, especially private sector productivity, in the long-run. The other complicating factor is the equity aspect of the exercise. Should the reduction in the budget for roads be applied equally across regions? Should poorer regions be cut back in road expenditures proportionately to richer ones? Should richer regions be spared because infrastructure spending has to be supported in view of agglomeration and dispersion forces that to a large extent determine the spatial distribution of economic activity?

To improve the country's infrastructure, the following are among tasks needing immediate government attention: (i) expanding the narrow fiscal space by improving the tax effort, eliminating inefficiencies in government procurement procedures and implementation, and combating graft and corruption; (ii) reducing political risks and uncertainties that deter potential private sector investments or delay the implementation of vital infrastructure projects—specifically, reviewing the BOT Law and its implementation, with particular focus on the provisions on government guarantee and incentives to private sector participation in infrastructure; (iii) establishing a policy environment that promotes competition, improving procurement, and developing effective and independent regulatory institutions that safeguard both consumer welfare and investor interest; (iv) addressing implementation bottlenecks, especially focusing on innovative use of ODA and PPP–BOT for financing projects and improving the targeting and prioritization of projects in view of limited resources and the need to address the regional imbalance in infrastructure; and (v) ensuring the support of LGUs in providing infrastructure through such mechanisms as (a) using ODA to fund infrastructure in poor areas and PPP–BOT for urban projects, (b) developing appropriate incentives for better LGU performance in infrastructure projects, (c) linking access to ODA funding to the attainment of MDGs, and (d) providing capability-building funds for project development to implementing agencies and especially to poor LGUs, and other appropriate incentives.

In view of the findings showing the specific type of infrastructure that matters most to economic growth, the following discussion summarizes issues surrounding energy, telecommunications, and transport that the government must address.

Transport

Considering the archipelagic geography of the Philippines, a fully integrated transport system plays a very important role in facilitating economic activities and integrating local economies. The Philippines' transport system relies heavily on the road network, which handles about 90% of the country's passenger movement and about 50% of freight movement (NEDA 2004). The road network provides the most common means of transporting passengers and economic goods within and between the islands, using the RORO shipping facilities inaugurated under the Strong Republic Nautical Highway Program. A light rail transport system is concentrated in the Metro Manila area. A partly functioning heavy rail system operates to some points on Luzon from Metro Manila. Domestic ports and airports form the remaining components of the network of transport infrastructure to major economic centers in the country.

Roads. There are several outstanding issues. While the Philippine road network is extensive, a large portion is in poor condition—only 70% of it is paved.[14] The national road network is a mere 12% of the total public road network. Barangay roads are mostly unpaved and in poor condition and comprise more than half of the network. Most of the road network has been devolved to LGUs. Table 6.1 presents comparative statistics on road quality, as indicated by the percent of paved roads to total roads. Only a little over 20% of Philippine roads are paved, compared with Indonesia's 58%, Malaysia's 81%, and Thailand's 98%. Poor roads and ports contribute to the high cost of doing business and to the relative isolation of local economies from the country's major urban markets.

In general, the road network has deteriorated due to the national government's and LGUs' neglect of basic maintenance and due to underinvestment in new roads. This is ironic because the problem does not lie with insufficiency of funds for road maintenance. Republic Act 8794 created the Road Fund, earmarked for the maintenance of national and local roads and the control of air pollution from motor vehicles. The Road Fund has accumulated a substantial amount of money since the collection of a motor vehicle user charge (MVUC) from motor vehicle owners started in May 2001. Data from the Road Board show MVUC collections from May 2001 to April 2005 of about P22.6 billion on a cumulative basis. The Land

---

[14] Paved roads refer to the length of all roads that are surfaced with crushed stone and hydrocarbon binder or bituminized agents (macadam), concrete, or cobblestones.

Transportation Office forecasts that total vehicle registration will grow at an average 3% per year and, thus, about P44.5 billion of MVUC collections are expected in 2005–2010. Therefore, the issue lies not with funding, but with maintenance. The uncoordinated road works, e.g., excavation, digging, and paving, by various utilities (telecommunications, water supply, and sewerage) in the urban centers contribute to the deterioration of already poor roads. Poor road maintenance, poor traffic management, and uncoordinated and wasteful road works produce the daily congestion on many urban roads, especially in the NCR.

Table 6.1. Paved Roads as Percent of Total Roads, 1990–2004

Year	Indonesia	Korea, Rep. of	Lao PDR	Malaysia	Myanmar	Philippines	Singapore	Thailand	Viet Nam
1990	45.1	71.5	24.0	70.0	10.9	–	97.1	55.3	23.5
1991	45.3	76.4	16.0	73.0	11.2	–	97.1	88.4	23.9
1992	53.6	80.8	16.0	75.0	11.4	–	97.1	89.7	24.4
1993	53.8	84.7	16.0	75.0	11.6	–	97.2	92.8	24.9
1994	53.8	77.8	16.0	75.0	11.9	16.6	97.2	94.7	25.4
1995	52.4	76.0	13.8	74.4	12.1	16.7	97.3	97.4	25.9
1996	46.3	72.7	–	74.4	12.2	17.4	97.3	97.5	25.1
1997	56.4	74.0	–	74.9	–	17.7	97.3	97.5	25.1
1998	47.3	74.5	–	75.6	–	19.8	100.0	97.5	25.1
1999	46.3	74.5	44.5	75.3	11.4	20.0	100.0	97.5	–
2000	57.1	–	–	–	–	21.0	100.0	98.5	–
2001	58.9	76.7	–	77.9	–	21.0	100.0	–	–
2002	58.0	76.7	14.1	–	–	–	100.0	–	–
2003	–	76.9	14.4	80.8	–	21.6	100.0	–	–
2004	–	86.8	–	81.3	–	–	100.0	–	–

– = data not available, Lao PDR = Lao People's Democratic Republic.
Source: World Bank (various years).

Rail. Rail transport systems provide land-based alternatives to road transport, and are expected to cut road traffic congestion and air pollution, reduce travel times, and ultimately spur economic growth. The light rail system, a component of the rail transport system, can move large numbers of people efficiently, thereby reducing road congestion, air pollution, and business costs. The development of a light rail system in the NCR was envisioned to provide an alternative and efficient means of transport to the traffic-stricken metropolis and to address congestion by encouraging people working in the metropolis to reside outside the NCR. The Philippine light rail system is administered by the Light Rail Transit Authority.[15] The NCR has three light rail transit (LRT) lines: LRT line 1, LRT line 2, and the Mass Rail Transit (MRT). For the light rail subsector, security and safety are controlled and should be continuously monitored. The main issues in the subsector are (i) the failure to link the lines—e.g., a missing 5-kilometer portion from North Avenue, Quezon City, to Monumento, Caloocan City, to link the MRT with LRT 1; (ii) insufficient capacity and number of coaches, especially during peak hours; and (iii) interruption of operations due to mechanical and/or electrical failure, especially during adverse weather conditions, as the system does not have a dedicated power source.

Ports. Philippine ports handle a wide variety of goods that are essential to the economy, including petroleum and other critical imports such as food and pharmaceuticals. An efficient and effective port system is essential to the Philippine archipelago. As of 2005, the country had 414 registered ports, more than half of which (222) were privately owned. The remaining 192 public ports were classified as base ports, terminal ports, and other national or municipal ports (NSCB 2006). The port of Manila ranked 31st among the top 50 worldwide in the 2005 World Port Rankings in terms of container traffic, with a total of 2,665 twenty-foot equivalent units (World Container Port League 2005).[16] The Philippines is way behind other Asian ports in the top 50 list: Singapore (1st); Hong Kong, China (2nd); Busan, Republic of Korea (5th); Port Klang, Malaysia (14th); Tanjung Pelepas, Indonesia (19th); Laem Chabang, Thailand (20th); and Tanjung Priok, Indonesia (24th).

The Medium-Term Philippine Development Plan identified the following key policy issues for the port subsector (NEDA 2004):

- the restructuring of the port institutions to improve port service;
- amendment of Executive Order 170 to facilitate expansion of the RORO terminal system coverage;

---

[15] The Light Rail Transit Authority is a wholly government-owned corporation primarily responsible for the construction, operation, maintenance, and/or lease of light rail transit systems in the Philippines.

[16] The 20-foot equivalent unit is a standard linear measurement used in quantifying container traffic flows, e.g., one 20-foot container equals one unit while one 40-foot container equals two.

- privatization of the remaining government-owned RORO ports and terminals;
- deregulation of routes and rates to attract new entrants and to make maritime transport more cost-efficient;
- a comprehensive review of the present port tariff system to pave the way for a cost-based tariff system;
- modernization of vessels by providing incentives to owners pursuant to Republic Act 9295, intended to promote the development of domestic shipping;
- establishment of a maritime equity corporation to acquire modern RORO vessels that can be provided to qualified operators under a lease purchase agreement;
- transfer of regulatory functions to independent regulator(s), with jurisdiction over all ports; and
- amendment of the Philippine Ports Authority charter to address, among other things, the authority's dual role as port regulator and operator.

Power

The passage of the Electric Power Industry Reform Act (EPIRA) was instrumental in introducing important reforms in the power sector by

(i) separating the competitive from the monopolistic components of the industry, such as generation versus transmission and distribution versus supply of electricity;

(ii) unbundling the cost components of power rates to ensure transparency and to distinguish the efficient utilities from the inefficient ones; and

(iii) promoting efficiency and providing reliable and competitively priced electricity, while giving customers a full range of choices.

A few reforms have been achieved under the EPIRA:

- the National Transmission Corporation (Transco) was created,
- the Power Sector Assets and Liabilities Management Corporation (PSALM) was created,
- a wholesale spot electricity market (WESM) was established,
- power rates were unbundled, and
- the independent power purchase contracts of the National Power Corporation (NPC) were reviewed and renegotiated.

However, generation remains a regulated industry with NPC[17] plants (and its independent power purchase contracts) continuing to dominate generation (71%). NPC is expected to become privately owned as the privatization of generation assets picks up. On the transmission side, Transco is mandated to link power plants to the country's distribution utilities and electric cooperatives, which, in turn, deliver electricity to end-users, ensuring the reliability, adequacy, security, stability, and integrity of the grid. Transco has approximately 21,319 circuit-kilometers of transmission lines, including a submarine cable system (the first of its kind in Asia) and 93 substations with approximately 24,310 million volt amperes capacity (TransCo 2007). Due to eminent domain and right-of-way issues, the transmission assets cannot be auctioned completely. Instead, the assets (grid interconnections) and ancillary services are being offered through open, competitive bidding in the form of a 25-year concession, with the possibility of renewal for another 25 years. Under this arrangement, the government, through the PSALM, will retain the ownership of Transco's assets. The winning bidder will be responsible for improving, expanding, operating, and maintaining the assets, and operating any related business.

Section 30 of the EPIRA provides for the establishment of a WESM that will be the mechanism for determining the price of electricity not covered by bilateral contracts between sellers and purchasers. Because the WESM is a spot market, electricity is traded in real time. At the same time, as a wholesale market, it is open to distributors, directly connected customers, large users, and supply aggregators. The Luzon WESM operations started in June 2006, while the Visayas WESM is still under being tested. The Luzon WESM commenced operations when the government dominated the generation market and the Manila Electric Company (MERALCO) was the dominant buyer. The WESM has yet to evolve into an efficient electricity spot market.

The EPIRA provides for the privatization of NPC's transmission and generation assets by the PSALM. As of 2007, the PSALM had privatized eight plants with a combined capacity of 1,080 megawatts (MW) since 2003, despite some difficulties.[18] Five more plants were being firmed up for privatization by the end of 2007: Calaca Coal-Fired Power Plant (600 MW),

---

[17] NPC was first established under Commonwealth Act No. 120 approved by President Manuel L. Quezon on 3 November 1936 and reorganized pursuant to Republic Act 6395 as amended. NPC has evolved in response to the mainstream needs of the economy and will continue to maintain its mandated functions until its gradual privatization as stipulated under the EPIRA.

[18] Masinloc Power plant was bid out in December 2003 and was awarded to YNN Consortium for the purchase price of $561 million. However, YNN Consortium defaulted on its obligation to pay 40%, and Masinloc was rebid and awarded to AES Corporation. Initial privatization of the Transco concession was also unsuccessful.

Palinpinon Geothermal Power Plant (192.5 MW), Panay (Dingle) Diesel Power Plant (146.5 MW), Tiwi Geothermal Power Plant (275 MW), and Mak-Ban Geothermal Power Plant (410 MW). As of 2006, the Philippines had a total installed generation capacity of 15,803 MW, slightly above the previous year's 15,619 MW (DOE 2007).

Challenges remaining in the power sector include

- the financial viability of NPC and PSALM;
- attracting of new investments in the power sector, in view of a fore-cast power shortage in the near future;
- better management of and more players in the WESM;
- privatization of generation assets; and
- a more efficient regulatory framework.

Telecommunications

Removing monopoly and promoting competition has resulted in an impressive improvement in "tele-density": the number of telephone subscribers has increased dramatically since 1992–1999 with the implementation of Republic Act 7925. The advent of mobile technology has slowed the rate of subscription to fixed telephone lines because it provided the much-awaited access to telecommunications services at affordable prices. Despite the promotion of competition, the Philippine Long Distance Telephone Company (PLDT) continues to dominate the domestic exchange carrier market, the interexchange (domestic long distance) carrier market, and the international gateway facility (international long distance). In 2006, PLDT accounted for 41% of the total installed lines and 55% of the total subscribed lines nationwide (NTC 2006). The rest was divided among Innove (21% of installed, but only 9% of subscribed lines) and other small, private, or municipal companies.

The low cost of mobile handsets and short messaging service (SMS) has made mobile telecommunications more popular than fixed-line service in the Philippines. As of 2006, the country had 42 million cellular telephone subscribers. The number has been increasing significantly and the trend is expected to continue as incomes grow and as telephone companies establish a wider and more efficient cellular network. Among ASEAN countries, the Philippine mobile market is quickly catching up with the Indonesian and Korean markets. In 2005, Indonesia and the Republic of Korea registered a total of 47 million and 38 million subscribers, respectively, while the Philippines registered a total of 35 million (World Bank 2006).

The liberalization of the sector in the 1990s and the subsequent market-oriented stance of the National Telecommunications Commission (NTC) have yielded dividends in the greater accessibility of telecommunications services by more people and declining costs. A recent report funded by the United States Agency for International Development (USAID) states that in telecommunications, the Philippines has laid the foundations for a competitive market that has improved the public's access to efficient means of communication and other information technology–enabled services (EMERGE 2007). An example of NTC's desire for a competitive market is its ruling that making telephone calls through a computer—termed "voice over internet protocol" (VOIP)—is a value-added service and not a franchise, as maintained by the dominant telecommunications firms. This ruling, which was first subjected to public hearings where stakeholders' views were presented, has resulted in an increase of VOIP providers and a decline in telecommunications costs. Telecommunications carriers are offering rates as low as $0.05 per minute for overseas calls made using VOIP technology, an 87.5% drop from the $0.40 per minute by telephone. At least 17 firms have been given licenses to provide VOIP services.

The same report indicated that NTC issued, in December 2005, a consultative document on the development of a competition policy framework for the information and communications technology subsector. The NTC document cites the inequality in market power in the Philippine telecommunications subsector, where the 2 largest of the 73 local exchange carriers account for 75% of the subscriber base, and the 2 largest cellular operators control 96% of the mobile service market. In 2004, the 2 largest carriers showed a net income of P39.2 billion against the net loss of P2.3 billion of the next 2 largest carriers. While this extreme inequality in market shares and performance is not necessarily caused by a lack of fair competition, NTC points out that it provides opportunities for anticompetitive behavior, and, hence, grounds for regulatory attention. For example, a large supplier that owns and controls essential facilities that are costly to duplicate can eliminate competition by constraining rivals' access to the facilities. Rivals need access in order to provide telecommunications services to clients. NTC further recognized the advantages of incumbents that are first movers in the market. Incumbents control essential facilities and network standards and have vertically integrated facilities that may be used to cross-subsidize services and engage in predatory practices to ruin competitors.

Due to mergers since the late 1990s, the Philippine mobile market is currently dominated by two players—the PLDT–owned Smart Communications (and Pilipino Telephone Corporation) with 56%, and Ayala Group's Globe Telecom (and Isla Communications, or Innove Communications) with 38% (NTC 2006). Realizing the lack of effective competition in the market, the NTC consultative document considered introducing four pro-competition policies: (i) imposing obligations on carriers with significant market power, (ii) mandating local loop unbundling, (iii) requiring carriers to allow resale of their services, and (iv) changing the basis of price regulation from ex ante to ex post. An important component is the development of an instrument that will address the problem of interconnection agreements between the access provider and access seeker and the public's desire for relevant information on the subject. This instrument is the set of guidelines on reference access offers.

The guidelines will require all authorized public telecommunication entities to submit to NTC a reference access offer for certain access services. The offer will contain the terms and conditions under which an access provider is prepared to provide access to its telecommunications network or facility to any requesting service provider. The end goal is to increase competition in the telecommunications market in order to drive down communication costs for the consumer and business sector.

6.4. Comments and Policy Recommendations

This chapter provides an empirical basis for the popular assertion that poor infrastructure has a negative impact on economic growth. The empirical tests confirmed the assertion and provided specific results with deep policy implications. Notwithstanding the limitations imposed by severe data constraints, the tests showed that infrastructure is a binding constraint to economic growth on an aggregative basis and at the subnational level. In other words, the tests showed that infrastructure is an important channel for influencing the level and trajectory of growth. Together with investments in human capital, infrastructure is a significant conditioning variable for regional convergence. Regions with good infrastructure tend to have higher economic output and lower poverty incidence. The empirical tests also showed which types of infrastructure matter most to economic growth—electricity, telecommunications, and roads. Finally the chapter identified broad policy and sector-specific issues that the government must address in the near future.

Given these findings, immediate tasks facing the government include

(i) expanding its narrow fiscal space by improving the tax effort, eliminating inefficiencies in government procurement procedures and implementation, and combating graft and corruption;

(ii) reducing political risks and uncertainties, which deter potential private sector investments and delay the implementation of vital infrastructure projects—specifically, reviewing the BOT Law and its implementation, with particular focus on the provisions on government guarantee and incentives to private sector participation in infrastructure;

(iii) establishing a policy environment that promotes competition, for example, by implementing transparent procurement processes and developing effective and independent regulatory institutions that safeguard both consumer welfare and investor interest;

(iv) addressing implementation bottlenecks, especially by (a) providing capability building funds for project development to implementing agencies, (b) focusing on innovations in using the ODA and PPP–BOT mix for financing projects, and (c) improving targeting and prioritization of projects in view of limited resources and the need to address the regional imbalance in infrastructure; and

(v) ensuring the support of LGUs in providing infrastructure through such mechanisms as (a) using ODA to fund infrastructure in poor areas and PPP–BOT for urban projects; (b) developing appropriate incentives for better LGU performance in infrastructure projects; (c) linking access to ODA funding to the attainment of MDGs; and (d) providing capability building funds for project development to poor LGUs, and other appropriate incentives.

References

Aaron, H.J. 1990. Why Is Infrastructure Important? Discussion. In Alicia H. Munnell ed. *Is There a Shortfall in Public Capital Investment?* Conference Series No. 34. Boston: Federal Reserve Bank of Boston.

Aschauer, D. A. 1989. Is Public Expenditure Productive? *Journal of Monetary Economics.* 23 (September): 177–200.

Asian Development Bank (ADB). 2005. *Philippines: Moving Toward a Better Investment Climate.* Manila.

ADB, Japan Bank for International Cooperation (JBIC), and World Bank. 2005. *Connecting East Asia: A New Framework for Infrastructure.* http://siteresources.worldbank.org/INTEAPINFRASTRUCT/ResourcesorLinks/20792371/Cover-TOR-ForwardNote.pdf

Asian Development Bank and World Bank (ADB–WB). 2005. *Improving the Investment Climate in the Philippines.* Manila.

Basilio, L., and D. Gundaya. 1997. The Impact of Collective Public Infrastructure on Regional Income Disparities. Quezon City: University of the Philippines, School of Economics. Unpublished undergraduate thesis.

Boarnet, M. 1996. The Direct and Indirect Economic Effects of Transportation Infrastructure. Working Paper, UCTC No. 340. Berkeley, CA: University of California at Berkeley, University of California Transportation Center.

Clark, X., D. Dollar, and A. Micco. 2001. Maritime Transport Costs and Port Efficiency, World Bank and Inter-American Development Bank. Unpublished.

Center for Research and Communications (CRC). 2006. A Review of Development Bank of the Philippines' Industrial Restructuring Program. Unpublished.

Cuenca, J. 2004. An Empirical Analysis of Factors Affecting Regional Economic Growth and Convergence in the Philippines. Manila: De La Salle University. Unpublished thesis.

Department of Energy (DOE). 2007. *Philippine Energy Plan 2005–2014.* www.doe.gov.ph/PEP/default.htm

EMERGE. 2007. EMERGE Quarterly Report 2007. Report submitted to the National Economic and Development Authority. Unpublished.

Ertekin, D., J. Berechman, and K. Ozbay. 2003. Empirical Analysis of Relationship between Accessibility and Economic Development. Final Report for the US Department of Transportation, Research and Special Programs Administration.

Gramlich, E. M. 1994. Infrastructure Investment: A Review Essay. *Journal of Economic Literature.* 32(3): 1176–96.

Hill, H. 2007. Regional Development: Analytical and Policy Issues. In A. Balicasan and H. Hill. eds. *The Dynamics of Regional Development: The Philippines in East Asia.* Cheltenham: Edward Elgar.

Holtz-Eakin, D., and A. E. Schwartz. 1995. *Spatial Productivity Spillovers from Public Expenditure: Evidence from State Highways.* NBER Working Paper No. 5004. Cambridge, MA: National Bureau of Economic Research.

Hulten, C. R., and R. M. Schwab. 1991. Public Capital Formation and the Growth of Regional Manufacturing Industries. *National Tax Journal.* 44 (4): 121–134.

International Institute for Management Development (IMD). 2007. *World Competitiveness Yearbook.* www.imd.ch/research/publications/wey/index/cfm

Infrastructure Canada. 2007. Infrastructure and Productivity. Research and Analysis Division. Unpublished.

Japan External Trade Organization (JETRO). 2006. *FY2006 Survey of Japanese Firms' International Operations.* www.jetro.go.jp/en/stats/survey/pdf/2006_04_biz.pdf

Lamberte, M., F. Alburo, and E. Patalinghug. 2003. Private Sector Assessment Study: The Philippines. Report for the Asian Development Bank. Unpublished.

Lamberte, M., R. Manasan, and G. M. Llanto. 1993. *Decentralization and Prospects for Regional Growth.* Makati City: Philippine Institute for Development Studies.

Limao, N., and A. J. Venables. 1999. Infrastructure, Geographical Disadvantage and Transport Costs. Policy Research Working Paper No. 2257. Washington, DC: World Bank.

Llanto, G. M. 2004. *Infrastructure Development: Experience and Policy Options for the Future*. Makati City: Philippine Institute for Development Studies.

———. 2007a. Infrastructure and Regional Growth. In A. Balisacan and H. Hill, eds. *The Dynamics of Regional Development*. Cheltenham: Edward Elgar.

———. 2007b. Dealing with Contingent Liabilities: The Philippines. In T. Ito and A. Rose. eds. *Fiscal Policy and Management in East Asia*. Chicago: University of Chicago Press.

Llanto, G. M., and J. Lasam. 2004. Decentralized Planning in the Visayas: Issues, Opportunities and Directions. Report submitted to the National Economic and Development Authority (NEDA) and Deutsche Gesellschaft für Techische Zusammenarbeit (GTZ). 26 July.

Manasan, R. 2004. Fiscal Reform Agenda: Getting Ready for the Bumpy Ride Ahead. PIDS Discussion Paper No. 2004-26. Makati City: Philippine Institute for Development Studies.

Manasan, R., and S. Chatterjee. 2003. Regional Development. In A. Balisacan and H. Hill, eds. *The Philippine Economy: Development, Policies and Challenges*. Quezon City: Ateneo de Manila University Press.

Manasan, R., and R. Mercado. 1999. Regional Economic Growth and Convergence in the Philippines: 1975–1997. In E. Gonzalez, ed. *Reconsidering the East Asian Economic Model: What's Ahead for the Philippines*. Pasig City: Development Academy of the Philippines.

Munnell, A. H. 1992. Policy Watch: Infrastructure Investment and Economic Growth. *Journal of Economic Perspectives*. 6(4): 189–98.

National Economic and Development Authority (NEDA). 2004. *Medium-Term Philippine Development Plan 2004–2010*. Pasig City.

———. 2007. *ODA Portfolio Review*. www.neda.gov.ph/progs_prj/16thODA/16th_odamain.htm

National Statistical Coordination Board (NSCB). 2006. *Philippine Statistical Yearbook*. Makati City.

National Telecommunications Commission (NTC). 2006. *National Telecommunications Commission Annual Report*. http://portal.ntc.gov.ph/wps/portal

O'Fallon, C. 2003. Linkages between Infrastructure and Economic Growth. Report submitted to the New Zealand Ministry of Economic Development. December.

Reyes, C. 2002. Impact of Agrarian Reform on Poverty. PIDS Discussion Paper Series 2002-02. Makati City: Philippine Institute for Development Studies.

Rodriguez, J. F. P. 2006. Public Investment in Infrastructure and Productivity Growth: Evidence from the Venezuelan Manufacturing Sector. http://frrodriguez.web.wesleyan.edu/docs/working_papers/Infrastructure_

Rosik, P. 2006. Transport Infrastructure, Public Capital and Regional Policy: Review of Studies. Paper presented at the International Conference on Shaping EU Regional Policy: Economic Social and Political Pressures. Leuven, Belgium. June.

Shiu, A., and P.L. Lam. 2003. Electricity Consumption and Economic Growth in China. Hong Kong, China: Hong Kong Polytechnic University, Department of Business Studies. Unpublished.

Sturm, J., J. Jacobs, and P. Groote. 1999. *Productivity Impacts of Infrastructure Investment in the Netherlands 1853–1913*. Groningen: University of Groningen, Department of Economics.

Sturm, J., G. Kuper, and J. de Haan. 1996. *Modeling Government Investment and Economic Growth on a Macro Level: A Review.* CCSO Series No. 9. Groningen: University of Groningen, Department of Economics. September.

TransCo. 2007. *Transmission Development Plan.* Quezon City.

Wang, E. 2002. Public Infrastructure and Economic Growth: A New Approach Applied to East Asian Economies. *Journal of Public Policy Modeling.* 24(5): 411–35.

World Bank. 2005. *Philippines: Meeting Infrastructure Challenges.* Washington, DC.

———. 2006 and various years. *World Development Indicators.* Washington, DC.

World Container Port League. 2005. *Containerisation International Yearbook.* www .iaphworldports.org/world_port_info/WorldPortTrafficLeague(2005).pdf

World Economic Forum (WEF). 2004, 2006, and various years. *Global Competitiveness Report.* http://gcr.weforum.org/gcr

Yoo, S. H. 2004. Electricity Consumption and Economic Growth: Evidence from Korea. Tokyo: Hoseo University, School of Business and Economics. Unpublished.

7. Human Capital

Hyun H. Son

7.1. Introduction

According to modern growth theory, the accumulation of human capital is an important contributor to economic growth. Numerous cross-country studies extensively explore whether educational attainment can contribute significantly to the generation of overall output in an economy. Although macro studies have produced inconsistent and controversial results (Pritchett 1996), several micro studies that look into the same problem have shown a positive relationship between the education of working individuals and their labor earnings and productivity. To put it differently, the general finding is that individuals with more education tend to have a higher employment rate and greater earnings and to produce more output than those who are less educated. These findings provide a strong rationale for governments and private households to invest substantial portions of their resources in education with the expectation that higher benefits will accrue over time. In this context, education is deemed an investment, equipping individuals with knowledge and skills that improve their employability[1] and productive capacities, thereby leading to higher earnings in the future.

The Philippine education system is characterized by high attendance rates, implying that, unlike in other developing countries, social interest in education is widespread in the Philippines. As a result, the average years of schooling of the labor force has increased over time and excellent performance in education by the Filipinos has been widely acknowledged in international circles. Yet, the performance in labor productivity contrasts with the increasing level of education of the country's workers. The country's poor growth performance is puzzling given the educational attainment of the labor force. Thus, this study raises the question: To what extent does education contribute to growth in the Philippines? Both macro and micro approaches are used to deal with this complex issue. The main objective of

---

[1] Employability in this book is defined as the proportion with a given set of skills and educational attainment levels that is employed.

this chapter is to analyze whether human capital is a binding constraint to investment and growth in the Philippines.

From a macro perspective, the chapter reviews studies on growth accounting, looking into the contribution of education to the total output of the economy. Cross-country comparisons are provided to determine whether there is evidence that human capital plays an important role in explaining the poor performance in output growth that the Philippines has experienced over the years.

From a micro perspective, this study utilizes the results of investment climate surveys conducted by the Asian Development Bank and the World Bank in 2003 and 2005 in examining whether human skills and education are major obstacles for firms considering investment in the Philippines (ADB–World Bank 2005). Further, this study investigates the relationship between education and labor earnings and productivity at the household level—the level at which decisions on education and labor force participation are made. The analysis will determine whether education matters not only for employment, but also for individual earnings and productivity.

This chapter attempts to address the following questions:

(i)   Are human skills and education major obstacles to attracting private investment in the Philippines?
(ii) Is human capital a major contributor to the growth performance of the Philippines as compared to other countries?
(iii) Does human capital or education matter for labor productivity over time within the Philippines?
(iv) Does education matter for employability in the Philippine labor market?
(v)   To what extent is per capita productivity able to explain per capita labor earnings?
(vi) Does higher education give rise to higher earnings in the Philippine labor market?

Section 7.2 discusses the macro links between education and economic growth. Section 7.3 is devoted to the micro analysis looking into the relationship between education and the labor market. Section 7.4 investigates the issues of rates of returns to education. Section 7.5 concludes the study.

7.2. Education and Economic Growth

Early neoclassical growth models did not consider education as an input to production. Only in the 1960s did economists begin to see education as one of the variables that account for the unexplained residual in growth accounting exercises. Toward the middle of the 1960s, microeconomic studies based on the concept of human capital investment began to measure education's rates of return. The endogenous growth theory provides explanations about why human capital investments are important to economic growth (Barro and Sala-i-Martin 1995). However, the cross-country empirical estimations that tested the endogenous growth theory have yielded mixed results.

In the Philippines, several attempts have been made to quantify the contribution of education to economic growth. The studies in recent years include those of Alonzo (1995), Cororaton (2002), and Bosworth and Collins (2003).

As discussed in other chapters, economic growth in the Philippines has been sluggish compared with that of other major economies in East Asia. While the Philippines' real gross domestic product (GDP) grew by 3.8% per year during 1961–2003, the country's labor force also expanded by an annual rate of 2.8%. Thus, on average, real GDP per capita—a proxy measure of standard of living—increased by only 1% a year during that period (Table 7.1). This was even lower than the 1.4% average growth rate achieved by all developing countries, and far below the 2.4% in the developed economies and the 4.4% in seven other major East Asian economies.

The Philippines' output per worker increased about 50% during the last four decades or so. In comparison, the corresponding figure for the other East Asian economies rose more than four fold on average (i.e., 450%). The results shown in Table 7.1 outline the approximate sources of the difference in growth between the Philippines and its East Asian neighbors. The table points to the conclusion that the difference was not primarily due to educational attainment or the growth of human capital. In the Philippines, the average years of education of people aged 15 and over almost doubled, from 4.4 years in 1960 to 8.0 years in 2000. It increased on average from 3.4 years to 7.8 years for the other 7 East Asian economies. Filipinos are largely considered to be highly educated in Asia. For example, the median years of education among taxi drivers is about 6 in Thailand, 9 in Indonesia, and 10 in the Philippines (ADB 2007).

Similarly, the Investment Climate Survey confirmed that education and worker skills were not a major impediment to a good investment climate in the Philippines (ADB–World Bank 2005). As Figure 5.3 in Chapter 5 shows, the severe constraints to attracting investment in the Philippines have to do instead with factors such as macroeconomic instability, corruption, and institutional quality (e.g., security and regulatory uncertainty). These constraints are discussed further in Chapters 3, 4, and 11.

Growth in both physical capital and total factor productivity (TFP) in the Philippines has been much lower than in the rest of East Asia (Table 7.1). While average TFP growth in the Philippines was slightly negative over the

Table 7.1: Growth Accounting (percentage points)

	Growth in Output per Worker	Contributions to Growth of		
		Physical Capital	Human Capital	Total Factor Productivity
Philippines				
1961–2003	1.0	0.8	0.4	–0.2
1961–1980	2.3	1.2	0.4	0.7
1981–1985	–1.9	1.5	0.2	–3.6
1986–2003	0.9	0.1	0.4	0.3
Comparators 1961–2000				
OECD	2.4	1.0	0.4	1.0
Developing economies	1.4	0.8	0.3	0.3
East Asia (7)	4.4	2.4	0.5	1.4
Comparators 1986–2000				
OECD	1.9	0.7	0.3	0.8
Developing economies	1.0	0.3	0.4	0.3
East Asia (7)	4.8	2.3	0.5	2.0

OECD = Organisation for Co-operation and Development.
Note: Calculations of growth and contributions to growth draw on the database that covers 22 developed and 62 developing economies during the 1960–2000 period. The 7 other East Asian economies referred to in the table are the People's Republic of China; Indonesia; Republic of Korea; Malaysia; Singapore; Taipei,China; and Thailand.
Source: Bosworth and Collins (2003).

entire period, TFP growth in the seven other East Asian economies averaged 1.4 percentage points per year. The findings of the Philippines' low or negative TFP growth since the early 1960s are essentially similar to those found in recent detailed studies of the Philippines' growth performance, e.g., Alonzo (1995) and Cororaton (2002).

Earlier, Alonzo (1995) carried out a growth accounting analysis for the 1961–1991 period, which was divided into four subperiods: 1961–1965, 1965–1976, 1976–1981, and 1981–1991. In the exercise, he used the growth in net domestic product at 1985 prices, physical capital based on estimates in Sanchez (1983), labor quantity based on third quarter employment, and index of labor quality based on average years of schooling embodied in the employed labor force weighted by the observed relative earnings by schooling completed based on the 1988 Labor Force Survey. He also employed the assumption in Sanchez (1983) that gave equal weight to total output for labor and capital. Alonzo also found that labor accounts for more output growth than does capital. When quality of labor is also considered, he concluded that much of the output growth is explained by both the quantity and the quality of the labor force. The contribution of education ranged from 11.8% in 1961–1965 to 59.2% in 1981–1991. The contribution of raw labor ranged from 18.2% in 1961–1965 to 110.4% in 1981–1991. The contribution of physical capital, on the other hand, ranged from 5.5% in 1961–1965 to –18.7% in 1981–1991.

Later, Cororaton (2002) used empirically estimated production functions to compute the contribution of labor quality to TFP from 1967 to 2000, which was divided into seven periods. Workers were disaggregated into skilled and unskilled to capture labor quality. Skilled workers refer to those who are at least high school graduates. Cororaton found that the contribution of labor quality to TFP had declined from 2.11% in 1967–1972 to 0.16% in 1991–1993, but rose slowly to about 0.52% in 1998–2000 (Figure 7.1).

Although Alonzo and Cororaton used different methods to estimate the contribution of education to economic growth, both provided evidence that education matters for output growth or productivity. This evidence only holds at the aggregate level. The following section provides micro evidence as to whether there is a positive or negative relationship between the education of working individuals and their labor earnings and productivity in the Philippines.

Figure 7.1: Contribution of Labor Quality to Total Factor Productivity Growth (%)

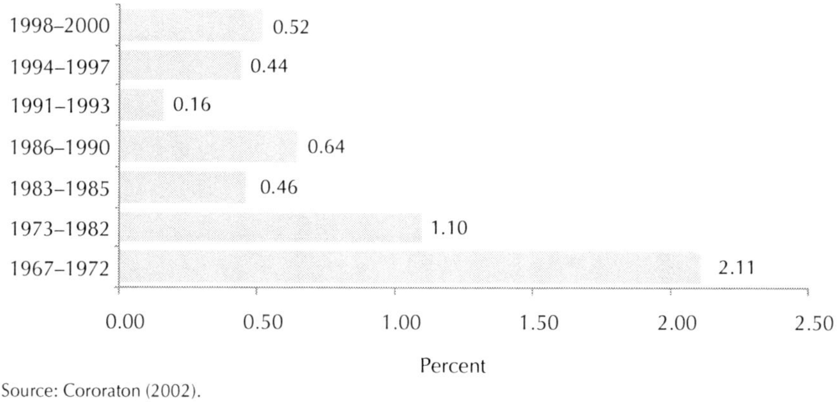

Source: Cororaton (2002).

7.3. Education and the Labor Market

The objective of this section is twofold: first, it seeks to investigate whether labor productivity is an important factor in explaining the earnings and productivity of employed people who belong to a household; second, it explores the extent of labor productivity's contribution to growth in real wage income.

Because households decide on education and labor force participation, it makes sense to use a micro approach to look into the relationship among education and labor productivity and earnings. The primary motivations to attend school are better future income prospects and personal well-being. Education is known not only to lead to higher earnings but also to other non-labor-market benefits, for example, better nutrition and health and better capacity to enjoy leisure (Haveman and Wolfe 1984). Higher earnings are compensation for increased productivity through education. This is the human capital view of education.

Before going into the issues of productivity and individual labor earnings, it will be useful to discuss the educational attainment of the working-age population within households as well as educational attainment by sector and gender.

Table 7.2 shows the education levels for people employed per household during 1997–2003. The figures presented in the table are all expressed in

Table 7.2: Per Capita Household Employment by Education Level and Gender (%)

Level and Gender	Actual Values			Annual Growth Rate	
	1997	2000	2003	1997–2000	2000–2003
Primary Education	16.5	15.2	15.0	-2.9	-0.3
Male	10.9	9.8	9.9	-3.4	0.4
Female	5.7	5.4	5.1	-2.0	-1.6
Secondary Education	12.5	13.1	14.1	1.7	2.5
Male	8.2	8.5	9.1	1.0	2.3
Female	4.3	4.6	5.1	2.9	2.8
Tertiary Education	8.5	9.1	9.3	2.3	0.7
Male	4.5	4.8	4.9	1.7	0.8
Female	3.9	4.3	4.4	2.9	0.6
Total Employment	37.5	37.3	38.4	-0.1	0.9

per capita terms per household. For example, per capita household employment was 38.4% in 2003. This means that on average, about 38.4% of household members were employed in 2003; almost two members living in a five-member household were engaged in some form of employment in the labor market.

Table 7.2 presents an interesting point. The per capita employment increased from 37.5% in 1997 to 38.4% in 2003, yet this was not sufficient to lower per capita unemployment given a rise in labor force participation in the economy. Son (2008) notes that per capita labor force participation grew by 0.9% per year, while per capita unemployment jumped at 10.0% per year during the crisis period (1997–2000) and rose slightly, by less than 1% annually, afterward (2000–2003). Overall, the number of jobs available in the labor market has not been growing fast enough to absorb the number of new entrants to the labor force.

Similar to the earlier findings (section 7.2), Table 7.2 indicates that household members are becoming more educated in the Philippines. During 1997–2003, the proportion of employed household members who had secondary and tertiary education increased, while those who had acquired only primary education declined. This suggests that higher education matters for employment in the Philippine labor market. In terms of gender, the proportion of employed female members tends to be higher among those who have achieved secondary- and tertiary-level education. Moreover, the gender gap in the employment rate within household narrows particularly at the tertiary level, but is still higher for male members.

Based on the foregoing, the reason for the differences in the employability of males and females by educational level remains unanswered. Son (2008) notes that educational attainment is higher for women than for men but does not seem to result in women's greater employability in the labor market. This issue will be discussed below.

In general, one would expect employability to increase with a higher level of education. Such a pattern is indeed observed from Table 7.3. For example, in 1997, employability among people with only primary-level education is 47.8%, rising to 48.9% among those with secondary education and reaching 56.6% among people with tertiary education. More importantly, at all education levels, women have much lower employability than men. The male–female gap, however, is much lower among people with tertiary education.

Interestingly, employability among the labor force with only primary education declined sharply during 1997–2003, while it increased for those with secondary and tertiary levels. This suggests that as the labor force is becoming more educated, job opportunities for those with less education have become increasingly scarce. The two explanations for this are that

(i) demand increased for jobs requiring secondary and tertiary education, and (ii) low-productivity jobs are taken over by the educated labor force.

If the latter is true, the foregoing observations suggest that the labor productivity of educated workers has been on the decline. As indicated in Table 7.2, per capita employment has remained roughly constant during the period. This implies that employment has increased merely in line with the population growth. Hence, if there is no improvement in labor productivity, then growth in per capita real labor earnings is expected to be stagnant. To achieve positive growth, labor productivity has to increase. Total labor productivity depends on the pattern of employment by sector and gender.

Table 7.3: Employment by Education Level and Gender (%)

Education Level Gender	1997	2000	2003
Primary Education	47.8	45.4	34.3
Male	61.5	57.5	43.6
Female	33.6	32.8	24.3
Secondary Education	48.9	48.1	49.8
Male	64.0	60.9	63.9
Female	33.6	34.8	35.7
Tertiary Education	56.6	54.3	56.8
Male	64.5	61.0	64.1
Female	49.6	48.4	50.4

Sources: Author's calculations based on the Family Income and Expenditure Surveys and Labor Force Surveys (NSO n.d.).

Table 7.4 reports per capita household employment by sector and gender. It shows that, in terms of magnitude, the proportion of household members employed in agriculture has declined, in industry has remained virtually unchanged, and in services has risen. This suggests a structural change where the labor force is moving away from the agriculture sector toward the service sector. Overall, average household members are largely employed in services. The employment of female household members in the service sector increased significantly during the period. This may be supported by a claim that the proportion of female college graduates employed in finance, insurance, and real estate has increased over time (Orbeta 2002).

As the findings clearly suggest, the working-age population is increasingly engaged in the service sector. Although the service sector tends to create more jobs, the quality of job matters for individual earnings in the labor market: taxi drivers belong to the service sector, but so do lawyers and doctors.

Employment within households varies according to education level, gender, and sector of work. All these factors determine the level of individual labor earnings. In this context, the study attempts to explain per capita earnings in terms of four key labor indicators.

Table 7.4: Per Capita Household Employment by Sector and Gender (%)

Sector	Actual Value			Annual Growth Rate	
Gender	1997	2000	2003	1997–2000	2000–2003
Agriculture	14.7	13.8	14.0	−2.2	0.5
Male	10.9	10.4	10.6	−1.6	0.6
Female	3.8	3.4	3.4	−3.8	0.2
Industry	6.3	6.1	6.1	−1.0	0.0
Male	4.5	4.3	4.4	−2.0	0.6
Female	1.8	1.9	1.8	1.3	−1.4
Service	16.4	17.4	18.3	1.9	1.6
Male	8.1	8.3	8.9	0.9	2.2
Female	8.3	9.1	9.4	2.9	1.1
Total Employment	**37.5**	**37.3**	**38.4**	**−0.1**	**0.9**

Table 7.5: Explaining Growth Rates in Real Labor Income (%)

	1997–2000	2000–2003
Labor Force Participation Rate	0.89	0.92
Employment Rate	−1.02	0.02
Work Hours per Employed Person	2.15	−0.63
Real Productivity	−4.76	−1.42
Real Labor Income	−2.73	−1.10

Sources: Author's calculations based on the Family Income and Expenditure Surveys and Labor Force Surveys (NSO n.d.).

Another objective of this exercise is to find out to what extent productivity contributes to growth in real wage income. In this regard, productivity is thought to be a proxy for assessing the quality of labor. For this study, productivity is estimated as per capita wage income adjusted for the number of working hours per week. As can be seen from Table 7.5, the decline in the productivity factor has contributed largely to the negative growth in real wage income among the employed population during the 1997–2003 period.

7.4. Rates of Return to Education

Policy makers in almost all countries agree on the importance of education and skills to ensure future economic prosperity. Studies show that countries with higher levels of education and skills have, on average, higher levels of productivity and economic growth (Machin and Vignoles 2005). However, proving a causal relationship between education and skills and economic growth has been quite problematic at a country level, because countries vary in many dimensions, not just in their levels of education and skills (Sianesi and Van Reenen 2000).

As shown in the Philippine context, the more educated labor force may be taking jobs that were previously held by the less educated labor force, particularly in the service sector. This scenario is likely to have contributed to declining labor productivity in the Philippines. As noted in the previous section, declining productivity is the major contributing factor to the negative growth in per capita real labor earnings.

There is evidence that with the rising education levels of the labor force, college graduates have increasingly taken on low-skilled work such as driving taxis, jeepneys, buses, and motorized tricycles in the Philippines (ADB 2007). It appears that a large proportion of highly educated workers are employed in jobs that do not match their educational attainments; hence, there is a mismatch between the labor market and the education sector. To enhance long-term growth prospects, the government needs to formulate policies to address this issue.

In evaluating the rates of return to education, education is analyzed as an investment, which involves individuals and the state incurring costs now (lost income or direct costs of tuition) in order to reap gains in the future, in the form of higher income. So how does education and training actually enhance individuals' earnings? Human capital theory suggests that when individuals invest in education and training, they make themselves more productive in the labor market, which leads them in turn to have higher earnings. This assumes that the labor market is fully competitive so that wages will fully reflect the productivity of workers, and that any gain in productivity due to education will subsequently result in higher earnings for the worker. These assumptions are subject to question, however. For example, signaling theory (Spence 1973) hypothesizes that individuals acquire education merely to signal to potential employers that they have superior productivity, although education itself does not necessarily enhance productivity. There are also a number of theoretical reasons as to why wages may not reflect an individual's true productivity. However, the bulk of the empirical evidence on this issue broadly supports the human capital perspective (Machin and Vignoles 2005). Just like any other investment, returns on education at different levels and in various fields of specialization have been computed and compared to guide policy makers in assessing the appropriateness of allocating labor within and across sectors.

This chapter will not dwell at length on the technical details of how rates of return are actually calculated, but will provide a brief explanation to help the reader interpret the evidence base. Regression analysis is most commonly used to estimate or approximate the return to education. Information is generally collected on a cross section of individuals working in the labor market, including data on their earnings, education, work experience, age, and other personal characteristics such as gender. A statistical model of wages is then estimated, which relates individuals' current wages to their education and training, as well as their characteristics.

The Philippine rate of return to education has always exhibited unusual behavior: though classified as a developing nation, the country's rate of return approximates that of a more developed country (Gerochi 2002). Figure 7.2 indicates that the Philippines has very high returns to education. Workers with 1 more year of schooling in the Philippines earn about 15% more in terms of wages. This is far higher than the pooled average returns, where an additional year of schooling is worth just 5%. These findings suggest that an additional year of education offers rewards to a working individual in terms of higher labor earnings in the Philippines.

Figure 7.2 considers the average return to a year of schooling during 1985–1995, which coincides with a significant expansion in the supply of skilled labor. Of great interest to policy makers is whether the rate of return differs significantly between levels of education. A latest estimate from Schady (2001) arbitrarily limits the sample to the male population based on the 1998 Annual Poverty Indicator Survey that was conducted by the National Statistics Office. This gets around the selection problem in the labor market that is essentially more established in estimating returns for women and approximating the potential experience that could lead to an upward bias of years of experience for women. The author attempts to determine the convexity in the relationship of the age and years of completed schooling and to measure the effect. Partial controls for ability, measured by parental education and within-sibling estimates, are also specified. The reported coefficient of schooling (i.e., 12.6%) may not be comparable to estimates in Figure 7.2 due to the specification of the earnings function used. Nevertheless, a more detailed result from a spline function indicates that the smallest coefficient has resulted for primary education, a slightly higher one for secondary education, and a much higher one for tertiary education. The author found significant sheepskin effects, in terms of higher wages, especially in the last year of schooling.

Figure 7.2: International Comparison of the Returns to Education, 1985–1995

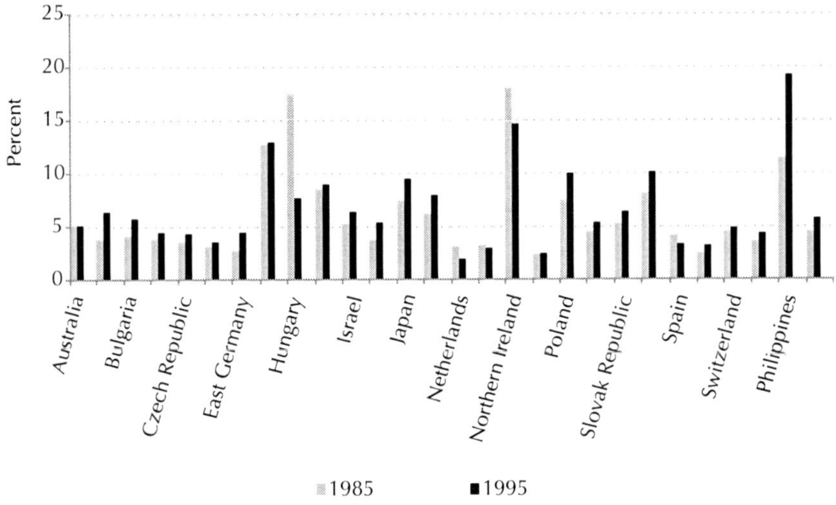

Source: Trostel, Walker, and Woolley (2002).

Similarly, the study estimated rates of return to different education levels during 1997–2003. The concern lies in marginal rates of returns rather than average returns to see if higher education is disproportionately rewarded in terms of higher returns. The estimates are presented in Table 7.6. As would be expected, returns rose with higher levels of education. The increase in returns was relatively small, moving from primary to secondary level. The returns to education increased substantially, moving from the secondary to the tertiary level—consider the period 1997–2003, when real labor household income per hour increased by more than three times from the secondary to the tertiary level, from P5.16 to P16.57.

Table 7.6: Rates of Return by Education Level and Sector (pesos per hour)

	1997	2000	2003
By Education Level			
Primary	2.50	2.42	2.22
Secondary	6.75	5.57	5.16
Tertiary	19.80	17.62	16.57
By Sector			
Agriculture	0.84	0.96	0.89
Industry	7.57	7.01	7.23
Service	11.42	9.90	9.36

More interestingly, the returns to education at all levels fell during the period. Noticeably, the decrease for tertiary education was much greater than that for the lower levels. This confirms the conjecture that a large expansion in the supply of qualified workers lowered the price for skilled labor over the period. As discussed earlier, this is an issue of mismatch between the labor market and the education sector. Thus, the education sector did not produce appropriate skill sets that were in demand by the labor market.

Returns are also calculated for different sectors. The results reveal that returns were highest from the service sector, followed by the industry sector. There was a big difference in returns between agriculture and the industry and service sectors, while the difference between the industry and service sectors was relatively small.

7.5. Conclusions and Policy Implications

In the Philippines, the supply of qualified labor has expanded massively. Nevertheless, the performance in labor productivity contrasts with the fact that the market has been endowed with highly educated (and by implication highly skilled) labor. Moreover, the country's poor growth performance becomes even more puzzling given the education effort made.

First, the study shows that education and labor skills are not a major constraint to attracting investment to the Philippines. This finding was drawn from the Investment Climate Survey of more than 700 firms conducted jointly by the Asian Development Bank and the World Bank in 2005. The survey indicated that the severe impediments to a good investment climate were not human capital, but constraints related to macroeconomic instability, corruption, and institutional quality.

Second, the study shows that the difference in growth between the Philippines and other countries—including growth in the Organisation for Economic Co-operation and Development (OECD) and East Asian neighbors—was not primarily due to educational attainment or the growth of human capital. Rather, cross-country difference in growth in output per worker was largely attributable to changes in physical capital and TFP over time.

Third, education matters for output growth or productivity in the Philippines. Other studies looking into the macro linkage of the contribution of education to productivity indicate that the quality of labor played an important role in determining TFP in the Philippines. Yet this evidence only holds at the aggregate level. Thus, the present study was extended to micro analysis to investigate the link between the education of working individuals and their labor earnings and productivity. The analysis was done at the household level because households decide on education and labor force participation. The major findings on the micro link are summarized as follows.

The study found that higher education is an important determinant of employment in the Philippine labor market. Employability among the labor force with only primary education declined sharply during 1997–2003, but increased for the labor force with secondary and tertiary education. This indicates that people with higher education have crowded out the less educated in terms of job opportunities. The study premised this finding on two explanations: that demand for people with secondary and tertiary education has increased in the Philippine labor market, and that low-productivity jobs are being taken over by the more educated labor force. If the second explanation is valid, then the findings support a scenario wherein the labor productivity of educated workers declines.

So far, the analysis has proven this argument to be true. That per capita labor productivity fell during 1997–2003 confirms the previous conjecture that a large expansion in the supply of qualified workers lowered the price for skilled labor during the period. This is an issue of mismatch between the labor market and the education sector, indicating that the current education sector does not supply the kinds of skills that are demanded by the labor market.

In addition, the study found a structural change where the labor force is moving away from the agriculture sector toward the service sector. The share of people employed in agriculture has declined, remains virtually unchanged in the industry sector, and is rising in the service sector. Within the service sector, employment among the female working population increased significantly during the period. This supports the view that the proportion of female college graduates employed in finance, insurance, and real estate has increased over time.

The labor mismatch is an issue that government needs to reckon with in order to accelerate and sustain economic growth. The major findings in this study clearly show that a policy of expanding the aggregate supply of skills is not sufficient to address the decline in labor productivity, which in turn, has slowed the pace of economic growth. From a policy perspective, going beyond universal coverage in education is imperative because what is required is an expansion of the supply of the right kinds of skills. For this to happen, employers, individuals, and policy makers need robust, up-to-date information on the real labor market value of different qualifications in order to help them navigate through the increasingly complex education system and make the optimal kinds of investment decisions.

References

Alonzo, R. 1995. Education and National Development: Some Economic Perspectives. In E. de Dios ed. *If We're So Smart Why Aren't We Rich?* Congressional Oversight Committee on Education. Quezon City.

Asian Development Bank (ADB). 2007. *Asian Development Outlook: Change Amid Growth.* Manila.

Asian Development Bank and World Bank (ADB–World Bank). 2005. *Investment Climate Survey.* Manila: ADB.

Barro, R., and X. Sala-i-Martin. 1995. *Economic Growth.* New York: McGraw-Hill.

Bosworth, B., and S. Collins. 2003. *The Empirics of Growth: An Update.* Washington, DC: Brookings Institution.

Cororaton, C. 2002. Research and Development and Technology in the Philippines. PIDS 25th Anniversary Symposium Series on Perspective Papers. Manila. August–September.

Gerochi, H. 2002. Rate of Return to Education in the Philippines. Preliminary Estimates for PDE Paper. Quezon City: University of the Philippines, School of Economics.

Haveman, R., and B. Wolfe. 1984. Schooling and Economic Well-Being: The Role of Nonmarket Effects. *Journal of Human Resources.* XIX (3): 377–407.

Machin, S., and A. Vignoles. 2005. What's the Good of Education?: *The Economics of Education in the UK.* Princeton, NJ and Oxford: Princeton University Press.

National Statistics Office (NSO). n.d. *Index of Family Income and Expenditure.* www.census.gov.ph/data/sectordata/dataincome.html

————. n.d. *Index of Labor Force Statistics.* www.census.gov.ph/data/sectordata/datalfs.html

Orbeta, A. 2002. Education, Labor Market and Development: A Review of the Trends and Issues in the Past 25 Years. PIDS 25th Anniversary Symposium Series on Perspective Papers. Manila. August–September.

Pritchett, L. 1996. Where Has All the Education Gone? World Bank Working Paper No. 1581, Washington, DC: World Bank.

Sanchez, A. 1983. Philippine Capital Stock Measurement and Total Factor Productivity Analysis. Quezon City: University of the Philippines. PhD. Dissertation.

Schady, N. 2001. Convexity and Sheepskin Effects in the Human Capital Earnings Function: Recent Evidence for Filipino Men. World Bank Working Paper No. 2881. Washington, DC: World Bank.

Sianesi, B., and J. Van Reenen. 2000. *The Returns to Education: A Review of the Macro Literature.* CEE Discussion Paper No. 20. London: London School of Economics.

Son, H. H. 2008. Explaining Growth and Inequality in Factor Income: The Philippines Case. ERD Working Paper No. 121. Manila: ADB.

Spence, M. 1973. Job Market Signalling. *Quarterly Journal of Economics.* 87(3): 355–74.

Trostel, P., I. Walker, and P. Woolley. 2002. Estimates of the Economic Returns to Schooling for 28 Countries. *Labor Economics.* 9(1): 1–16.

8. Equity and the Social Sector

Hyun H. Son and Jane Carangal-San Jose

8.1. Introduction

Gross domestic product (GDP) per capita and related aggregate income measures are widely used to assess the economic performance of countries. Economic growth that measures the rate of change in per capita real GDP has become a standard economic indicator. Despite the popularity of economic growth as a measure of success, there is increasing recognition that it is an inadequate measure of a population's well-being. Higher economic growth does not necessarily mean a higher level of well-being.

GDP, as conventionally measured, excludes many factors that contribute to well-being while incorporating other factors that have an adverse effect on it. For example, GDP does not include nonmarket production in the economy. The contribution made by housewives to output can be quite substantial, but is not included in measuring GDP. As growth leads to increased air and water pollution, people spend more money protecting themselves from these ill effects. These expenditures are included in GDP, but they do not add to well-being. Instead, pollution contributes to people's ill-being.

Economic growth is important for well-being. It provides people with a greater command over goods and services, which translates into greater utility. Economic growth gives people more choices. However, these do not necessarily or automatically translate to well-being.

Furthermore, the benefits of economic growth are seldom shared equally. Some people may enjoy a large share of benefits, while many others may be completely bypassed by growth. Thus, economic growth does not necessarily imply a higher level of well-being for everyone in the society. If the objective is to enhance the well-being of everyone, then economic growth indicators should be supplemented with other indicators that are more closely related to individual lives, such as, "achievements in the most basic human capabilities—leading a long life, being knowledgeable, and enjoying a decent standard of living" (UNDP 1999, 127). According to the 1990 Human Development Report, "Economic growth is a means and not an end of development" (UNDP 1990). There is no automatic link between high GDP growth and progress in human development, at least in the short to medium term.

This study focuses on identifying the obstacles or constraints to achieving sustainable and equitable growth that contribute to human well-being in the Philippines. The study posits that ultimately, such constraints could be related to human capital, i.e., in terms of education and health (Figure 8.1).

Figure 8.1: Problem Tree for the Social Sector

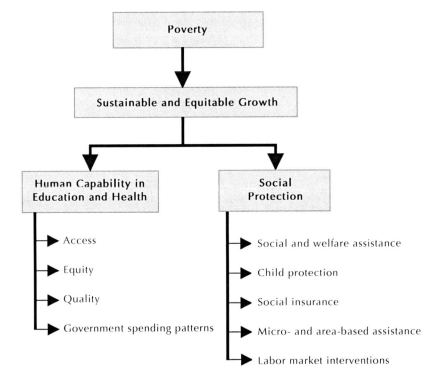

Source: Authors.

Households decide on schooling, health care, and labor force participation. These decisions relate closely to the households' well-being. Such decisions, moreover, have direct impacts on the economy as a whole: for example, households' decisions on schooling are directly related to the production of skilled and unskilled labor for the economy. Although GDP (obtained from national account statistics) and household welfare (coming from unit record household surveys) are not comparable and do not always provide the same trend in growth, it is widely accepted that people's well-being is better reflected in welfare measures obtained from micro household surveys than in national accounts. This study explores what constrains the achievement of sustainable and equitable growth with a particular focus on basic social services such as health and education.

The key questions of interest in this study are as follows:

(i) Is spatial disparity a major constraint to growth and poverty reduction?
(ii) Have spatial disparities in opportunities been serious constraints to achieving equitable growth?
(iii) Do people have access to primary education and health services?
(iv) Does everyone in society benefit equally from primary education and health services?
(v) Is the pattern of government budget allocation equitable across regions and income groups?

This study uses two types of nationally representative household surveys: the Family Income and Expenditure Survey (FIES) and Annual Poverty Indicator Survey (APIS), both conducted by the National Statistics Office. This study used the FIES conducted in 1994, 1997, 2000, and 2003 and the APIS of 1998 and 2004.

The study is organized in the following manner. Section 8.2 analyzes trends on average welfare, inequality, and poverty in the Philippines. Section 8.3 explains changes in poverty in terms of growth and distribution effects, and examines whether the growth process in the Philippines has been pro-poor or anti-poor. Section 8.4 discusses human development in health and education and economic growth. In this section, major findings from cross-country and cross-regional regression analyses are discussed. Section 8.5 investigates the education sector, particularly issues including access to and equity of education, quality of education, and government resource allocations to it. Section 8.6 deals with similar issues for the health sector. Section 8.7 reviews the social protection stance and major poverty reduction programs, child protection programs, labor market interventions, and micro-based programs. Section 8.8 also discusses issues of programming, budgeting, and institutional arrangements and compares them with similar issues in other Asian countries, especially Indonesia, Thailand, and Viet Nam. The final section contains conclusions and policy recommendations based on the major findings of the study.

8.2. Average Welfare, Inequality, and Poverty

It is widely held in the Philippines that development policy has favored Luzon and discriminated against the Visayas and, particularly, Mindanao. Moreover, the poor performance of the Philippine economy has been blamed partly on the relatively large gap in access to infrastructure and social services between the major urban centers and rural areas (Balisacan 1996, Bautista 1997). Spatial variation in certain summary measures of human development is also evident (HDN 1996 and 2005).

If spatial income disparities are indeed at the core of the poverty problem in the Philippines, then policy reforms aimed at reducing these disparities need to be central to the country's poverty reduction program. This may also promote efficiency goals: important dynamic externalities can arise from targeting by region or according to sector-specific characteristics (Bardhan 1996, Ravallion and Jalan 1996). Channeling physical infrastructure investments—such as roads, communications, and irrigation—to less developed areas, or the rural sector in general, may improve the productivity of private investments, promote the development of intangible "social capital", and mitigate erosion in the quality of urban life by discouraging rural–urban migration.

However, if spatial income disparities result from variations in human development within each of the regions of the country, then a different approach to poverty reduction needs to be found. For example, systematic differences in levels of human capital between low- and high-income groups within a geographic region may translate into considerable differences in earning opportunities. In this case, a policy prescription to reduce overall income inequality and poverty would require expanding the access of low-income groups to basic social services and infrastructure.

This section seeks to test if spatial disparity is a binding constraint to growth and poverty reduction in the country. The analysis begins with studying trends in average standard of living or welfare, poverty, and inequality during 1994–2003, with a particular focus on regional disparities.

8.2.1. Average Standard of Living

Average standard of living can be measured either by per capita income or by per capita consumption. The latter is widely preferred, however. On theoretical grounds, consumption is better than income in reflecting the current and long-term standard of living. Income is subject to large fluctuations due to transitory components, while consumption is more stable as people tend to smooth out their consumption over time, albeit partly, through savings and dissavings. Consequently, consumption is deemed a better measure of permanent income; it is less influenced by transitory income and is thus more stable.

212

From a practical perspective, consumption is measured more accurately than income. In an economy largely characterized by self-employment and the informal sector, income is hard to estimate accurately. Moreover, it tends to be reported inaccurately for tax advantage or illegal activities. Based on both theoretical and practical reasons, international practitioners have relied increasingly on consumption or expenditure-based measures to analyze poverty and inequality. Nevertheless, this analysis will use both measures for completeness.

For the analysis, per capita nominal income and expenditure were adjusted by the costs of living that differ across regions and over time. The adjustment was achieved by dividing per capita nominal income or expenditure by the per capita poverty line, expressed as a percentage. This measure is commonly referred to as the per capita welfare of income or expenditure, which could be interpreted as real income or expenditure. The poverty lines used are consistency-conforming provincial poverty lines developed by Balisacan (2001).[1] Per capita welfare of income or expenditure is thus equivalent to the per capita income or expenditure that is above or below the poverty line. For example, a per capita welfare income of 250 means that an individual's income is 2.5 times greater than the poverty line. Similarly, a per capita welfare income of 70 can be interpreted as the per capita income that is 30% lower than the poverty threshold.

According to the analysis as estimates from FIES, both welfare measures show that people's average standards of living improved during 1994–2003. In this period, per capita welfare of income and expenditure grew at annual rates of 1.43% and 1.70%, respectively. The estimates also reveal that both welfare indicators increased sharply in the 1994–1997 period, flowing from the restoration of political stability and deepening of policy and institutional reforms. However, because of the combined impact of the 1997 Asian financial crisis, the El Niño phenomenon in 1998, and political uncertainty, the overall growth in average welfare fell during 1997–2000 and continued to decline in 2000–2003. Per capita welfare based on income fell more rapidly than per capita welfare using expenditure.

Figure 8.2 shows the disparity in the level of average welfare across the 16 regions of the Philippines. Clearly, average welfare varies substantially across regions, with the National Capital Region (NCR) having the highest mean living standard during the 9-year period. In 2003, the NCR's average per capita welfare of expenditure was almost 47% higher than the national average and about three times the mean living standard for the Autonomous Region in Muslim Mindanao (ARMM), the poorest region of

---

[1] Although there have been debates on official poverty lines versus other poverty lines, this is not the main objective of the current study. For detailed discussions on the poverty lines, see Balisacan (1999) and ADB (2005).

Figure 8.2: Per Capita Welfare of Income and Expenditure by Region, 2003 (as % of National Capital Region levels)

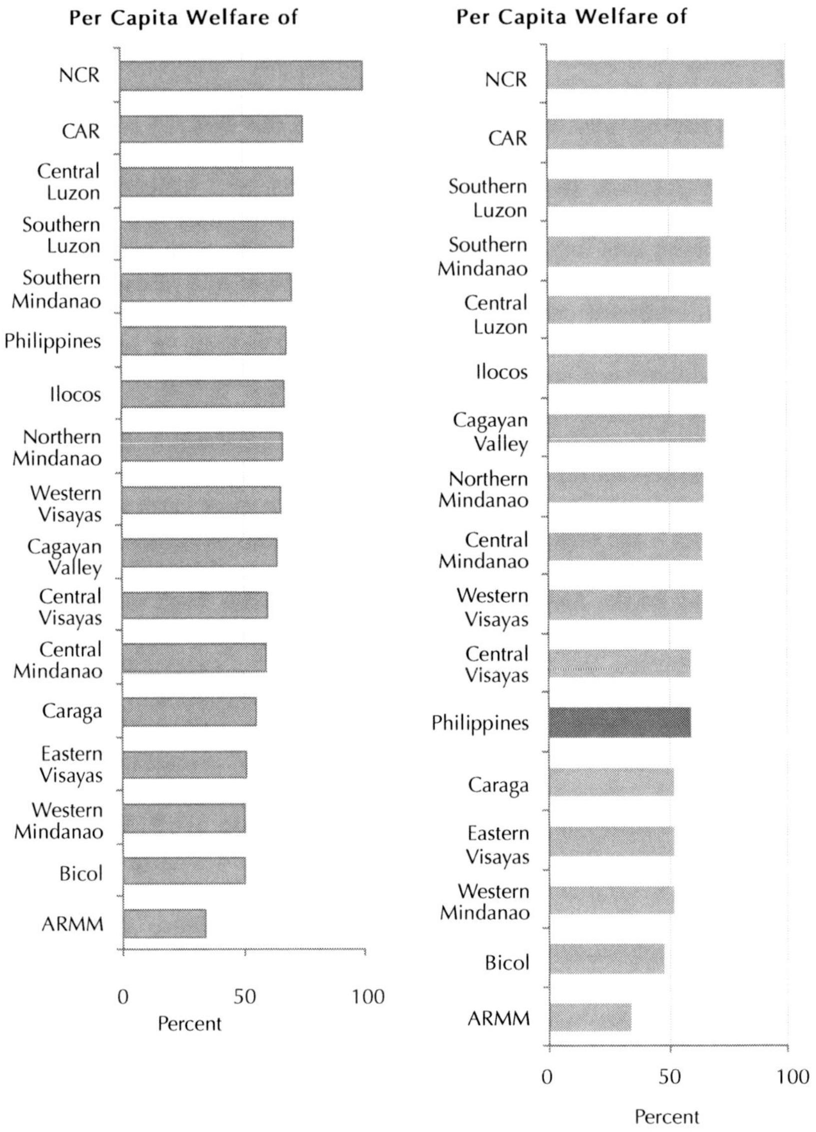

Per Capita Welfare of

Per Capita Welfare of

ARMM = Autonomous Region in Muslim Mindanao, CAR = Cordillera Administrative Region, NCR = National Capital Region.
Note: Per capita welfare is expressed in terms of NCR, i.e., per capita welfare of NCR is taken as 100.
Source: Authors' calculations based on the Family Income and Expenditure Surveys 1994 and 2003 (NSO various years).

the country. Overall, the average welfare for the Luzon regions surpassed those in the Visayas and Mindanao. While the welfare ranking of most regions changed between 1994 and 2003, the NCR remained in its relative position during the period. This suggests that the prevalence of regional disparity remains a major challenge to the country.

In terms of growth in average welfare, Figure 8.3 does not suggest that richer regions grew faster than poorer ones during 1994–2003. The NCR, the richest region, grew sluggishly during that period (0.26% per year), far slower than the other regions except ARMM. The poorest region, ARMM, is the only region that had negative growth during the period (–2.54% per year). Such trends have widened the disparity in the standards of living between the NCR and ARMM. Along with material well-being, disparity in human development in education and health could have increased between the two regions, which will be investigated in sections 8.4 and 8.5. Such changes highlight the need to address economic hardships suffered by people living in the ARMM.

The foregoing shows that average welfare has improved nationwide, but growth in welfare has declined over time. Moreover, disparities in regional welfare pervade the Philippines.

Figure 8.3: Annual Growth Rates in Per Capita Welfare of Expenditure by Region, 1994–2003 (%)

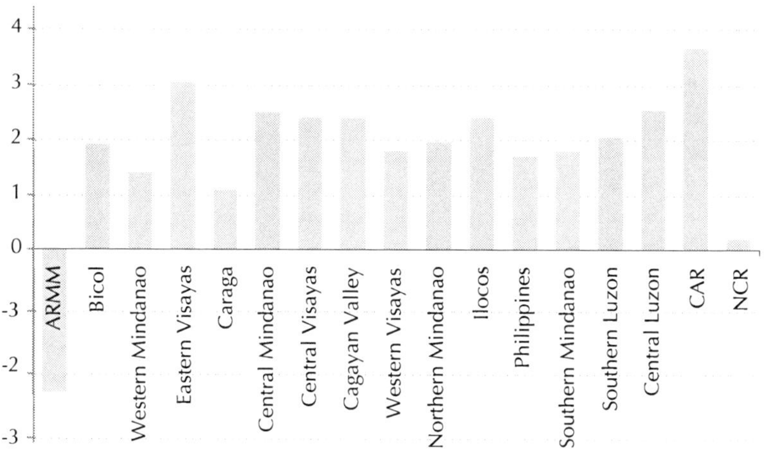

ARMM = Autonomous Region in Muslim Mindanao, CAR = Cordillera Administrative Region, NCR = National Capital Region.
Note: Regions are arranged in ascending order of their per capita expenditure in 2003 price.
Source: Authors' calculations based on the Family Income and Expenditure Surveys (NSO various years).

8.2.2. Inequality

In this study, inequality in per capita welfare of income and expenditure is measured using the Gini coefficient, which is the most widely used measure of inequality. Figure 8.4 shows that inequality is high in the Philippines in terms of both income and expenditure. As expected, distribution based on income is more unequal than that based on expenditure. More importantly, the distribution of both income and expenditure worsened during 1994–2003; the Gini coefficient rose by 7.0% and 4.2% for per capita welfare of income and expenditure, respectively. This increase was mainly attributed to the rise in Gini in the earlier period (1994–1997). While inequality fell in the latter period (2000–2003), the 2003 level was still higher than that in 1994. These findings indicate that, while average per capita welfare increased in the Philippines during 1994–2003, the benefits of growth were not equally shared by all segments of the population.

Figure 8.4: Gini Coefficients Based on Per Capita Income and Expenditure Adjusted for Regional Costs of Living Indexes

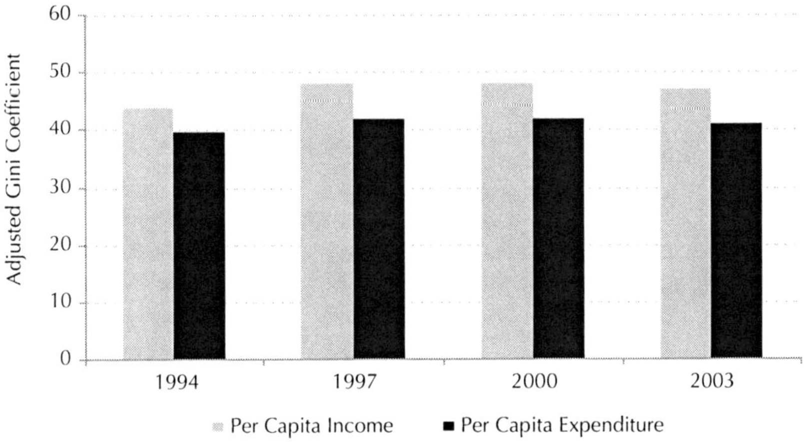

Source: Authors' calculations based on the Family Income and Expenditure Surveys (NSO various years).

Figure 8.5 shows the annual growth rates of per capita welfare of income and expenditure by quintile shares. The growth rates are positive for all quintiles during the entire period (1994–2003). The rates increase monotonically as one moves toward the richer quintile shares: per capita welfare had grown the slowest for the poorest quintile, and fastest for the richest quintile. However, more recently (2000–2003), the growth rates were negative for the richest quintile, suggesting that the standard of living of the top 20% of the population declined during the period while that for the poorest quintile remained unchanged. These findings indicate that, generally, inequality in the Philippines had worsened in the 1994–2003 period, although it slightly improved in the later years.

Figure 8.5: Annual Growth Rates of Per Capita Real Income and Expenditure by Quintile, 1994–2003

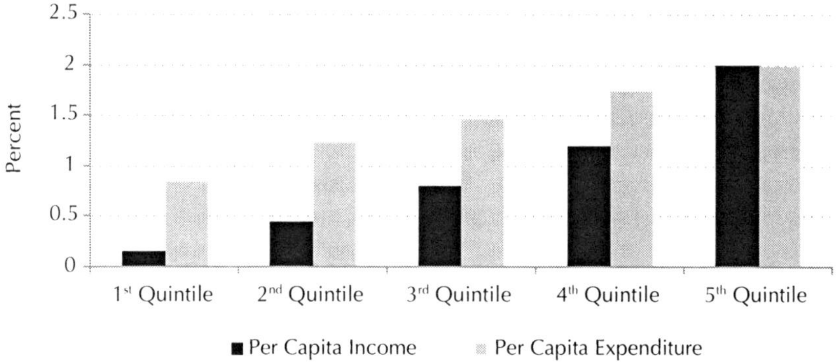

Source: Authors' calculations based on the Family Income and Expenditure Surveys (NSO various years).

A way of understanding inequality is to calculate the contributions of various socioeconomic groups to aggregate inequality. A commonly used tool is Theil's index (Theil 1967). This index decomposes total inequality into between- and within-group inequality. Decomposition is useful in separating the relative contribution of between- and within-group inequality to the overall inequality in society. This technique can be most helpful in examining changes in intra- and inter-regional inequality over time.

Table 2.11 in Chapter 2 shows a decomposition of national inequality of per capita welfare of income and expenditure into two components: inequality between regions and inequality within region. The results show that the contribution of the between-group (i.e., between regions) component to overall inequality is small, despite the large regional differences in average welfare of income and expenditure. Hence, removing between-group inequality by equalizing all regional mean incomes or expenditure will not do much to reduce total inequality. In 2003, for example, equalizing all regional mean incomes and expenditure by removing between-group inequality would have reduced total inequality by only 7.2% and

9.2%, respectively. On the other hand, removing within-region inequality by making everyone's income or expenditure within a region equal to the mean for that region would lower total inequality substantially—for example, by 92.8% in 2003.

Clearly, disparity in average welfare and human achievement within each of the regions is the major problem. Within-region inequality arises from differences in possessions of both physical and human capital, including public goods. Differences in educational attainment alone raise the contribution of between-group inequality to more than one third of the observed national inequality (Table 2.12). In 2003, for example, between-group inequality of per capita welfare accounted for 34.2% and 35.7% of overall inequality in income and expenditure, respectively. Unfortunately, while the distribution of human and physical capital is within the influence of government policy, public investments have fallen short of creating a highly favorable environment for capital formation, especially for those at the bottom end of the distribution.

In sum, inequality during 1994–2003 stemmed mainly from differences within geographical boundaries and sectors, not from differences in mean incomes or expenditures between boundaries and sectors in the Philippines.

Although income or consumption is an important component of the standard of living, it will be useful to look into inequality based on non-income dimensions. Non-income dimensions of living standards may include various housing characteristics, such as access to safe drinking water, sanitary toilet, and electricity. As illustrated in Figure 3.41 in Chapter 3, inequality in the endowment of modern housing amenities can be seen between regions, wherein the NCR is far better equipped than ARMM.

Water scarcity accentuates poverty by directly constraining people's access to a basic necessity and indirectly limiting access to food and employment. Improved household and community water security, safe environmental sanitation, and better hygienic practices are among the most effective approaches to minimizing the transmission of and exposure to pathogens and wastes in and around communities and households. When access to water and sanitation is suboptimal, the levels of disease, mortality, and morbidity in the population are likely to be high.

As expected in the Philippine context, richer households tend to have better access to various basic infrastructure services than the poorer ones (Figure 3.41, Chapter 3).

To recap, inequality persists in the Philippines and worsened during 1994–2003. Much of the inequality is attributed to within-group inequality. In assessing further how welfare has changed in the Philippines, this study shows that inequality persists in terms of both income and non-income dimensions (e.g., access to housing amenities such as safe drinking water and electricity). As pointed out earlier, this reflects much of the bias in government spending that favored the northern regions in the country. As the next section shows, inequality has yielded disparities in poverty incidence across Philippine regions. Well-being in the Philippine economy has on the whole remained largely uneven.

8.2.3. Poverty

This study focuses on three aspects of poverty: incidence, depth, and severity. These are captured by the general class of Foster-Greer-Thornbecke poverty measures. The incidence of poverty is measured by the headcount ratio, which simply estimates the percentage of population living below the poverty line (Foster, Greer, and Thornbecke 1984).

The depth of poverty is estimated by the poverty gap ratio. The poverty gap ratio can be defined by the average distance below the poverty line as a proportion of that line, where the average is formed over the entire population, counting the non-poor as having zero poverty gap. Thus, the sum of poverty gaps (aggregated across all individuals) reflects the minimum amount of consumption that is required to bring all the poor up to the poverty line.

The severity of poverty measure represents the mean of the squared proportionate poverty gaps. Unlike the headcount ratio and the poverty gap ratio, it considers inequality among the poor. The severity of poverty measure is sensitive to the distribution of consumption among the poor, in that its calculation gives more weight to those whose consumption falls far below the poverty line. Hence, the severity of poverty index is more sensitive to changes in the standard of living of the ultra-poor than of the moderately poor.

Table 8.1 shows poverty incidence across regions of the country from 1994 to 2003, as well as the contribution of each region to total poverty. Despite the huge gaps, the NCR consistently recorded the lowest poverty, while ARMM, Bicol, and Western Mindanao were the highest. As shown in Table 8.1 and Figure 8.6, the highest concentration of poor people was in the Visayan and Mindanao regions in 2003, where 48.3% of the poor lived. In particular, the highest concentration of the ultra-poor—as measured by the poverty gap and severity of poverty ratio—was in Western Mindanao. High poverty—in all three aspects—in Western Mindanao and ARMM was brought about largely by instability: toward the end of the 1990s, the region was at the center of violent conflicts between the military and armed dissidents.

Table 8.1: Poverty Incidence in 16 Regions
(%, based on per capita welfare of expenditure)

Region	1994	1997	2000	2003			
				Poverty Incidence	Population Share	Contribution to Total Poverty (% points)	Share of the Poor
Ilocos	26.4	20.9	20.3	16.9	5.3	0.9	3.6
Cagayan Valley	41.8	30.1	29.6	26.2	3.4	0.9	3.3
Central Luzon	24.4	13.4	16.3	13.9	11.1	1.5	5.8
Southern Luzon	28.8	19.6	19.7	20.7	16.0	3.3	12.7
Bicol	50.2	45.6	49.6	45.7	6.1	2.8	11.4
Western Visayas	34.5	22.1	28.6	26.7	7.6	2.0	8.4
Central Visayas	42.9	35.6	39.5	36.6	7.4	2.7	9.4
Eastern Visayas	51.4	50.6	47.0	45.0	4.7	2.1	7.8
Western Mindanao	47.1	35.3	47.0	48.2	3.6	1.8	7.0
Northern Mindanao	35.1	26.1	27.7	32.9	4.5	1.5	5.7
Southern Mindanao	30.5	27.6	25.1	25.9	4.9	1.3	4.9
Central Mindanao	45.2	32.9	36.7	29.3	4.3	1.3	5.2
NCR	5.6	3.5	5.6	4.9	13.5	0.7	2.3
CAR	26.6	23.4	20.9	15.3	1.7	0.3	1.1
ARMM	48.9	51.1	61.9	63.9	3.3	2.1	7.6
Caraga	41.3	37.1	34.0	36.9	2.6	1.0	3.8
Philippines	32.2	25.2	27.1	26.0	100.0	26.0	100.0

ARMM = Autonomous Region in Muslim Mindanao, CAR = Cordillera Administrative Region, NCR = National Capital Region.

This study began by positing that education can ultimately bear on poverty reduction. Table 8.2 reaffirms that education can be a powerful shield against poverty. As in most countries, the Philippines shows a negative

Figure 8.6: Poverty Estimates by Region in 2003 (%)

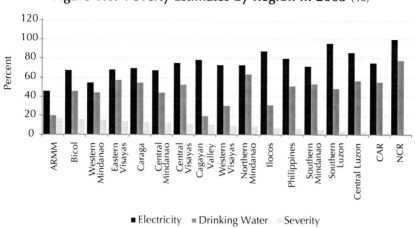

ARMM = Autonomous Region in Muslim Mindanao, CAR = Cordillera Administrative Region, NCR = National Capital Region.
Source: Authors' calculations based on the Family Income and Expenditure Surveys (NSO various years).

Table 8.2: Poverty Incidence by Education Level of Household Head
(%, based on per capita welfare of expenditure)

Education Level	1994	1997	2000	2003			
				Poverty Incidence	Population Share	Contribution to Total Poverty (% points)	Share of the Poor
No Education	54.7	46.9	57.5	60.2	2.8	1.7	6.7
Primary Incomplete	48.9	41.9	45.0	46.5	21.9	10.2	39.0
Primary Graduate	39.3	31.7	33.3	32.8	20.5	6.7	26.2
High School Incomplete	31.5	24.5	28.6	26.3	12.9	3.4	12.8
High School Graduate	18.3	13.6	17.0	14.5	21.3	3.1	11.9
College Incomplete	8.8	6.3	7.5	6.6	11.2	0.7	2.7
College Graduate	2.8	1.8	1.3	2.0	9.4	0.2	0.6
Philippines	32.2	25.2	27.1	26.0	100.0	26.0	100.0

correlation between poverty and the household head's level of education. The incidence of poverty falls continuously from households whose head has no formal education (60.2% in 2003) to those with a tertiary education (2.0% in 2003). This suggests that human capital accumulation has important impacts on individual earnings, and thus on mitigating poverty.

So far, the analysis shows that Philippine economic growth is unbalanced, with some regions growing faster than others, and that poverty is more severe in the southern regions of the country such as Bicol, Mindanao, and the Visayas. That spatial disparity could be a binding constraint to sustainable and equitable growth and ultimately to poverty reduction appears valid. The analysis also indicates that addressing inequality within, rather than between, each region would considerably reduce inequality nationwide. This suggests the need for government policies to be region-specific, to ensure success in curbing aggregate inequality.

8.3. Changes in Poverty by Growth and Inequality

8.3.1. Poverty Decomposition into Growth and Distribution

In general, the poverty level depends on two factors: the average level of mean income or expenditure and the extent of inequality in the income or expenditure distribution. While an increase in average income reduces poverty, an increase in inequality increases poverty. According to Kakwani (2000), the total change in poverty can be explained in terms of the exact sum of the growth and inequality components. The growth component captures the change in poverty given a constant distribution, and the inequality component measures the change in poverty that occurs due to a change in inequality when the average income does not change. Table 8.3 presents the results of decomposing national poverty in terms of growth and distribution effects during 1994–2003.

Clearly, in 1994–1997, the period when poverty reduction was comparatively large, the growth component contributed to the reduction in poverty incidence by 12.85% per year, assuming the distribution of expenditure remained unchanged. However, the change in inequality during 1994–1997 had an offsetting effect on poverty reduction. If growth were distributionally neutral in 1994–1997, the headcount ratio would have fallen by 4.76% per year. In other words, the increase in inequality in that period offset the impact of growth on poverty. On the other hand, if the distribution of expenditure had not changed in 2000–2003, poverty incidence would have increased rather than decreased, which was observed. Inequality actually fell during this period, thereby offsetting the adverse

Table 8.3: Explaining Changes in Poverty, 1994–2003
(%, based on per capita welfare of expenditure)

Period Poverty measure	Growth Effect	Inequality Effect	Total Effect
1994–1997			
Headcount Ratio	–12.85	4.76	–8.10
Poverty Gap Ratio	–17.77	7.83	–9.94
Severity of Poverty	–21.23	9.49	–11.74
1997–2000			
Headcount Ratio	2.03	0.30	2.33
Poverty Gap Ratio	2.73	0.35	3.08
Severity of Poverty	3.28	0.73	4.01
2000–2003			
Headcount Ratio	0.73	–2.03	–1.31
Poverty Gap Ratio	0.94	–1.76	–0.83
Severity of Poverty	1.12	–1.68	–0.56
1994–2003			
Headcount Ratio	–3.36	1.00	–2.36
Poverty Gap Ratio	–4.62	2.05	–2.56
Severity of Poverty	–5.50	2.74	–2.76

Source: Authors' calculations based on the Family Income and Expenditure Surveys (NSO various years).

impact on poverty of the fall in mean expenditure. However, in most periods, the growth effect tended to dominate the distribution effect in explaining the observed changes in any of the poverty measures. The only exception occurred in the later period (2000–2003), when the distribution component outweighed the growth component. For the entire 1994–2003 period, the increase in inequality reduced the impact of growth on poverty. While this effect was quite substantial, it was small relative to the reduction attributable to expenditure growth. Thus, the changes in both real mean expenditure and its distribution contributed to the changes in poverty during the 9-year period. Corollary to this finding, the next section investigates the extent to which recent episodes of growth in the Philippines have benefited the poor or the non-poor.

Figures 8.7 and 8.8 present changes in the headcount index and the poverty gap ratio in terms of growth and inequality effects in 16 regions during 1994–2003. Growth effect tends to dominate inequality effect in each region. Growth effect is greatest in the Cordillera Administrative Region,

Figure 8.7: Explaining Changes in Headcount Ratio by Region, 1994–2003 (%, based on per capita expenditure)

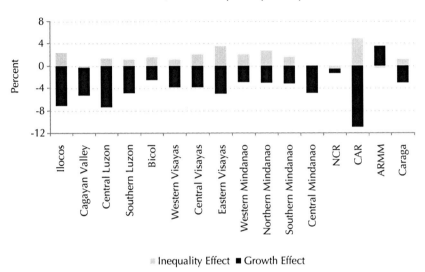

ARMM = Autonomous Region in Muslim Mindanao, CAR = Cordillera Adminstrative Region, NCR = National Capital Region.
Source: Authors' calculations based on the Family Income and Expenditure Surveys (NSO various years).

while ARMM, Bicol, Caraga, and Western Mindanao had a smaller growth effect than the other regions. The growth effect in ARMM was positive, meaning that its growth during 1994–2003 had contributed to increasing both the incidence and depth of poverty.

While the impact of the change in expenditure distribution is relatively small, its effect on changes in poverty varies quite substantially across regions. In most regions, inequality had increased within region. The inequality effect on poverty had been particularly large in the Cordillera Administrative Region, Eastern and Central Visayas, and Northern and Western Mindanao. On the contrary, a fall in inequality within region in areas such as the Cagayan Valley and ARMM resulted in a positive contribution to changes in poverty. Figures 8.7 and 8.8 show that ARMM is different from the rest in terms of the contributions of growth and inequality effects on changes in poverty—ARMM is the only region that shows an increase in poverty due to the growth effect and a fall in poverty due to a slight improvement in the distribution of expenditure.

Overall, there are spatial differences in changes in mean expenditure, distribution of expenditure, and poverty reduction across regions during 1994–2003. The findings also show that, in all 16 regions, poverty reduction had been largely due to the contribution of the positive growth effect in mean expenditure, with the distribution being constant. This suggests that growth is vital for poverty reduction within region. For instance, ARMM had the least impressive growth; it is also one of the poorest regions in the Philippines.

Figure 8.8: Explaining Changes in Poverty Gap Ratio by Region, 1994–2003 (%, based on per capita expenditure)

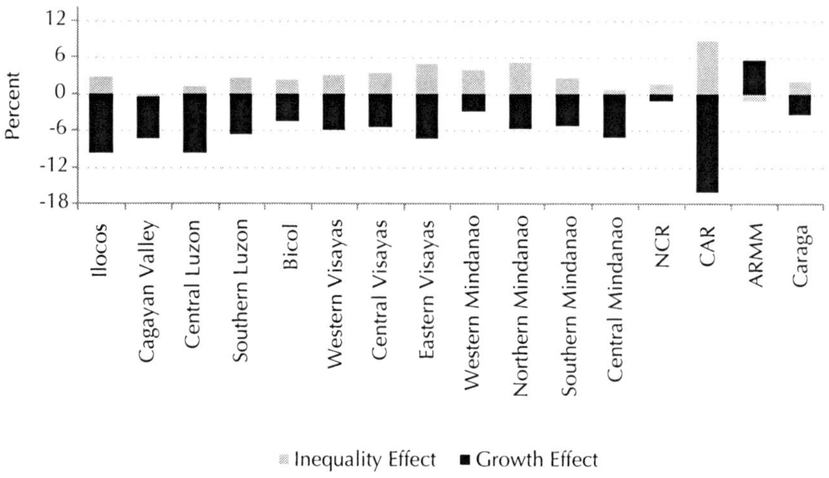

ARMM = Autonomous Region in Muslim Mindanao, CAR = Cordillera Administrative Region, NCR = National Capital Region.
Source: Authors' calculations based on the Family Income and Expenditure Surveys (NSO various years).

8.3.2. Pro-Poor Growth

There are various views on pro-poor growth. This study takes the perspective that growth is pro-poor if it benefits the poor proportionally more than the non-poor. Hence, pro-poor growth occurs when growth reduces poverty; inequality concurrently falls during the growth process. This study uses the poverty equivalent growth rate (PEGR) to measure the degree of pro-poorness of economic growth in the Philippines in 1994–2003.

The PEGR is the growth rate that results in the same level of poverty reduction as the present growth rate if the growth process had not been accompanied by any change in inequality, i.e., when everyone in society received the same proportional benefits of growth. It may be also called an effective growth rate for poverty reduction. The PEGR can be separately computed for the entire class of poverty measures—including headcount ratio, poverty gap ratio, and severity of poverty index. The PEGR addresses both the magnitude of growth and the benefits the poor receive from growth. There is a monotonic relationship between the PEGR and poverty reduction: the proportional reduction in poverty is a monotonically increasing function of the PEGR. Thus, to achieve rapid poverty reduction, the PEGR ought to be maximized rather than growth rate alone.

Table 8.4: Poverty Equivalent Growth Rate, 1994–2003
(based on per capita welfare of expenditure)

Period Poverty Measure	Poverty Equivalent Growth Rate	Actual Growth Rate (%, per year)
1994–1997		
Headcount Ratio	4.02	6.39
Poverty Gap Ratio	3.57	
Severity of Poverty	3.53	
1997–2000		
Headcount Ratio	–1.10	–0.96
Poverty Gap Ratio	–1.09	
Severity of Poverty	–1.18	
2000–2003		
Headcount Ratio	0.61	–0.34
Poverty Gap Ratio	0.30	
Severity of Poverty	0.17	
1994–2003		
Headcount Ratio	1.19	1.70
Poverty Gap Ratio	0.94	
Severity of Poverty	0.85	

Source: Authors' calculations based on the Family Income and Expenditure Surveys (NSO various years).

Table 8.4 presents PEGRs for the entire period and its subperiods. During 1994–2003, the PEGRs of any poverty measure were lower than the actual growth rate of per capita welfare of expenditure (1.70% per year). This suggests that the growth process in 1994–2003 had not been pro-poor; the non-poor had benefited from growth proportionally more than the poor. A similar conclusion is drawn from the growth pattern of the economic boom period, 1994–1997. The same non-poor growth pattern continued during the crisis period. But the picture changed in the 2000–2003 period: the average welfare of expenditure fell, but its adverse impact was much greater on the non-poor than the poor.

There is no question that overall economic growth benefits the poor and that it is crucial to poverty reduction in both the short and long term. Indeed, no country has ever won the war against absolute poverty without first getting its economy to sustain growth at rates higher than its population growth rate over a reasonably long period of time. The key to success in poverty reduction in the major East Asian countries was their rapid economic growth—averaging 6–9% per year—sustained for 2–3 decades. Seen from this perspective, the main reason for the high level of absolute poverty in the Philippines is primarily the short duration of and the slowness of economic growth. Moreover, the growth pattern during 1994–2003 shows that growth had not favored the poor.

8.4. Economic Growth and Human Development in Education and Health

The link between human capital development and economic growth cannot be undermined. Higher levels of human development affect the economy by enhancing people's capacities and, consequently, their creativity and productivity. Ample evidence suggests that as people become healthier, better nourished, and more educated, they contribute more to economic growth through higher labor productivity, improved technology, attraction of more foreign capital, and higher exports. This, of course, does not detract from the intrinsic value of improving the lives of those who cannot find employment because of disability or age, for example.

As discussed in Chapter 8, increases in earnings are associated with additional years of education, with the rate of return varying with the level of education. In agriculture, moreover, evidence suggests the positive effects of education on productivity among farmers using modern technologies (Schultz 1975, Rosenzweig 1995).

There is also positive return from improved education to greater income equality. As education becomes more broadly based, people with low incomes are better able to seek economic opportunities, which improves income distribution over time. For example, a study of the relationship between schooling, income inequality, and poverty in 18 Latin American countries in the 1980s concluded that education has the strongest impact on income inequality (Psacharopolous et al. 1992). Improved income distribution, in turn, has been found to be positively associated with economic growth, even though the empirical basis for this appears to be rather inconclusive (Alesina and Rodrik 1994, Alesina and Perotti 1994).

Improved health and nutrition have also been shown to have direct effects on labor productivity, especially among poorer individuals (Behrman 1996). For instance, calorie increases have been widely shown to raise productivity, including among farmers in Sierra Leone, sugarcane workers in Guatemala, and road construction workers in Kenya (Cornia and Stewart 1995). A longitudinal study of children in Chile concluded that providing nutritional supplements to children to prevent malnutrition would generate benefits in terms of additional productivity 6 to 8 times the cost of the intervention (Selowsky and Taylor 1973). At the aggregate level also, health has been shown to be an important input into economic growth (Bloom, Canning, and Sevilla 2004).

Education and health alone, of course, cannot transform an economy. The quantity and quality of investment, domestic and foreign, together with the overall policy environment, form other important determinants of economic performance. Yet, the level of human development in health and education has a bearing on these factors, too.

This study investigates whether empirical evidence shows that economic growth is related to human capital in education and health. For this purpose, the study used data from 69 developing countries including the Philippines, though for some variables, a smaller number of observations was used due to lack of data (Boozer et al. 2004). Regression using the ordinary least squares method can show the extent to which indicators of human capital had a bearing on growth in GDP per capita during 1960–2001. The variables chosen to measure progress in human capital are the adult literacy rate and life expectancy. The results showed that GDP per capita growth was significantly related to improvement in the literacy rate at both 1% and 5% levels. Similar results were derived for life expectancy.

The study also used regression to test the link between growth and income distribution (using average Gini coefficient) and poverty (using average headcount ratio) in 69 developing countries for the same period (1960–2001). The results showed that the average Gini coefficient during the period did not prove significant, while the average poverty headcount ratio was highly significant at the 1% level. The regression results were robust particularly for the 12 Asian countries included in the model.[2]

Overall, the study showed significantly positive effects of progress in education and health indicators on growth. While useful, cross-country

---

[2] The People's Republic of China; Hong Kong, China; Indonesia; Republic of Korea; Lao People's Democratic Republic; Malaysia; Mongolia; Papua New Guinea; Philippines; Singapore; Thailand; and Viet Nam.

analysis suffers from insufficient attention to country heterogeneity in the relationship among growth, human capital, inequality, and poverty. The analysis is also empirically unable to generate robust determinants of growth that are valid across the developing world. Therefore, policy recommendations emerging from cross-country analysis should not be prescribed for individual countries without further analysis at a specific country level.

Balisacan (2007) used a similar regression methodology to investigate the impact of human capital on regional income growth in the Philippines. His findings echoed the results of our cross-country regression analysis. A major conclusion from his analysis was that improvements in health and schooling have positive effects on regional income growth rates in the Philippines. In his regression model, Balisacan included basic literacy rate and under-5 mortality rate as explanatory variables to capture their impacts on regional growth.

Findings from both the foregoing cross-country and within-country analyses suggest that progress in health and education affects growth. This provides impetus for investigating the relationship between human capital and growth. The main objective of this study is not to establish the casual relationship between the two. To do so can be an endless exercise if its objective is to find the causation between human capital and growth. In fact, economic literature suggests that causation runs in both directions, from human capital to growth and vice versa. Rather, this study focuses on investigating the link between growth and human capital in health and education at a micro level.

8.5. Education

For decades, the Philippines has ranked among the most highly educated developing countries. At first glance, it appears that the Philippines has made significant progress in education as reflected in the levels of basic and functional literacy. While basic literacy (i.e., ability to read and write) increased from 90% in 1989 to 93% in 2003, functional literacy (i.e., ability to read, write, compute, and comprehend) improved from 73% to 84% during the same period.

However, a closer look reveals a number of disturbing trends. Of particular concern in recent years is the continued decline in primary participation, from 90% in school year 2001–2002 to 84% in school year 2005–2006. The drop is more pronounced in urban areas, threatening the likelihood of the Philippines attaining its Millennium Development Goal target of universal primary education by 2015. More depressing has been the drop in cohort survival rates for both primary and secondary schools, from 66% and 71%, respectively, in school year 1981–1982 (NSCB 1990) to 58% and 59% in 2004–2006. The sharp fall in secondary schools has been blamed on increasing tuition fees and the need for poor students to forego studies in order to work.

Most problematic has been the persistence of poor quality education in the Philippines as evident in low average scores achieved by primary students in 2002–2003. Achievement rates in primary schools are measured by the National Achievement Test and its predecessors, the National Elementary Assessment Test and the National Secondary Assessment Test. These tests assess students in three subjects—mathematics, English, and science. In addition, the quality of education has suffered as a result of the country's high pupil–teacher ratio at the primary school level, with 35 students per teacher (Department of Education 2007). The ratio for the secondary level is even higher, at 39 students per teacher. By comparison, the primary pupil–teacher ratios in other Southeast Asian countries in 2004 were 19 for Malaysia, 21 for Thailand, and 23 for Viet Nam.

While the foregoing depicts the Philippines' progress in achieving education nationwide, a different picture emerges at the regional level. The following discussions shed light on variations in access to education across the regions and income classes within the country. Further, it will discuss the government's resource allocation in education.

8.5.1. Access to and Equity

Education is known to promote social mobility, thereby improving equity. This is one of the frequently used justifications for public intervention in the education sector. Whether the education system is indeed serving this end can be ascertained using two measures: (i) average access to education by school-age children, over time and across space; and (ii) distribution of educational opportunities across socioeconomic and income groups. This section deals with both access to and equity of education at primary and secondary levels.

According to the 2004 Annual Poverty Indicators Survey (APIS), the Philippine primary education system provides impressively wide access to children aged 7–12 years. Almost 96% of school-age children attended a primary school in 2004. However, the proportion of school attendance by children aged 13–16 years drops at the secondary level (73%). As Figure 8.9 shows, the most frequent reasons for dropping out of school are lack of personal interest (35%), affordability (32%), and the need for employment (16%). At the primary level, the main reason for not attending school is lack of personal interest. The lack of interest results from a number of factors that discourage students from studying, including inadequate curriculum,

Figure 8.9: School-Age Children's Reasons for Not Attending School
(%)

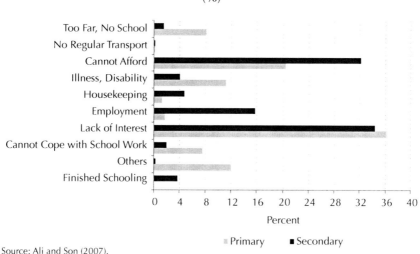

Source: Ali and Son (2007).

unqualified teachers, and lack of learning materials. Such factors are largely related to the quality of education.

In the Philippines, regional differences in school attendance exist at both the primary and secondary levels (Figure 8.10). While the gap among regions is smaller for primary education, it increases at the secondary level. These results reveal a degree of correlation between children's school attendance and poverty across regions. Indeed, poor regions—such as Bicol, Mindanao (particularly ARMM), and the Visayan regions—tend to have lower school attendance, falling below the national average, while richer regions such as the Cordillera Autonomous Region and NCR exhibit the best performance on this account. These gaps persist because the high cost of education has made it impossible for the poor to attend school, without sacrificing their basic needs.

The correlation between children's school attendance and poverty is evident further when examining access to education by income class in the Philippines. Some studies argue that there are pronounced differences in access to education between income groups. For instance, Balisacan (1994) suggests that while almost 100% of children aged 7–10 years were enrolled, the figure drops beyond that age, particularly for the three poorest deciles. More recently, Manasan (2001) found that the poor have much lower access to education than the non-poor, and the disparity becomes greater at the higher educational level.

Figure 8.10: School-Age Children Attending Primary
and Secondary School, 2004 (%)

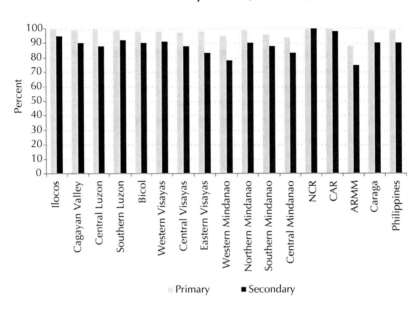

ARMM = Autonomous Region in Muslim Mindanao, CAR = Cordillera Administrative Region, NCR = National Capital Region.
Note: Figures are normalized to the NCR, i.e., access to primary and secondary school in the NCR is equal to 100.
Source: Authors' calculations based on NSO (2003a and b).

An attempt by this present study to assess the equity of access to primary and secondary education by income deciles reveals similar findings to those of the foregoing studies. This study uses the methodology of the opportunity curve proposed by Ali and Son (2007). The methodology was applied to two periods of the APIS, 1998 and 2004.

The slope of the opportunity curve may be helpful in assessing the extent to which opportunities are distributed equally or unequally among people at a given time. A downward sloping opportunity curve suggests that opportunities are distributed equally among the population; an upward sloping curve suggests an inequitable distribution. Figure 3.38 in Chapter 3 presents the opportunity curves for 1998 and 2004. In this case, opportunities are assessed in terms of access to primary and secondary education.

There are two points to consider on these curves. First, when the entire population is covered (i.e., a variable on the horizontal axis is 100), the opportunity curve coincides with the average access to primary (or secondary) education among children aged 7–12 years (or 13–16 years). Hence, access to primary education by 7–12-year-old children averaged 95.7% in 1998, increasing slightly to 96.5% in 2004. Similarly, 73.4% of the children aged 13–16 years attended secondary school in the Philippines in 1998; slightly more children, 74.8%, attended in 2004. These results can be seen from the upward shifts in the opportunity curve. Such changes in both educational levels are quite small over a 6-year period, particularly for the secondary level.

Second, in terms of the equity of access to education, children at the bottom end of the income distribution have lower access to primary and secondary education. Such inequity can be seen from the upward sloping opportunity curves for both education levels.

Figure 3.38 shows clearly that the average opportunity in primary education expanded during 1998–2004 among children aged 7–12 years. The opportunity in primary education remained inequitable, but its degree was almost constant over the period, as suggested by the parallel shift of the opportunity curves across the income distribution.

Figure 3.38 also clearly depicts an expansion of the average opportunity in secondary education, available among children aged 13–16 years between 1998 and 2004. The shift in the opportunity curve is greater for households with higher incomes than for those with lower incomes. This suggests that secondary education has been utilized increasingly by children from richer households, supporting earlier claims that education has become unaffordable to the poor.

Hence in terms of access, the Philippines has achieved almost universal coverage at the primary education level, but remains far from doing so at the secondary level. Disparities in access are prevalent across regions within the country, particularly in secondary education. That the gaps persist among income groups suggests the need to reallocate resources to the most needy.

8.5.2. Quality

Wide access to education, which means a larger number of student enrollees, brings with it concerns over class size, bottlenecks in teaching, and (most importantly) quality. Ensuring the quality of the labor force by providing quality education is particularly important in the Philippine context as it exports professionals, technicians, and other skilled workers. In 2004, overseas Filipino workers accounted for 10% of the country's population, the highest in the world (Lam 2005). Moreover, remittances from the overseas workers have accounted for about 8% of gross national product (GNP) in recent years.

Undoubtedly, the low quality of education is likely to be most visible in poor areas and regions. Hence, it is critical to improve the coverage and quality of the education system in the most impoverished parts of the country. Education is valued highly by Filipinos, rich and poor alike. For the poor, education is a means of getting a good job and thus escaping poverty and deprivation. For the rich, the state of public education, except for a few coveted state schools at the secondary and tertiary levels, is largely irrelevant. Rich families normally send their children to private schools, local or abroad. Indeed, the education policy for primary and secondary levels has largely been about schooling for the poorer segments of the population. Nevertheless, the rich have good reason to worry about the quality of public education because it contributes to the quality of labor force and, hence, economic growth in future.

That quality has remained low is evident in completion levels of primary and secondary education in the Philippines. A large number of children who enter school (about 30% of those who enter grade 1 and about 25% of those who enter the first year of secondary school) do not reach the last grade in the level. With the low transition rates, less than 50% of children who enter grade 1 complete secondary school.

There is little direct evidence—using household survey data and school data—in the Philippines on the impact of improved school quality on school enrollment (and completion). There is, however, convincing evidence of its impact on learning outcomes. A World Bank report (1996) using provincial data showed that some school staffing characteristics—particularly related to teachers—have an impact on elementary school completion rates. The report also suggests that provincial imbalances in school staffing characteristics are correlated with provincial income.

Regional disparity in the quality of education is apparent further in cohort survival rates and average scores on the National Elementary Assessment Test and National Secondary Assessment Test. Cohort survival rates tend to be lower in the poorer regions. For instance, the survival rate was lowest, at 32.2%, for primary education in Western Mindanao (Lam 2005). The test scores reflect a similar result—the NCR had the highest achievement rate in 1998, and Mindanao regions had the lowest. Thus, more effective targeting of available educational resources in poor areas is needed to reduce the disparities in schooling outcomes. However, the way governments spend on education is likely to have negative effects on the quality of education, as will be discussed in the next section.

In addition, a study by De Guzman and Cortes (1995) using the Household and School Matching Surveys data showed that having experienced school administrators (with tenure of 10 years or more), teachers who use innovative teaching methods, and schools that offer remedial classes reduces the rate of student absenteeism in grade 1. Also, the availability of textbooks and the presence of a guidance counselor lower the likelihood of absenteeism among grade 4 students. Glewwe and Jacoby

(1996) showed that, in Viet Nam, where enrollment rates are also very high and primary school completion rate is 80%, poor school quality (as proxied by the lack of supplies, poor quality buildings, and insufficiently trained teachers) significantly lowers the probability of students completing primary school. A higher percentage of trained teachers showed otherwise. Mason (1994) similarly showed that, in Indonesia, the lower the quality of the school (as proxied by a high ratio of run-down classrooms to maintained classrooms), the lower the probability of students completing primary education.

8.5.3. Government Resource Allocation

The Philippines' total (government and private) expenditure on education has increased in real terms during the last 15 years or so. The increase was due to larger enrollments at the primary and secondary levels as a result of the rapid growth in the number of school-age children.

Education has always ranked highest among the government's budgetary priorities. The newly launched Basic Education Sector Reform Agenda underpinned a substantial increase in spending on education, close to 8% in real terms for 2007. However, when benchmarked against major countries of the Association of Southeast Asian Nations (ASEAN), education spending appears insignificant. Education spending as a share of Philippine GDP fell from 4.0% to 2.4% during 1998–2005 (World Bank 2007). This is far lower than in countries such as Malaysia (8.1%), Thailand (4.2%), and Viet Nam (4.4%). Similarly, the Philippines lags behind its neighbors (e.g., Malaysia and Viet Nam) when it comes to per capita spending on primary and secondary education. In 2004, the national government spent 11.1% of GDP per capita for every elementary student and 9.2% for every secondary school student. The corresponding figures for Malaysia were 20.2% and 28.3%, respectively. This casts doubts on the quality of secondary education in the Philippines.

Recent evidence supports the view that the low quality of education has resulted from lack of clear priorities in allocating public resources. For example, the share of government spending on primary education fell during the period, with private households paying for the shortfall. Moreover, as a share of total spending on education, national government spending on primary school dropped from 68% in 1986 to 59% in 1994, and recovered to 61% in 1997. Between 1986 and 1997, shares of spending for secondary education increased from 12% to 20% and remained unchanged for tertiary education, at 20%. Per budget item, education spending appears to have shifted in favor of personal services, whose share rose substantially, from 74% in 1990 to 88% in 1999, on account of salary increases for teachers. During the same period, the share of maintenance and operating expenditure fell from 17% to 9%. The squeeze on maintenance and operating expenditure has resulted in the short supply of key educational inputs, including textbooks, teaching and instructional materials, science laboratory equipment and supplies, desks, teacher training, and school building maintenance.

While the above analysis suggests broad directions for the efficient and equitable allocation of public resources, it also stresses the need for a sound institutional environment to implement effective educational reforms in the Philippines. One such factor pertains to having adequate accountability mechanisms to ensure good performance in the sector (Luz 2004). Teachers' salaries need to be increased, and their capabilities need to be strengthened. Unlike the current practice, an adequate probationary period must be introduced for teachers before they can attain permanent status. It is critical to address teacher issues in educational policy because these directly impact student achievement. The education system needs to look carefully into the process of recruiting teachers, focusing on their competencies and ability to deliver good-quality education.

8.6. Health

Similar to the experience of the education sector, the Philippine health sector achieved modest gains at the national level. Life expectancy increased from 62.8 years in 1990 to 64.1 years in 2000–2005 for males and from 66.4 years in 1990 to 70.1 years in 2000–2005 for females. Infant and child mortality rates declined significantly. The infant mortality rate was reduced from 57 per 1,000 live births in 1990 to 24 in 2006. The mortality rate among children below 5 years old was also reduced, from 80 per 1,000 children under 5 years old to 32 in 2006. At the regional level however, disparities are evident in these health indicators—child mortality in ARMM is twice that in the NCR. The maternal mortality rate nationwide remains high despite the decline from 209 per 100,000 live births in 1993 to 162 in 2006. The rate for ARMM is extremely high at 320, almost triple that in the NCR. The mortality data suggest that where access to primary health care may be limited by geography or conflict, the risk of dying is double that in areas where health care is more available.

Access to health care is fundamental to improving the Philippines' health status. Using the opportunity curve methodology, this study investigates the extent people have access to health facilities, including primary health care; and whether the access to health services is equitably provided to the population. The study also explores whether government spending on health suffices to address the issues related to quality health services and if government expenditure on health is allocated toward poorer regions.

8.6.1. Access and Equity

Figure 3.39 in Chapter 3 shows access to and equity of health services in the Philippines. In 1998–2004, about 44–46% of ill people sought treatment in one of the available health facilities—e.g., government hospital, private hospital, private clinic, rural health unit (RHU), *barangay* health station (BHS),[3] or other health facilities. Access to overall health services in the Philippines appears to be inequitable in that the services are largely used by people at the top end of the income distribution. This is depicted by the upward sloping opportunity curves in Figure 3.39.

Moreover, the proportion of people who sought treatment in a health facility declined over 1998–2004, with the shift far greater at the bottom end than at the top end of the income distribution. This implies that the provision of health services became more inequitable between 1998 and 2004.

Services for ill people are provided by government hospitals, private clinics, RHUs, and BHSs. However, the quality of services among these facilities differs vastly. Those offering better quality service are likely to be used mainly by rich individuals. Such use of health facilities is expected to show an opportunity curve that steeply slopes upward.

Figure 8.11 clearly shows that health services provided by private clinics tend to be highly inequitable, becoming more so during 1998–2004. This suggests that private clinics are heavily used by the richer segments of the society. A similar result emerges with private hospitals. As Figure 8.12 suggests, access to private hospitals has fallen across income groups, declining more for those at the bottom end, while government hospitals tend to be used more by poor people. Moreover, the study's calculations suggest that poor Filipinos sought treatment more often in government hospitals than in private health facilities (Table 8.5). Compared with private facilities, the quality of health care in government hospitals is generally much lower, especially in the NCR. This is disconcerting, especially because a large share of the national government budget for health is spent on NCR hospitals.

Public health services are used mainly by people who cannot afford private health care—the poor in society. Compared with government facilities, clients ranked private facilities superior in all aspects of quality (e.g., care, facility, personnel, medicine, and convenience) to public facilities. Government facilities cater to the poor because of low costs of treatment, cheaper medicines and supplies, and flexibility in paying health bills.

---

3   The *barangay* is the Philippines' lowest administrative unit, part of a municipality or city.

Figure 8.11: Opportunity Curve of Access to Private Hospitalization, 1998–2004

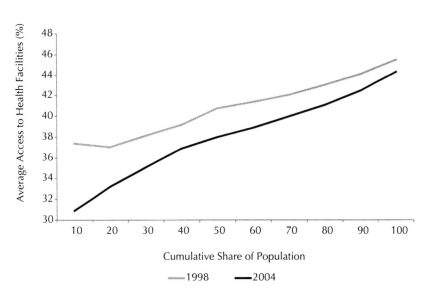

Source: Ali and Son (2007).

Expectedly, public health facilities such as RHUs and BHSs are used more by people at the lower end of the income distribution. This is evident in the downward-sloping and flat opportunity curves for BHSs (Figure 8.12). Moreover, the opportunity curve shifted upward during 1998–2004, with the shift far greater at the bottom end of the distribution. This suggests that poor people use health services provided by BHSs and RHUs. That the poor use these facilities does not mean they have access to quality health care. RHUs and BHSs are generally perceived to provide low quality health services (World Bank 2001). Diagnosis is poor, resulting in repeat visits. Medicines and supplies are inferior and rarely available. Staff members are often absent, especially in rural areas, and are perceived to lack medical and people skills. Waiting time is long, schedules are very inconvenient, and facilities are rundown.

Moreover, results from the 2004 APIS also show that use of health facilities varies across regions. People living in Mindanao tended to underuse health services during 1998–2004. Health status indicators show large differentials across regions and provinces within the country. For example, the NCR has an infant mortality rate of about 20, which is very close to the norm of developed countries, whereas some parts of Mindanao have mor-

Table 8.5: Opportunity Index of Access to Hospitals and Clinics, 1998–2004

	Government Hospital		Private Hospital		Private Clinic	
	1998	2004	1998	2004	1998	2004
Average Opportunity (for society)	20.22	26.12	15.38	14.40	27.02	25.15
Opportunity Index	20.16	25.60	9.55	8.37	19.52	16.41
Equity Index of Opportunity	0.99	0.98	0.62	0.58	0.72	0.65
Comments	Not equitable	Not equitable	Not equitable	Not equitable	Not equitable	Not equitable

Figure 8.12: Opportunity Curve of Access to Barangay Health Stations, 1998–2004

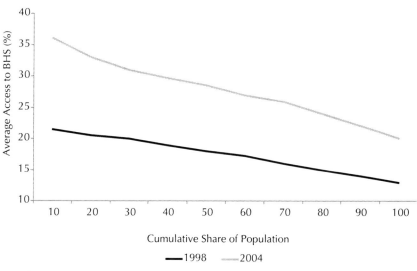

BHS = barangay health station.
Source: Ali and Son (2007).

tality rates close to 100, similar to least-developed countries. Given that Mindanao is one of the poorest areas in the country, the wide gap in health status calls for an effective system of health service delivery that will reach the disadvantaged areas and regions.

Disparity (i.e., between regions and income groups) persists in the Philippines due to fragmented administration, as well as the high costs of operating public hospitals. Administrative fragmentation of health services occurs at different levels because of a lack of referral networking among health care providers. In the past, the national government controlled all public health facilities, from the central office down to the regional districts. Today, however, the regional health units such as RHUs and BHSs are run by the municipalities, while the provincial and district hospitals are controlled by the provinces. This proves disadvantageous because the less capable health centers have difficulty getting the services of the hospitals that have well-trained doctors and better facilities. In some cases, health units are linked because of informal personal contacts and not institutionalized arrangements. Thus, technical fragmentation happens. Increased networking would not be necessary if relationships among the health units were formally established.

It is also claimed that public hospitals could lose their competitive edge over private hospitals due to the higher costs of operating them if quality adjustments are to be factored in. Such adjustments include necessities like running water and reliable supply of electricity. A comparison of hospital bills showed that primary and secondary public hospitals have lower utility bills than private hospitals. It is not the price of medical services that lead to the higher expense but the cost of running the hospital. This means that public tertiary hospitals need to spend more on electricity and water supply for them to match the quality of service private hospitals offer. Unfortunately, pubic hospitals are subject to budgetary allocations by local governments for utilities—electricity and water supply. Less funding for utilities will certainly affect the efficiency and quality of service provided by these hospitals, whose main clientele are the poor.

8.6.2. Government Budget Allocation

Low spending and persistent poor quality of health services—which have led to lagging achievement in important health targets of the Millennium Development Goals (e.g., infant mortality rate)—are the focus of health sector reforms in the Philippines.

Total health expenditure has been increasing in real per capita terms, outpacing the growth in GNP from 2.9% of GNP in 1991 to 3.3% in 2000. However, public spending on health remains low relative to that in other countries with similar per capita income. Despite the growth in health spending, access to health services remains highly inequitable, with many poor households unable to receive care. As a consequence, households pay (out of their own pockets) the largest share of the country's health care costs, accounting for almost 47% in 2003–2004 (Table 8.6). This places a heavy financial burden on families, mostly penalizing the poor. Also, the share of the national health insurance program in total health expenditure has been relatively small, at about 9–10% for 2003–2004, although it increased sharply during the period.

In 1995, the new National Health Insurance Law was enacted to expand the coverage of the national health insurance program. This law replaced the Medicare Commission and created a public corporation to manage the system. By 1998, the Philippine Health Insurance Corporation (PhilHealth) formally took over all activities previously performed by the Medicare Commission. Delays in processing claims during that year lowered the national health insurance program's share of total health expenditures (3.8% in 1998). In 1999, PhilHealth caught up with the backlog of claims and was able to restore its share of total health spending, and increased it to 9.4% in 2004, partly as a result of an increase in health benefits.

Table 8.6: Total Health Expenditure by Source of Funds, 2003–2004

Source of Funds	Amount (billion pesos)		Percent of Total		Growth Rate (%)
	2003	2004	2003	2004	
Government	**47.5**	**50.1**	**32.0**	**30.3**	**5.5**
National	24.0	26.3	16.2	15.9	9.9
Local	23.5	23.8	15.8	14.4	1.0
Social Insurance	**12.9**	**15.7**	**8.7**	**9.5**	**21.1**
Medicare	12.8	15.5	8.6	9.4	21.3
Employees' Compensation	0.2	0.2	0.1	0.1	5.7
Private Sources	**86.4**	**97.5**	**58.1**	**59.0**	**12.9**
Out-of-Pocket	69.2	77.5	46.6	46.9	12.0
Private Insurance	3.4	4.1	2.3	2.5	21.3
Health Maintenance Organizations	7.0	8.0	4.7	4.8	14.0
Employer-Based Plans	5.0	5.9	3.4	3.6	18.1
Private Schools	1.8	2.0	1.2	1.2	12.9
Other	**1.8**	**2.0**	**1.2**	**1.2**	**8.3**
All Sources	**148.6**	**165.2**	**100.0**	**100.0**	**11.2**

Source: NSCB (2004).

National government spending on health mainly goes to the Department of Health. The department's budget decreased immediately after the responsibility for health care was devolved to the local government units in 1994, but rose rapidly thereafter to reach P19.6 billion in 2000 and further to P26.3 billion in 2004. While local government spending on health has increased beyond what is needed to maintain the devolved health functions, local efforts remain uncoordinated. The devolution of administrative powers has also led to fragmented health services (Solon et al. 1999).

The foregoing findings call for a change in the sourcing of funds for the Philippine health system. First, the financial burden on families needs to be shifted to societal risk pools, particularly the national health insurance program. Second, the coverage of the national health insurance program should be expanded to cater to the needs of the poor. This suggests securing adequate funding for premium subsidies to ensure that the poor can afford to participate in the program. The benefits of health insurance should also be enhanced to make the program more attractive to the rest of the population, including groups not yet covered, such as the self-employed.

8.7. Social Protection Programs

In a broader sense, social protection is defined to consist of policies and programs designed to reduce poverty and vulnerability by promoting efficient labor markets, diminishing people's exposure to risks, and enhancing their capacity to protect themselves against hazards and interruption or loss of income (Ahmed et al. 2006). Social protection in the Philippines consists of a set of interventions—both formal and informal—that help the poorest and most vulnerable communities lessen their exposure to risks. Compared to other Asian countries, the Philippines is seen to have a wide scope of programs for social protection (Sta. Ana III 2002, Ortiz 2001). Although many of the programs were in place even before the 1997 Asian financial crisis, some argue that the crisis exposed the weaknesses of the Philippines' social protection system as evident in low coverage, absence and/or weakness in targeting methodologies and techniques, and operational constraints due to the lack of coordination among the agencies that implement the programs (Torregosa 2005). These issues cut across the social protection programs discussed here.

8.7.1. Social Assistance and Poverty Reduction Programs

Social welfare and assistance in the Philippines cover a wide range of services and target sectors. Overall, it aims to provide welfare-enhancing opportunities to poor groups, households, communities, wage and nonwage earners, and formal and informal sectors. Subsectors covered include health, education, food, livelihood, disaster management and response, social security, and housing.

But while such forms of assistance appear to be relatively generous compared with those in other Asian countries (Appendix A), they do not always achieve their targets. For example, the Indonesian food subsidy program was assessed to be more successful than the Philippine program in reaching needy households. Geographical targeting of public works programs in the Philippines did not always provide jobs to the poorest.[4] Poor targeting and lack of funding was common in most Asian countries (Cook, Kabeer, and Suwannarat 2003).

While coverage seems adequate given the multisector nature of social assistance in the Philippines, issues include weak programming and limited outreach lacking clarity about target beneficiaries: who the poor are, how they are determined to be poor, and where they are located. This makes monitoring and evaluating program benefits difficult. Duplication and overlaps in welfare programs are rife. Moreover, heavy dependence on government funding and assistance from multilateral institutions threatens financial sustainability. Support from community-based, people's, and nongovernment organizations is lacking (Torregosa 2005).

The foregoing issues also manifest in many of the government's poverty reduction programs, particularly the KALAHI–CIDSS, which is the country's main vehicle for social assistance. The agenda has evolved from alleviating to eradicating poverty, with each President owning a flagship poverty reduction project (summarized in Appendixes B and C). Despite the variety of antipoverty measures, the programs suffer from weak programming, low budgets, and poor coordination. Programming is weak because antipoverty programs are often short-lived and coterminous with a President's tenure; poorly targeted; lacking in accountability; and wanting in key ingredients such as programs that differentiate between chronic and transient poverty, well-designed and well-targeted scholarships for the poor, stronger population management policy, and programs that enhance agricultural productivity to help reduce rural poverty (Reyes 2002). The Comprehensive Agrarian Reform Program forms part of the latter, but this has remained inadequate. Chronic budget deficits meant the government had less funding to allocate for poverty reduction. Institutions that carry out antipoverty programs have been weakened by high staff turnover, politicization, and redundancy.

---

4   Work-fare programs, although seen as theoretically efficient in targeting the poorest, were not always effectively implemented (Cook, Kabeer, and Suwannarat 2003).

8.7.2. Child Protection Programs

Across Asian countries, the major issue in further developing and improving child protection strategies, and in implementing relevant programs, is the lack of knowledge and data concerning the lives of children living in adverse conditions. This includes a lack of experience in how to work with children and youth. The profound lack of knowledge and dearth of research affect governments' ability to craft relevant national child protection strategies and national policy issues on children in adversity.[5] They also affect the ability to clearly identify and define relevant indicators—qualitative as well as quantitative—for interventions in child protection (Ortiz 2001).

8.7.3. Social Insurance Programs

As in many Asian countries, social insurance in the Philippines offers wide protection including for health and crops (the latter is included under micro-based protection programs). Health insurance is provided to the population at large to protect people from risks associated with the sudden onset of illness. Social health insurance has specific programs targeted to the poor and the informal sector.

All four main comparators—Indonesia, Philippines, Thailand, and Viet Nam—provide social security for old age, disability, and death insurance. All but Indonesia provide maternity benefits and insurance against illness and work-related injury. The Philippine social security program serves the largest proportion of the workforce nationally within the region,[6] and is more comprehensive as its protection includes both formal and informal workers, farmers, and overseas workers. Moreover, the Philippines is less discriminating as it offers similar social security benefits for workers in the private and public sector—including those in the armed forces (Asher 1999). In all these countries (including the Philippines), however, coverage is low, being largely limited to workers in the formal sector. Fiscal constraints discourage the countries from offering universal coverage and adequate benefits, although the Philippines is pilot testing insurance for informal workers

---

[5] Scholarships offered after the 1997 Asian financial crisis in Indonesia and Thailand averted school dropout problems, but education participation rates remained low. In Thailand, press reports indicated that relatives of both national and local politicians received scholarships, limiting access of those most deserving of such benefits (Cook, Kabeer, and Suwannarat 2003)

[6] The program covered 38% of the work force in 1999 (Cook, Kabeer, and Suwannarat 2003). Previous estimates put the coverage of 20% of the labor force in Indonesia in 1996, 27.8% of the population in the Philippines in 1997, and 20% of the total labor force in Thailand in 1999 (Asher 1999, 8).

in selected provinces, and Thailand has committed to do the same. Low coverage is also due to many workers being unaware of their social security entitlements (Cook, Kabeer, and Suwannarat 2003; Fritzen 2003).

While the policy and program design of social insurance in the Philippines seem sufficient, as these programs continue to expand, reaching the poorest and the informal sector is problematic. Beneficiaries are not clearly identified in the absence of sound poverty indicators and mechanisms to effectively target beneficiaries. The beneficiary base needs to be expanded to achieve economies of scale to offer more benefits and coverage. While the poor and vulnerable are protected from health and agricultural risks, there is no direct form of support for sudden loss of employment. Moreover, social insurance remains largely provided by the government, subjecting workers to inefficiencies in the public sector (Torregosa 2005). Critics indicated the Philippine Social Security System faces questions of governance and equity. In 2001, huge investments by the Social Security System in subsidized loans eroded the optimal yield for the pension contributions of its members. Other investments (e.g., in the stock market) were deemed to be politically motivated or posed conflict of interest issues (Sta. Ana III 2002).[7]

8.7.4. Micro-Based Programs

In terms of scope, the Philippines is innovative and remains at par with Viet Nam in mobilizing community social funds, anchored on explicit poverty reduction programs. In addition, the Philippines offers insurance for farmers, although it remains insufficient to cover risks. Several microcredit programs have been established in the Philippines since the mid 1990s, modeled on the Grameen Bank in Bangladesh. While many are effective in targeting clients, the programs suffer from weak institutional capacity, weaknesses in the delivery system, a limited financial base, and high training investments needed to reach a large number of clients (Cook, Kabeer, and Suwannarat 2003).

8.7.5. Labor Market Interventions

Labor market interventions in the Philippines are embodied in policies and programs that seek to strengthen the institutional environment to support

---

[7] Asher (1999) criticized aggressive investments by the Philippine Social Security System in the domestic stock market affecting, in some cases, the control of some corporations. While this situation had improved the investment returns of the Social Security System, it raised difficult issues of corporate governance and control, and of political considerations in the investment decision of social security institutions. This could burden the Social Security System's members directly or indirectly.

employment generation and to protect the labor sector from work-related abuses and hazards. These interventions are largely financed by the government, including job placements and searches. Compliance with labor laws is the responsibility of the employee.

While unemployment and job displacements were more acute and received greater attention in Indonesia and Thailand following the 1997 Asian financial crisis, the Philippines and Viet Nam lagged behind in addressing such issues despite experiencing similar job losses and diminished work prospects for younger and less educated workers (Cook, Kabeer, and Suwannarat 2003). Moreover, while Indonesia and the Philippines pioneered sending workers overseas especially after the crisis, the lack of harmonized policies with employing countries often permitted job acquisition through informal recruitment practices, heightening the risks faced by migrant laborers (Ortiz 2001).

Low coverage characterizes labor market interventions in the Philippines. While the labor code is relatively rich and developed, it lacks policies that address the rights of and welfare of workers in the informal sector,[8] who are unorganized and are prone to abuse and income disruptions. Moreover, the scope of regulation is limited to organized formal labor. The main issue is monitoring compliance with the labor law. While organized labor has one or more unions to look after members' rights, subcontracted labor lacks such mechanisms. In terms of coverage, labor market interventions have yet to devise an effective monitoring system to keep track of unemployment. Skills training is too costly to be solely provided by the government.

8.7.6. General Assessment

The scope of social protection in the Philippines seems to address essential risks adequately, including causes that are manmade, natural, economic, political, and due to health status. The Philippines' allocation of social expenditures appears to be comparable with that in its Asian neighbors (Appendix A). However, the number of beneficiaries covered and the per capita level of benefits remain inadequate due first to insufficient funding and second to poor targeting, often resulting from the lack of reliable poverty measures, especially at the local level. National surveys, often conducted at wide intervals, generate poverty statistics only at the provincial

---

[8]   These include domestic help, clerks in small-scale enterprises, and workers who are subcontracted or are home-based.

level,[9] making it difficult to identify and validate the poorest families being targeted (Torregosa 2005, Reyes 2002). Third, programs lack built-in monitoring and evaluation components, rendering impact assessment impossible. Fourth, financing for social protection is limited by the government's budget problems, but continued reliance on foreign grants and funding can threaten program sustainability. Finally, social protection programs in the Philippines are not well coordinated and are often implemented on a piecemeal basis, due to their individual mandates. This causes wastage because of overlaps and redundancies in sectoral or geographical beneficiaries, which also occur in other Asian countries. These programs should be consolidated to harmonize implementation.

8.8. Conclusions and Policy Recommendations

This study shows that the Philippines achieved modest success in average welfare, poverty reduction, and human development during 1994–2003. Life expectancy has gone up and mortality rates have gone down. While school participation rates have gone up, the decline in the primary participation rate in the 2000s is a particular concern. Moreover, spatial disparities remain large and some regions have lagged behind—particularly ARMM, Bicol, Eastern Visayas, and Western Mindanao. Due to the disparities, neighboring Asian countries overtook the Philippines based on income as well as non-income indicators in human development.

This study focuses on identifying constraints to achieving sustainable and equitable growth in the overall well-being of the people, with a particular focus on the basic social services of health and education. Because of the strong two-way relationship between human capital and growth, both must be promoted to sustain progress in either. Economic growth is both an important input into human capital improvement and is required for human capital to continue to improve. Economic policy has often tended to focus on getting the economic fundamentals right as a necessary precondition for economic growth, arguing that human capital improvement must await such growth. However, if human capital is not improved, economic growth will be not sustained. Therefore, the study has focused on investigating the links between growth and human capital in education and

---

9   In the absence of data on the dimensions of well-being, the programs implemented by local government units seldom correspond to the priorities of the local chief executives. For example, some local government units headed by engineers tend to prioritize infrastructure over health and education (Reyes 2002).

health at the micro level. The study has carried out a systematic analysis to test a few hypotheses to establish such links. Major findings can be summarized as follows.

First, disparity in incomes and human capital within each region of the country is the major problem in the Philippines. While there is a large variation in income and non-income indicators between regions, this study found that disparity within each region largely explains the aggregate inequality, i.e., by almost 90%. Hence, a policy that aims to reduce poverty requires a targeted approach to address intraregional disparity, which poses a major constraint to achieving equitable growth. To put it slightly differently, it is possible, for example, that systematic differences in the levels of human capital between income groups within a geographical region can translate into considerable differences in earning opportunities. Thus, the policy prescription to reduce overall inequality and poverty should focus on expanding the access of low-income groups to basic social services and infrastructure.

Second, although enrollment in basic education is high in the Philippines relative to that in its Asian neighbors, recent trends are alarming. Specifically, the continued decline in elementary participation, from a high of 90% in school year 2001–2002 to a low of 84% in school year 2005–2006, can hamper achieving the Millennium Development Goal of universal primary education by 2015. More disturbing is the poor access to secondary education among children living in poorer regions (e.g., ARMM and Western Mindanao) and those aged 13–16 years. As noted, a major reason for not attending secondary school was the high cost of education.

The opportunity costs of sending children aged 13–16 years to school are high, and are even greater for poor households. The need to improve access to basic education by children living in the poorer regions has become pressing. This calls for financial schemes that can cater to poor enrollees. Well-designed and well-targeted scholarships for the poor—particularly those in ARMM and Western Mindanao—are most urgently needed to address intraregional disparity in the Philippines. Schemes similar to conditional cash transfers could be options to consider. Strict monitoring of such schemes is essential to ensure their success.

Third, while access to primary education is of less concern, its equity dimension requires attention. Although disparity in access to primary education is not very large between the poor and the non-poor, children from poor families tend to have fewer opportunities in primary education than the non-poor. The APIS indicated that poor families have more children aged 7–12 years than do non-poor ones. This finding is also consistent with the common view that larger families tend to be poorer in the Philippines, highlighting the need for a stronger population management policy as an important component of a poverty reduction program.

Fourth, there is ample scope for policy makers to think about accessibility and equity in the health sector. The study found that Filipinos do not have equitable access to health services, which are largely used by people at the top end of the income distribution. The poor use primary health facilities such as RHUs and BHSs more than the rich do, and these facilities are poorly equipped and staffed, depriving the poor of quality health care. Although RHUs and BHSs are categorized as primary government facilities that can appropriately provide preventive health services and treatment for minor illnesses and accidents, a sizable number of Filipinos still prefer to seek treatment in government hospitals and private clinics and hospitals. Thus, government hospitals end up providing the same services as primary facilities. It is critical to ensure that primary health services are delivered efficiently so that they can help prevent diseases such as bronchitis, diarrhea, influenza, pneumonia, and tuberculosis. Preventive health care services do much more in the long run in protecting the people's health, and require less budgetary allocation than does curative treatment.

Fifth, the Philippine health sector is beset with problems of low spending and persistent poor quality of services. Public spending on health remains low relative to that in other countries with similar per capita income. As a result, health services are inequitably provided, with many poorer households unable to receive care. Consequently, households pay out of their own pockets, accounting for the largest share in the country's health care costs—almost 47% of the total in 2003–2004. This places a heavy financial burden on families and makes access to health care highly inequitable. It remains vital, therefore, to make the health system more pro-poor by (i) expanding health insurance coverage for the poor, (ii) improving the quality and accessibility of health care for the poor in public health facilities, (iii) reducing the cost of medicines and expenditures on hospital stays, and (iv) improving quality by giving government hospitals more autonomy in setting budgets.

Finally, the government's social protection and antipoverty measures have remained weak in issues related to programming, budgeting, and institutional arrangements. Poor targeting is foremost among these issues. It is often claimed that targeted programs are seldom carried out in accordance with the design, because the data needed to operationalize

249

the criteria for selecting eligible beneficiaries are not available. To address intraregional disparity, well-targeted programs are of critical importance. This calls for further research to identify the beneficiaries. With limited resources, it is critical to minimize leakages of the benefits to nonbeneficiaries on the one hand, and to maximize the benefits to the targeted beneficiaries on the other.

Appendix 8.A: Summary of Social Protection Programs

Cost and Indicators	Philippines	Indonesia	Nepal	Viet Nam
Total Value	not available	Rp40,232 billion	NRs9.385 billion	D18,680 billion
Indicators of Social Protection Expenditure in 2003				
Social Protection Expenditures as % of GDP	no data	1.9%	2.2%	3.5%
Social Expenditure as % of GDP (in 2005)	3.5%	not available	not available	not available
Social Protection Expenditure Per Capita	P303 (in 2002)[a] ($5.87)[b]	Rp187,800 ($22.1)	NRs408 ($5.5)	no data
Social Protection Expenditure Per Poor Person	not available	Rp149,000	NRs434	D223,300
Per Capita Social Protection Expenditure as % of Income of Poor Beneficiaries	not available	15%	28%	11.6%[c]

GDP = gross domestic product.

Notes: Percent of GDP is estimated using GDP in current local currency data from the World Bank's World Development Indicators online for 2003. Social expenditures in the Philippines include expenditures on four components: (i) social security and welfare, (ii) housing and community amenities, (iii) education, and (iv) health. A list of individual country programs and projects is available at http://www.adb.org/Projects/Country-Diagnostic-Studies/country-studies.asp

[a] in Reyes-Cantos (2001).

[b] Estimated using conversion rate of P51.60/$1.

[c] Per capita social protection expenditure as a percentage of per capita poverty line income.

Source: World Bank (2007).

Appendix 8.B: Poverty Goals, Targets, and Strategies in Medium-Term Development Plans of Philippine Administrations, 1987–2004

MTPDP Administration	Goals/Priorities	Targets	1985	1992	Main Poverty Strategies and Activities
1987–1992 Corazon Aquino	• poverty alleviation • generation of more productive employment • promotion of equity and social justice • achievement of sustainable economic growth	Reduce poverty incidence National Rural areas NCR Urban outside NCR	50.8% 63% 48% 56%	45.4% 48% 44% 49%	Employment-oriented, rural-based development strategy Activity: Tulong sa Tao Program ("help for the poor")
Update 1990–1992 Corazon Aquino	• poverty alleviation • increased productivity and growth • equitable distribution of opportunities, income, wealth, and means of production	Reduce poverty incidence from 58.9% in 1985 to 46.1–49.3% in 1992			Employment-oriented, rural-based development strategy that maximizes the complementarities between agriculture and industry Activities: provide physical infrastructure, enhance social services delivery, implement agrarian reform and decentralization
1993–1998 Fidel Ramos	• human development • improved quality of life	Reduce poverty incidence from 39.2% in 1997 to about 30% by 1998			Main strategies were people empowerment and acceleration of global competitiveness Activity: Social Reform Agenda

continued on next page

Appendix 8.B (continued)

MTPDP Administration	Goals/Priorities	Targets	Main Poverty Strategies and Activities
2001–2004 Gloria Macapagal Arroyo	• macroeconomic stability with equitable growth based on free enterprise • agriculture and fisheries modernization with social equity • comprehensive human development • protection of the vulnerable • good governance and rule of law	"Healing the Nation: First 100 Days of the Macapagal-Arroyo Administration," said that the MTPDP included the goal of reducing poverty to 28% by 2004. The final MTPDP failed to mention any target.	Main strategy is convergence Activity: Kapit-Bisig *Laban sa Kahirapan* (KALAHI)

MTPDP = medium-term Philippine development plan, NCR = National Capital Region.
Source: Reyes (2002).

Appendix 8.C: Objectives and Components of Flagship Government Poverty Reduction Programs, 1986–2004

	Tulong sa Tao (Corazon Aquino)	*Social Reform Agenda* (Fidel Ramos)	*Lingap Para sa Mahihirap* (Joseph Estrada)	*Kapit-Bisig Laban sa Kahirapan* (KALAHI) (Gloria Arroyo)
Key objectives	• increase employment and income of low-income groups • strengthen self-help groups • encourage savings mobilization among low-income groups • increase production of goods and services by members of the low-income groups • strengthen NGOs to service credit needs of low-income groups	• poverty alleviation • quality basic social services • institutional development	• For government and private sector to converge efforts and resources for poverty alleviation	• address inequities in ownership, distribution, management, and control over productive resources • meet basic human needs • strengthen capacities of marginalized groups to engage in productive enterprises and livelihood • eliminate all forms of discrimination • institutionalize and strengthen participation of basic sectors in all levels of governance • asset reform • human development services • employment and livelihood • social protection • participation of the poor in governance
Program components	Some components include • Micro credit program • Community mortgage program • Nutrition (*Lalakas ang Katawang Sapat sa Sustansya*)	Flagship programs: • agricultural development, fisheries and aquatic resources management • ancestral domains • socialized housing • workers' welfare and protection • livelihood and credit • institution building and effective participation in governance	• potable water • socialized housing • health care • protective services for children • livelihood/cooperative development • food subsidy	

continued on next page

Appendix 8.C (continued)

	Tulong sa Tao (Corazon Aquino)	Social Reform Agenda (Fidel Ramos)	Lingap Para sa Mahihirap (Joseph Estrada)	Kapit-Bisig Laban sa Kahirapan (KALAHI) (Gloria Arroyo)
Poverty reduction target	Not explicit	Reduce poverty incidence to 30%	Reduce poverty incidence to 25–28%	Win the war against poverty within the decade
Coordinating agency	Department of Trade and Industry (DTI)	Social Reform Council	National Anti-Poverty Commission (NAPC)	National Anti-Poverty Commission (NAPC)
Target area	Low-income municipalities	Special priority areas: 20 poorest provinces' 5th and 6th class municipalities; Special Zones of Peace and Development (Mindanao and Palawan)	Nationwide	Poorest barangays[a] in the KALAHI convergence areas
Target beneficiary	Low-income groups in rural areas	Poor and vulnerable groups	100 poorest families in every province and city	14 "basic sectors": children, women, urban poor, persons with disabilities, farmers, fisherfolk, indigenous peoples, informal labor, formal labor and migrant workers, youth and students, senior citizens, victims of disasters and calamities, cooperatives, NGOs
Delivery Mechanism	National government agencies with NGOs as conduits	Flagship program agencies	National government agencies	National government agencies

NGO = nongovernment organization.

[a] The barangay is the lowest government administrative unit, part of a municipality.

Source: Adapted from ADB (2005).

References

Ahmed, K., B. Baulch, S. Bhatta, N. Danzan, T. Nguyen, H. Quyen, A. Rahman, S. Sharma, S. Sherani, H. Sigit, S. Surbakti, E. Uuganbileg, and J. Wood. 2006. *Social Protection Index for Committed Poverty Reduction*. Manila: Asian Development Bank (ADB).

Asher, M. 1999. *Social Security Reforms in Southeast Asia*. Manila: ADB.

Asian Development Bank (ADB). 2005. *Poverty in the Philippines*. Manila.

Alesina, A. and R. Perotti. 1994. The Political Economy of Growth: A Critical Survey of the Recent Literature. *The World Bank Economic Review*. 8(3): 351–71.

Alesina, A., and D. Rodrik. 1994. Distributive Politics and Economic Growth. *Quarterly Journal of Economics*. 109(2): 465–90.

Ali, I., and H. H. Son. 2007. Measuring Inclusive Growth. *Asian Development Review*. 24 (1). pp. 11–32.

Balisacan, A. M. 1994. Urban Poverty in the Philippines: Nature, Causes, and Policy Measures. *Asian Development Review*. 12(1): 117–52.

———. 1996. Poverty, Inequality and Public Policy. In de Dios, E., ed. *If We're So Smart, Why Aren't We Rich? Essays on Education and Economic Success*. Manila and Quezon City: Congress of the Philippines.

———. 1999. Poverty Profile in the Philippines: An Update and Reexamination of Evidence in the Wake of the Asian Crisis. Manila: University of the Philippines. Unpublished.

———. 2001. Rural Development in the 21st Century: Monitoring and Assessing Performance in Rural Poverty Reduction. In Canlas, D. B. and S. Fujisaki, eds. *The Philippine Economy: Alternatives for the 21st Century*. Quezon City: University of the Philippines.

———. 2007. Local Growth and Poverty Reduction. In Balisacan, A. M. and H. Hill, eds. *The Dynamics of Regional Development: The Philippines in East Asia*. Cheltenham: Edward Elgar.

Bardhan, P. 1996. Efficiency, Equity and Poverty Alleviation: Policy Issues in Less Developed Countries. *Economic Journal*. 106(1): 344–56.

Bautista, R. M. 1997. Income and Equity Effects of the Green Revolution in the Philippines: A Macroeconomic Perspective. *Journal of International Development*. 9 (2). pp. 151–168.

Behrman, J. 1996. Impact of Health and Nutrition on Education. *World Bank Economic Observer*. 11(1): 23–37.

Bloom, D. E., D. Canning, and J. Sevilla. 2004. The Effect of Health on Economic Growth: A Production Function Approach. *World Development*. 32(1): 1–13.

Boozer, M., G. Ranis, F. Stewart, and T. Suri. 2004. *Paths to Success: the Relationship between Human Development and Economic Growth*.

Economic Growth Centre Discussion Paper. New Haven: Yale University.

Cook, S., N. Kabeer, and G. Suwannarat. 2003. *Social Protection in Asia.* New Delhi: The Ford Foundation and Har-Anand Publications PVT Ltd.

Cornia, G. A., and F. Stewart. 1995. Two Errors of Targeting. In Stewart, F. *Adjustment and Poverty: Options and Choices.* London: Routledge.

De Guzman, E. A., and J. Cortes. 1995. *Correlates and Determinants of Absenteeism and Dropping Out among Public Elementary School Pupils.* HSMS 11 Report No. 5. Bureau of Elementary Education, Department of Education, Culture and Sports. Pasig City.

Department of Education. 2007. *Basic Education Statistics Fact Sheet.* August. Pasig City.

Foster, J. E., J. Greer, and E. Thornbecke. 1984. A Class of Decomposable Poverty Measures. *Econometrica.* 52(3): 761–66.

Fritzen, S. 2003. Escaping the Low Income–Low Social Protection Trap in Developing Countries: What Are the Options? *Indian Journal of Social Development.* 3(2).

Glewwe P., and H. Jacoby. 1996. *A Delayed Primary School Enrollment and Childhood Malnutrition in Ghana, an Economic Analysis.* LSMS Series Paper No. 98. Washington, DC: World Bank.

Human Development Network (HDN). 1996. *Philippine Human Development Report 1996.* Quezon City.

———. 2005. *Philippine Human Development Report 2005.* Quezon City.

Kakwani, N. 2000. On Measuring Growth and Inequality Components of Poverty with Application to Thailand. *Journal of Quantitative Economics.* 16 (1). pp. 67–79.

Lam, L. T. A. 2005. *Human Resource Development and Poverty in the Philippines.* Discussion Paper Series No. 2005-17. Makati City: Philippine Institute for Development Studies.

Luz, J. M. 2004. Reflections on Institutional Reform at the Department of Education. *The SGV Review.* 2(1): 19–35.

Manasan, R. G. 2001. *Budget Allocation for Human Development Expenditures: Measuring Progress on the 20:20 Initiative of Provinces and Cities 1995–1998.* Manila: United Nations International Children's Emergency Fund.

Mason, A.D. 1994. Schooling Decisions, Basic Education, and the Poor in Rural Java. Stanford, CA: Stanford University, Food Research Institute. PhD thesis.

National Statistical Coordination Board (NSCB). 1990. *Philippine Statistical Yearbook.* Makati City.

———. 2004. *National Expenditure on Health Accounts.* National Statistical Coordination Board. Makati City.

National Statistics Office (NSO). 2003a. *Functional Literacy, Education, and Mass Media Survey.* www.census.gov.ph/data/sectordata/dataedlit.html

———. 2003b. School Attendance of Children and Youth in the Philippines, Philippines: 2003. www.census.gov.ph/data/sectordata/fl03_sacy.html

———. various years. *Annual Poverty Indicators Survey.* Manila.

———. various years. *Index of Family Income and Expenditure Surveys.* www.census.gov.ph/data/sectordata/dataincome.html

Ortiz, I. 2001. *Social Protection in Asia and the Pacific.* Manila: ADB.

Psacharopolous, G., S. Morley, A. Fiszbein, H. Lee, and B. Wood. 1992. *Poverty and Income Distribution in Latin America: The Story of the 1980s.* Washington, DC: World Bank.

Ravallion, M., and J. Jalan. 1996. Growth Divergence due to Spatial Externalities. *Economics Letters.* 53:. 227–32.

Reyes, C. 2002. *The Poverty Fight: Have We Made an Impact?* Discussion Paper Series No. 2002-20. Makati City: Philippine Institute for Development Studies.

Reyes-Cantos, J. 2001. *A Glimpse of the Philippine Economy.* Social Watch Philippines 2001 Report. Manila: Social Watch-Philippines.

Rosenzweig, M. R. 1995. Why Are There Returns in Schooling? *American Economic Review.* 85(2): 153–8.

Schultz, T. W. 1975. The Value of the Ability to Deal with Disequilibria. *Journal of Economic Literature.* 13(3): 827–46.

Selowsky, M., and L. Taylor. 1973. The Economics of Malnourished Children: an Example of Disinvestment in Human Capital. *Economic Development and Cultural Change.* 22(1): 17–30.

Solon, O., A. N. Herrin, R. H. Racelis, M. G. Manalo, V. N. Ganac, and G. V. Amoranto. 1999. *Health Care Expenditure Patterns in the Philippines: Analysis of National Health Accounts, 1991–1997.* Discussion Paper No. 9908. Quezon City: University of the Philippines, School of Economics.

Sta. Ana III, F. 2002. Briefing Paper: Social Protection in the Philippines. Paper presented at United Nations Development Programme Social Protection in an Insecure Era: A South–South Exchange on Alternative Policy Responses to Globalization Interregional Workshop. Santiago de Chile. 14–16 May.

Theil, H. 1967. *Economics and Information Theory.* Amsterdam: North-Holland.

Torregosa, C. L. 2005. *Looking into Social Protection Programs in the Philippines: Towards Building and Implementing an Operational Definition and a Convergent Framework.* Manila: United Nations Development Programme.

United Nations Development Programme (UNDP). 1990. *Human Development Report 1990*. New York: Oxford University Press.

———. 1999. *Human Development Report 1999*. New York: Oxford University Press.

World Bank. 1996. *World Development Report 1996*. Washington, DC.

———. 2001. *World Development Report 2001*. Washington, DC.

———. 2007. *World Development Indicators 2007*. http://web.worldbank .org/WBSITE/EXTERNAL/DATASTATISTICS/0,,contentMDK: 20398986~menuPK:64133163~pagePK:64133150~piPK:64133175 ~theSitePK:239419,00.html

9. Poverty Reduction: Trends, Determinants, and Policies

Arsenio M. Balisacan

9.1. Introduction

While economic growth in most East and Southeast Asian countries has been remarkably rapid during the past 25 years, the same cannot be said for the Philippines. The country's economic growth has barely exceeded the population growth rate, which has continued to expand relatively rapidly at 2.04% a year so far in the current decade (2000–2009). Economic growth quickened in the first half of the decade, but questions linger about its sustainability. Even at the 2004–2006 pace (5–6% per year), the Philippines has not come close to the growth trajectories of its neighbors. Thus, serious students of Philippine development contend that shifting the economy to a higher growth path—and keeping it there for the long term—should be first and foremost on the development agenda.

The country's disappointing performance in poverty reduction mirrors its growth performance. This is not unexpected. Every country that has chalked up significant achievements in poverty reduction and human development has also done quite well in securing long-term economic growth. Such a correlation is expected: economic growth is an essential condition for generating the resources needed to sustain investments in health, education, infrastructure, and good governance (law enforcement, regulation, etc.).

That achieving economic growth should be in the forefront of the policy agenda does not imply that nothing else can be done to lick the poverty problem. On the contrary, cursory evidence indicates that much can be done to enhance the poverty-reducing effects of growth. For example, some countries have been more successful than others in reducing poverty, even after controlling for differences in income growth rates.

The response of poverty to economic growth in the Philippines is quite muted compared with that in its Asian neighbors, especially Indonesia, Thailand, and Viet Nam (Balisacan 2003a, Balisacan and Fuwa 2004). Why is this so? What conditions need to be changed, or what policy responses have to be evolved, to make poverty reduction more responsive to economic growth?

This chapter examines the sources and causes of poverty reduction from an intranational perspective. Going beyond cross-country averages, it exploits the increasingly available wealth of subnational data to shed light on the determinants of poverty reduction, especially on the effectiveness of policies and programs intended to address the poverty problem by way of income growth, redistribution, or both. Section 9.2 provides an overview of the aggregate poverty trends and characteristics. Of particular interest here are the spatial diversity and the sectoral attributes of poverty. For section 9.3, subnational panel data are used to explore the determinants of local growth and poverty reduction. In light of the regression results, section 9.4 assesses the country's major antipoverty programs, focusing on "high-profile" programs of recent years. Finally, the chapter provides some concluding remarks.

9.2. Poverty Trends

Poverty reduction in the Philippines has lagged far behind that in its East Asian neighbors, particularly the People's Republic of China (PRC), Indonesia, Thailand, and Viet Nam (Figure 9.1). Both the PRC and Viet Nam had a higher poverty incidence than the Philippines during the early 1980s, but their absolute poverty soon dwindled and became much lower than the Philippines' during the early 2000s. Malaysia and Thailand also virtually eliminated absolute poverty during the last 20 years. Interestingly, while the Philippines had a much higher average income (purchasing power parity $4,381) in the mid 2000s than Indonesia ($3,402) and Viet Nam ($2,683), the Philippines' absolute poverty rate was actually much higher than that in either of the two countries.[1]

Figure 9.2 shows national poverty estimates, both in terms of incidence (proportion of the population deemed poor) and the number of poor people,

---

[1]   Purchasing power parity is the preferred measure when comparing incomes of countries. It considers differences in the prices of goods and services and is used by multilateral institutions such as the World Bank.

Figure 9.1: Poverty Reduction in East Asia (%)

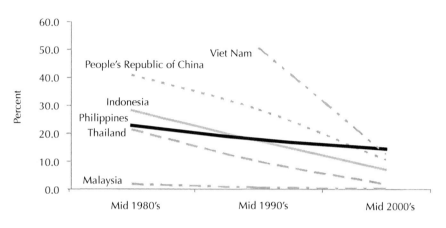

Note: World Bank estimates based on a poverty line of $1 (purchasing power parity) per day.
Source: Data from World Bank (various years).

for the recent years when nationally representative data are available.[2] The estimates are based on consistent poverty lines and family expenditures per capita adjusted for provincial cost-of-living indexes. Hence, this series is not strictly comparable with that in Figure 9.1 or with official estimates. The estimates in Figure 9.2 show two contrasting faces of the poverty problem in the Philippines: the incidence has been declining, albeit slowly, but the number of poor people has risen in recent years. Indeed, the number of poor people in 2003 was as high as that in 1988. This observation generally holds true for other decomposable aggregate measures of poverty, such as those that are sensitive to the depth and severity (distribution) of poverty, as well for other equally plausible poverty lines.

---

[2]   The comparable national household surveys used in constructing Figure 9.2 are available only for 1985 and every 3 years thereafter. The latest survey pertains to 2006, but the data were not available as of this writing. Poverty estimates are those used in Balisacan (2007c) and Balisacan and Fuwa (2004). These are not comparable with official poverty data released by the National Statistical Coordination Board. As shown in Balisacan (2003b), the official estimates are not an accurate guide to ascertaining changes in poverty over time or across the country's regions—or provinces, or between rural and urban areas. By construction, the official methodology uses poverty lines that are not consistent, that is, the standard of living implied by the poverty lines varies for each region as well as over time. In contrast, Balisacan (2003b) used poverty lines that are fixed for various subpopulation groups and periods in terms of the level of living they imply. Moreover, he used expenditure per capita as a proxy measure for individual welfare, while the official methodology uses income per capita as the relevant indicator.

Figure 9.2: Number of Poor People and Poverty Incidence, 1985–

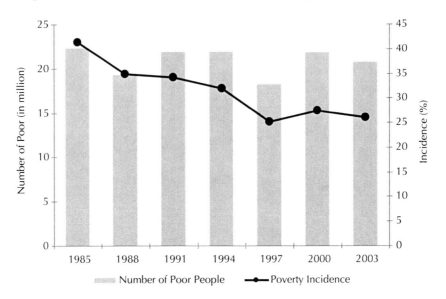

Source: Balisacan and Hill (2007).

The Philippines' poor performance in economic growth and poverty reduction has often been attributed partly to the relatively large variation in access to infrastructure and social services across regions and island groups. A widely held view, for example, is that development efforts have favored Luzon and discriminated against the Visayas and (especially) Mindanao. The view's proponents say that this development pattern has led to substantial regional differences in access to economic opportunities, in rates of poverty reduction, and in the incidence of armed conflict. For instance, the Philippine Human Development Report 2005 shows that measures of deprivation—such as disparities in access to reliable water supply, electricity, and especially education—predict well the occurrence of armed encounters (HDN 2005).

Table 9.1 shows the patterns of income poverty across regions of the Philippines during 1988–2003, as well as the contribution of each region to national poverty. As expected given the regions' very diverse growth records (see the last column), considerable variations occur across regions. However, the National Capital Region (NCR) consistently had the lowest poverty while Bicol, the Eastern Visayas, and Western Mindanao had the highest—their incidence was roughly 10 times that in the NCR. Some significant re-rankings also occurred, such as the Autonomous Region in

Table 9.1: Poverty Incidence and Income Growth, Philippine Regions, 1988–2003 (%)

Region	Poverty Incidence						Contribution to National	Annual Per Capita Income Growth Rate, 1988–
	1988	1991	1994	1997	2000	2003		
Philippines	34.4	34.3	32.1	25.0	27.5	26.1	100.0	2.7
NCR	9.5	5.9	5.6	3.5	5.5	4.8	2.6	2.1
CAR	39.1	46.5	26.6	22.1	19.8	14.8	1.0	2.3
Ilocos	25.5	24.3	26.4	20.8	20.3	16.8	3.4	2.3
Cagayan Valley	39.2	39.1	41.8	30.1	29.9	26.9	3.5	3.3
Central Luzon	15.3	15.4	24.3	13.2	16.1	13.7	5.4	2.2
Southern Tagalog	31.7	22.9	28.6	19.6	19.5	20.9	12.2	3.9
Bicol	60.9	62.2	50.2	45.6	53.3	45.6	10.8	2.9
Western Visayas	34.4	31.6	34.5	21.8	28.1	26.5	8.2	3.6
Central Visayas	55.2	53.2	42.8	35.2	39.4	37.5	10.4	3.3
Eastern Visayas	53.7	54.4	51.5	50.6	46.8	45.6	8.8	4.3
Western Mindanao	47.6	47.1	47.1	35.2	47.0	48.9	7.6	2.0
Northern Mindanao	44.9	55.7	34.4	26.0	27.3	30.3	4.2	1.7
Southern Mindanao	46.9	56.8	30.4	26.7	25.4	27.2	7.4	3.5
Central Mindanao	35.8	46.9	45.2	33.1	38.0	34.0	4.3	2.8
ARMM	23.4	34.0	48.7	50.5	60.7	60.5	6.1	−0.5
Caraga	30.1	45.7	41.0	37.0	33.8	38.4	4.1	2.1

ARMM = Autonomous Region in Muslim Mindanao, CAR = Cordillera Administrative Region, NCR = National Capital Region.

Note: The provincial composition of the regions has changed over the years. For comparability over time, the provinces are grouped consistently according to the 2000 regional classification. Estimates are not comparable with official figures.

Source: Author's estimates based on data from the *Family Income and Expenditure Survey* (NSO various years). Details of the estimation method employed are shown in Balisacan (2003b).

Muslim Mindanao (ARMM) becoming the poorest region in 2003 from being the third least poor (i.e., third richest) of 16 regions in 1988. Even more significant is the differential evolution of poverty over time. In ARMM, Caraga, and Western Mindanao, poverty was higher in 2003 than in 1988. This increase also shows up in measures reflecting human development deprivation, particularly in the areas of health and education (HDN 2005). Toward the close of the 1990s, these two regions, particularly ARMM, were at the center of violent confrontations between the military and armed dissidents.

As in most of Asia's developing countries, poverty in the Philippines is a largely rural phenomenon. Two of every three poor people in the country are in rural areas and depend predominantly on agricultural employment and incomes. The poverty incidence among agricultural households is about four times that of the rest of the population (Table 9.2). Although the share of agriculture in the total labor force has gone down from about one half in the late 1980s to only a little more than one third by the mid 2000s, the sector continues to account for nearly two thirds of total poverty.

Table 9.2: Poverty by Sector of Employment, 1985–2004

Sector	Poverty Incidence (%)							Contribution to Total Poverty	
	1985	1988	1991	1994	1997	2000	2003	1985	2003
Agriculture	57.7	51.2	51.9	49.9	42.3	45.9	46.0	67.2	65.9
Mining	46.4	34.4	44.7	37.1	30.0	58.4	43.4	1.0	0.7
Manufacturing	31.4	21.9	20.9	16.5	13.5	16.1	15.0	4.9	4.1
Utility	17.5	10.8	12.5	9.5	9.5	6.7	3.7	0.2	0.1
Construction	39.6	33.8	33.8	34.5	23.1	29.8	26.3	5.3	7.5
Trade	27.3	18.6	21.3	17.8	13.5	15.4	13.0	4.4	5.6
Transportation	27.8	24.1	22.5	21.2	13.7	18.2	15.1	4.7	5.8
Finance	13.2	8.5	6.9	7.1	3.0	9.1	5.9	0.5	0.9
Services	20.0	15.4	15.2	12.7	9.9	10.5	11.0	5.6	4.1
Unemployed	21.5	18.3	16.8	17.1	12.1	14.0	11.1	6.1	5.3

Source: Author's estimates, based on data from the *Family Income and Expenditure Survey* (NSO various years).

Because poverty is pervasive and has declined quite slowly, the common presumption is that most of the poor in the Philippines must be chronically poor.[3] Moreover, since the lion's share of total poverty is found in agriculture, the poor in agriculture are deemed to be chronically poor. Indeed, this has a ring of truth. In an earlier work, Balisacan (2007b) showed that multidimensional deprivation in the Philippines—as manifested in low incomes and inadequate human capabilities, as reflected in poor health, low educational achievement indicators, and limited access to the means to achieving these capabilities—is closely linked to agriculture. Results of cluster analysis of provincial data indicate that the share of agriculture in employment increases with the level of provincial deprivation, being lowest (about 6%) in the least deprived provinces and highest (about 65%) in the extremely deprived provinces. This suggests that targeting agriculture for poverty reduction has the potential advantage of capturing many dimensions of deprivation at the same time.

9.3. Determinants of Local Growth and Poverty Reduction

The link running from economic growth to poverty reduction is well articulated in policy discussions. The same is not true for the other link from poverty reduction (equity) to growth. What is casually presumed is that high inequity in incomes and assets, combined with imperfection in financial markets, inhibits the poor's access to profitable investments and human capital formation. That is, because physical assets are usually the acceptable collateral, the poor who do not have these assets may be unable to access credit and, hence, take advantage of income-enhancing technologies and production processes. They may also not have the means to smooth household consumption—especially food, health, and education services for children—in the event of downside risks, hence effectively preventing them from escaping the poverty trap from one generation to another. Put differently, investing in equity (poverty reduction) is a necessary condition for the economy to move to a higher growth path. Indeed, there is increasing evidence that such investment has a high payoff in terms of human capital accumulation and, hence, economic growth (Deininger and Squire 1998, Bourguignon 2004, Barro and Sala-i-Martin 2004, Sachs 2005).

---

3   By definition, chronic poverty is simply extended poverty. That is, a person is deemed chronically poor if his or her income, defined broadly to include cash and in-kind incomes, always or usually falls below a predetermined poverty line. Chronically poor people are usually multidimensionally deprived, falling short of income to meet the poverty line and lacking capabilities such as educational achievement and good health.

Until recently, the examination of the growth–poverty nexus usually involved data on cross-country averages (i.e., average growth rates for a specified period regressed against initial income and other explanatory variables, including infrastructure, human capital, and policy regime). However, data comparability is a serious problem in cross-country averages. For example, observation units on income are often measured differently across countries. Political factors influence economic performance, but comparing political characteristics across countries also proves to be difficult owing to differences in historical experience, cultures and norms, and institutional contexts. Moreover, some unobserved factors at the country level may be correlated with the observed variable of interest (e.g., the country's initial income), thereby biasing any measured effects of that variable on steady-state growth and poverty reduction.

In this chapter, a unique subnational "panel data" set is used to explore the determinants of income growth and poverty reduction. The observation units are provinces, which show remarkable diversity in terms of economic performance and poverty reduction. The units and variables are consistently defined, both across space and over time. The historical and institutional contexts are largely similar across these units (e.g., same legal system, same political administration). Moreover, the major sources of heterogeneity—i.e., technologies and tastes—are likely to be less severe for these data than for data across countries. Hence, the estimation problems concerning data across countries are likely to be less serious for the subnational panel data set.

The long-term relationship between Philippine poverty and income growth is evident for data on the country's 77 provinces. This is shown in Figure 9.3, which plots the change in poverty incidence during 1985–2003 and the corresponding percent change in real family income per capita, adjusted for provincial cost-of-living differences.[4] Clearly, as in cross-country data on growth and poverty, the pace of poverty reduction at the provincial level is closely linked to local economic performance. However, there are significant departures from the fitted line (i.e., provinces not conforming to the "average pattern"), suggesting that factors other than the local economic growth rate are influencing the evolution of poverty. One set of such factors may have to do with the relatively large variation in access to infrastructure and social services across regions and island groups.

Adopting the growth framework developed by Barro and Sala-i-Martin (2004), Balisacan (2007c) traced the quantitative significance of the channels by which income growth, together with a host of other factors, influ-

---

4   Poverty estimates are those used in Balisacan (2007c) and are not comparable with official data released by the National Statistical Coordination Board.

ences poverty reduction. In his model, these other factors affect the speed of poverty reduction either directly by changing the distribution of a given economic pie (the redistribution channel), indirectly by expanding the economic pie for each person in society (the growth channel), or both. These factors can be grouped into two types:

(i) initial economic and institutional conditions (in or around 1988)— initial mean provincial per capita income, initial distribution of per capita income, initial human capital stock, political "dynasty" (as a proxy for political competitiveness), and ethnolinguistic fragmentation; and

(ii) time-varying policy variables (difference during 1988–2003): simple adult literacy rate, agricultural terms of trade (as a proxy for economic incentives), access to infrastructure (represented by electricity and good-quality roads), and Comprehensive Agrarian

Figure 9.3: Income and Poverty Reduction, Philippine Provinces, 1983–2003

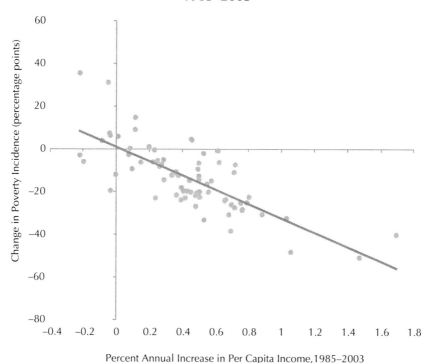

Percent Annual Increase in Per Capita Income, 1985–2003

Source: Data from the Family Income and Expenditure Survey (NSO various years).

Reform Program (CARP) implementation.

The income growth regression is specified as in the standard Barro and Sala-i-Martin framework. The poverty reduction regression adds the income growth rate variable to the set of explanatory variables associated with the rate of poverty reduction. This amounts to estimating the income growth and poverty reduction equations simultaneously using the three-stage least squares estimation technique. Only variables that are significant in the reduced-form estimates of the growth and poverty reduction equations are retained. The regression results are summarized in Table 9.3. The appendix shows the complete list of variables, including descriptive statistics.

Among the initial conditions, the level of human capital stock (as proxied by the child mortality rate) is found to be statistically significant at conventional levels. This finding of a positive association between growth performance and human capital is consistent with most other studies on determinants of income growth. The magnitude of the coefficient, however, is comparatively small. An increase of 10% in the mortality rate relative to the mean for all provinces (84.7 in 1988) would reduce the rate of provincial income growth by 0.2 percentage points per year. Put differently, if the mortality rate in the province with the highest rate (Western Samar) were to fall to the average level for all provinces, that is, from 121.1 to 84.7, or by 30% (Appendix), the income growth rate for that province would increase by 0.7 percentage points per year, all other things remaining equal.

All the time-varying policy variables are significant and have the expected signs. In conformity with theory and most cross-country regressions, improvements in literacy and access to infrastructure (electricity and roads) have a positive effect on income growth. The magnitude of those effects, however, is surprisingly small. In the case of literacy, even a 20% improvement in the overall provincial average increase of 3.8 percentage points per year (Appendix) would increase income growth by only 0.05 percentage points. This limited gain can be attributed to the already relatively high rate for the provinces as a group (91.4% in 2003). The average, however, conceals the large variation across provinces. For provinces that are well below the national average, an improvement in the literacy rate to, say, the national average could have a major impact on local income growth. For example, if the province with the lowest literacy rate in 2003 (Tawi-Tawi, at 63.3%) were to achieve the average rate for all provinces (91.4%), the income growth rate of that province would increase by 1.8 percentage points per year, all other things remaining the same.

Increments in land reform implementation (CARP) have a positive and significant effect on the mean income growth rate. A 25% increase in the pace of CARP implementation (that is, an increase in the average change for all provinces from 80% to 100%, thereby effectively completing imple-

Table 9.3: Determinants of Local Growth and Poverty Reduction

Explanatory Variable	Mean Income Growth	Rate of Poverty Reduction
Mean income Growth		−1.30161[a]
		(−5.18)
Change in Literacy	0.00066[a]	−0.00077
	(2.66)	(−1.45)
Change in Electricity	0.00031[a]	
	(2.81)	
Change in Road Density	0.04649[a]	−0.07067[a]
	(2.41)	(−1.95)
Change in CARP	0.03211[a]	0.00748
	(3.55)	(0.38)
Change in Agricultural Terms of Trade	0.01346[a]	
	(1.95)	
Initial Per Capita Income (Log)	−0.02106[a]	
	(−3.29)	
Initial Mortality	−0.00019[b]	0.00035[b]
	(−1.89)	(1.86)
Landlocked	0.00754[a]	0.00615
	(2.29)	(1.05)
Initial Gini Ratio	0.00806[a]	
	(3.02)	
Initial Gini Ratio Squared	−0.00012[a]	
	(−2.98)	
Constant	0.06261	−0.01666
R[2]	0.62850	0.64880
Sample Size	71	71

CARP = Comprehensive Agrarian Reform Program.
[a] Statistically significant at the 5% level.
[b] Statistically significant at the 10% level.
Notes:
The procedure used to estimate mean income growth is three-stage least squares regression. Figures in parentheses are t-ratios. Other variables that are included in the estimation but are not significant in both growth and poverty regressions are not shown.
The poverty measure used is headcount, defined as the proportion of the population deemed poor. The dependent variable is the average annual rate of headcount reduction between 1988 and 2003 so that a negative coefficient for a variable implies that the variable has a positive effect on poverty reduction.
Source: Balisacan (2007c).

mentation) would raise the income growth rate by 0.6 percentage points per year. This is a significant result considering that land reform is often seen as a policy tool mainly for achieving noneconomic objectives. The result suggests that addressing access to productive assets would improve efficiency, thereby raising the economy's subsequent income growth rates, as argued cogently by Bourguignon (2004).

The regression results also reveal cracks in poverty reduction efforts. The policy variables and the variables representing initial conditions, except those pertaining to human capital and infrastructure, are found mainly to exert an indirect effect on poverty reduction through their effect on overall income growth. For infrastructure, particularly transport, and, to some extent, initial human capital, both direct and indirect effects are operative and, taken together, have positive impact on the pace of poverty reduction. Particularly remarkable is the lack of direct response of poverty to the CARP. Considering that the agrarian reform program is touted as an equity tool, this result is not only surprising but also inconsistent with earlier findings. The CARP does affect the poor, but its effect is mainly through the income growth channel. Taken together, the regression results show very limited direct effects of recent policies and institutions on the speed of poverty reduction; their effects are transmitted to poverty reduction indirectly, mainly through overall income growth.

Another interesting observation from the foregoing study, as well as other studies using the same provincial data (e.g., Balisacan and Fuwa 2004), concerns the extent by which poverty reduction responds to overall income growth, after accounting for the influences of other factors just noted. This response can be aptly summarized by what is referred to as the "growth elasticity" of poverty reduction. This elasticity clusters around 1.3, i.e., a 10% increase in the income growth rate increases the poverty reduction rate by roughly 13%. Significantly, these estimates are much lower than those reported for other developing countries. For example, using parameter estimates of inequality distribution for each country, Cline (2004) obtained growth elasticities of 2.9 for the PRC, 3.0 for Indonesia, and 3.5 for Thailand.[5] Ravallion (2001) obtained a growth elasticity of 2.5 for 47 developing countries, based on a bivariate regression of the proportionate changes in their poverty rates and mean incomes. A similar bivariate regression of the data used in this chapter gives an elasticity of 1.5. Hence, by all these indications, the growth elasticity in the Philippines has been low by international standards.

Clearly, the very low income growth in recent years is a key factor in the country's sluggish rate of poverty reduction. Still, even this modest

---

[5]   Cline's estimate for the Philippines was 2.2. While higher than the other estimates quoted here, it is still low by Asian standards.

level of income growth could have delivered more poverty reduction than was actually realized if the growth elasticity in the Philippines had come close to the elasticities of neighboring countries.

The finding that certain policy levers often identified as tools for achieving equity objectives—human capital and asset reform through the CARP—have rather weak discernible direct effects on poverty reduction is quite disturbing. Their effects are felt mostly indirectly through the income growth process. In other words, even programs supposedly targeted at poverty, such as the CARP, have actually been largely neutral from an income distribution viewpoint. One interpretation of this result is that the implementation of such programs has been poorly targeted. The next section takes a closer look at some of the country's direct antipoverty programs to validate this disturbing result.

9.4. Antipoverty Programs

As noted, the roots of the country's economic malaise during the last 25 years have been well articulated (that is, weak governance, low investment in basic infrastructure, political and macroeconomic instability, a highly unequal distribution of productive assets such as land, and a persistently rapid population growth). This is not the case for programs intended to deliver assistance efficiently to the poor, especially in the event of adverse shocks such as during a macroeconomic crisis or natural calamities. In short, how must programs intended for the poor be designed so as to achieve the desired objective? What lessons have been gleaned from recent experience to serve as input to this design?

Efficiency in the use of funds for poverty reduction underlies the principle of targeting, in which benefits are channeled to the high priority group that a program aims to serve. Targeting requires that the poor be distinctly identified from the non-poor, and that the program be monitored so that its benefits flow to the intended beneficiaries. As such, targeting is a potentially costly activity, both in terms of time and administrative outlay.

The literature distinguishes between two types of targeting—broad and narrow. Broad targeting specifies the intervention. The effectiveness of broad targeting lies in the comparative propensity of the poor to utilize the intervention vis-à-vis the non-poor. Narrow targeting stipulates inclusion and exclusion criteria to distinguish the qualified beneficiaries (the poor) from the others (the non-poor). Broad targeting may result in substantial leakages, but narrow targeting may entail significant administrative costs. In practice, the design of antipoverty projects employs both types of targeting.

273

9.4.1. An Overview of Poverty Reduction Programs

Poverty reduction has always been a central element of the government's development effort, as articulated in its development plans and official policy statements. By and large, only the emphasis and the strategy to achieve these goals have changed during recent decades.[6]

The development program of the Aquino administration (1986–1992) primarily stressed the alleviation of poverty, the generation of more productive employment opportunities, and the promotion of equity and social justice. Unlike previous programs, which emphasized import-substituting development, the new program called for the removal of policy biases against agriculture and the rural sector, with agrarian reform serving as its centerpiece. For its direct poverty reduction strategy, the administration launched the *Tulong sa Tao* Program (Help for the Poor), with provision of subsidized credit as a focal point.

The Ramos administration (1992–1998) focused on accelerating the pace of economic growth by building the international competitiveness of domestic industries, reforming regulation in services and industry, and investing in basic infrastructure. For achieving human development objectives, the Ramos administration implemented the Social Reform Agenda. The Social Reform Agenda contained a package of government interventions organized around flagship programs for the country's 20 poorest provinces, and is considered to be the first effort of the Philippine public administrative system to organize the various sectors of government toward securing so-called minimum basic needs before attending to other demands of priority sectors.

The Comprehensive and Integrated Delivery of Social Services (CIDSS) was the flagship antipoverty project of the Ramos administration. The CIDSS basic strategy was to empower the poor by directly engaging them in the design and implementation of antipoverty programs. Previous programs were ineffective either due to underutilization, or, if use was high, impacts were not sustained. This may have been because the projects did not coincide with the perceived needs of the target beneficiaries, who had no sense of ownership of the antipoverty projects involved. Under the CIDSS, beneficiary communities, with the help of full-time community workers, were organized and taught to identify their problems, prepare a work program, mobilize additional funding resources as necessary, and implement projects themselves. Civil society groups were involved in all the project stages.

The CIDSS employed the minimum basic needs approach in project prioritization. The approach used a set of 33 indicators, spanning the different

---

6   Balisacan (2003a) reviews postwar development planning vis-à-vis poverty reduction. ADB (2005) provides an overview of poverty reduction programs since the mid 1980s.

basic needs for survival (food and nutrition, health, water and sanitation, and clothing), security (shelter, peace and order, and income and employment), and an enabling environment (basic education and literacy, people's participation, family care, and psychosocial needs). Priority was given to projects that addressed the top unmet needs. In practice, the most common projects were day care centers, water supply systems, sanitary toilet facilities, shelter assistance, and credit provision. Other projects entailed skills training and provision of school facilities. Of course, the CIDSS's innovative contribution was mobilizating the community to participate in all the project stages. Within priority provinces, preference was given to the poorer municipalities and within these, to poorer districts (*barangays*).[7]

The Estrada administration (1998–2001) came to power with a lavish pro-poor agenda. It recognized the imperative of broad-based rural development to win the war against poverty. Its Medium-Term Philippine Development Plan for 1999–2004 identified the main elements of the development strategies required to spur growth and to achieve sustainable development in rural areas. The plan envisioned, for example, an aggressive delivery of basic social development services, removal of policy and regulatory distortions, sustained development of rural infrastructure, improvement in governance, and macroeconomic stability. The administration's flagship program for poverty alleviation was the *Lingap Para sa Mahihirap* (Care for Poor) Program, which involved identifying, in each province and city, the 100 poorest families. These families were to be provided with a package of assistance, including livelihood development, price support for staple foods, medical assistance, socialized housing, and a rural waterworks system. Several modalities were employed in selecting beneficiaries, but in principle, the aim was to use data on the unmet minimum basic needs. If such data were not available, the local social worker was consulted to identify the poorest families. Overall, the program turned out to be far less effective—in terms of impact on national poverty—than either the *Tulong sa Tao* Program of the Aquino administration or the CIDSS of the Ramos administration (Balisacan and Edillon 2005).

The ascension to power of the Arroyo administration (2001) has revived the push for economic growth as the principal vehicle for addressing the poverty problem. The current administration also initiated a new national strategy of direct poverty alleviation, dubbed *Kapit-Bisig Laban sa Kahirapan* (KALAHI), literally translated as "Linking Arms Against Poverty." The strategy encompasses asset reform, provision of human development services, creation of employment and livelihood opportunities, social protection and security against violence, and participation of basic sectors in

---

7   A *barangay* is the lowest administrative unit, below a municipality.

governance. Interventions are delivered using the administrative apparatus of national government agencies and local government units (LGUs), but the emphasis, as in earlier programs, is on local community empowerment.

The KALAHI interventions are grouped into four programs: (i) KALAHI–CIDDS, which seeks to empower poor communities through enhanced participation in community governance and involvement in the design, implementation, and management of antipoverty initiatives; (ii) KALAHI–Agrarian Reform Zone, which focuses on acquiring lands for qualified farmers, improving tenancy, and providing agricultural support services; (iii) KALAHI–KALAYAAN, which aims to address the needs of poor communities in conflict areas; and (iv) KALAHI–Poverty-Free Zones, which provides livelihood opportunities for people in targeted areas. As of mid 2006, these programs cover about 12,800 barangays (nearly 30% of all barangays), of which 29% are served by KALAHI–CIDSS and 71% by KALAHI–Agrarian Reform Zones.[8] The two other programs are present in 600 and 44 barangays only, respectively.

9.4.2. Government Expenditure on Antipoverty Programs

As previously discussed, the policy and institutional response to poverty requires more than growth-mediated (i.e., long-run) poverty reduction initiatives. It likewise involves direct intervention to meet short-run poverty reduction objectives, including avoiding transient poverty, as well as provision of the conditions for some groups to escape poverty traps.

Socioeconomic conditions and circumstances of households vary considerably. Some groups are usually unable to participate—either partially or fully—during episodes of growth, or may in fact be hurt by public decisions chosen to move the economy to a higher and sustainable growth path. These groups may include

- individuals who do not have the assets, particularly skills, necessary to take advantage of the opportunities offered by growth;
- households in geographic areas bypassed by growth—geographic poverty traps may systematically prevent population subgroups from escaping poverty;
- households whose entitlements are shrunk by public actions chosen to bring the economy to a higher growth path; and

---

8   Of the KALAHI barangays, 100 are beneficiaries of at least three KALAHI agency programs, 1,210 barangays have at least two KALAHI agency programs, and 11,249 barangays have one KALAHI agency program (NAPC 2006).

- households falling into poverty traps owing to the reinforcing effects of adverse shocks and imperfect capital markets, the latter leading to a failure to smooth consumption—for example, the 1997 Asian economic crisis tended to hit hardest the poorest groups in society (Balisacan and Edillon 2001, Reyes et al. 1999).

Estimates of the total expenditure on the types of directly (narrowly) targeted interventions discussed above suggest that they account for a very modest share of government expenditure. Recent figures are not available, but data for the late 1990s show poverty-related measures at no more than 0.60% of central government expenditure. When the cost of the National Food Authority (NFA) operations are added, the figure comes to about 1.5%.[9] Expenditure by local governments on poverty programs was tiny, at only P0.60 per capita, compared with P37.00 per capita by the central government (Manasan 2001).

For broad targeting of expenditure categories, real public expenditure per capita on key activities has declined in recent years. While total spending per capita in real terms (in 1985 prices) on social services rose from P480 in 1991 to P807 in 2000, it then fell to P664 in 2005. In particular, education expenditures per capita dropped from about P440 in 2001 to P390 in 2004.

The trends simply reflect the broader picture—expenditures for social services as a percentage of the total government expenditures declined in the first half of the current decade, from 31% in 2000 to 27% in 2005 (Figure 9.4). The decline came mainly from the national government, not from LGUs. Historically, of the total national government spending for social services, a little over 50% has gone to education. However, education's share declined in the first half of the current decade.

---

[9] NFA implements a number of subsidy schemes, of which the most important is that for rice. NFA aims to meet potentially conflicting objectives of maintaining a floor price of rice for producers and a ceiling price for consumers. NFA buys the grains from the farmers during times of bumper harvest, when NFA's buying price is higher than the market price. The program essentially provides a subsidy to farmers, so that they are assured of a stable income, independent of the supply situation in the market. However, in recent years, NFA has been able to procure less than 5% of total rice production. On the consumer side, subsidies are provided for sales of supported goods in selected retail outlets and NFA rolling stores. The main objective of the program is to protect consumers against large increases in the price of basic commodities, not just rice but also sugar, cooking oil, and (more recently) common drugs. NFA has a monopoly control over rice imports, and its import quota has combined with relatively high import tariffs on rice to keep domestic consumer prices well above world prices.

Figure 9.4. Percent of Social Services Expenditures in Total Government Expenditures, 1991–2005

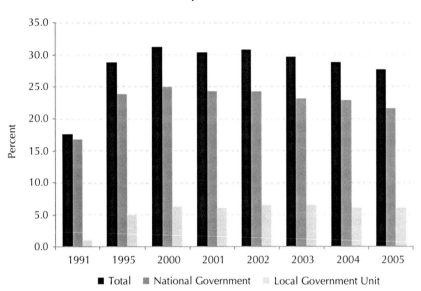

Source: Based on data from DBM (various years).

Disasters, both natural and man-made, have been a major source of poverty and vulnerability in the Philippines. An average of 20 typhoons, accompanied by strong winds, intense rainfall, and flooding, buffet the country every year; in recent years, hydrologic events have become more intense and more frequent (presumably arising from global climate change). The most vulnerable areas of the country are the Eastern Visayas and Southern, Central, and Northen Luzon, the first two being among the poorest regions in the country. Agriculture, the sector on which two thirds of the poor depend for income and sustenance, is most vulnerable to vagaries of climate and weather and to the incidence of pests and diseases. In 2004–2006, disasters, particularly typhoons and associated hydrologic events, adversely affected about 8 million people annually, mostly in rural areas—over 50% more than during 1994–2006. Only about half of the affected people received assistance from government and private relief institutions, and the value of the assistance was miniscule—not even representing 1% of the average income during "normal" times of the poorest 30% of the population (Table 9.4). This is a serious concern considering that disasters often inflict serious damage to and losses of property, and destroy the only means of livelihood for the poor. Failing to receive assistance, they risk falling to perpetual poverty traps.

Table 9.4: Disaster Occurrences and Assistance

Type of Disaster	Number of Persons Affected (annual average)		Number of Persons Assisted (annual average)		Assistance Per Affected Person (pesos)		As % of Income of Poor Person	
	1994–1996	2004–2006	1994–1996	2004–2006	1994–1996	2004–2006	1994–1996	2004–2006
Typhoon	4,092,023	5,928,979	2,221,036	2,992,873	7	16	0.14	0.18
Flooding	829,560	1,864,245	326,826	1,039,266	6	20	0.12	0.22
Strong Wind/Waves	2,877	14,381	1,936	10,304	21	83	0.41	0.92
Sea Tragedy	515	906	271	411	2,083	170	39.56	1.88
Tremors/Landslides	6,761	7,778	289	7,109	11	977	0.21	10.78
Volcanic Activity	35,872	15,811	28,210	15,811	117	630	2.23	6.95
Others	71,386	1,332	14,748	1,182	0	260	0.00	2.87
Total	5,038,994	7,833,432	2,593,316	4,066,955	8	19	0.15	0.21

Note: Average income of a poor person is average of the poorest 30% of the population.

Sources: Disaster and assistance data: Response Operations Monitoring and Information Center, Department of Social Welfare and Development (2007); Income data: Family Income and Expenditure Survey (NSO various years).

9.4.3. Impact Evaluation of High-Profile Antipoverty Programs

As noted, the core of the Arroyo administration's KALAHI strategy is poverty reduction through asset reform, access to basic services by way of community empowerment, and generation of livelihood opportunities. Concretely, the main vehicle for the asset reform is the country's land reform (CARP). For delivering basic services through community empowerment, the flagship program is the KALAHI–CIDSS. Microfinance programs take the front seat for generating employment and livelihood opportunities. While many other poverty-oriented programs are implemented by the various national government agencies, the CARP and KALAHI–CIDSS programs have acquired high-profile status owing to their extensive coverage (national in scope), budget outlays, and projection in media and national development forums. To be sure, the three programs preceded the inception of the KALAHI. The CARP, for example, was created by a landmark law passed in the late 1980s by the Aquino administration, and the CIDSS was the implementing vehicle for the Social Reform Agenda of the Ramos administration. Microfinance programs have been around since at least the mid 1980s, though in a smaller scale than those operating at present. But under the Arroyo administration, through the KALAHI strategy of convergence of resources, programs and projects, and stakeholders and sectors, the three programs have served as the main vehicles for directly addressing the problems of inequity and poverty. The following subsections focus on the CARP and CIDSS.

The Comprehensive Agrarian Reform Program. By East Asian standards, land inequality in the Philippines, as gauged from estimates of the Gini coefficient for operational landholding, is comparatively high (Balisacan 2007a). The median Gini coefficient for East Asia is 0.41; for the Philippines, it is 0.57. Moreover, despite the country's three decades of land reform programs, the inequality has hardly changed (Table 9.5). Meanwhile, for most of the postwar period, rapid population growth, combined with slow growth of productive employment opportunities outside of agriculture, has put pressure on average farm size.

The CARP has been the government's landmark agrarian initiative since the late 1980s. At its inception, expectations were high that the CARP would serve as a social program to reduce rural income disparities and as part of the government's counterinsurgency campaign. The Philippine Congress enacted what was to become the Comprehensive Agrarian Reform Law (Republic Act 6657) in 1988 to govern the program's implementation.

Table 9.5: Average Farm Size and Landholding Distribution

Year	Ave. Farm Size (ha)	Land-Labor Ratio	Percent of Farms		Percent of Area		Gini Ratio
			Above 10 ha	Above 25 ha	Above 10 ha	Above 25 ha	
1960	3.6	1.34	5.5	0.5	38.3	15.4	0.53
1971	3.5	1.16	4.8	0.6	33.8	17.1	0.54
1980	2.8	1.08	3.5	–	26.0	–	0.54
1991	2.2	0.88	2.3	0.3	23.5	10.6	0.57
2002	2.0	0.69	1.8	0.2	19.4	8.1	0.57

– = data not available, ha = hectare.
Sources: Author's estimates based on the Philippine Census of Agriculture (NSO various years).

The CARP departs from all previous land reform initiatives by (i) including all agricultural lands, regardless of the commodity produced; and (ii) going beyond tenancy arrangements to include other alternative production arrangements, such as production or profit-sharing, labor administration, and distribution of shares of stock.

At the beginning of its implementation, the CARP was expected to cover about 9.77 million hectares. Subsequent reassessments of potential areas led to a downward revision to 8.2 million hectares. Of the revised scope, the Department of Agrarian Reform (DAR) was tasked to distribute 4.4 million hectares of private agricultural and government-owned lands to about 3 million farmers, while the Department of Environment and Natural Resources was tasked to distribute 3.7 million hectares of public agricultural and integrated social forestry and community-based forest management lands to about 2 million farmers.

The CARP was intended to be completed in 10 years, i.e., by 1998. Cognizant of the remaining tasks to be done, Congress extended the program's implementation by another 10 years (until 2008). Even so, in 2007, the program was far from completed. At the end of December 2006, only 86% of DAR's scope of 4.4 million hectares had been distributed. However, even this level of accomplishment is exaggerated. The end results expected from the land redistribution program are individual ownership titles, which would be instrumental in bringing about incentive effects that redound to increases in farm investments, household incomes, and opportunities for human development. However, instead of individual titles, about 2.15 million hectares—about 50% of the distributed lands or 72% of the combined individual and collective titles—are still under collective land ownership awards (CLOAs), or "mother" certificates. These collective titles are supposed to have been subdivided to individual titles for distribution to agrarian reform beneficiaries. The program's performance system does not distinguish between hectarage under individual titles and that under CLOAs.

Land distribution was particularly slow for private agricultural lands (other than rice and corn lands) under compulsory acquisition, which total 1.5 million hectares or roughly one fifth of the program scope. Only about 18% of this program component was accomplished. The main problems were the slow process involved in land acquisition and distribution, insufficient technical capacity of implementing agencies, legal disputes relating to coverage and land valuation, landowners' resistance, harassment and unstable peace and order conditions, and budget constraints. And most of the remaining problems with landholding inequality relate to these lands (particularly lands planted to sugarcane, coconut and other tree crops, and nontraditional export crops).

In the case of public lands defined as "alienable and disposable," where only 69% of the target had been achieved after 20 years of CARP implementation, the bottlenecks were delays in undertaking land surveys, slow reconstitution of land records, and sluggish resolution of land conflicts among competing claimants. Public alienable and disposable lands and forested lands are not vacant—they are being tilled by farmer "squatters" who only need to be given security of tenure.

Too-frequent changes in the leadership of implementing agencies, especially of DAR and the Department of Environment and Natural Resources, have also constrained the program's implementation.

Financing the program has likewise become a major bottleneck. At the beginning of program implementation, the required funding was estimated at P221 billion. The average annual budget represented about 30% of the national government's total appropriations for 1987. The total budget was subsequently pared down to about P153.07 billion. Funds were to be drawn from proceeds of the government's sale of nonperforming assets. This was not realized to the extent intended. The CARP's extension to 2008 came with an additional allocation of P50 billion. Likewise, the additional budget requirement was still insufficient or unavailable.

The funding problem, together with the limited technical capacity of the agencies tasked to implement the program, bred uncertainty about the effective scope of the CARP. Invariably, successful land reform programs elsewhere, especially in East Asia, were implemented swiftly. The uncertainty is magnified by the continued efforts of certain sectors to lobby in Congress for exclusion from the program. In early 1995, Congress granted an exemption to fishery and prawn farms. The uncertainty surrounding the program has discouraged the flow of investment into agriculture and encouraged leaving agricultural lands unplanted and converting them into nonagricultural uses. Moreover, the program could have effectively weakened the private market for agricultural lands, thereby diminishing their collateral value.

The CARP is distinct from previous agrarian initiatives in another major respect: it provides a comprehensive program of beneficiary development, especially the delivery of basic services (capacity building, credit and marketing assistance, farm infrastructure, etc.) needed to transform the beneficiaries into efficient agricultural producers and entrepreneurs. However, because the funds available to support the program had been very limited, the government, through DAR, launched in 1993 the agrarian reform community (ARC) approach to beneficiary development. The approach involves focusing the delivery of support services on selected areas, rather than dispersing the delivery to all areas covered by the CARP. It is also a mechanism to fast-track investment in basic social infrastructure, such as water, power supply, education, and health.

About 1,780 ARCs have been established since the program's launch (DAR 2006). They cover roughly 42% of the total agrarian reform beneficiaries (ARBs) nationwide. Foreign-assisted projects for the agrarian reform program have been concentrated in the ARCs. These projects have provided support to 58% of the ARCs, covering 62% of the ARBs in all ARCs, or roughly 30% of all ARBs nationwide. Owing to the government's fiscal constraint, ARCs receiving support services through foreign-assisted projects are expected to be better off than those without.

Despite the implementation problems, evidence tends to show that the CARP's impact on farm household welfare and poverty reduction has been positive, although not as large as expected. The latest and most comprehensive assessment is that by a team of researchers of the Asia Pacific Policy Center (APPC 2007a).

The APPC study reexamined earlier findings in light of available national household surveys, agriculture and population censuses, updated panel data, and related community-level data. From these extensive data, a nationally representative group of ARCs (treatment group) was matched with an initially comparable, nationally representative group of non-ARCs (control group). The matched set—consisting of 1,467 barangays for each group, or a total of 2,934 barangays—was then used to determine whether the ARC barangays were better off than the non-ARC barangays. Regression analysis was also performed to examine the independent effects of ARCs and of land ownership on the welfare of ARBs and non-ARBs.

The study found that the net effect of the CARP through the ARCs on the economic welfare of beneficiaries was positive, albeit rather small, compared with the comparable group of nonbeneficiaries and with findings in previous studies (e.g., Lim 2003). The annual increase in income attributable to the CARP was, on the average, P223 per person (at 2006 prices). For the 1990–2000 period, the increases sufficed to cause a slightly faster reduction of poverty incidence in ARCs than in comparable non-ARCs. Further, the increase in per capita income was significantly higher for farmers owning land than their counterparts not owning land, all other things remaining the same. This was the case whether the comparison was made for farmers residing in ARCs or in non-ARCs.[10] Moreover, the odds for a farmer owning land being non-poor were 1.7–2.6 times more than for one not owning land.

Evidently, while the CARP had been a positive force for social reform and poverty reduction, the welfare gains had been rather small. The major impediment to realizing the full benefits of asset reform, as envisioned by Republic Act 6657, was the extremely slow program implementation. This gave rise to bureaucratic inertia; provided room for legal disputes, lobbying by landowners for exemption from the program, and rent-seeking activities by elite groups for the resources made available to the program; and led to dwindling financial support from the political regime as the prime trigger (e.g., rural unrest) for the program receded. Moreover, the long-drawn-out implementation discouraged private investment in agriculture and encouraged the conversion of agricultural land to other uses. In contrast, successful East Asian land reform was rooted mainly in its speedy implementation.

High on the agenda for faster implementation should be completion of the division of the CLOAs into individual ownership titles, along with improved access to production support services. This move should enhance the incentives of land ownership for farm investment, productivity, and household welfare. For private agricultural lands, the political economy is likely to continue to stand in the way of completing compulsory acquisition of large plantations. Other modalities of implementing reform for these lands need to be explored. In any case, a firm timeline for a closure of the program has to be set. Finally, land reform should be seen as only one of the elements of a comprehensive strategy for economic and social development. No land reform program can effectively achieve its goals unless the economic and political environment is conducive to sustained economic growth and development.

Kapit-Bisig Laban sa Kahirapan–Comprehensive and Integrated Delivery of Social Services (KALAHI–CIDSS). The KALAHI–CIDSS is the government's second major direct antipoverty program. The program, which was launched in January 2003, aims to reduce poverty in poor areas

---

[10] Not all members of an ARC are ARBs.

by providing basic social services through local communities, which take the key role in identifying, designing, and implementing projects responsive to their development needs. Conceptually, the program is similar to other community-driven development initiatives in which the poor and vulnerable are given greater voice in development decisions by empowering communities while improving services and reducing poverty.

The program was planned for implementation during a 6-year period in 4,216 rural barangays and 183 municipalities in the country's 42 poorest provinces, benefiting an estimated 1.1 million poor households. The provinces were selected based on the poverty data of the National Statistical Coordination Board. The poorest one fourth of the municipalities were selected from each of the 42 provinces, based on municipal poverty mapping methodology developed by the Manila-based APPC (Balisacan, Edillon, and Ducanes 2002). All the barangays within the selected municipalities were eligible to participate in the program.

The total program cost is $182.4 million, of which $100.0 million comes from the World Bank through a loan window, $31.4 million from the national government, and $51.0 million from LGUs (mainly in-kind contributions). This is the first program of its kind the World Bank has financed, by way of loan, in the Philippines, and among the few it has in its global operations. Multilateral finance instititutions still do not commonly lend to national governments for projects intended mainly for empowering communities, especially because such projects are not easily adaptible to the usual financial and economic viability filters (e.g., loan repayment and benefit–cost ratios). The KALAHI–CIDSS provides a window for understanding the intricate economics of building social capital. For the Philippines, the program offers an opportunity to try new approaches to generating and implementing local projects that address the pressing needs of poor communities. Indeed, the many high-profile antipoverty initiatives in recent decades have been costly to administer (not sustainable), had high benefit leakage, and were geared for top-down implementation (Balisacan and Edillon 2005).

The program is implemented in four phases, with coverage broadened as the program progresses from one phase to the next. The midterm progress report noted that in 2006, the KALAHI–CIDSS had reached 3,080 barangays in 129 municipalities across 42 provinces (World Bank 2005). It financed about 2,300 subprojects amounting to $41 million. Basic infrastructure (roads, footpaths, bridges, culverts, flood control, drainage) comprises 51% of the subprojects and essential services (water supply, health stations, school buildings, day care centers) 39%. The remaining 10% is mainly for common service facilities (postharvest facilities and community enterprises).

The KALAHI--CIDSS Update for the Second Quarter 2007 showed that a total of 2,770 community projects in 2,947 barangays, for a combined cost of $67 million, had been funded (DSWD 2007). Of this amount, about 34% ($23 million) was shouldered by the local governments and communities as counterpart. The completed subprojects, numbering 2,062 of the 2,770 funded subprojects, amounted to approximately $48 million.

Midterm internal monitoring and evaluation of the KALAHI–CIDSS indicates that the subprojects had addressed the pressing development needs of the targeted communities. Moreover, the program's capacity development component had built social capital and improved local governance, as indicated by improvements in LGU officials' capabilities, participation in barangay assemblies, the practice of LGU accountability and transparency in implementing projects, and community–LGU relations (World Bank 2006). While obtaining positive results from a program's own monitoring and evaluation system is usually predictable (at least in the Philippine context), two independent external evaluations of the KALAHI–CIDSS provide similar qualitative results, though one shows much lower impacts than does the other.

The first of the two external evaluations, that by Araral and Holmemo (2007), focused on the program's economic effects. Drawing from program field reports and rapid appraisals, they concluded the following.

- Overall, the program is economically beneficial, with an economic internal rate of return of 21%. At this rate, the program passes the National Economic and Development Authority's threshold for economically justifiable investments.
- The projects tend to be more cost-effective than traditionally implemented infrastructure projects of other government agencies. Unit costs under them are lower than those of other agencies' comparable projects, ranging from 8% for school buildings to 76% for water supply.
- Investment in the capability development of communities and LGUs can be beneficial. This was shown to be positively associated with collective action, inclusive access to local public goods, maintenance of projects, and trust among community members.
- The program's social mobilization process led to more efficient resource allocation through improved matching of demand for and supply of local public goods.

The other external evaluation, conducted by APPC (2007b), points to a far more subdued program impact. Unlike the Araral-Holmemo study, the APPC study used carefully designed panel data of treatment and control groups, thereby allowing a more informed attribution of program benefits (and costs). The treatment group consisted of beneficiary municipalities, while the control group was composed of municipalities that were chosen from within the same sample provinces and with similar characteristics as the treatment municipalities, but that were not part of the project. The control municipalities were selected using cluster analysis in which the "discriminators" were the variables that proxy for quality of life. The baseline survey of 2,400 households in four selected provinces was conducted in late 2003, and the follow-up (midterm) survey was implemented in late 2006. The APPC study results on the effects of the KALAHI-CIDSS on social capital formation and local governance are broadly consistent with those reported by the Araral-Holmemo study. However, on income and other economic welfare measures, the APPC results are mixed, i.e., the treatment municipalities were not deemed consistently better off than the control municipalities. Moreover, in cases where the economic gains are significantly higher for the beneficiary municipalities than for the others, the benefits are perceived to have resulted mainly from the projects supported by the program (basic infrastructure and essential community services), not from empowerment and participation in governance per se. However, it may be too early to see such links, especially significant gains in economic welfare terms.

The KALAHI–CIDSS experience provides interesting insights and issues for the design of poverty reduction strategies. First, investment in community empowerment and local governance as a path out of poverty potentially has high payoffs, but the risks are also high. The translation of community empowerment into economic welfare gains appears not to be as clear-cut as often assumed. The question arises as to whether it would have been more appropriate to anchor the flagship antipoverty program to something that is already well understood in the literature and development practice. For example, the connection between access to basic education and health services, on the one hand, and poverty, on the other, is well understood, as is what it takes to improve this access to the poorer segments of the Philippine society. Also, a question arises as to whether the KALAHI–CIDSS implementation infrastructure is replicable without high-level funding and technical support, i.e., in a regime of fiscal bind.

9.5. Conclusion

Poverty in the Philippines has to do largely with the country's inability to achieve—and sustain—an income growth substantially higher than its population growth. Economic growth is good for the poor, but it alone is not good enough. The response of poverty reduction to income growth in the Philippines has been low by international standards, especially compared with that in the country's neighbors. Hence, the Philippines' unenviable record in poverty reduction in recent years is the outcome not only of its comparatively low per capita growth rate of gross domestic product but also of its weakness in transforming any rate of income growth into poverty reduction. The quality of economic growth has to be improved to enhance the benefits of growth to the poor.

Even given the fiscal constraints, there are wide avenues for improving the response of poverty to overall income growth. For example, agricultural and rural development are strongly connected to poverty reduction. Investments in social services, such as in basic health and education especially in rural areas, also have high payoffs in poverty reduction.

The Philippines' high spatial diversity is quite remarkable. This chapter has shown that, indeed, poverty has a strongly spatial dimension, with some regions and provinces far more multidimensionally deprived than others. Some areas of the country have human development outcomes comparable with those found in more economically advanced countries; for example, the Human Development Index (HDI) for the National Capital Region for 2003 is comparable with that of Thailand, and the province of Rizal's with Ukraine's. Conversely, in many other areas, HDI ranks are comparable with those of the poorest countries of the world—the ARMM provinces have HDI scores similar to those of Ghana, Myanmar, and Sudan. In recent years, some regions have done well in attaining high per capita income growth and reducing poverty, but in others, the average per capita income has fallen and poverty has increased. Viewed from an international perspective, such disparities could breed regional unrest, armed conflicts, and political upheavals, thereby undermining the progress in securing sustained economic growth and national development. The *Philippine Human Development Report 2005* shows that measures of deprivation—such as disparities in access to reliable water supply, electricity, and (especially) education—predict well the occurrence of armed conflict (HDN 2005).

The reform effort has to go beyond simply raising the level of public investment in basic infrastructure and social services, particularly health and education. It has to be made pro-poor as well. The country's public spending on basic infrastructure (particularly in rural areas), education, and health, whether seen in terms of share in gross domestic product or in expenditure per person, has been lagging well behind that of its East Asian neighbors with similar per capita income. To catch up with these countries in terms of poverty reduction and human development outcomes, the government has to give high priority to spending in basic infrastructure and the social sector, especially in education and health. More than that, however, targeting of public spending must be improved so that poorer individuals receive proportionately more opportunities to benefit from publicly funded social services and infrastructure. Unfortunately, the country's record in administering direct antipoverty programs—such as agrarian reform and food, credit, and housing subsidy programs—has been disappointing.

The programs have been afflicted by high leakages to the non-poor, were administratively costly to implement, and encouraged unintended rent-seeking processes.

To be sure, a number of direct antipoverty programs had been successfully pilot-tested in various areas or sectors of society, especially at the LGU level. Scaling these success stories up appears to be a major challenge, especially if they are to be implemented without using significant funding from foreign sources.

Overall, the country has not been lacking in the thrust and zeal to achieve poverty reduction and sustainable growth. By and large, only the emphasis and the strategy to achieve these goals have changed over the years, at least as indicated by development plans and official policy statements. However, development plans are one matter; the development record is another. Implementing the plans in a regime of accountable and pro-poor governance has long been a challenge for the Philippines. The country can ill afford to again forego opportunities for reforms—and inclusive growth.

Appendix 9: Determinants of Growth and Poverty Reduction—Descriptive Statistics

Variable	Description	Mean	Standard Deviation	Minimum	Maximum
Income 1988	Log of per capita income, 1988	9.868	0.270	9.168 (Romblon)	10.562 (National Capital Region)
Income 2003	Log of per capita income, 2003	10.059	0.290	9.058 (Sulu)	10.717 (Nueva Vizcaya)
Headcount 1988	Proportion of the population deemed poor, 1988	0.394	0.175	0.075 (Kalinga-Apayao	0.852 (Romblon)
Headcount 2003	Proportion of the population deemed poor, 2003	0.321	0.176	0.044 (Nueva Vizcaya)	0.884 (Sulu)
Average Income Growth Rate	Average annual growth rate of per capita income,1988–2003	0.012	0.016	–0.030 (Maguindanao)	0.049 (Batanes)
Average Headcount Growth Rate	Average annual rate of change in poverty incidence, 1988–2003	–0.008	0.032	–0.0568 (Batanes)	0.115 (Mindoro Occidental)
Gini 1988	Expenditure Gini ratio, 1988	33.594	5.077	21.190 (Tawi-Tawi)	43.230 (Iloilo)
Gini Squared 1988		1,153.988	339.961	449.016	1,868.833
Dynasty	Proportion of provincial officials related by blood or affinity	0.140	0.246	0	1.000
Ethnic Fragmentation 1988	Herfindahl index	0.579	0.190	0.287 (Catanduanes)	0.884 (Palawan)
Mortality	Mortality rate per 1,000 children aged 0–5 years, 1988	84.688	14.847	55.920 (Pampanga)	121.120 (Western Samar)
Landlock	Dummy variable (1 if a landlocked province, 0 otherwise)	0.203	0.405	0	1.000

continued on next page

Appendix 9 (continued)

Variable	Description	Mean	Standard Deviation	Minimum	Maximum
Change in Literacy	Change in simple literacy rate, 1988–2003	3.847	5.288	–8.960 (Zamboanga del Norte)	16.0000 (Abra)
Change in Road Density	Change in (concrete-equivalent) road density, 1988–2003	0.123	0.286	–0.076 (Romblon)	2.466 (National Capital Region)
Change in Electricity	Change in share of households with electricity, 1988–2003	18.761	13.931	–11.800 (Agusan del Sur)	67.380 (Batanes)
Change in CARP	Change in CARP accomplishment, 1988–2003	0.802	0.144	0.263 (Sulu)	1.000 (Batanes, Squijor)
Change in Agricultural Terms of Trade	Change in agricultural terms of trade, 1988–2003	–0.004	0.186	–0.310 (Northern Mindanao provinces)	0.460 (CAR provinces)

CAR = Cordillera Administrative Region, CARP = Comprehensive Agrarian Reform Program.
Note: The last two columns show the provinces with the lowest and highest scores, respectively.
Source: Balisacan (2007a).

References

Araral, E., and C. Holmemo. 2007. *Measuring the Costs and Benefits of Community Driven Development: The KALAHI–CIDSS Project, Philippines.* Paper No. 102, Social Development Papers. Washington, DC: World Bank.

Asian Development Bank (ADB). 2005. *Poverty in the Philippines: Income, Assets, and Access.* Manila.

Asia Pacific Policy Center (APPC) 2007a. *Study on the Impact of the Comprehensive Agrarian Reform Program on Poverty Reduction and Prospects for Long-Term Growth.* Quezon City.

———. 2007b. *Tracking Progress towards Community Empowerment and Welfare: KALAHI–CIDDS Midterm Evaluation Report.* Quezon City.

Balisacan, A. M. 2003a. Poverty and Inequality. In A.M. Balisacan and H. Hill, eds. *The Philippine Economy: Development, Policies, and Challenges.* New York: Oxford University Press.

———. 2003b. Poverty Comparison in the Philippines: Is What We Know about the Poor Robust? In C. Edmonds, ed. *Reducing Poverty in Asia: Emerging Issues in Growth, Targeting, and Measurement.* Cheltenham: Edward Elgar.

———. 2007a. Agrarian Reform and Poverty Reduction in the Philippines. In *Agrarian Reform and Rural Development: Sharing Experiences from the Philippines.* Policy Dialogue Report 2. Dhaka: Centre on Integrated Rural Development for Asia and the Pacific.

———. 2007b. *An Analysis of Chronic Poverty in the Philippines.* Quezon City: University of the Philippines.

———. 2007c. Local Growth and Poverty Reduction. In A.M. Balisacan and H. Hill, eds. *The Dynamics of Regional Development: The Philippines in East Asia.* Cheltenham: Edward Elgar.

Balisacan, A. M., and R. Edillon. 2001. Socioeconomic Dimension of the Asian Crisis: Impact and Household Response in the Philippines. In Y-P. Chu and H. Hill, eds. *The Social Impact of the Asian Financial Crisis.* Cheltenham: Edward Elgar.

———. 2005. Poverty Targeting in the Philippines. In J. Weiss, ed. *Poverty Targeting in Asia.* Cheltenham: Edward Elgar.

Balisacan, A. M, R. G. Edillon, and G. Ducanes. 2002. *Poverty Mapping and Targeting for KALAHI–CIDSS.* Final Report for the Department of Social Welfare and Development. Quezon City.

Balisacan, A. M., and N. Fuwa. 2004. Going Beyond Cross-Country Averages: Growth, Inequality and Poverty Reduction in the Philippines. *World Development.* 32(11): 1,891–907.

Balisacan, A. M., and H. Hill. 2007. *The Dynamics of Regional Development: The Philippines in East Asia.* Cheltenham: Edward Elgar.

Barro, R. J., and X. Sala-i-Martin. 2004. *Economic Growth.* 2nd Edition. Cambridge, MA: MIT Press.

Bourguignon, F. 2004. The Poverty–Growth–Inequality Triangle. Paper presented at the Indian Council for Research on International Economic Relations, New Delhi.

Cline, W. R. 2004. Technical Correction. In *Trade Policy and Global Poverty.* Washington, DC: Institute of International Economics.

Deininger, K., and L. Squire. 1998. New Ways of Looking at Old Issues, Inequality, and Growth. *Journal of Development Economics.* 57(2): 259–87.

Department of Agrarian Reform (DAR). 2006. *CARP Situationer.* Quezon City.

Department of Budget and Management (DBM). various years. *Budget Expenditure and Sources of Financing.* Manila.

Department of Social Welfare and Development (DSWD). 2007. *KALAHI–CIDSS Update for the Second Quarter 2007.* Quezon City.

Human Development Network (HDN). 2005. *Philippine Human Development Report 2005.* Quezon City.

Lim, J. A. 2003. An Integration of the First Round of CARP Impact Assessment Studies. In *CARP Impact Assessment Studies.* Vol. 1. Quezon City: Department of Agrarian Reform.

Manasan, R. G. 2001. *Budget Allocation for Human Development Expenditures: Measuring Progress on the 20:20 Initiative of Provinces and Cities 1995–1998.* Manila: United Nations International Children's Emergency Fund (UNICEF).

———. 2003. *Analysis of the President's Budget for 2004: Looking for the Complete (Fiscal) Picture.* Discussion Paper Series No. 2003-17. Makati City: Philippine Institute for Development Studies.

National Anti-Poverty Commission (NAPC). 2006. *Kapit-Bisig Laban sa Kahirapan.* www.napc.gov.ph/kalahi.htm

National Statistics Office (NSO). various years. *Family Income and Expenditure Survey.* Manila.

———. various years. *Philippine Census of Agriculture.* Manila.

Ravallion, M. 2001. Growth, Inequality, and Poverty: Looking beyond Averages. *World Development.* 29(11): 1,803–15.

Reyes, C. M., A. Orbeta, R. G. Manasan, and G. de Guzman. 1999. *Social Impact of the Regional Financial Crisis in the Philippines.* Discussion Paper Series No. 1999-14. Makati City: Philippine Institute for Development Studies.

Sachs, J. 2005. *The End of Poverty: How We Can Make It Happen in Our Lifetime.* London: Penguin Books.

World Bank. 2005. *Community Driven Development and Social Capital: Designing a Baseline Survey in the Philippines.* Report No. 32405-PH, Social Development Department. Washington DC.

———. 2006. *KALAHI–CIDSS: KKB Project Progress Report, As of 30 June 2006.* Quezon City: Department of Social Welfare and Development.

———. various years. *World Development Indicators.* Washington, DC.

10. Governance, Institutions,and Political Economy

Emmanuel S. de Dios

10.1. Introduction

I t is difficult, in principle, to controvert the simple statement that institutions play a role in explaining growth. An institution, after all, is "a system of rules, beliefs, norms, and organizations that together generate a regularity of (social) behavior" (Greif 2006, 30).[1] Viewed at this fundamental level, institutions are pervasive, and, therefore, affect all behavior manifesting any semblance of regularity, including behavior by politicians, bureaucrats, and the citizenry itself. In particular, to the extent that formal rules, informal norms, beliefs and convergent expectations, and organizations are implicated in the acquisition and exercise of political authority, then governance itself—"the manner in which public officials and institutions acquire and exercise the authority to shape public policy and provide public goods and services" (World Bank 2007, i)—must be understood as being an institutional outcome. This is straightforward, since the institutional elements just mentioned directly affect political behavior. At the most formal and superficial level, constitutions and statutes place obvious limits on the mode of acquiring and exercising authority (e.g., elections and executive–legislative relations). In many instances, of course, behavior will appear to deviate from or spill over the limits imposed by formal laws—a problem endemic to many developing countries—such as when clientist or patriarchal relations swamp outwardly democratic processes.

---

[1] This definition amplifies the more cursive definition, provided originally by Douglass North (1990), of institutions as constraints on behavior or as "rules of the game" and of organizations as players in the game. The distinction highlights the point that for people to be guided by rules, they must be motivated by beliefs, while rules must often be sanctioned or implemented by organizations, notably those involved in the political and legal system. In more recent work, North (2005, 48ff) has acknowledged the crucial importance of beliefs.

Closer analysis, however, will typically reveal that such behavior[2] actually accords with some other (perhaps competing) set of de facto institutions that operate alongside or in lieu of de jure institutions. In the event, institutions of one form or another are implicated.

The term "political economy" is taken here to mean the analysis of the effects of political constraints on economic policies and economic outcomes (Drazen 2000, 7). "Political constraints" is shorthand for conflicting or heterogeneous interests, because, upon closer consideration, complete homogeneity of interests would imply an almost axiomatic absence of conflict. Viewed from this aspect, the content of policies themselves assumes second-order importance, because whether or not policies are implemented, and the degree to which they are, become matters that are endogenous to prevailing institutions and political economy. But although definitions of institutions and their pervasiveness appear unexceptionable, exactly what kinds of institutions do matter for economic performance, how their effects are transmitted, and how they may be changed is less clear.

Section 10.2 briefly recapitulates what is known conceptually and empirically regarding the role institutions play in development. Section 10.3 changes tack by sifting through evidence to suggest that economic growth in the Philippines has indeed been hobbled by issues relating to institutional outcomes or the performance of institutions. Section 10.4 applies a framework based on new institutional economics for understanding the historical roots of the problem. Section 10.5 concludes with some implications for policy.

10.2. Institutions and Development—the Argument

The crucial importance to economic development of the rule of law, the enforcement of contracts, and the protection of property rights stems from Douglass North's earliest observations (1990, 1981, and 1973 [with Thomas]) of how such institutional outcomes appear to have been historical preconditions for the support of anonymous exchange and long-term contracting, especially for credit, venture capital, and technological innovation. Without the preconditions, the risks and costs associated with consummating market transactions beyond spot exchange and local markets would have been prohibitively high, and technological innovation likely stifled. North distinguished between contracts that are self-enforcing between parties, e.g., those based on credible commitments (hostage

---

[2] That is, to the extent it is regularly observed behavior. In another paper (de Dios 2007), the author applies this observation to local political relationships in the Philippines.

exchange, collateral, and repeat transactions) and contracts that rely on third-party enforcement. Contracts of the former type are frequently supported by customs and norms in the context of a "dense social network where people have an intimate understanding of each other" (North 1990, 39) such as those prevailing in small and close-knit communities. But for transactions that are more complex, entail large amounts, are spread out over time and space, and involve large jurisdictions, self-enforcing contracts become increasingly difficult to write and to enforce. Instead, there is increasing reliance on sanctions by third parties, which points to the rise of impersonal legal systems and specialized institutions to enforce them. These outcomes were historically achieved in the now-developed economies in conjunction with the rise of a legal and penal system and a bureaucratic state in the sense of Weber.[3] Even Adam Smith's vision of laissez-faire was underpinned by a state that performed a night watchman's role of enforcing the law, providing defense, and providing a number of public goods.

Coercive force and revenues must be conceded to the state for it to fulfill its functions of property rights protection, contract enforcement, and defense. The perennial problem, however, is that of constraining state power. Rules and organizations have had to evolve to exact accountability from rulers, who could otherwise use their powers for expropriation and abuse. In one sense, therefore, the institutional design required for growth entails a careful balance between vesting the state with sufficient power to enforce, yet not so far as to make it oblivious to its citizens' interests and allow it to act with impunity. In much of the history of Western Europe and North America, these constraints on the powers of the state were imposed by the emergence of electoral democracy, checks and balances between branches of government, a professional bureaucracy, and the guarantee of civil rights and liberties (North and Thomas 1973, North 1981). On the other hand, whether and how the transplantation or emulation of such institutions will work for developing countries remains a festering question in development.

---

3   This historical account is not entirely unchallenged, of course. Greif (2006) contended that the impersonal state did not, per se, guarantee long-distance trade, credit, and impersonal exchange and instead cited the role of corporate bodies or associations, such as merchant groups (e.g., those of the Maghribi traders or the German Hansa), town-communes bound by community responsibility systems, and finally joint-stock corporations. These same observations tie in with similar work on *guanxi* networks in Chinese society that also originally facilitated trade. On the latter, see Fabella (2007).

Econometric tests of the above hypotheses from Barro (1991) onward have, for the most part, consisted of cross-country data[4] that repeatedly display significant influences on the long-run growth (or investment) record of different variables representing institutions or their outcomes. However, attempts to measure variations in economic performance across explicit types of institutions (e.g., forms of constitution and types of electoral rules, as found in the important work of Persson and Tabellini [2003]), are impaired in principle and, in fact, by divergences between the formal specification of institutions and actual conditions on the ground. For instance, while presidential systems of government on paper represent relatively more constraints on the executive than do parliamentary systems, they can (and do) mask a great deal of unilateral executive power in some real instances, e.g., *caudillismo* in Latin America and the strong presidency (as will be discussed later) in the Philippines.

Such difficulties have led to attempts at measuring the impact of institutions, rather than specifying them directly. Barro's original work, for example, found significant influence of variables that measure the rule of law and political stability. Since then, the list of institutional variables that plausibly appear to enhance growth has come to include the degree of protection of property rights; civil liberties; political rights and democracy; and measures of social cooperation, such as trust, religion, and clubs and associations (see, e.g., the survey by Aron [2000]).

One difficulty with the interpretation of such results, however, is that they represent at best only an indirect test of the hypothesis, since the variables included are not institutions per se but rather outcomes of institutions or their performance (Shirley 2005). Such reservations apply even to the most comprehensive collection of such variables currently available for a large number of countries (Kaufmann, Kraay, and Mastruzzi 2007). Kaufmann, Kraay, and Mastruzzi assembled data representing institutional quality or institutional performance from a wide array of sources and defined indexes delineating six aspects of institutional quality for various years (since 1998 and annually beginning 2002). The aspects were voice and accountability, political stability, government effectiveness, regulatory quality, rule of law, and control of corruption. Here, indexes of political instability, for example, measured not institutions per se but rather the results of the weakness or lack of legitimacy of institutions. Likewise, the scope of corruption (typically measured through subjective-expert or public opinion) was not by itself an institution but rather the signal of institutional weakness, in the sense that widespread corruption reflects the

---

[4]   Subsequent work includes Barro and Sala-i-Martin (1995); Mauro (1995); Keefer and Knack (1995); La Porta et al. (1998); Kaufmann, Kraay, and Zoido-Lobatón (1999); Rodrik, Subramanian, and Trebbi (2002); and Easterly, Ritzen, and Woolcock (2006).

extent to which rules do not exist, are badly designed, go unheeded, or are vendible. As a result, even as the econometric evidence suggesting the importance of institutions continues to mount, it is quite another thing to determine exactly which institutions matter, why, and how.

An early attempt to address such questions was the significant work of La Porta et al. (1998), which used cross-section data to explain how a series of institutional outcomes or indicators of institutional performance—such as respect for property, corruption, bureaucratic efficiency, and political rights—could be related to prevailing legal systems, geography, social or ethnic heterogeneity, and belief systems. Their findings suggest that, even controlling for per capita incomes, countries (i) with legal systems derived from civil code traditions (ultimately of French or Spanish origins) rather than common law, (ii) that have predominantly Islamic or Roman Catholic religious backgrounds, (iii) that are ethnically fragmented, and (iv) that are geographically close to the equator, generally perform poorly on most indexes of governance outcomes.

Important exceptions and qualifications can, of course, be made with respect to any of these conjectures. Notable counterexamples are some of the major Western industrialized countries—Belgium, France, Italy, Portugal, and Spain, after all, maintained their unhelpful civil codes and predominantly Roman Catholic traditions yet managed to join the ranks of the wealthiest nations, even if this is nuanced by the fact that within Europe, civil code and Roman Catholic countries were often relative laggards or latecomers compared to England and the Netherlands (North and Thomas 1973). Be this as it may, the historical experience of these countries shows that the mechanisms of causation can be modified by such factors as the external pressures of intra-European rivalries and competition among fragmented states (Diamond 1997); the remarkable cross-fertilization of ideas among the European intellectual (particularly its scientific) elite (Mokyr 2004); and the peculiar history of violent religious wars those countries underwent. The rise of a secular state in France and Germany, for example, cannot be understood separately from the struggle against temporal claims of the papacy and the need to preserve national unity amid violent internal strife between Roman Catholics and Protestants. Ultimately, even institutional economists concede that they know very little about the mechanisms through which the rules implemented by these institutions diffuse to governance structures and contribute to the shaping of how transactions are organized. Therefore, we know very little about comparative costs of different institutional schemes (e.g., the cost of running different kinds of judiciary systems for implementing contractual laws) (Menard 2001, 86–7).

The problem is rendered more complex when one recognizes the significant differences in the development of institutions in the present developed Western countries, on the one hand, and the postcolonial developing countries, on the other. The costs of operating institutions in today's developing countries are difficult to appreciate without understanding the historical processes that molded them. North made the important (but somewhat heretical) point that institutions proven to work in the current industrialized countries—such as democratic rules for selection of leaders, non-kin-based organizations, impersonal third-party enforcement, and prices as the primary means of resource allocation—will not necessarily provide an improvement when simply imported (and imposed from without) in today's poorer countries, one of the most important reasons being that this may simply disrupt a preexisting social order without installing a feasible replacement (North, Wallis, and Weingast 2006). The difficulties the United States (US) encountered in introducing the formal institutions of Western democracy in its recent interventions in Afghanistan and Iraq should serve as sufficient food for thought.

Two historical factors complicate the understanding of institutions in developing countries: a country's colonial heritage; and the preexisting degree of social or national cohesion (Shirley 2005) or its opposite, the degree of social heterogeneity. The effect of the former is partly reflected in the differences between various legal traditions and religious beliefs, which, as already noted, created a measurable impact on the relative growth trajectories of the Western industrial countries. The hierarchical and authoritarian structures of traditional Roman Catholicism render it less accessible to the masses and more the preserve of initiates and trained specialists. Such a "scholastic" or prescriptive tradition contrasts with the "pietism" of many Protestant sects, many of whose observances emanated from the communities of the faithful themselves.[5] A similar contrast presents itself in a comparison of the common law and civil code traditions. The common law tradition presumes greater openness to the community's evolving customs rather than (as in the civil code) the delineation of right by an interpretation and application of a fixed code by learned individuals. This is partly evident, for instance, in the practice of judgment by jury in most common law systems, rather than by specialist judges and magistrates as under the civil code tradition. It is reasonable to conclude, therefore, that common law traditions are, all else being equal, more accessible to communities than the civil code.

More important, however, is the fact that such institutions (whether common law or civil code) have been transplanted and imposed (largely

---

5   Nelson (2004, 474) uses "scholastic" to describe the situation where "a church hierarchy interprets the ways of God to the faithful," as exemplified by the Roman Catholic Church, and "pietistic" to describe "a more direct relationship between the individual and God," a notion more closely associated with the tendencies of early Protestantism. Nelson cites the theologian Paul Tillich for these assessments.

through conquest and coercion) by colonizers. This raises the real cost to the indigenous peoples of using or accessing any of them. This is one way to view the findings (notably by Acemoglu, Robinson, and Johnson 2001) that persuasively relate subsequent growth to the density of the external settlers relative to the native population. Where the areas colonized by outsiders were densely populated to begin with (e.g., South and Central America, sub-Saharan Africa, and parts of Asia), a greater cost was obviously involved before borrowed or imposed institutions could gain legitimacy or be internalized among the majority of the inhabitants. By contrast, where new settlers constituted the larger proportion or a majority of the population, such as in Australia or North America, the cost of establishing functioning institutions was lower, since this largely entailed transplanting forms of rules and traditions that were, in many respects, already familiar to and accepted by the colonists.

The degree of social or national cohesion is another factor potentially affecting the subsequent hold of formal institutions in developing countries. Greater ethnic, cultural, or economic homogeneity—itself an outcome of common history or experience—is more likely to facilitate convergent beliefs and an appreciation for a common set of rules. However, many developing countries today are handicapped in this respect by their more recent national experience and by the almost capricious partitioning and assignment of territory among the new nation states by the quondam colonial powers. In the Philippines, for example, Mindanao and its Islamic populations were effectively incorporated into the Philippine territory only after the sultanates came under US military occupation (Corpuz 1989), while the thorny claims and counterclaims over Sabah arose from what were ultimately British colonial decisions. Such a problem is even more pronounced in other parts of the world, i.e., most of Africa, the Middle East, Central Europe, and the Indian subcontinent, where multiethnic states have been the remnants from the postcolonial experience.

This observation regarding the cost of using institutions may also explain the earlier-mentioned findings of La Porta et al. (1998) that associated ethnic fragmentation with poor governance outcomes. From the viewpoint of access and the cost of internalizing and trusting institutions, a heterogeneous population is more likely than a homogeneous one to encounter difficulties in reconciling preexisting traditions, beliefs, and aspirations with rules that have been crafted and imposed from outside. More recently, Easterly, Ritzen, and Woolcock (2006) also pointed to the significance of social equality and the size of the middle class as determinants of subsequent growth. Interestingly, colonial heritage and economic geography may again be partly implicated, since certain economic formations in colonial times were conducive to the persistence of highly unequal distributions of political power and economic wealth. In an attempt to elaborate earlier work by Engermann and Sokoloff (2000), Easterly, Ritzen, and Woolcock (2006) hypothesize that geography and factor endowments encouraged certain types of settlement and colonial economic exploitation that strongly influenced subsequent social structures. In particular, factors conducive to wheat farming encouraged small farms and a more equitable asset distribution in North America; by contrast, the massive labor requirements and large scale of operations entailed by sugar plantations produced slavery and social inequity in the Caribbean, Central and South America, and the southern US.

From the viewpoint represented here, factors that have been alluded to in the literature (e.g., colonial heritage, social cohesion, and even geography) therefore matter primarily because they affect the ease of access by the majority of the population to the formal or codified institutions that were ultimately able to support anonymous exchange, long-term investment, and technological innovation in the manner described by North. The analytical upshot of this, however, is that an assessment of institutional performance cannot simply consist of an a priori specification of what are "good" and "bad" institutions, per se; rather, one must additionally consider the degree to which the greater part of population grants credibility and are able to gain access to existing institutions to guide their behavior, given their current beliefs, historical experience, proximate expectations, and interests. It then follows that mismatch or conflict between prevailing institutions—particularly of the formal kind—and the beliefs, history, expectations, and interests can be expected to result in cognitive dissonance at the societal level, at the very least, and in social strife and collapse, at the worst. The succeeding sections document how such a framework may provide part of the explanation for the long-run record of Philippine economic performance.

10.3. Current Evidence

In applying such a framework to the Philippines, the study initially seeks to establish whether and to what extent institutions—as expressed through governance outcomes—currently represent first-order causes hindering investment and economic growth. A further pursuit of the argument becomes important, after all, only if institutional factors or outcomes can be shown to significantly hinder current performance.

Toward this end, indicators for governance outcomes for recent years were assembled to determine whether the Philippines fares significantly better or worse than other countries (Kaufmann, Kraay, and Mastruzzi 2007). As already described, these indicators pertain to six dimensions: voice and accountability, political stability, government effectiveness, regulatory quality, the rule of law, and control of corruption. As a further control, however, Philippine scores on each dimension are compared to those of other countries based on a regression controlling for levels of per capita income. The results of this comparison[6] are summarized in Chapter 3, Table 3.5, which is reproduced here. The negative (or positive) entries indicate that in that particular year, the Philippines' score is comparatively worse (or better) on that particular governance outcome indicator than countries with a similar level of income per capita.

Table 3.5: Governance Indicators for the Philippines, Selected Years

Governance Indicator	1996	1998	2002	2003	2004	2005	2006
Voice and Accountability		+	+	+	+	+	+
Political Stability	–	–	–	–	–	–	–
Government Effectiveness	+					+	+
Regulatory Quality	+	+	+	+		+	+
Rule of Law	+	+	–	–	–	–	–
Control of Corruption	–	–	–	–	–	–	–

Note: + or – denotes a governance score for the Philippines that is significantly better (+) or worse (–) at the 5% level or less, compared to countries with similar gross domestic product per capita for the period. No entry indicates no significant difference.
Source: ADB staff computations using data from Kaufmann, Kraay, and Mastruzzi (2007).

For all years reported except in 2006, the Philippines rated above the norm in voice and accountability. This largely reflects the country's long-established democratic traditions and the formal guarantees of civil liberties, a free media, regular elections, and checks and balances as prescribed in the country's current constitution (in force since 1987). The deterioration in the most recent period coincides with the perceived government restrictions of civil liberties and extraordinary assertions of executive power in response to corruption allegations and threats to stability. The recent period also corresponds with deterioration in the rule of law as noted by the United Nations Commission on Human Rights, which appointed a special rapporteur to periodically review each country's fulfillment of its human rights obligations and commitments. The government also recognized the deterioration of the rule of law—in particular, extrajudicial killings—as a serious problem, and constituted the Melo Commission to investigate the allegations.

The other dimension in which the Philippines appears to rate fairly well is regulatory quality, referring to the ability to formulate and implement policy that encourages private enterprise. Political vagaries notwithstanding, all administrations since 1986 have invariably committed to a formal policy of promoting private enterprises and reducing government

---

[6]   Details can be provided by the author upon request.

involvement in business. The more substantive aspects have included the sustained efforts at privatization, deregulation, and trade liberalization in various industries. The quality and qualifications of the bureaucracy are also vindicated by ratings of "government effectiveness" that are broadly in line with what is typical for the Philippines' level of income.

By contrast, the country falls consistently below the norm in political stability and the absence of violence, the control of corruption, and the rule of law. Unlike other aspects previously mentioned, it is significant that the latter pertain less to formal policies and declarations of principle and relate more to performance. For example, while regulatory policy may be liberal with respect to the private sector, the actual assignment of economic rights and concessions may be biased and subject to elite capture. As a result, above-average ratings in the quality of regulatory policy may be diluted—as in this case—by below-average scores in the control of corruption. Likewise, although civil liberties and a resort to the courts and administrative or legal channels may be constitutionally guaranteed, real access may be limited or the application of the law may be biased, which could cause resentment and possibly violence. The result—as in this case—would be a poor showing in the rule of law, despite the de jure affirmation of "voice and accountability".

Ultimately, the most acute manifestation of these disjunctions is political instability itself, which would otherwise be difficult to explain, given the existence of what one might think are democratic avenues for voice and accountability. The low ratings for political stability coincide with a recent history marked by consummated or attempted popular uprisings, disputes of electoral results, attempted coups d'état and military mutinies, cabinet resignations, and impeachment threats.

A sharper contrast is gained by comparing the Philippines to a smaller set of neighboring countries. Using the same data from Kaufmann, Kraay, and Mastruzzi, Figures 10.1 and 10.2 show the ranking of the Philippines on two crucial governance aspects where it has performed consistently below average—control of corruption and political stability—and maps these against indicators for comparable countries in the region. The shifting pattern across countries becomes apparent particularly in the last few years. In the control of corruption, Thailand has remained several notches above the Philippines, which has typically been rated better than Indonesia in the recent past. The Philippines' loss of momentum is apparent, however, with the People's Republic of China (PRC), Viet Nam, and (soon) Indonesia catching up with the Philippines in this governance aspect.[7] In terms of stability and absence

---

[7]   Strictly speaking, the Kaufmann, Kraay, and Mastruzzi indicators are not ideally suited to measuring changes over time, as Kaufmann, Kraay, and Mastruzzi themselves admit. This is because they are constructed to reflect not only changes in absolute performance levels but also changes in ranking. See Arndt and Oman (2006).

Figure 10.1: Indicator for Control of Corruption for Selected

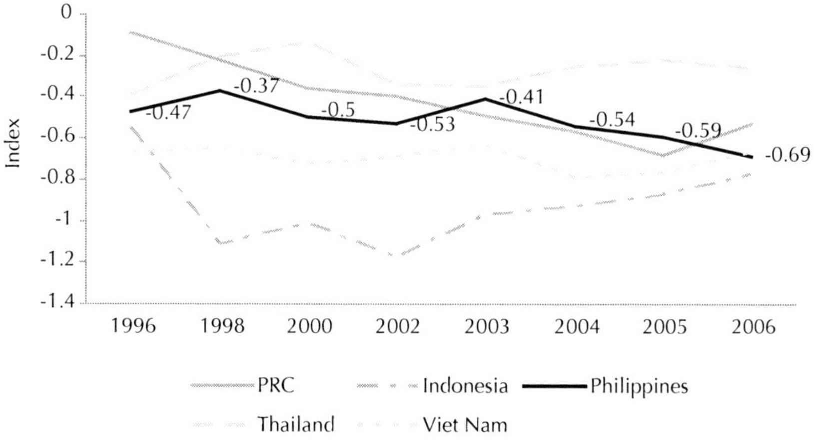

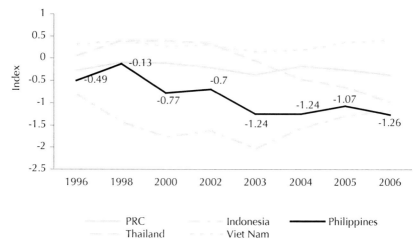

PRC = People's Republic of China.
Note: Higher scores indicate better control of corruption.
Source: Kaufmann, Kraay, and Mastruzzi (2007), generated from World Bank Governance Indicators.
(http://info.worldbank.org/governance/wgi2007)

Figure 10.2: Indicator for Political Stability For Selected Countries

PRC = People's Republic of China.
Note: The range is from 2.5 (best) to –2.5 (worst).
Source: Kaufmann, Kraay, and Mastruzzi (2007), generated from World Bank Governance Indicators.
(http://info.worldbank.org/governance/wgi2007)

305

of violence, Viet Nam rates best among the countries included, doing consistently better than the 50th percentile. Again, the Philippines' loss of ground is apparent, particularly relative to 1998. (Political stability in Thailand deteriorated in the years immediately preceding the successful generals' coup of 2006 that deposed the civilian government.)

Compared to countries in other regions and subregions, the Philippines's corruption indicators are better than those of Afghanistan, Bangladesh, and Pakistan, but worse than India's and Sri Lanka's. The Philippines performs worse than major Latin American countries such as Argentina, Brazil, Chile, Colombia, Mexico, and Peru; better than Venezuela; and similar to Bolivia and some smaller Central American states.

Broadly similar patterns can be found in other data sets. For example, Transparency International's Corruption Perceptions Index—which, like the Kaufmann, Kraay, and Mastruzzi data, is a composite indicator based on several sources—rates the Philippines as similar to Indonesia and Viet Nam, but significantly worse than the PRC and Thailand, not to mention Malaysia and Singapore (Table 10.1). Overall, the Philippines is in the lowest 20th to 30th percentile of all countries in the Transparency International sample.

Table 10.1: Corruption Perceptions Index and Ranking for Selected Asian Countries and Years

	2001	2003	2005	2007
Philippines	2.9 (65)	2.5 (92)	2.5 (125)	2.5 (131)
Singapore	9.2 (4)	9.4 (5)	9.4 (5)	9.3 (4)
Malaysia	5.0 (36)	5.2 (37)	5.1 (39)	5.1 (43)
People's Republic of China	3.5 (57)	3.4 (56)	3.2 (79)	3.5 (72)
Thailand	3.2 (61)	3.3 (70)	3.8 (59)	3.3 (84)
Viet Nam	2.6 (75)	2.4 (100)	2.8 (116)	2.6 (123)
Indonesia	1.9 (88)	1.9 (122)	2.2 (137)	2.3 (143)
No. of Countries	91	133	158	180
Percentile Rank of the Philippines	28%	31%	21%	27%

Note: Figures in parentheses represent ranking among countries in the sample. Index ranking varies from 10 (least corrupt) to 1 (most corrupt).

Source: Transparency International (various years).

Figure 10.3: Overall Political Risk—Philippines (1984–2006)

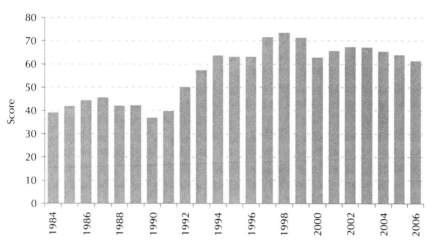

Note: Risk score: 0–less than 50 = very high; 50–less than 60 = high; 60–less than 70 = moderate; 70–less than 80 = low; 80–100 = very low.
Source: Political Risk Services *International Country Risk Guide* (various years).

Finally, a longer historical perspective is obtained from a series of indicators generated by the *International Country Risk Guide* (gathered and maintained by the private risk-rating firm, Political Risk Services), which is the same set of indicators used by Keefer and Knack (1995). The total political risk score in this case consists of 12 subindexes including political stability, corruption, internal conflict, external threat, law and order, and bureaucratic quality,[8] the sum of which is constructed to range from 0 to 100. Figure 10.3 plots this overall index for 1984–2006. The Philippines was in the "very high risk" category during 1984–1994, attaining its worst standing in 1990. The Philippines' score improved gradually thereafter—coinciding with the successful elections in 1992—and the country reached "moderate risk" levels by 1997 and even "low risk" during 1998–2000, coinciding with the holding of credible elections in 1998. There was a noticeable decline in 2001 following the EDSA[9] 2 events that led to the removal of President Estrada. Notwithstanding a minor improvement in 2001–2002, perceived overall political risk in the country increased after

[8]   The other six components are socioeconomic conditions, investment profile, the military in politics, the role of religion in politics, ethnic tensions, and democratic accountability.
[9]   EDSA is the abbreviation by which Epifanio de los Santos Avenue is best known. EDSA is the major thoroughfare where much of the protest action took place during the "people-power revolutions."

the election in 2004, running contrary to the typical expectation that a successful holding of elections would reduce political risk.

10.3.1 Political Instability

The most evident and dramatic manifestation of the effect of institutions on Philippine economic performance has been the impact of political instability on growth, particularly as it affects investment. Episodes of overt political instability during the last 50 years have involved attempted or consummated changes in political regime through the declaration of martial law and emergency rule, civilian–military uprisings, coups d'état, cabinet crises, and impeachments. Apart from this, the country is host to Muslim secessionist and communist-led agrarian insurgencies that are among the longest running in the world.

As the preceding section has suggested, large-scale political regime changes can unsettle distribution and property rights and, in this manner, affect investment. A major hypothesis, therefore, is that investment decisions should generally be sensitive to the actual or threatened political regime changes that have characterized recent Philippine history.

The decline and then virtual stagnation in per capita income in the 1980s must be regarded as the single most significant episode that caused the Philippines to fall behind its neighbors in economic performance. This is immediately evident to anyone viewing the comparative record of long-term growth, such as those provided by Angus Maddison or by Summers and Heston and their associates (CICUP various versions). The 1980s and 1990s can justifiably be regarded as the Philippines' "lost decades," when it became the exception in a region in which rapid economic growth was the rule (Figure 10.4). As a result, the country lost economic ground in both relative and absolute terms. Indonesia and Thailand overtook the country in per capita income terms in 1985; the PRC did likewise by 1998.

It was no accident that this very period was also marked by episodes of severe political instability. The most notable and extended period of political turbulence was associated with the events culminating in the popular uprising known as the EDSA People Power Revolution of 1986, which led to the toppling of the Marcos regime. The regime's policies of crony capitalism and excessive foreign borrowings led to the worst postwar decline in Philippine output and investment; ultimately, the Marcos dictatorship collapsed under a wave of popular protest.

The installation of a new government headed by President Corazon Aquino, however, failed to produce immediate political stability owing to the fragile and tentative nature of the coalition that stood behind it. In particular, military elements that had originally broken with the Marcos

Figure 10.4: Relative Per Capita Income Levels in East and Southeast

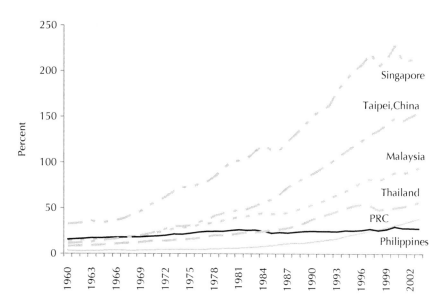

PRC = People's Republic of China, US = United States.
Source: CICUP Penn World Tables (various issues).

regime and initiated the uprising sought to assert what they perceived as their prior claims to govern and sought continually to swamp and ultimately depose the civilian politicians behind President Aquino. Such claims were behind numerous attempted putsches, the major ones occurring in August 1987 and December 1989.

The putsch attempts of 1987 and 1989 could not have come at a worse time, as they coincided with a period of huge increases in Japanese outsourcing investments throughout the region that resulted from the yen appreciation following the Louvre Accord of 1985 and the Plaza Accord of 1989. Events in the Philippines effectively resulted in the perception that the newly installed Aquino Administration was not yet fully in control. The impact of the attempted coup of December 1989 was particularly devastating, because it occurred in the country's financial district.[10]

---

[10]   Contemporary anecdotal accounts recount that the putsch attempt caught a large delegation of prospective Japanese investors at the Makati hotel that the rebellious soldiers had taken over.

Figure 10.5 shows the behavior of the government stability index taken from the data set of the *International Country Risk Guide* for comparable countries covering the years after the Louvre and Plaza accords until the eve of the 1997 Asian financial crisis. Clearly, the country's perceived level of stability had already been badly affected by the political crisis in 1984 and was well below levels of other countries in the region. An incipient improvement until 1987 was interrupted by a sharp decline after 1987 and 1989, lasting until 1991 and coinciding with the period of violent coup attempts against the Aquino Administration.

The Philippines failed to benefit from the foreign direct investment (FDI) that boosted other regional economies, particularly Indonesia, Malaysia, and Thailand, and provided them with a valuable stimulus for growth during the period leading up to the 1997 Asian financial crisis. During 1984–1997, FDI flows to Malaysia, Indonesia, and Thailand averaged $3.31 billion, $1.86 billion, and $1.6 billion annually, respectively, with an accelerating trend. In contrast, the Philippines averaged only $808 million in annual FDI in the same period (Figure 3.30 in Chapter 3).

This hypothesis can be tested in a straightforward manner, the results of which are reported in Table 10.2. Per capita FDI flowing into comparable

Figure 10.5: Government Stability Index for Selected Countries

Note: 1 = least stable to 12 = most stable.
Source: Political Risk Services *International Country Risk Guide*.

countries of the region (Indonesia, Malaysia, and Thailand) relative to that of the Philippines is regressed against the political stability scores of those countries relative to the Philippines, with a one-period lag. For 1985–2006, the index of relative political stability is positively and significantly related to the relative amounts of per capita FDI entering the country—that single factor alone explaining as much as 20% of the variation in relative shares of FDI. If the sample is restricted to the critical period following the Plaza and Louvre accords, the size of the coefficient of relative political stability is larger and the explanatory power of the equation far greater (up to 50%). This suggests the critical nature of the period following the Plaza and Louvre accords, owing to the one-time investment surge that occurred. That was a tide that the Philippines unfortunately failed to "take at the flood."

Table 10.2: Foreign Direct Investment and Political Stability

Dependent Variable	Relative Per Capita FDI[a]	
	1985–1992	1985–2006
Constant	1.84103 (1.01)	4.07829*** (4.45)
Lagged Relative Political Stability[b]	1.59409** (2.50)	1.01625** (2.16)
Sigma	2.51775	2.40543
R^2	0.509704	0.1976747
Log-Likelihood	−17.5877	−47.1784
F-test (d.f.)	6.237; (1,6)	5.447; (1,19)
Durbin Watson	1.32	1.28

** = significant at the 5% level, *** = significant at the 1% level.
FDI = foreign direct investment.
Note: Ordinary least squares regression, 1985–2006.
[a] Relative per capita FDI: mean of annual per-capita of FDI into Indonesia, Malaysia, and Thailand as a proportion of the annual per capita FDI of the Philippines.
[b] Relative political stability: mean *International Country Risk Guide* Government Stability scores of Indonesia, Malaysia, and Thailand as a proportion of the *International Country Risk Guide* Government Stability score of the Philippines.
Source: Author's calculations.

Table 10.3: Dependent Variable—First-Difference in Lending Interest Rates (ordinary least squares estimation; annual data: 1986–2006)

	Model 1	Model 2	Model 3	Model 4	Model 5
Constant	−0.412692	−0.28575	−0.273362	−0.415578	−0.231485
	(−0.707)	(−0.512)	(−0.513)	(−0.776)	(−0.474)
Difference in Inflation	0.417040***	0.409148***	0.371635***	0.402492***	0.344901***
	(4.03)	(4.22)	(3.82)	(4.17)	(3.89)
Lagged Difference in Logs of Governance 1	−7.89052				
	(−1.15)				
Lagged Difference in Logs of Governance 2		−7.76819*			
		(−1.88)			
Lagged Difference in Logs of Governance 3			−8.54232**		
			(−2.28)		
Lagged Difference in Logs of Governance 4				−8.55233**	
				(−2.00)	
Lagged Difference in Logs of Governance 5					−8.15274**
					(−3.05)
Sigma	2.57284	2.43709	2.34798	2.41008	2.16209
R^2	0.54002	0.587371	0.616992	0.596466	0.675237
Log-likelihood	−48.0244	−46.886	−46.1038	−46.652	−44.3717
$F_{(2,18)}$	10.57	12.81	14.5	13.3	18.71
Durbin Watson	1.89	1.89	2.0	1.95	2.04

* = significant at the 10% level, ** = significant at the 5% level, *** = significant at the 1% level.
Notes:
Governance 1: Total score on 12 governance components (Political Risk Survey).
Governance 2: Governance 1 less scores on socioeconomic conditions, external conflict, religion in politics, and democratic accountability (Political Risk Survey).
Governance 3: Sum of scores on government stability, corruption, internal conflict, and investment profile (Political Risk Survey).
Governance 4: Score on government stability.
Governance 5: Score on government stability, corruption, and internal conflict (Political Risk Survey).
Source: Author's calculations.

Nor has the impact of political instability been limited to FDI. Table 10.3 shows estimates of the effects of sets of governance variables on lending interest rates, which, of course, affect investment more generally. The signs of the coefficients of variables associated with governance outcomes are consistently negative, implying that better governance outcomes are associated, other things being equal, with declining lending rates. Table 10.3 also shows that a combination of variables relating particularly to government stability, corruption, and internal conflict (Model 5) performs best in explaining the penalty on investment, as measured by changes in the lending rate. Indeed other aspects of governance outcomes, such as democratic accountability and bureaucratic efficiency, do not appear to contribute to the explanation, as their inclusion actually reduces the explanatory power of governance indicators (Models 1–3). On the other hand, as previously suggested, special attention must be paid to the government stability variable (Model 4): changes in this variable alone account for the bulk of the impact of governance indicators on changes in the interest rate, and therefore, investment and growth more generally.

Even as the problem of political stability subsided significantly during 1992–2000 (Figure 10.5), it reappeared in 2001 (Figure 10.5). The situation deteriorated owing to the controversy over the 2004 election results, leading to street protests, a failed cabinet coup (2005), attempts at impeachment (2006 and 2007), and abortive military mutinies or revolts (2006, 2007, and 2008).

10.3.2. Corruption

Corruption is the second institutionally rooted governance outcome that has most palpably influenced Philippine economic performance. But while examples of corruption and their impact on investment are numerous, they are inherently difficult to document and systematize, much less quantify— owing in no small measure to the illegal and clandestine nature of such transactions. An important distinction should be made between "petty" and "grand" corruption. Petty corruption, as practiced among the lower to middle echelons of the bureaucracy, partakes of the nature of a regular activity. It is typically implemented through implicit collusion among agency insiders who exercise discretion through the selective implementation of otherwise well-known rules. Examples of these occur in the revenue collecting agencies and some large line departments that routinely engage in large-scale purchasing, recruitment, or front-line dealings with the transacting public (see, e.g., Chua [1999] on education; for a survey, see de Dios and Ferrer [2001]). Such phenomena are largely predictable and can be comprehended as a "going concern", the channels of which are well known, albeit difficult to close off, because they are integral to the regular mandated functions of these agencies. Left to fester at that level, however, such activities are unlikely to cause large enough shifts in investment behavior to change the trajectory of a country's growth. This is because the scope of the functions of low- to mid-level bureaucrats is well defined, transactions are limited in scale, and large deviations would, in principle, be relatively straightforward for higher-ups to monitor. For such activities to be ratcheted up substantially and the off-take enlarged, the initiative and protection of highly placed "backers" will be typically required. Smuggling, for example, or even the protection racket for the widespread illegal numbers game (popularly known as *jueteng*), can assume an unusually large scale only when the customary operators obtain implicit support and protection from the highest places in the political establishment and are thus able to expand the scope of operations well beyond what is customary. At the point where routine corruption of this sort becomes elevated to a national scale, it graduates into "grand corruption."[11]

More typically, however, the conduits of "grand corruption"—involving "a substantial expenditure of funds with a major impact on a government budget and growth prospects" (Rose-Ackerman 1998)—are projects and deals of a one-off nature involving the disbursement of huge sums (typically running into billions of pesos). Again these could occur only through the witting or unwitting complicity of centrally placed politicians and administrators. Major corruption allegations that have hounded successive post-Marcos administrations were under the purview of executive discretion: these include the Public Estates Authority–Amari deal and power purchase agreements in the electricity sector, e.g., the Caliraya–Botocan–Kalayaan Hydropower Project by Industrias Metalurgicas Pescarmona S.A.I.C.&F (IMPSA); the Ninoy Aquino International Airport Terminal 3 Project; the Northrail Project; and the National Broadband Network–ZTE Project. These are either foreign assisted or build–operate–transfer (BOT) projects involving the private sector. The explicitly political (rather than routine bureaucratic) nature of decisions taken at higher levels of government also means that the bases for objective evaluation of such decisions become more elusive to the public at large, and the distinction between well-meant executive discretion and corruption becomes blurred.[12]

Corruption discourages investment in that it effectively functions like a tax on the proponent, with the rent being transferred to politicians, bureaucrats, or deal makers rather than the treasury. The rent itself adds to the cost of any project and therefore reduces the incentive to invest. A corruption rent is inferior to a tax, however, to the extent that it can be unpredictable in the magnitude of payoffs asked and unreliable in the (illegal) delivery of the contract to the briber. Cross-country evidence (Campos, Lien, and Pradhan 2001) suggests that the "predictability" of corruption matters. Shleifer and Vishny (1993) explicitly suggest that the

---

[11] The plunder case filed against former President Estrada serves as an illustration. Estrada was convicted in 2008 of being at the top of the pyramid of bribes involving the running of the illegal jueteng numbers game in different parts of the country. While the running of the jueteng racket and its protection by local politicians have existed for decades and are common knowledge, the attempted national organization of its protection and its implicit sanction by the President was an unprecedented leap in scale.

[12] This point was also made in de Dios and Ferrer (2001).

creation of overlapping jurisdictions and multiple centers of veto in the post-Marcos Philippines—to the extent that enforcement of rules remained weak—may have increased the scope for uncertainty and the extent of corruption.

Beyond such effects, corruption also undermines fair competition by causing the award of vital projects on considerations other than entrepreneurship and productivity (e.g., rent-seeking and political extortion), leading to distortions in market incentives and misallocation of resources. Decisions are more likely to correspond to the priorities and conveniences of corrupt insiders than to those of the public at large: the over-specification in recent proposals for information technology for a government broadband project and for "cyber-education" is the most glaring example in the recent period (Fabella and de Dios 2007).

Another aspect of corruption with an investment impact that is similarly difficult to specify or quantify is the effect of "regulatory capture." Unlike the situation of overpriced equipment purchases, for example, there is no natural benchmark (e.g., a competitive price) that can serve as a point of comparison to detect the occurrence of an illicit sale of rights and rules for political or financial considerations. Regulations typically affect specific sectors, and a proper specification needs to posit pre- and post- or counterfactual situations that are quite idiosyncratic. As a result, the evaluation of the consequences of decisions by regulatory bodies—which are frequently empowered to make such decisions—will inevitably be conditional, so that the integrity of process itself must be ensured.

The reasonable values that the Philippines obtains—close to or better than the income-adjusted norm—for regulatory quality and government effectiveness in the Kaufmann, Kraay, and Mastruzzi data suggest that little, if any, institutional problems exist from this aspect. A shortcoming of such data, however, is that they are based on assessments of a general situation, without allowing for a more nuanced appreciation of actual practice in strategic or critical sectors. As already noted, the worsening assessment of corruption tends to dilute the favorable assessment of regulation in principle with the reality of regulation as practiced.

After the Marcos period, successive Philippine administrations (especially under President Fidel Ramos) embarked on a spate of liberalization and deregulation reforms in many sectors. Notable successes have been registered in telecommunications, for example, where the dismantling of a monopoly, notwithstanding an imperfect reform, resulted in increased investment and customer access. However, Llanto and Gonzales (2007) and Patalinghug and Llanto (2005) documented how this initial pace of reforms subsequently decelerated and even faltered in such sectors as shipping, power generation, and telecommunications, with the pertinent regulatory agencies hesitating to take what are thought to be essential next steps to complete the reform process and create more competition in their industries. It has been suggested that at least some part of this must be traced to the intrusion of political agenda in what ought to be independent regulatory agencies.

Llanto and Gonzales (2007) call regulatory agencies "a point of political access for purchasing major influence over government policy" on the part of affected firms or special interests, with entrée being provided by the fact that, in almost all cases, such regulatory and quasi-judicial bodies are made up of presidential appointees with no fixed tenure. In the power industry, for example, new private investment has been held up owing to a badly designed law that allowed cross-ownership between distributors and generators. This has created uncertainty among potential investors who are at a disadvantage vis-à-vis parties that have secure contracts with their affiliate distributors. Similarly, telecommunications rules have allowed established telecommunications companies to offer value-added services to their own subsidiaries on terms not made available to third parties. The popular suspicion cannot then be avoided that regulatory agencies tend to treat dominant firms in their industry depending on the political accommodation these have reached with the appointing powers. Ultimately, the question is to what extent an independent and professional bureaucracy continues to exist in the Philippines given the extraordinary political influences and the nature of political institutions and transactions.

A worsening of corruption differs in its effect from deteriorating political stability in that the latter can develop quite rapidly and is therefore more prone to affect volatile price variables, such as interest rates and exchange rates, as well as potential new investment, particularly FDI. A rise in corruption, on the other hand, is likely to be more gradual and to be felt and recognized by investors who are already present in the domestic economy. It is therefore more likely to affect the overall investment or accumulation rate, e.g., investment as a proportion of gross domestic product, rather than potential investment. (Separate tests—not reported here—show the corollary: that political instability variables are not a strong influence on the investment rate.)

Empirically, therefore, it is possible to test whether corruption, as measured, contributes significantly to explaining the rate of accumulation or of investment. Table 10.4 contains specifications using either current or lagged measures of the corruption index, together with the variables typically included such as real interest rates, lagged investment, or some measure of predicted or past levels of output. In the great majority of these specifications, the corruption index, whether current or lagged, emerges as an important variable explaining the investment rate, sometimes overshadowing more traditional explanatory variables such as real interest rates or predicted or lagged gross domestic product. Perceived corruption ratings easily explain a quarter to a half of the variation in the investment ratio.

Table 10.4: Dependent Variable—Investment Ratio
(ordinary least squares estimation; annual data)

	Model 1 1984–2006	Model 2 1984–2006	Model 3 1985–2006	Model 4 1985–2006	Model 5 1985–2006
Constant	19.7433 (0.688)	18.24999 (0.647)	10.6855** (3.26)	8.90129** (2.74)	7.93916* (2.45)
Lagged Investment Ratio	0.438040** (2.90)	0.454500** (3.32)	0.276124 (1.60)	0.354844* (2.05)	0.355959** (2.22)
Lagged Gross Domestic Product	−0.891797 (−0.420)	−0.814160 (−0.387)			
Real Interest Rate	−0.107748 (−0.312)				0.326867 (1.17)
Lagged Real Interest Rate		−0.0560761 (−0.181)	−0.107073 (−0.2678)		
Lagged Nominal Interest Rate				0.0511975 (0.628)	
Inflation Rate				−0.0852405 (−0.896)	
Corruption Score	1.88295*** (3.88)	1.87210*** (3.86)			
Lagged Corruption Score			2.12317*** (4.05)	2.00497** (3.46)	2.17246*** (4.39)
R^2	0.629827	0.6285	0.734012	0.745481	0.750745
Log-likelihood	−46.0585	−46.0997	−40.8054	−40.3206	−40.0907
F-test; (d.f.)	7.656; (4,18)	7.613; (4,18)	16.56; (3,18)	12.45; (4,17)	18.07; (3,18)
Durbin Watson	1.94	1.91	1.61	1.52	1.52

* = significant at the 10% level, ** = significant at the 5% level, *** = significant at the 1% level.
Source: Author's estimates.

To sum up the foregoing, political instability and corruption have had measurable effects on Philippine economic performance in the recent past, affecting investment directly and indirectly through interest rates. New FDI has historically been deterred by the country's record of political instability, particularly causing it to miss the relocating Japanese investments in the wake of the Plaza and Louvre accords. In a gross sense, the country's rate of accumulation is influenced negatively and significantly by the extent of perceived corruption.

10.4. Legitimacy and Political Economy

What are the likely institutional and historical bases of the recurring problems of instability and corruption in the Philippines? Many hypotheses and explanations have been put forward by economists and political scientists. This section focuses on the following areas: constitutional issues; intra-elite rivalry; inequality, poverty, and the middle strata; and concentration of power.

10.4.1.   Broad Legitimacy

One hypothesis is that the occurrence of political events in recent decades in the Philippines (described in the previous section) may be due to the country's failure to attain one of the important "doorstep conditions" that North posited for institutions that sustain growth, i.e., the willingness of elites themselves to abide by the rule of law (North, Wallis, and Weingast 2006). Hutchcroft and Rocamora (2003) argued that the tenuous hold of formal political institutions in the Philippines cannot be divorced from a historical failure to justify their existence to broader sections of the population, which have at critical points become alienated from a system that has often failed to respond to their interests and imperatives. The potency and appeal of competing elite projects for change often draws upon the larger sea of discontent and cynicism among the poor and marginalized. It could be argued, therefore, that existing institutions have been continually tested by how they have accommodated two types of conflict: (i) contests for political power and rent redistribution between opposing factions of the elite, and (ii) demands for redistribution and economic redress originating from the masses and their political representatives.

It has been argued that historically, an important effect of formal independence and the introduction of democratic forms was to release centrifugal tendencies that had been suppressed by the superior force of the colonial government. Preexisting networks based on kinship and clientelist relations became operative, even though these were ill-suited to a super-imposed political system that nominally aspired to democratic politics and a meritocratic bureaucracy. Families and clans to this day remain the most stable form of social organization, often trumping anonymous, interest-based organizations in important spheres of public life.[13] Despite the decline of the feudal agrarian settings in which relations of personal dependence were indispensable, personal ties and kinship nonetheless continue to be major organizing principles in current politics and business organizations.[14] Using 1997 data, for example, Saldaña (2000) found that half of the 50 largest corporate entities in terms of sales were affiliated with large family-based groups and that these accounted for more than one third of the sales of the top 1,000 corporations. Through pyramiding structures, such family-based groups managed to retain disproportionate control of many publicly listed corporations.

A further initial condition that has influenced subsequent development is the social inequality that already existed in the colonial period but was reinforced with the formation of modern political institutions. Originally rooted in unequal ownership of agricultural land, these inequalities have been preserved, even as the asset base of elites has through time gradually shifted away from agriculture to extractive industries, finance and trade, manufacturing, real estate, and other services. Privileged access to the legal system has historically allowed members of the social elite to establish de jure rights over property that was de facto owned by the indigenous poor population. Such privileged access has only been moderated but not offset by subsequent economic growth and the spread of literacy and education. Examples range from the *pacto de retroventa* (wherein land owned by a debtor was turned over to a creditor) during the Spanish occupation, to the introduction of the Torrens land-titling system under the Americans, to recent headlines on an agrarian dispute between indigenous farmers and a land-owning family and a diversified conglomerate. The dissonance between the application of the formal law (based on the less accessible civil code tradition) on the one hand, and common usage and the sense of traditional moral entitlement, on the other, has been a major obstacle to the widespread acceptance of formal institutions in the Philippines. Persistent inequality and mass poverty have, as a result, formed the basis for a peren-

---

[13] Here, families and clans are broadly defined to include blood relationships and close personal ties.

[14] Clan-based politics are described by McCoy (1994), Coronel et al. (2004), and de Dios (2007). Less has been written on closely-held businesses in the Philippines and their implications. But, see Saldaña (2000) for patterns in the Philippines and Claessens, Djankov, and Lang (2000) for a more general survey. Origins of the resilience of kin-based organizations include (i) pre-Hispanic kin- and ethnicity-based social divisions; (ii) the coordination required of labor requirements in rural rice farming; (iii) ideological reinforcement from Roman Catholicism and the organization of large-scale landownership under colonial rule; and (iv) preexisting Chinese ethnic business practices (guanxi, see Perkins [2000]) combined with emergence of the Chinese-mestizo class as the business sector at the turn of the century.

nial demand for social redress (and the expectation of state intervention in many economic sectors) that place severe constraints on social decision making, as well as posing constant challenges to regime legitimacy. The intensity and pervasiveness of this social demand are still evident in the various incarnations of reformist and revolutionary movements for agrarian reform and Islamic secession.

From a new institutional economics viewpoint, the exogenous introduction via colonial experience of political and economic institutions amid great and persistent social inequities and a parallel network of informal, personal, and kin-based institutions, clearly placed such institutions beyond the reach of the larger part of the population, for whom these forms can be little more than abstractions beyond the periodic exercise of voting rights (de Dios and Hutchcroft 2002/2003). Largely absent are the real means of social control of members of the political elite on a regular basis, which in mature democracies are provided by political parties.

It is not surprising, therefore, that the introduced institutions would command weak allegiance, at most. Moreover, where the foundations of secular and impersonal state institutions are historically weak, primordial parallel institutions, such as the clan or family, or religious and ethnic affiliations, become dominant by default, with their workings being superimposed upon the formal political processes.

10.4.2. Intra-Elite Rivalry

A distinct but closely related hypothesis focuses on the problem of intra-elite rivalry in the Philippines. It has been argued (see, e.g., de Dios 2007) that unique historical features contributed to the inchoateness of common goals among elite leaders in the Philippines. In many postcolonial countries, protracted struggles for independence (e.g., India or Viet Nam) or the need to respond to perceived threats (e.g., South Korea) have often served as a crucible to form a broad common vision and to extract a coordinated effort among political leaderships that ultimately prove durable and dominant. Both were absent in the Philippines, as independence had already been promised by the US ab initio, with the arenas for political competition expanding almost as a matter of course. As a result, intra-elite activity tended to focus not on cooperation for a common purpose against adverse odds, but upon gaining differentially favorable political treatment from the foreign occupier at the expense of other factions. Indeed, competition among provincial elites for national political power was virtually encouraged by the occupying regime. Hutchfroft and Rocamora (2003, 265) regard this circumstance as unique and significant, since it allowed the operation of patronage-based politics and intra-elite competition before an effective and autonomous bureaucracy could be put in place that could "resist the depredations of patronage-seeking politicians."[15] This reverses the pattern seen in other instances of colonial rule (India being a good example), in which colonizers first perfect the bureaucratic machinery before instituting institutions of political representation.

It has been argued that because the political elite historically lacked a clear articulation of common goals and convergence of ideas regarding the state (de Dios 2007), and because bureaucracies provided no effective checks (Hutchcroft and Rocamora 2003), no clear limits were placed on the pursuit of clan or even narrow personal agendas, which could and frequently did spring the bounds of what was permissible under formal political rules. The result is that historically political processes could be used to expand the interests of informal institutions, while the state's deployable resources provided a substantial addition to any elite faction or clan's means in pursuit of its goals. Through elite capture, state institutions could become major instruments of wealth accumulation by the elite (i.e., the "booty capitalism" described by Hutchcroft [1992]). If one takes this view, then the well-known Philippine phenomena of clan politics, cronyism, corruption, and instrumentalization of the bureaucracy become comprehensible consequences rather than aberrations.

Intense rivalry among factions of the elite for a larger share of political power at various levels may be the result of unrestrained and unstructured pursuit of clan and individual interests and the treatment of state power and resources as a common pool and as a means of wealth accumulation. While intra-elite rivalry may be contained in constitutionally ordained processes, such as regular elections in "normal" periods, this competition could also burst normal bounds and threaten political stability, at times resulting in sudden upheavals. The latter could occur when the state's legitimacy crisis worsens. Historically in the Philippines, periods of visible and vocal mass discontent, disillusionment, or political paralysis have tended to be associated with attempts by opposing elite factions to seize power extra-constitutionally, with weaker or stronger appeals to popular support. The clearest and most important example was Marcos' declaration of martial law, a major part of the agenda of which entailed suppressing and dispossessing rival elite factions. Such measures, however, were founded on the specious argument that they were meant to head off a Leftist rebellion that threatened to co-opt the demands of the poor and undermine government.

The intensity of intra-elite political rivalry is influenced by the scale and ambition of some incumbent faction's project to redistribute corruption and other rents. In a "normal mode," only regular flows and incremental rents are up for redistribution, with an implicit commitment to a terminus, as evidenced, say, in the observance of presidential term

---

15   The phrase is Martin Shefter's, quoted by Hutchcroft and Rocamora (2003, 63).

limits to turn over power to other elite factions. This was the "revolving-door" regime originally described by Landé (1965) that characterized the two-party system under the 1935 constitution, with "ins" and "outs" alternating in power in a more or less regular manner.[16] The authoritarian project of Marcos, however, broke with this pattern in two ways: first, it sought not only to redistribute incremental rents but to reassign even existing property rights (i.e., dispossessing "oligarch" families); second, it sought to extend the term of the incumbent indefinitely through a de facto dictatorship, introducing the military for the first time as an intervenor in deciding political outcomes. Apart from the other abuses committed by that regime, this historical break was a principal reason that led to the EDSA 1 Revolution and Marcos's removal.

It has been argued that the threat of an opposing section of the ruling elite acquiring unlimited power has been a fundamental reason that elite political conflict in the Philippines intensified to the point of threatening stability. This threat has gained credibility owing to the actual experience of the declaration of one-man rule by Marcos. A willingness to consider extra-constitutional courses of action could be especially provoked by the perception that normal rules and processes have been co-opted and legitimate state agencies have been captured by some incumbent, so that the path to a normal turnover has been blocked off. It stands to reason that the perceived independence of the military and police, the electoral commission, and the judiciary (particularly the Supreme Court) will be regarded as crucial indicators of whether normal avenues of change remain open. Historically, the unprecedented politicization of such agencies, beginning with martial rule under Marcos, was a defining event that led even the formal political opposition to mistrust and ultimately abandon constitutional change processes.

10.4.3. Inequality, Poverty, and the Middle Strata

De facto legitimacy has been measured historically and in popular cultural beliefs by the government's ability (or credible promise) to provide decent material standards of living among the population. Such beliefs and traditions are of long standing and are continuously reinforced in literature, religion, and the press. The ideology of the Philippine revolution, for example, was founded partly on religious and semi-millenarian hopes of earthly salvation among its mass followers (Ileto 1979). Moreover, reflecting various ideological streams flowing through it, the predominant Roman Catholic

---

[16]   Between 1949 and 1965, the Liberal and Nacionalista parties more or less alternated as the party in power, with no incumbent president winning reelection until Marcos in 1969.

Church has reinforced the ideal of a government with a social activist role performing a patrimonial role on behalf of the poor.[17]

Owing to erratic economic growth and a long-delayed demographic transition, however, the actual reduction of mass poverty in the Philippines has been far slower than the East Asian norm, while the historic legacy of inequality has persisted. Indeed, in the most recent period, the incidence of poverty increased, as moderate growth tended to benefit the already-affluent.[18] Given the high ideal expectations of government among the masses and the failure of its most recent strategies, it is unsurprising to find ready political fodder for instability in the large numbers of poor people, particularly in urban centers such as Metro Manila, where inequality of incomes is most evident. Festering mass disaffection can be and has been used to tilt the balance against incumbent administrations at critical junctures. In the aftermath of President Estrada's ouster from office, for example, the urban poor in Metro Manila—many of whom regarded Estrada as an icon of pro-poor populism—formed the main force in the massive demonstrations seeking to topple the new administration and reinstate the arrested former president, culminating in the violent siege of the presidential palace on 1 May 2001 known as "EDSA 3" or "Poor People Power."[19]

Recent experience has made clear, however, that poverty and inequality are not sufficient conditions for political instability since, one can argue, while mass poverty has always been present, political instability has not been equally acute in all periods. This suggests that the more decisive conditions are the perceived failure of formal institutions and the willingness of the elite and the middle classes to undertake extra-parliamentary or even extra-constitutional courses of action. From a political viewpoint, the existence—and indeed even worsening—of mass poverty and disaffection assumes the character of a pervasive background—a "red-shift" that is ubiquitous and conditioning but perhaps not decisive in importance.

In these circumstances, the middle classes and the intelligentsia (which includes some elements of the political elite) have often displayed a moral and ideological stake in constitutional and democratic processes. This is

---

[17] Most notably, the "liberation theology" current from Latin America, which sympathized with socialism and national liberation movements, was influential in the Philippine church in the 1960s and 1970s, a period during which many members in the present Roman Catholic hierarchy were educated.

[18] The Philippines's Gini coefficient was a relatively high 44.5 in 2003. Official poverty incidence (headcount) actually rose from 24.4% to 26.9% of all families between 2003 and 2006.

[19] After Estrada's arrest on 25 April 2001, a growing crowd, consisting largely of the urban poor, massed on the main thoroughfare, EDSA, from 25 to 30 April, then marched on the presidential palace on 1 May. The violent dispersal and street battles that ensued resulted in four deaths and hundreds injured. On this, see Bautista (2001, 26ff.).

aligned with the regularity, observed by Easterly, Ritzen, and Woolcock (2006) in cross-country data, that a broad middle class is an important factor for the stability of formal governance, largely due to the implied consensus that stratum maintains regarding the efficacy of impersonal institutions. Unlike the masses, whose quotidian existence is rarely affected by the results of intra-elite contests, the middle classes have a material stake in outcomes of policy, on which their future progress may depend; and, unlike the elite, who can actively intervene and lobby in their own behalf, the middle classes must seek refuge in the uniform application of rules. Thanks to the historical legacy of great inequality, however, the numerically small middle class in the Philippines has often been squeezed in an electoral environment between the numerous poor for whom the prescriptive rules of a formal democracy tend to be reduced to mere forms and abstractions, and an elite that is willing to distort such rules to preserve its economic and political privileges.[20] The country's two major popular uprisings, for example, had very distinct middle-class characteristics and agendas and were directed particularly against authoritarianism (EDSA 1) and grand corruption (EDSA 2).[21] In both cases, middle-class rage, culminating in direct action, was provoked by evident attempts to frustrate otherwise legitimate processes: by a manipulation of the results of a snap election in EDSA 1 and the obstruction of evidence in an impeachment trial in EDSA 2. From the viewpoint of the middle classes, therefore, the provocation to extraordinary action was the blockade or frustration of legitimate means of redress—hence the paradoxical point that an extra-constitutional action is needed to reaffirm the constitution itself.

Evidence suggests that the middle class has been disenchanted with the political processes, and this has instead given way to a growing apathy and reticence regarding political action even when it was not satisfied with the government's performance. The weakening political engagement and growing cynicism regarding the integrity and efficacy of existing institutions among the middle classes must be counted among the important reasons for heightened political instability. On the one hand, the trend of growing middle-class apathy may mean less volatility, to the extent that a constituency for extraordinary and direct action is no longer available. On the other hand, without positive developments—and taken together with intra-elite rivalry and even political agnosticism and pragmatism of

---

[20] Virola (2007) reckoned that the middle class, defined based on a fixed living standard or expenditure pattern in 1997, actually shrank as a share of the population, from about 23% in 1997 to 20% by 2003.

[21] Bautista (2001) estimated that as many as 56% of those who participated in the EDSA 2 rallies in Metro Manila in 2001 could be classified as middle class if non-income characteristics such as level of education and type of occupation are taken into account.

the broad masses—middle-class passivity could also render the country's institutions vulnerable to extra-constitutional political projects, particularly power grabs by elite leaders (whether incumbent or out of power) or autonomous action on the part of the military.

10.4.4. Allocation of Political Power

If political economy influences the degree of receptiveness by various groups to formal institutions, the distribution of power implied by those institutions also affects the behavior and motivation of the political actors themselves. It has been argued that a central inducement to corruption and political instability in the Philippines stems from the centralization of power in the executive branch (de Dios and Esfahani 2001). More powerful than his or her US counterpart, the Philippine President exercises unprecedented fiscal discretion and powers of appointment. The fiscal powers vested in the executive branch of the Philippine government are particularly crucial. In addition to a line-item veto, the chief executive exercises the power to withhold or impound the actual release of already appropriated funds, allowing him or her to effectively pursue or realign priorities quite independently of Congress.[22] Apart from this, the chief executive can directly dispose of large lump-sum funds (e.g., intelligence funds, social funds, and calamity funds) with minimal congressional oversight, as well as the earnings of government-owned and -controlled corporations. Other features enhancing the chief executive's fiscal discretion include the automatic appropriation of a previous year's budget if Congress should fail to pass a new one, automatic appropriation of debt-service, and the power to approve financing for projects involving official development assistance or BOT schemes involving the private sector.

Some studies suggest that the President's appointing powers are staggering as well. David (2007), a former chair of the civil service commission, estimated that presidential appointments may number as many as 10,000, ranging from supreme court justices to members of the military and police hierarchy, members of the Commission on Elections, board members in government corporations, and staff of regulatory agencies, down to minor officials in far-flung cities and municipalities. The depth of the chief executive's political appointments—to as far down as the level of assistant director in a government bureau—is unprecedented. In comparison, most systems in the British mold (e.g., India) allow political appointments only up to the

---

22 Many of these powers were established by authoritarian decrees under the Marcos regime, particularly Presidential Decree 1177, which was largely retained by the Aquino administration particularly during the period of its "revolutionary government" (1986–1989) prior to the election of the first legislature under the 1987 Constitution.

level of secretary or minister. Discretion in presidential appointments is virtually absolute. Furthermore, weaknesses in the system even allow for an individual to be appointed as an acting member of the cabinet after he or she failed to secure the required confirmation from the Congress.

An obvious danger is that the wide appointing power of the executive branch could open the system to possible manipulation and corruption. Career civil servants who fail to toe an administration's line or do the bidding of powerful politicians may be placed in the "freezer," assigned to nonstrategic or insignificant positions, and replaced with more pliant political appointees. The result would be a weakening of the independence and integrity of decision making among the bureaucracy, whose members gradually realize that retaining their position and seniority depends less on inherent merit and more on being in the good graces of the appointing power. It has been suggested that such a phenomenon is most developed and regular in the revenue collection agencies, where the quest for political patronage and protection originates from the bureaucracy itself and corruption is part of a going concern. The larger upshot, of course, is that the government's perennial problem with revenue efficiency is never permanently addressed. Doing so, after all, would require dismantling the carefully built web of clientelism and corruption that have become the raison d'être of the bureaucrats that populate those agencies. The problems or perception of problems associated with executive appointments could also lead to potential conflict of interest and eventually could lead to destabilization, especially when these involve (particularly constitutional) bodies that guarantee and moderate the political process.[23]

10.5. Conclusions and Policy Implications

From some perspectives, the foregoing may be seen as vindication of a point made by North, Wallis, and Weingast (2006), who argued that economic and political institutions are mutually reinforcing, so that "limited-access order" societies like the Philippines may find it difficult to move forward by means of social and political institutions that seek to enforce impersonal rules, meritocracy, and democratic processes—institutions that presuppose societies with highly-developed economies, contestable markets, and pervasive social organizations based on objective secular interests beyond kinship. The country's failure to bring the actions of its elites to heel under

---

[23] Apart from the major branches of government, independent offices specified under the Constitution include the Commission on Elections, the Commission on Audit, the Civil Service Commission, the public prosecutor (Ombudsman), and the antigraft court (Sandiganbayan).

the rule of law; its difficulties in forming enduring social organizations that go beyond personal ties and kinship; and its erratic record in controlling violence, particularly from the military—all point to the distance Philippine society needs to traverse before it can create the conditions to escape underdevelopment.[24]

The momentous question is whether attaining those threshold conditions is more likely if the country pursued a different institutional path. To be sure, the "Asian values" debate of some decades past suggested that greater social order and congruence with grassroots beliefs and expectations—hence more rapid growth—might be better achieved under authoritarian and paternalistic institutions that regularly create and dispense rents in order to buy social peace.[25] Nor has there been a shortage in the Philippines of harbingers of retro-authoritarianism (as well as a few thoughtful independent individuals[26]) who point to the all-too-obvious inadequacies of formal democratic institutions to advertise the potential benefits of more authoritarian political institutions.

This chapter contends it would be foolhardy and costly to radically change the country's direction of institutional development. Such an argument is based on the simple assessment that the traverse is itself likely to be costly, chaotic, and fraught with social risk. The difficulty presented by the Philippines to social scientists lies in its ambivalence: on the one hand, is the observable disconnect between the real behavior of the majority of the populace and that prescribed by formal institutions; on the other hand, is an almost hegemonic clamor for and acceptance of "open-access order" political institutions in public discourse and rhetoric. This is strongest among the middle classes and the intelligentsia (including the Roman Catholic Church), who have been educated and socialized into democratic values; but it also finds support among the more conservative sections of the elite who fear the challenge that radical changes pose for existing property rights. Thus, it may be more prudent to inquire instead into the possibilities for incremental change under the present institutional set-up that could bring the country closer to threshold conditions. The three broad directions

---

24   This enumeration closely corresponds to what North, Wallis, and Weingast (2006) termed "doorstep conditions" for the transition from "limited-access orders" to "open-access orders".

25   North, Wallis, and Weingast (2006, 36) argued that rents are an indispensable feature of limited-access orders, because these are necessary to secure the elite's political ends, e.g., buying political support from the masses or from allies. As a corollary, the proscription of rents in such a context would undermine social order. Some writers (e.g., Jomo and Gomez [2000]) have sought to explain Malaysia's discriminatory *bumiputra* policy under Mahathir Mohammed in this fashion.

26   The most consistent has been the prominent business leader Washington Sycip. On this, see Fabella (2007).

in which the change might occur are (i) greater adherence to constitutional processes, (ii) a reduction of presidential prerogatives within the present constitution, and (iii) a rebuilding of civil society and the spread of political education and organization.

10.5.1. Elections and Adherence to Constitutional Processes

First, is the obvious need to promote greater adherence to constitutional processes and limits. This is required if society is to escape the downward spiral of diminishing legitimacy, where incumbent elite factions and those who oppose them constantly threaten to infringe on normal constitutional limits in order to retain power or seize it. Moving forward, people and government both need to make a common investment in the infrastructure of secular constitutional processes that should be allowed to operate normally and regularly, regardless of whether the results fail to conform to immediate elite interests, or to middle-class or religious ideals.

The crucial condition is the restoration of the credibility of the electoral process, which has been severely tarnished by recent electoral controversies. Reforms in this area are particularly urgent in the light of approaching presidential elections in 2010. Toward this end, it may be worthwhile to consider thoroughly revamping the Commission on Elections by appointing competent and professional members who command the acceptance and assent from all parties and civil society. The government may also consider transferring the appointing power to a special body for the purpose of involving both the legislature and the Supreme Court, in the spirit of electoral tribunals.[27] As an interim measure, the government could adopt a practice of appointing members of the commission from a small set of nominees openly submitted and scrutinized by an impartial public body.

Operationally, the completion of the long-delayed modernization and computerization of voting and canvassing is indispensable.[28] The currently tortuous process of manually tallying and canvassing votes (with a tedious stepwise aggregation of election returns at municipal or city, provincial, and national levels) is the single most important circumstance that renders the present system highly vulnerable to the manipulation and misrepresentation of election results. That it is still possible to delineate spheres of public life and place them beyond the operation of narrowly partisan

---

[27] Article VI, section 17 of the Constitution specifies the composition of electoral tribunals.

[28] As of this writing, there has only been agreement to implement a computer-aided system during the special elections in the autonomous Muslim region. Computerization of the 2010 elections hangs in the balance.

interests is demonstrated by the transformation of the central bank into an independent agency and the abiding public trust vested in the Supreme Court. The electoral commission probably needs radical reform that will professionalize its lower echelon personnel and expand its coverage and organizational capacities. A professionalization of the electoral commission is also necessary if the role of the military and the police in elections is to be clearly delineated and substantially reduced.

Beyond the conduct of elections, reforms pertaining to campaigns and election finance should also be placed on the agenda of a national debate. Particularly important are effective disclosure requirements for large campaign contributions imposed on both candidates and donors. Candidates may be required to agree to disclosures of assets and interests, while extraordinarily large campaign contributions could be monitored administratively as part of the country's money laundering laws.

Serious questions regarding the integrity of elections have repeatedly been the trigger for prolonged political instability. The recent series of controversies over election irregularities and the involvement of high electoral officials, particularly the large public outcry it provoked, has caused instability, but also provides a unique opportunity for action—a political crisis that is the impetus that galvanizes multisectoral action on an issue.

10.5.2. Balancing Power and Strengthening the Bureaucracy

Key steps must include an effort to reduce by statute the executive branch's powers of appointment in favor of ensuring the integrity and security of tenure of the career civil service and enlarging the role of the other branches of government and civil society organizations in the selection of members of constitutional bodies. A landmark step would be sharpening the civil service law to limit direct appointments by the executive branch to the level of assistant secretary or its equivalent. Members of regulatory bodies should generally be appointed to fixed terms (the monetary board being an exemplary success in this respect). Strengthening the independence and professionalism of the subcabinet bureaucracy should permit it to resist political behests to justify grand corruption. This weakness in the bureaucracy and the lack of clarity and integrity in internal processes was, after all, what allowed the intervention of hangers-on and high-level fixers to intercede and pervert policy and project decisions.

In the same spirit, and as part of an effort to extricate the revenue agencies from the milieu of political patronage, earlier proposals to corporatize them (while binding agency heads to a system of performance contracts) should be seriously revived in the legislature. The point is to improve incentives as well as to strengthen those agencies' hiring and firing powers as part of the plan for massive recruitment of new personnel for them.

Appointments to offices dealing with the investigation and prosecution of corruption cases within government are particularly crucial and should be treated with the same circumspection as those for constitutional bodies. The independence of the department of justice, the solicitor general, the ombudsman's office, the police, and the higher courts is particularly sensitive and would benefit from a transparent selection process that involved civil society and other branches of government. The point is to reverse the current situation, in which the independence and integrity of agencies with a role in anticorruption efforts are highly suspect, owing to the perception that these offices have been thoroughly politicized and co-opted to favor the incumbent administration.

Equally important are the appointments to agencies vested with regulatory powers that draw up guidelines for strategic economic sectors. Chief among these are regulatory or quasi-judicial bodies dealing with power; telecommunications; and air, sea, and land transport. The quality of appointments to these bodies and investment in the investigative and analytical capacities of their professional staffs could be enhanced to create a countervailing force within the government against the capture of such bodies by vested interests. For the same reason, a larger investment in professional staff and an independent capacity to undertake feasibility studies is needed in the National Economic and Development Authority (NEDA) to offset the bias in favor of donor- or supplier-driven projects. A credible commitment to exercise executive discretion prudently could be a published set of procedures for approving foreign-assisted or BOT projects, as well as the disclosure of feasibility studies and other supporting documents leading up to project approvals.

The vast fiscal powers of the executive branch and the role of the legislative branch in the budget process should be reviewed. To ensure that funds are being allocated and used appropriately, the executive should systematically involve Congress in a year-round review of national expenditures (i.e., engaging legislators beyond the budget period); reducing lump-sum allocations over which the executive branch has discretion; and instituting congressional oversight to review prospective foreign borrowing for various projects.

A major step to increase congressional responsibility for the government's spending program would involve passing legislation, e.g., a law limiting or removing the executive branch's discretion in the release of funds appropriated by Congress; this would essentially constrain any administration to fully spend for each fiscal year whatever appropriations Congress has passed and limit the spending according to the priorities outlined by the executive during budget deliberations.[29] Such a measure would obviate the need for individual legislators to become subservient to the executive branch simply to have the funds released for their constituencies.

A further reduction of power imbalances would be helpful if applied to devolving more power to local governments; in particular, the formula for internal revenue allotments to local governments should be redesigned to at least partly reward local governments that effectively exert their own revenue efforts.

In principle, many of these changes could be addressed in one fell swoop through constitutional amendments or perhaps a shift from a presidential to a parliamentary system. In practical terms, however, any proposal to change the constitution at this time will—for good or ill—be suspected as self-serving. The more prudent course, therefore, is to seek smaller changes within the ambit of the current constitution; this will be less destabilizing than open-ended charter reforms that have historically been an opportunity for the realization of ulterior motives and extra-constitutional projects.

On a more general note, the reduction in the powers of the executive is compatible with and reinforces a smaller role for the government in the economy. Fewer government corporations and the sale of government shares in companies not inherently imbued with a public goods character would be a step toward curtailing the patronage that comes with the appointment of government representatives to these entities, as well as reducing economic inefficiency and promoting competition. As North and his co-authors have suggested, such rents may be essential in sustaining a limited-access order, so that the demand for smaller government disturbs the correspondence between economic and political spheres. On the other hand, real progress will require upsetting that equilibrium in any event; and in this instance, the almost universal political outcry against corruption—an outcome of a history of scandals and anomalies—may motivate a real economic change, reconstituting the political–economic equilibrium on a slightly higher plane.

10.5.3.　Rebuilding the Constituency for Reform and Political Education

Ultimately, convergent expectations that the rules governing public life do work—and the fact that these are normally serviceable—yield political stability, stabilize investor expectations, and give a fair chance for superior economic growth to occur. The historical heterogeneity of Philippine society, however, currently militates against this occurring—instead, it causes

---

[29]　This would require a review and revision of sections 43, 44, 38f, and other provisions of Presidential Decree 1177.

dangerous feedback from inequality to divergent beliefs, to political instability and corruption, to low growth and high poverty, and thence again to further differentiation.[30]

The crucial questions then are: Where will the constituency for future changes and reforms come from, and what will induce elite factions to moderate their conflict so as not to become destabilizing?

One source of anxiety in the present situation lies in the growing mood of despair among many of the intellectuals and middle classes and their waning interest in further participation in the political system itself—i.e., the decimation of civil society. This is particularly true for those with the option of "voting with one's feet" to seek institutions more in accord with one's beliefs.[31] Left unchecked, such a trend would mean an even smaller and weaker constituency in support of formal political institutions that are accountable to the public interest—which would be an invitation to greater impunity and more intense rivalry among the political elite, hence a deeper legitimacy crisis.

On the other hand, the present stability in the economic situation (caused partly by that very trend, i.e., the migration overseas with the resulting return flow of remittances) may provide a small opening, to the extent that it affords upward social mobility and a higher education among a larger number in society. In one sense, therefore, even the middle-class Diaspora may be helping recreate the future middle classes. If the example of successful middle-class civic organizations (e.g., Gawad Kalinga) are any guide, then the process of repoliticization begins not from explicitly political organizations themselves but from common professional, business, civic, or local interests that build up a sufficient solidarity to hold political institutions to account. Economic differentiation during the past decades due to the liberalization of goods and capital flows has created a section of big business with a greater stake than before in long-term political stability. Typically, larger, more established, and diversified interests (e.g., conglomerates such as the Ayalas and the *taipans*, or Filipino-Chinese large-business people) have emerged that are less bound up with lobbying for advantage in narrow economic sectors. Like the middle classes, these are potentially a part of a reform constituency insisting on adherence to constitutional rules regarding transition and turnover (since political unrest could

---

30   The gulf in political values becomes evident, for example, as between the middle classes and the *masa* (masses) in their differing appreciations of the judicial fate of former President Estrada, both before and after conviction—what was perceived by some as the operation of the rule of law is regarded by others as unusual and demeaning punishment for a popular leader (Bautista 2001).

31   In some public opinion surveys, as many as a fourth of adults from the rich to upper-middle classes and from the educated express a preference for living and working abroad permanently.

endanger the value of their holdings) and an even-handed policy thereon (since their size and ubiquity imply they need not cater for any sector in particular).

The Philippines will have made significant political progress when powerful elite interests come to realize that the common cost to them of seeking large changes in rules may be far greater than simply operating under existing ones. But, such a point cannot be reached without a re-involvement of other social sectors that are willing to stake a claim in the existing order. The remaining question then becomes whether and how to speed up the reengagement of such new emerging elements in the rebuilding of the country's ravaged institutions.

References

Acemoglu, D., J. Robinson, and S. Johnson. 2001. Colonial Origins of Comparative Development: An Empirical Investigation. *American Economic Review.* 91 (December): 1369–401.

Arndt, C. and C. Oman. 2006. *Uses and Abuses of Governance Indicators.* Development Center Studies. Paris: Organisation for Economic Co-operation and Development.

Aron, J. 2000. Growth and Institutions: A Review of the Evidence. *World Bank Research Observer.* 15(1): 465-490.

Barro, R. 1991. Economic Growth in a Cross-Section of Countries. *Quarterly Journal of Economics.* 106(2): 407–43.

Barro, R., and X. Sala-i-Martin. 1995. *Economic Growth.* New York: McGraw-Hill.

Bautista, C. 2001. People Power 2: 'The Revenge of the Elite on the Masses'? In Doronila, A., ed. *Between Fires: Fifteen Perspectives on the Estrada Crisis.* Pasig City: Anvil and *Philippine Daily Inquirer.*

Campos, J. E., D. Lien, and S. Pradhan. 2001. Corruption and Its Implications for Investment. In Campos, J. E., ed. *Corruption: The Boom and Bust of East Asia.* Quezon City: Ateneo de Manila University Press.

Center for International Comparisons of the University of Pennsylvania (CICUP). various issues. Penn World Tables. http://pwt.econ.upenn.edu

Chua, Y. 1999. *Robbed: an Investigation of Corruption in Philippine Education.* Quezon City: Philippine Center for Investigative Journalism.

Claessens, S., S. Djankov, and L. Lang. 2000. The Separation of Ownership and Control in East Asian Corporations. *Journal of Financial Economics.* 58(1–2): 81–112.

Coronel, S., Y. Chua, L. Rimban, and B. Cruz. 2004. *The Rule-Makers: How the Wealthy and Well-Born Dominate Congress.* Quezon City: Philippine Center for Investigative Journalism.

Corpuz, O.D. 1989. *The Roots of the Filipino Nation*. 2 vols. Quezon City: Aklahi Foundation.

David, K. 2007. Politics, Perils, and the Pain of Building Institutions. Lecture before the General Assembly of the Human Development Network. 28 March. www.hdn.org.ph/files/karina_david.pdf

de Dios, E. 2007. Local Politics and Local Economy. In A. Balisacan and H. Hill, eds. *Dynamics of Regional Development*. London: Edward Elgar.

de Dios, E., and H. S. Esfahani. 2001. Centralization, Political Turnover and Investment in the Philippines. In J. E. Campos, ed. *Corruption: The Boom and Bust of East Asia*. Quezon City: Ateneo de Manila University Press.

de Dios, E. and P. Hutchcroft. 2002/2003. Political Economy. In A. Balisacan and H. Hill, eds. *The Philippine Economy: Development, Policies, and Challenges*. Quezon City: Ateneo de Manila University Press (2002) and New York: Oxford University Press (2003).

de Dios, E., and R. Ferrer. 2001. Corruption: A Framework and Context. *Public Policy*. 5(1): 1–42.

Diamond, J. 1997. *Guns, Germs, and Steel*. New York: W. W. Norton.

Drazen, J. 2000. *Political Economy in Macroeconomics*. Princeton, NJ: Princeton University Press.

Easterly, W., J. Ritzen, and M. Woolcock. 2006. Social Cohesion, Institutions, and Growth. *Economics and Politics*. 18(2): 103–20.

Engerman, W., and K. Sokoloff. 2000. Institutions, Factor Endowments, and Paths of Development in the New World. *Journal of Economic Perspectives*. 14(3): 217–321.

Fabella, R. 2007. Deconstructing Mr. Sycip. CNaPS Discussion Paper. Quezon City: Center for National Policy and Strategy.

Fabella, R., and E. de Dios. 2007. Lacking a Backbone: The Controversy Over the National Broadband Network and Cyber-Education Projects. Discussion Paper No. 2007-07. University of the Philippines, School of Economics. Quezon City.

Greif, A. 2006. *Institutions and Path Economic Modernity: Lessons from Medieval Trade*. Cambridge: Cambridge University Press.

Hutchcroft, P. 1992. *Booty Capitalism*. Quezon City: Ateneo de Manila University Press.

Hutchcroft, P. and J. Rocamora. 2003. Strong Demands and Weak Institutions: The Origin and Evolution of the Democratic Deficit in the Philippines. *Journal of East Asian Studies*. 3 (2). pp. 259–292.

Ileto, R. 1979. *Pasyon at Rebolusyon*. Quezon City: Ateneo de Manila University Press.

Jomo, K. S., and E. Gomez. 2000. The Malaysian Development Dilemma. In M. Khan and K. S. Jomo, eds. *Rents, Rent-Seeking, and Economic*

Development: Theory and Evidence in Asia. Cambridge: Cambridge University Press.

Kaufmann, D., A. Kraay, and M. Mastruzzi. 2007. Governance Matters VI: Indicators for 1996–2006. Policy Research Working Paper No. 4280. Washington, DC: World Bank.

Kaufmann, D., A. Kraay, and P. Zoido-Lobatón. 1999. Governance Matters. Policy Research Working Paper 2196. Washington, DC: World Bank Development Research Group.

Keefer, S., and P. Knack. 1995. Institutions and Economic Performance:. Cross Country Test Using Alternative Institutional Measures. *Economics and Politics*. 7(3): 207–27.

La Porta, R., F. Lopez-de-Silanes, A. Shleifer, and R. Vishny. 1998. The Quality of Government. *Journal of Law, Economics, and Organization*. 15(1): 222–79.

Landé, C. 1965. *Leaders, Factions, and Parties: The Structure of Philippine Politics*. Southeast Asia Studies series. New Haven: Yale University.

Llanto, G., and E. Gonzales. 2007. *Policy Reforms and Institutional Weaknesses: Closing the Gaps*. Makati City: Philippine Institute for Development Studies.

Mauro, P. 1995. Corruption and Growth. *Quarterly Journal of Economics*. 110(3): 681–712.

McCoy, A. 1994. *An Anarchy of Families*. Quezon City: Ateneo de Manila University Press.

Menard, C. 2001. Methodological Issues in New Institutional Economics. *Journal of Economic Methodology*. 8(1): 85–92

Mokyr, J. 2004. *The Gifts of Athena: Historical Origins of the Knowledge Economy*. Princeton, NJ: Princeton University Press.

Nelson, R. 2004. Scholasticism and Pietism: The Battle for the Soul of Economics. *Economic Journal Watch*. 1(3): 473–97.

North, D. 1981. *Structure and Change in Economic History*. New York: W. W. Norton.

———. 1990. *Institutions, Institutional Change, and Economic Performance*. Cambridge: Cambridge University Press.

———. 2005. *Understanding the Process of Economic Change*. Princeton, NJ: Princeton University Press.

North, D., and R. Thomas. 1973. *The Rise of the Western World*. Cambridge: Cambridge University Press.

North, D., J. Wallis, and B. Weingast. 2006. A Conceptual Framework for Interpreting Recorded Human History. NBER Working Paper 12795. Cambridge, MA: National Bureau of Economic Research. www.nber .org/papers/w12795

Patalinghug, L., and G. Llanto. 2005. Competition Policy and Regulation in Power and Telecommunications. Discussion Paper No. 2005-18.

Makati City: Philippine Institute for Development Studies. http://dirp4.pids.gov.ph/ris/dps/pidsdps0518.pdf

Perkins, D. 2000. Law, Family Ties, and the East Asian Way of Business. In Harrison, L. and S. Huntington, eds. *Culture Matters: How Values Shape Human Progress*. New York: Basic Books.

Persson, T., and G. Tabellini. 2003. *The Economic Effects of Constitutions*. Cambridge, MA: Massachusetts Institute of Technology.

Political Risk Services. various years. *International Country Risk Guide*. http://ssdc.ucsd.edu/ssdc/iri00001.html (accessed in October 2007)

Rodrik, D., A. Subramanian, and F. Trebbi. 2002. Institutions Rule: The Primacy of Institutions Over Geography and Integration in Economic Development. NBER Working Paper No. 9305. October. Cambridge, MA: National Bureau for Economic Research.

Rose-Ackerman, S. 1998. Corruption and Development. Paper presented at the Annual World Bank Conference on Development Economics. World Bank, Washington. D.C.

Saldaña, C. 2000. The Philippines. In M. V. Capulong, D. Edwards, and J. Zhuang, eds. *Corporate Governance and Finance in Asia*. Vol. 2: Country Studies. Manila: Asian Development Bank.

Shirley, M. 2005. Institutions and Development. In C. Menárd and M. Shirley, eds. *Handbook of New Institutional Economics*. Berlin: Springer Verlag.

Shleifer A., and R. Vishny. 1993. Corruption. *Quarterly Journal of Economics*. 108(3): 599–617.

Transparency International. various years. *TI Corruption Perceptions Indices*. www.transparency.org/policy_research/surveys_indices/cpi

Virola, R. 2007. Anti-Poverty? How About Pro-Middle Class? www.nscb.gov.ph/headlines/StatsSpeak/default.asp

World Bank. 2007. *Strengthening World Bank Group Engagement on Governance and Anticorruption*. www.worldbank.org/html/extdr/comments/governancefeedback/gacpaper-03212007.pdf

Index

Lightning Source UK Ltd.
Milton Keynes UK
23 December 2010

164807UK00001B/94/P